| | | | |
|---|---|---|---|
| Central Library | | | |
| Cecil Road | | | |
| Enfield | | | |
| 366 2244 | | | |
| 28. JAN. 1986 | −1. JUN 1987 | | |
| 14. FEB. 1986 | −1. OCT 1987 | | |
| 19. APR. 1986 | −1. DEC. 1987 | | |
| | 01. SEP 88 | | |
| 17. MAY 1986 | | | |
| −1. JUL 1986 | | | |
| −9. AUG 1986 | | | |
| −3. MAR 1987 | | | |
| 21. APR. 1987 | | | |
| | | | |
| | | | |

## LONDON BOROUGH OF ENFIELD
## LIBRARY SERVICES

This book to be RETURNED on or before the latest date stamped unless a renewal has been obtained by personal call or post, quoting the above number and the date due for return.

# The Evolution of the Agency from Roosevelt to Reagan

# The CIA Under Reagan Bush & Casey

### Dr. Ray S. Cline
Former Deputy Director of the Central Intelligence Agency

ACROPOLIS BOOKS LTD.
Washington, D.C. 20009

© *Copyright 1981 by Ray S. Cline*

*All right reserved. Except for the inclusion of brief quotations in a review, no part of this book may be reproduced or utilized in any form or by any means, electronic or mechanical, including photocopying, recording or by any information storage and retrieval system, without permission in writing from the publisher.*

**ACROPOLIS BOOKS**
*Colortone Building, 2400 17th St., N.W.
Washington, D. C. 20009*

*Printed in the United States of America by*
**COLORTONE PRESS, Creative Graphics Inc.**
*Washington, D. C. 20009*

Library of Congress Cataloging in Publication Data

Cline, Ray S.
   The CIA under Reagan, Bush, and Casey.

  Originally published as: Secrets, spies, and scholars: Washington: Acropolis Books, 1976.
  Includes index.
    1. United States.   Central Intelligence Agency.
I. Title.
JK468.I6C55  1981      327.1'2'06073      81-12857
ISBN 0—87491-442-6                             AACR2

# Dedication

*This book is dedicated to the three wonderful women who shared with me the pleasures and sacrifices of a life in the public service at home and abroad, my wife, Marjorie Wilson Cline, and my daughters, Judy and Sibyl; perhaps it will some day be of interest to my most captivating grandchildren, Elizabeth and Matthew.*

# Contents

Preface .................................................. 9
Overview: What Went Wrong ..................... 11
The Importance of Strategic Intelligence ........... 12
Illustrative Case Histories ........................ 14
Dark Days for CIA ............................... 18
The Reagan Agenda .............................. 19
Chronicle of the OSS and the CIA ................ 21

## CHAPTER 1  The Birth of "Central Intelligence" .......... 23

Perspective ....................................... 25
Rudiments of an Intelligence System .............. 28
Open Sources .................................... 30
Foreign Broadcasts ............................... 32
State Diplomatic Reporting ....................... 33
Army and Navy: Military Collection and
    Evaluation .................................... 34
Code Breaking: No Game for Gentlemen .......... 36
The Non-Barking Watchdog: The Joint
    Intelligence Committee ....................... 38
Counterintelligence: the FBI ..................... 39
Intelligence Gifts from Britain .................... 41
The Beginnings of a Central Intelligence
    System ....................................... 50

CHAPTER 2 **OSS: "Wild Bill's" Band of Secret Warriors** ............................... 59

    Research and Analysis ........................... 61
    Espionage ....................................... 63
    Other Elements .................................. 66
    Perspective ..................................... 72
    The Current Intelligence Staff .................. 75
    Intelligence Collection and Analysis ............ 80
    Covert Action Elements in the OSS ............... 86
    The TORCH Operation ............................. 89
    Worldwide Theater Operations .................... 92
    The Legacy ...................................... 96

CHAPTER 3 **Seeking National Security in the Postwar World, 1945-1952** .................... 103

    Perspective ..................................... 109
    A Pseudo-Central Intelligence System: 1946-1947 .. 112
    Creation of CIA ................................. 115
    Covert Action ................................... 119
    Perspective ..................................... 126
    The Bedell Smith Reforms: 1950-1953 ............. 129

CHAPTER 4 **Building an Intelligence System** ............. 141

    National Estimates .............................. 142
    Intelligence Liaison ............................ 146
    Covert Political Action ......................... 150
    Perspective ..................................... 155
    Drafting National Estimates ..................... 157
    The Net Estimate ................................ 163
    DDI Research and Analysis ....................... 166
    Perspective: Headquarters, CIA, 1955-1957 ....... 171
    Photographic Reconnaissance ..................... 178
    Open Skies ...................................... 181
    The CIA Overseas ................................ 182
    The Berlin Tunnel ............................... 184
    Khrushchev's Secret Speech ...................... 185
    Around the World ................................ 187

CHAPTER 5 **The CIA in High Gear** .......................... 195

    To Taiwan ........................................ 196
    The Quemoy Crisis, August 1958 ................. 198
    Station Operations .............................. 200
    Covert Action ................................... 203
    The Indonesian Operation ....................... 205
    Entering the Kennedy Era ....................... 207
    The Bay of Pigs and Assassination Planning ....... 208
    The McCone Period ............................. 215
    Close-in Analytical Work with the
        White House ................................ 219
    The DDI Domain ............................... 226
    The Raborn Interlude ........................... 234
    Helms at the Helm, June 1966-
        February 1973 .............................. 239
    Perspective ..................................... 240
    The Schlesinger-Colby Interregnum .............. 243

CHAPTER 6 **Time of Troubles** ............................ 247

    The CIA Flap: What Went Wrong ................ 252
    President Ford's Reforms ....................... 260
    The Carter-Mondale Era ....................... 268

CHAPTER 7 **A New Beginning for
               Central Intelligence** .......................... 277

    Accountability: Congressional Oversight .......... 279
    The CIA Charter ............................... 298
    Current Structure and Function .................. 303
    The Reagan Agenda ............................ 309
    The Casey Case ................................ 311
    Issues Ahead ................................... 315
    List of Charts .................................. 326
    List of Acronyms ............................... 327
    Footnotes ...................................... 332
    Index .......................................... 337

# *Preface*

It is hard for me to break the traditional silence of the professional intelligence officer after 30 years of keeping secrets. My aim in doing so is to try to explain what secret intelligence work in an open society is like, why it is needed, and how best it can be carried out in the service of the United States.

The story which follows is one of growth and achievement. It may sound immodest, even egocentric. If so, it is not because I am unaware of failures or shortcomings of intelligence agencies, or of mistakes of my own for that matter. The successes are emphasized here because they mark the long trail upward in the evolution of the American central intelligence system from conception to maturity.

I deliberately decided to drop the impersonal tone of political science and to write in the first person so that it would be very clear exactly what my personal perspective was at every stage of CIA's history. Readers thus can judge for themselves the legitimacy of my views in the light of my actual experience.

This personal approach probably appears to give too much importance to my own activities and to the colleagues I worked with most closely; it has the benefit, however, of permitting me to confine myself to telling only what I know at first hand to be true, avoiding both the romantic myth-making and the gossipy pseudo-exposures that make most of the literature of U.S. intelligence nearly worthless. There is just enough detail in my account to authenticate it and not enough to endanger any former colleagues or reveal any still viable espionage techniques. The names which can be mentioned are only a few of those I know to be deserving of high praise. The main point is that this book is not my story or the story of my friends and colleagues but rather an account of what I know of the development of the role and functions of central intelligence in the United States.

My original study of intelligence was made possible by a grant from the Ford Foundation and was sponsored by the Georgetown University Center for Strategic and International Studies (CSIS). In my capacity as Senior Associate, CSIS, I am continuing to do research and writing on intelligence topics as an aspect of strategic decision-making. This work has also been carried on as part of my responsibility as President of the National Intelligence Study Center, a non-profit institute established to encourage serious scholarly and journalistic writing on the subject of American intelligence.

Ray S. Cline

# Overview: What Went Wrong

Many subtle social, psychological, and bureaucratic forces shape the destinies of nations. Rarely are these perceived, except dimly and superficially, by the citizens whose lives are affected for good or ill. Systematically collected intelligence about foreign societies for government planning and decision-making by U.S. leaders is one of these forces which have greatly affected historic events of the past 40 years.

The course of World War II would have been entirely different were it not for American code and cipher work. The superior Japanese navy in the Pacific and Hitler's vast armies in Europe became vulnerable only because the U.S. and British commanders were better informed. Afterwards, the fluctuations in strategic equilibrium during the long, short-of-war conflict with the Soviet Union were substantially influenced by the effectiveness of the U.S. national intelligence system.

In the 1950s and 1960s, the Central Intelligence Agency (CIA) played a major role in the American political process by collecting, analyzing, and providing to policymakers in Washington sophisticated intelligence about the world. Yet, the real facts about U.S. intelligence activities remain arcane, misunderstood, and, in some instances — sometimes properly, often improperly — undisclosed. The CIA is still treated more as the subject of sensational headlines than as a normal part of the government.

The literature and doctrine of U.S. intelligence are only beginning to address the question of what kind of intelligence machinery is needed and how it should operate within our free political process. In the past, the lack of serious writing on the subject has forced the American people to derive their knowledge of intelligence from the fantasy world of cloak-and-dagger fiction. This situation is, fortunately, changing.

### The Importance of Strategic Intelligence

In his pioneer historical analysis of *Strategic Intelligence for American World Policy*, Sherman Kent, a veteran of the wartime Office of Strategic Services (OSS) and of the CIA, pointed out:

> Intelligence is a simple and self-evident thing. As an activity it is the pursuit of a certain kind of knowledge; as a phenomenon it is the resultant knowledge. In a small way it is what we all do every day. When a housewife decides to increase her inventory, when a doctor diagnoses an ailment — when almost anyone decides upon a course of action — he usually does some preliminary intelligence work.... But no matter whether done instinctively or with skillful conscious mental effort intelligence work is in essence nothing more than the search for the single best answer.
> .... And strategic intelligence, we might call the knowledge upon which our nation's foreign relations, in war or peace, must rest. If foreign policy is the shield of the republic, as Walter Lippmann has called it, then strategic intelligence is the thing that gets the shield to the right place at the right time. It is also the thing that stands ready to guide the sword.[1]

The importance of strategic intelligence activity, the capabilities of the actor or agency engaged in it, and the "resultant knowledge" is self-evident.

Intelligence on foreign affairs can be gathered from conventional sources, such as press reports, foreign radio broadcasts, foreign publications, and reports from our Foreign Service and military attachés. During the past few decades, these sources have been supplemented by technical data gathered by photographic satellites and electronic signals sensors.

Information on international activities is useful only if it is evaluated and analyzed in the context of U.S. national security and foreign policy concerns. It must be evaluated for accuracy and credibility in the light of its source or collection method, for the validity and significance of the content, once it has been collated with other available data, and for its impact on U.S. interests, operations, or objectives. The result of this process is a report intended to assist foreign and defense policy officers in making decisions.

Through the information provided in these reports, policymakers can trace developments in foreign affairs and forecast the consequences of those developments. The future estimate, a prediction of the probability of particular foreign activities, is the subtlest and most elusive kind of intelligence. If objectively and imaginatively conceived, it builds an indispensable floor under policymaking.

The collection of intelligence, including clandestine "undercover" espionage operations to find hidden or hard-to-get information, and its evaluation or analysis are seldom questioned as legitimate and essential parts of the Washington bureaucratic process. Occasionally, someone will admit to scruples about stooping to clandestine, illegal or immoral techniques of gathering information, but, generally, Americans feel it is only a fair game to try secretly to obtain data that other nations are withholding from us. They assume that the information is very likely to affect our relations with those nations and might, indeed, affect the security of American institutions or lives. Secret measures protecting the nation from unpleasant or dangerous surprise are commonly accepted as being neither immoral nor improper, simply prudent.

The public's fascination with the details of espionage often overshadows the acceptance of another facet of intelligence gathering. This is the need for analytical research to reduce raw data to meaningful ideas, seen as a normal function of government. If national decisions are to be made, national efforts to provide a sound and carefully articulated data base are clearly worthwhile. Information gathering and intelligence analysis have been, since the World War II beginnings of central intelligence coordination, the heart of intelligence work. It still is. In this field the CIA has chalked up many successes, some of which have provided evidence needed to counter Soviet moves abroad.

## Illustrative Case Histories

One of the most notable examples of successful intelligence work, still remembered for its worldwide effect in exposing the falsity of Soviet political propaganda, was the clandestine capture and public release of the secret speech Soviet Communist Party chief Nikita Khrushchev made to the 20th Party Congress in Moscow on February 25, 1956.

In a three-hour tirade, he startled the assembled members of the Communist Party by denouncing the crimes of Josef Stalin. The *New York Times* published the speech on June 4, 1956. Radio Free Europe, the CIA's covert radio station in Germany, broadcast the terrifying details about Stalinism behind the "Iron Curtain." Never before had such a damning indictment of a regime been made by its own ruler. No single document has better described the true Soviet methods of government and the horrible purges, based on falsified evidence by the Soviet intelligence apparatus, that were carried out over the years. Its release created chaos in the ranks of the Soviet secret intelligence services; for months, information about Communist Party desertions, arrests, and bloody uprisings poured in to the CIA analysts. It is no accident that the Hungarian revolution, an attempt to gain freedom from the Soviet yoke, came a few months after these disclosures nor that disillusionment with Soviet domination figured in the uprisings in Czechoslovakia in 1968. The brutality of the Soviet military liquidation of both Budapest and Prague demonstrated most conclusively the kind of Soviet behavior the CIA had been set up to study. In 1981, the unrest in Poland under the heavy Soviet political and military hand demonstrated how completely the existence of one-party dictatorships and Soviet imperialism have become accepted as facts of life.

Information gathering and analysis during the Cuba missile crisis of 1962 was also a first-class performance by the CIA. Espionage agents in Cuba provided the agency with some of the clues that unravelled the missile mystery as did an observant refugee debriefed by the CIA at Opa-locka, Florida. The U-2, the fast-flying queen of the skies in those days, finally brought home the bacon — the first picture of a Soviet MRBM being emplaced at San Cristobal—and launched the United States into the "13 days of October." When President Kennedy saw the U-2 photographs of the Soviets' medium-range offensive missiles, capable of reaching cities as far away as Washington, D.C., he had all the evidence he needed to force Nikita Khrushchev to withdraw the weapons.

The Cuba missile crisis was a case in which the United States triumphed because it had top-quality intelligence reporting that made clear exactly the nature of the Soviet threat as well as superior military forces. When the crisis was over, Vasiliy Kuznetsov, Soviet foreign service chief, said the USSR would never again enter a strategic contest at such a disadvantage. The Cuba defeat was one of the misjudgments that caused Khrushchev's downfall in 1964.

The overhead photographic reconnaissance used during the Cuba missile crisis supplemented the traditional disciplines of cryptanalaysis and espionage. It quickly came to equal, and in many ways surpass, the older intelligence methods. The marriage of the technology of the airplane with that of the camera took place in World War I, but the quantum jump in capability came in the 1950s. Then, pioneering efforts by the CIA culminated in the perfection of the precision camera lens, fine-grain fast film, high-flying aircraft, and, finally, the earth-orbiting satellite.

The history of the U.S. intelligence is complicated in many people's minds by the CIA's responsibility for a second, more controversial function — namely, covert political action abroad. "Covert action" includes all kinds of political, paramilitary, or propaganda moves undertaken secretly to gain support for U.S. foreign policies overseas or to thwart Soviet intelligence and security agents in their attempts to undermine the stability of governments in which the United States has economic, political, or military security interests. Such activities were taken for granted in World War II, but, in peacetime, critics have opposed secret operations involving intervention in foreign political situations even when hostile forces were clearly at work against the United States.

American political leaders in the late 1940s, including patriotic and conscientious statemen such as Harry S. Truman, George C. Marshall, and Dwight D. Eisenhower, were not content simply to note with dismay the Soviet conduct revealed by the CIA's intelligence reporting. They wanted to meet it, openly by economic and military aid where possible and secretly by covert political action. The National Security Council charged the CIA with the responsibility for secret operations to frustrate Communist plans and their conduct.*

In June, 1950, the outbreak of the Korean War caused the CIA to mount a major covert political action program which included paramilitary operations in Asia. By 1953, covert operations were being carried out by the CIA in 48 foreign countries. Some of these activities were small in scale and consequence; others were ambitious. Most were benign in my view (aimed at constructive, stabilizing political goals) and some achieved lasting results. For instance, the CIA helped the Shah of Iran regain his throne with the assistance of loyalist military leaders and oust a radical, pro-Soviet regime jeopardizing the flow of oil to West Europe. Iran prospered and remained comparatively stable for more than 25 years. The decision to withhold such a CIA effort when the Shah was deposed in 1979 has resulted in a situation that exemplifies how revolution and social anarchy can destroy the fabric of political order.

Regrettably, romantic gossip about the "coup" in Iran spread around Washington like wildfire. Allen Dulles basked in the glory of the exploit without ever verifying the accuracy of the impression it created of the CIA's power.

The CIA involvement, also benign and successful, in building up Eduardo Frei as a progressive, center-conservative political leader of a democratic, economically dynamic Chile epitomized how the legend of the CIA's power grew. In the two years prior to the 1964 presidential election, the CIA carried out some 15 covert action projects in Chile, including monetary support of about $3 million to Frei's Christian Democrats. The agency mounted anti-Communist propaganda campaigns — in the press, radio, films, pamphlets, direct mailings, and wall paintings. As a result, Frei won with 56 per cent of the vote.

His victory against Marxist, left-wing coalition leader Salvador Allende was an example of covert political assistance that activated and astutely advised center-conservative forces against the revolutionary dictatorship sought by a minority

---

*For details of early CIA responsibility for covert action, see Chapter 3, pp. 119-126.

being encouraged from outside, in this case, the USSR and Cuba. While reasonable men may differ, this secret intervention seems to have produced happier results for both Chileans and Americans than those which came about later when the CIA did not intervene, then intervened too urgently and without success.

The CIA played no part in the 1970 elections. However, when Allende was voted into office, the CIA tried to assist the Chilean opposition to resist his policies and to organize a politically coherent campaign to save parliamentary government. The Nixon White House approved this effort and granted over $7 million to support center-conservative radio stations, newspapers, magazines, and books.

Subsequent White House instructions to the CIA were to overthrow Allende. The CIA operatives doubted the feasibility of these orders at the time; those doubts were compounded by their misgivings about the morality and political wisdom of such action. Personal control by President Richard Nixon and his National Security Assistant Henry Kissinger, furthermore, caused confusion both in Chile and Washington, and the operation was a failure.

When a military coup in 1973 did overthrow Allende, the CIA merely reported the event; it had played no role in instigating or assisting it. Worst of all, the coup brought into power a right-wing military dictatorship, not the parliamentary coalition Washington had hoped for.

This was the beginning of the travail of the CIA. The emphasis on U.S. covert political action as an almost magic solution to difficult foreign political situations marked the end of covert action. The Chile story was publicized by the Church Committee of the U.S. Senate investigating the CIA in 1975. Richard Helms, then director of the agency, was trapped into misleading statements concerning Chile before the Senate's Committee on Foreign Relations; he eventually pleaded *nolo contendere* to a misdemeanor involving not testifying fully about a secret political operation. He felt his oath to prevent unauthorized disclosures of intelligence "sources and methods" had kept him from being totally forthcoming. In this dilemma lies the irony and tragedy of the covert action tale. By the end of 1980, the CIA was virtually dormant in this area and, indeed, under the influence of President Jimmy Carter and Vice President Walter Mondale had disbanded the network of intelligence officers and agents once able to intervene in support of U.S. foreign policy interests almost anywhere in the world. Vice President Mondale, who worked with Senator Frank Church on the disastrous Senate investigation, made it plain that the Carter Administration viewed covert action as an unwise and indecent "bludgeoning" of other countries — an activity to be assigned to a sinful past era of American history.[2]

## Dark Days for CIA

Covert action was the most controversial CIA activity but the real national crisis was the Watergate scandal. The U.S. intelligence system has not yet fully recovered from the effects of the overheated Washington atmosphere at the close of the Nixon era. At that time, the capital was hostile to any form of secrecy. In 1975, President Gerald R. Ford tried to protect the CIA during the storm of criticism that saw the agency castigated for things it had never done as well as for things it had done under direct orders from several different Presidents of the United States. Senator Church, chairman of the Senate committee investigating the CIA, opined that the agency might have been a "rogue elephant" running amok, a charge so thoroughly refuted in his own investigation that his final report retracted it. These were dark days for the whole intelligence community.

What went wrong has been discussed for more than five years in the halls of Congress, in the press, and on many street corners. The question now before the nation is what must be done as the United States prepares itself to face the threats of the 1980s.

Soviet intelligence forces, some 500,000 strong, and other Soviet-controlled national intelligence services, such as those of Cuba and East Germany, continue their activities worldwide. Their objectives are to collect intelligence, particularly on the economic and technological advances on which the future strength of free societies depends and to use this information covertly to influence economic, military, and political developments everywhere, including in the United States, to their strategic advantage.

At the same time, the Soviet Union and all Communist dominated powers consider nearly every aspect of their national policy and behavior to be prime state secrets. Policymakers in the United States must know what developments in these closed societies may be encroaching upon our security. Otherwise, they will eventually be forced to acquiesce in the unilateral disarmament, isolation, and, finally, destruction not only of our own nation but of all the relatively free, politically pluralist lands as well.

## The Reagan Agenda

President Ronald Reagan initiated a program as soon as he took office in 1981 to strengthen the international strategic posture and credibility of the United States by rebuilding and revitalizing the national intelligence system. Critical to this program was restoring the system to the level of competence it had achieved in the late 1960s and early 1970s.

By coincidence, Reagan's main challenger for the Republican nomination and his running mate in the 1980 campaign, Vice President George Bush, was as strongly supportive of intelligence functions as the President. He had served under President Ford as Director of Central Intelligence, giving the CIA the only boost in morale and confidence it had experienced in recent years. He had left the agency when President Carter assumed office in 1977 and the CIA had returned to the doldrums of uncertainty and mistrust for another four years.

To reverse the tide of deterioration in intelligence capabilities and morale that had run during the late 1970s, President Reagan turned to William J. Casey, a veteran of the first U.S. central intelligence coordinating agency, the wartime OSS. This action put the world on the alert that experience and professionalism in intelligence work would be valued and trusted in the Reagan administration.

William J. Casey assumed the leadership of the CIA on January 28, 1981, with the challenging mission of restoring its "ability to supply the President, senior U.S. officials, and the Congress with accurate and timely analyses concerning fundamental threats to our nation's security." He was charged with undertaking "an urgent effort to rebuild the intelligence agencies" across the board and to "improve U.S. intelligence capabilities for technical and clandestine collection, cogent analyses, coordinated counterintelligence, and covert action."[3]

The American public, having voted overwhelmingly for President Reagan, clearly thinks the 1980s demand strenuous efforts to protect the national security against military attacks, terrorism, and the subtler but equally dangerous forms of political subversion by revolutionary agents of the Soviet Union and its subordinates such as Cuba, North Korea, and East Germany. On Reagan, Bush, and Casey fell a heavy responsibility — to bring intelligence back to life as a dynamic and creative element in protecting the national security.

To understand the scope of the problem of rebuilding U.S. intelligence in the OSS-CIA tradition, one must start at the outbreak of hostilities in World War II. I have in this book outlined how the Pearl Harbor disaster demonstrated the need for a central coordinating intelligence system, how the CIA created a going concern to satisfy this need, and how fortune turned against the intelligence professionals during the 1970s. The Reagan-Bush-Casey agenda was to recapture the zest and skill of the CIA of 20 years ago and mold a competent modern intelligence community that would build on demonstrated strengths too long neglected.

How hard this task will be was well illustrated in July 1981 by a fire storm of Congressional and news media criticism over an early administrative decision by Casey to assign a politically oriented businessman to a top post in the line of command of clandestine operations. Media speculation about Casey's character and competence suddenly rose to a high pitch with very little substance to go on. For a time it appeared the new Director of Central Intelligence would be obliged to step down from his critically important post.

The long range damage to CIA would have been incalculable if its chief could be toppled so easily by casual Congressional comments and a flurry of speculative journalistic stories. Fortunately people who wanted to give CIA a chance to restore its earlier vigor rallied to call for fairness and due process of law, and the White House finally supported Casey firmly. The storm died down as quickly as it had appeared with a finding by the Senate Select Committee on Intelligence that no evidence had surfaced to suggest Casey was unfit for his job. The whole episode served to emphasize once more, however, the difficulty of managing secret intelligence in an open society.

## Chronicle of the OSS and the CIA

This book is a chronicle of the secrets of the CIA, the spies who collected them, and the scholars who interpreted them in the light of all other available knowledge for U.S. Presidents, foreign affairs experts, and military planners. It is, in a limited sense, a memoir, though not a full or systematic one. In the shadowy world of intelligence operations the truth is not always on paper; it is more apt to be in men's minds or apparent only in their actions. Accordingly, illustrations for the points I make about intelligence draw on my recollections of 30 years of government service working for the Navy and Army, with the Air Force, and in positions at a high level in the Central Intelligence Agency and the State Department. They spring from incidents I observed or learned of from colleagues I knew to be reliable observers. The romance of cloak-and-dagger tales is not part of this account of the real intelligence world in which real intelligence officers work, trying to discover crucial facts and evaluate objectively what they see, hear, and read.

These personal reflections would be of little value, however, it it weren't for the fact that they also constitute an outline history of the evolution of our central intelligence system as it developed over the 35 years from its bare bones beginning at the outbreak of World War II. As it happened, my professional career almost exactly coincides with this period of challenge and response by the men who made the CIA.

The United States was almost totally unprepared for the dangers and stresses of the 1940s in the field of intelligence as in so many others. It is almost a miracle that the United States built a creditable wartime record with its Office of Strategic Services, which served as a legacy for peacetime efforts, and then developed under the CIA during the 1950s and 1960s the best intelligence system in the world. The CIA's history comes to the brink of tragedy as a result of the near-destruction of this system in the mid-1970s. Flaws in its performance, comparatively minor when placed in perspective with its achievements, were widely and sensationally advertised. The whole U.S. intelligence apparatus became a political football for the news media and the Congress of the United States, lowering the morale and effectiveness of the CIA catastrophically.

Finally, this book is a contribution to political science, an analysis of how the main elements in American intelligence operations can contribute information and ideas to decision-making and national policy. It explains that scholars and spies can give to our national strategy and foreign policy the enormous benefit of objectivity if our national leaders wish to protect our open society by using, not abusing, a secret intelligence service. A free nation with accurate knowledge of the world around it, particularly of hostile and secretive closed societies, is more likely to survive and prosper than one that relies on wishful thinking.

The United States lives in an international environment that demands professional skills in penetrating the cloak of secrecy in unfriendly countries. It also requires the capability to keep our own intelligence operations safe from discovery by opposing intelligence services. Secrecy is not in and of itself good or bad. In the disciplined service of a good society, secret intelligence contributes to political aims set forth in the Preamble of the U.S. Constitution in efforts to "insure domestic tranquility, provide for the common defense, promote the general welfare, and secure the blessings of liberty."

Spies and scholars can give significant clues to future opportunities and dangers if kept at work on a systematic, stable, well-coordinated program calculated to find facts and interpret them as the foundation for military and foreign policy decisions.*

---

*This book is a revised edition of *Secrets, Spies, and Scholars: Blueprint of the Essential CIA* published in 1976. This version contains virtually all of the material in the earlier book but brings the story up to date (1981).

*Chapter One*

# The Birth of "Central Intelligence"

The U.S. central intelligence system came into being as a result of two critical surprise events. One was the Stalin-Hitler pact of August 1939, leading directly to the outbreak of the European war. The second was the Japanese assault on Pearl Harbor, December 7, 1941, eventually perceived as a tragic failure to piece together and interpret available intelligence about Japan's intentions.

The creation of the Office of Strategic Services (OSS) as a pioneer central espionage and evaluation service and its wartime record laid the foundation for the postwar birth of the Central Intelligence Agency (CIA). The story starts with the U.S. government's urgent need in 1941 to obtain and absorb more fully the complex geopolitical information vitally affecting the security and foreign policy of the United States.

In June and July of 1941 President Franklin D. Roosevelt, who had gingerly led his country away from fear of fear and through the worst of the Great Depression of the 1930s, was now even more delicately leading them to an awareness of the dangers to America from abroad. He described in a Presidential Directive dated July 11, 1941, a central information handling process whereby the President would be effectively informed about events on the international scene that might threaten the safety, or at least the foreign interests, of this country. Roosevelt established the position of Coordinator of Information and selected the dynamic World War I hero, William J. (Wild Bill) Donovan, to fill the job. Donovan was authorized to coordinate the activities of those parts of the U.S. Government which were collecting information and, after analyzing and correlating it, make the information available to the President.[1]

This Presidential Directive was revolutionary and farsighted. The new institution thus established was first called the Office of the Coordinator of Information in 1941; it became the Office of Strategic Services in 1942. It was the direct precursor of the Central Intelligence Agency. It never achieved half of what Roosevelt sketched out, but this was natural since the task was so complex and so little understood. Yet a beginning was made, experts in intelligence learned their trade, and the basic concept of central intelligence outlived Roosevelt and World War II to become a fixture of postwar Washington.

The order setting up this new institution came at a time when even the principle of military conscription, whereby Roosevelt and General George C. Marshall were trying to build up the minimal armed forces of the United States, was in serious question. In 1941 the law to continue the draft for a second year passed by only one vote in the House of Representatives. Many people, probably a majority, still felt in 1940 and 1941 that political movements and wars overseas were no business of Americans and that the Neutrality Act passed by the U.S. Congress would guarantee peace and security for the United States behind its two oceans despite the Japanese military incursions into China and the German conquest of much of Western Europe.

As a result of these sentiments, the Army and Navy in the 1939-1941 era were small and ill-equipped. There was no central intelligence system for gathering and analyzing data about the cataclysmic developments in Asia and Europe. The United States, although a great nation, possessed little of the power necessary to settle conflicts and protect its national interests in the international arena. By mid-1940, except for beleaguered Great Britain and sprawling, disorganized China, the United States faced the militant powers of the Tokyo-Rome-Berlin Axis alone. Worse, the dominant view in the country and the Congress was that isolation from the outside world was a good thing, that this isolation was sufficient protection from the ills of world war.

To these challenges the United States eventually responded vigorously, but only after the Pearl Harbor attack unified opinion behind the policies toward which Roosevelt had been edging since the European war broke out in 1939. It then took about 20 years to build the kind of central intelligence system that Roosevelt had authorized in 1941 to serve as a shield for the republic.

## Perspective

In the years 1939-1941, few Americans were ready to face up to the prospect of a new world war. To a generation still focusing on the Great Depression of the 1930s and brought up to believe that peace could be maintained with declaratory treaties, hemispheric isolation, and neutrality, the outbreak of large-scale hostilities in Europe in September 1939 was a rude shock. War was a grim intrusion upon the prevailing assumption that we were effectively insulated from the rest of the globe.

I felt this intrusion very personally and very strongly. Like most of my contemporaries, I had been taught that war was so destructive of human life in the age of the machine gun, tank, and combat aircraft that only a madman would turn to it. Today we often hear much the same argument based on the existence of different weapons.

We were also taught in the 1930s that the economies of Germany and Japan were inadequate to challenge the democracies of Western Europe, France, Great Britain, and the Low Countries, no matter how politically divided and militarily feeble the Western European nations were in the late 1930s. We deplored the brutality of Japan's attacks on China, Fascist Italy's conquest of African colonies, and Hitler's seizure of Austria and Czechoslovakia, but most of us thought it was not an American problem. Hence the U.S. armed forces, including Army, Navy, Marines, and the embryonic air force, in 1939 totaled only about 190,000 men. The defense budget was between $1 billion and $2 billion, mostly allocated for ships and airplanes that would be a long while building. Isolation, neutrality, and virtue were supposed to protect us. It was a cruel blow when they did not do the job.

The outbreak of war in Europe found me deeply concerned about what was happening. Born on a farm in Illinois and educated in public schools in Indiana, I had won a scholarship to Harvard, hopped a freight train to get there, adjusted to East Coast academia, and won an elegant prize fellowship for study at Oxford University in England. Not wishing to be done out of my European adventure by the likes of Hitler, I boarded a small Dutch freighter at Montreal on September 2, 1939, and headed for London. It turned out the ship was carrying scrap metal that was contraband of war, that the Captain intended to run the submarine blockade instead of heading home, and that a big passenger ship, the ATHENIA, was sunk right in our sea-lane just as we were heading out into the Atlantic.

The vast inhospitable waters of the North Atlantic bring one face to face with the imponderables of nature and are conducive to realistic philosophizing. I quickly came to admire the Dutch Captain of my ship, the PRINS WILLEM, because of the courageous way he accepted the dangerous situation he was in and faced the prospects of a Nazi military attack on Holland that he was sure would, in time, come. This cold-blooded talk about war was new to me. The Captain arranged for me to take meals with him, allowed me to take a turn at the wheel so I could get the feel of the sea, and let me help him forge a new ship's manifest that we could show, if boarded by Nazis, to deceive them into thinking our cargo was not contraband. Looking at the shimmering play of Northern Lights on the skies above the monstrously heaving seas at night is calculated to make anyone feel deeply the insignificance of a single human being. So did the realization that the sinking of the ATHENIA by German submarines, even though women and children were aboard, meant we might get a torpedo any moment.

We zigzagged across the Atlantic on an erratic course, hoping to escape notice, and finally were intercepted by British patrols. I was very glad Britain still ruled the waves, at least in the vicinity of the English Channel. We were on the water almost four weeks. I landed at Gravesend near London full of a new awareness of what was going on in Europe behind the alarming newspaper headlines.

Everyone I had encountered when leaving for Europe thought I was mildly insane for heading into the war zone, but it proved educational to be in England in 1939 and 1940 in every sense of the word. I returned to Harvard only when I was informed that my passport would be cancelled—shortly after the fall of France and just at the time of the British retreat from Dunkirk. I left knowing that England would continue to fight. Despite the fact that a few years before Oxford undergraduates had declared they would not fight for "King and Country," many of them soon were engaged in the air battle of Britain. Only later did I learn that this victory was due not only to the bravery and skill of the Royal Air Force but even more to the fantastic intelligence derived in large part from cracking Germany's ciphers. It is hard to see how Great Britain could have survived 1940 and 1941 except for the sophisticated intelligence system at Churchill's command for obtaining data and fathoming the enemy's intentions.

Back home again in mid-1940, I was firmly persuaded that the United States must help the British lest we be truly isolated in a "Fortress America," surrounded by more powerful, militant foes. Teaching and writing in 1940 and 1941, I had no doubt about the trials that lay ahead for our country. The brutal overrunning of Holland just before my return to America confirmed the judgment of my Dutch ship's Captain. What Americans needed was his foresight and his readiness to face up to the challenge. Firsthand knowledge of what was at stake in Europe had ended my naivete about the facts of military power and international conflict. The American people, less precipitately, were also being educated.

Under the cautious leadership of Franklin D. Roosevelt, who saw the dangers clearly, the nation moved uneasily and unwillingly, step by reluctant step, toward international responsibility—and war. "Intervention" became the slogan of his supporters. Bitter controversy between interventionists and isolationists persisted until the devastating Sunday morning raid on Pearl Harbor. All citizens came together only then, at the end of 1941, thus completing their two-year course in world affairs. Information about the balance of power in Europe and Asia, strategic analysis of the security interests of the United States, understanding of what militant totalitarian dictatorship would mean—all of these were not adequately in focus in American minds to permit adoption of a more prudent policy to protect U.S. interests. The die was finally cast when—in the aftermath of the disaster in Hawaii and the almost equally damaging assault on the Philippines—Japan, Germany, and Italy all openly declared war on the United States. Neutrality was over.

## Rudiments of an Intelligence System

Among the evidences of pitiful unreadiness for the challenges of the time was the state of U.S. intelligence agencies on the eve of World War II. Prior to mid-1941, when the new idea of central, coordinated intelligence machinery was born, there were only a few scattered, undermanned agencies engaged in activities designed to inform the President and his advisers about what other nations were doing that might affect the security of the United States. Of these, only the Army and Navy had any tradition of systematic collection and analysis of data. In only one area—code and cipher work—were there still extant some of the skills left over from U.S. participation in World War I and its immediate aftermath. I found all this out much later, but it is still frightening to think how devoid of adequate intelligence assets we were when war came to us.

A sketch of intelligence functions performed for policy-makers in Washington in 1940 would have looked something like the chart opposite.

This chart of functions does not look too bad on paper. On the face of it Roosevelt had a chance to learn something from these agencies, either directly or as filtered through his Cabinet advisers. Unfortunately, examination of the individual components of the chart reveals that the actual intelligence work being done was limited, that there really was no integrated system—no organized and coordinated machinery. Each component operated virtually independently with no sense of common mission nor any sense of responsibility for coordinating with one another to insure that essential coverage of foreign developments was provided and that all components could plan their activities and report their findings in the full light of what the others were doing. All in all, as of mid-1940, there were probably not many more than 1,000 people working

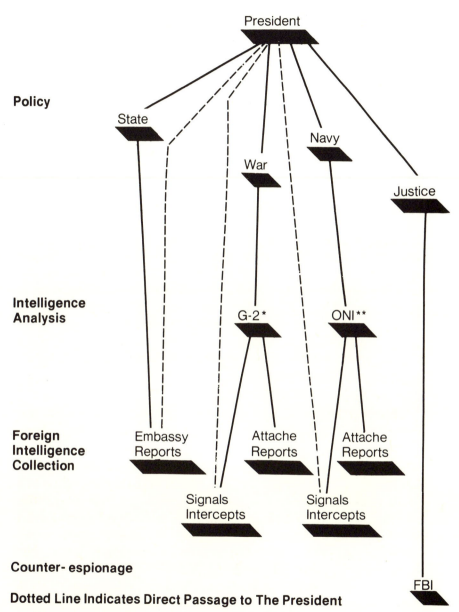

in what we would now classify as intelligence jobs, and most of these were radio intercept technicians.

What the President found out was simply what he could pick up from the occasional exceptionally broad-gauged interpretive report from a Foreign Service officer or from translations of the occasional foreign diplomatic message that the Army or Navy had succeeded in decoding. It was a rudimentary, unfledged intelligence process not even thought of as an integrated system.

The State Department conceived of itself as a staff primarily engaged in the conduct of diplomacy, and the embassies reported on events abroad only in enough depth to permit the Secretary of State and the senior officials under him to think about policies to regulate dealings with foreign capitals. The Army and Navy by tradition had intelligence units at the general staff level, but these were comparatively small, totally lacking in prestige for ambitious officers, and focused on providing basic military facts to military and naval war planning staffs. The upward flow to the Cabinet officials supervising the military agencies and on to the President was negligible, at most times nonexistent. When significant intercepts were available, they were shown to, but not left with, Roosevelt and a very few other senior officials, and they were not combined with other data in an evaluative and interpretive estimate except in a very narrow war plans context.

## Open Sources

Probably Roosevelt and the energetic, competent Secretaries of War and Navy, Republicans Henry L. Stimson and Frank Knox, whom he felt obliged to bring into his Cabinet in the conditions of emergency in June 1940, probably learned more from reading newspapers and periodicals than from any of the intelligence units. While the serious element of foreign news in the American press was pitifully small, there were from time to time perceptive articles from foreign correspondents sent abroad by the metropolitan daily journals and a few of the more opulent nonfiction periodicals like *Time* and *Life*. Private enterprise performs this reporting function fairly well concerning open societies like France and Great Britain, but most inadequately concerning closed societies where nearly all data about public affairs are treated as state secrets—as was the case in Nazi Germany and is today in the USSR, the People's Republic of China, and other Communist nations. The trouble with this asymmetry is—and was in the 1939-1941 period—that a great deal about open societies is reported but almost nothing about the workings of dictatorships. Only skillful intelligence operations can penetrate a ruthlessly secretive police state. There were no such operations being run by the United States prior to World War II.

One accidental reason the war in Europe and its alarming portents for the whole world impinged at all on the consciousness of Americans was that the end of the 1930s was the age of radio. This period saw the beginning of the first dramatic international news "roundups" ever to reach the ears of citizens of the United States direct from Berlin, Vienna, Rome, Paris, and London. The voice of Hitler screaming about Czechoslovakia's Sudetenland at Nuremberg in September 1938 came live across the airwaves while translated passages of the speech were broadcast and H. V. Kaltenborn analyzed their meaning for Europe's future. Edward R. Murrow and William L. Shirer quickly became household names in the United States, commanding enormous listening audiences. American broadcast news came of age. Roosevelt and most officials in Washington got most of their up-to-date information about foreign crises from this source or, a day or two later, from the foreign correspondents of the press.

These open source news items, plus the knowledge of foreign countries accumulated by the relatively small number of American university scholars, businessmen, missionaries, and enterprising tourists who travelled abroad constituted a large part of the information possessed by the citizenry of the United States and their officials in Washington. Beyond this, in the category of open sources, although not available to every citizen, was the reporting of the Foreign Service.

Some brilliant minds were in the State Department, as we later discovered when George F. Kennan, Charles E. (Chip) Bohlen, and Llewellyn E. Thompson educated a generation of officials on the Soviet Union in the postwar era. What was in these minds was a long way from percolating to the consciousness at the top of government in the prewar period, however, and courtly Cordell Hull, Roosevelt's choice as Secretary of State because of his qualifications as a popular politician from a Southern state, was able to contribute very little to the knowledge of foreign affairs needed by Roosevelt.

Everyone in Washington claimed to be an expert on Europe—as is still true today—so no one relied much on the Foreign Service for interpretation of the crucial events unfolding there. Hull concentrated mainly on Japan, where he had an exceptionally able Ambassador, Joseph Grew, but the Ambassador never received from Washington the benefit of the astonishing glimpses into the Japanese mind afforded by intercepted messages, and it is far from clear that Hull fully grasped the import of the messages shown him from time to time. There was no intelligence evaluation staff in the State Department to insure the Secretary was well informed and to tie together the best of Embassy reporting with the best of data from the military intelligence agencies.

## Foreign Broadcasts

In February 1941 an intelligence unit was created for collecting open source data of a particularly useful kind. This intelligence unit proved so useful in providing information to government officials who covered foreign affairs that it has been in operation ever since.

The Federal Communications Commission, at the suggestion of the State Department, established a Foreign Broadcast Monitoring Service to record broadcasts of foreign origin, translate speeches and news items, and report the important findings to other agencies. Being up-to-date and reliably filled in on the details of statements by foreign political and military leaders was obviously sensible for U.S. diplomats, policy planners, and military staffs. Thus was born the intelligence service that is indispensable to Foreign Service officers and ambassadors—and even to the American press—as a reference file. Its name was settled upon later as the "Foreign Broadcast Information Service" (FBIS) and it eventually ended up as a "service of common concern" managed by the CIA. Its reports, its analytical summaries, and its files are still invaluable.

Liaison was quickly established with a similar monitoring service for Europe that operated under the British Broadcasting

Corporation for the benefit of the government in London. Editors, translators, and information analysts began exchanging data and skills with the net result that the British record of broadcasts from Europe was exchanged for the U.S. take on other parts of the world. Throughout the war and for the next three decades, this unique information service covered a worldwide beat, copying and translating hundreds of thousands of words daily and transmitting the product electronically for prompt availability wherever needed in Great Britain, the United States, and their outposts overseas. It is a bread-and-butter service now taken for granted by intelligence officers and policy officials alike, but it is interesting that as early as 1941 an open source like radio broadcasting was recognized as a legitimate intelligence source for government along with diplomatic and military reporting and cryptanalysis. Government officials recognized that they needed this service of common concern. In a sense the FBIS was the first truly "central" element in a structure that cried out for better coordination of activities, collation of data, and systematic analysis.

## State Diplomatic Reporting

The State Department throughout the prewar years relied mainly for its appreciation of foreign events on reporting from the embassies it maintained in every major capitol abroad, staffed by American Foreign Service officers and—as an assist to the Army and Navy—military attaches. The numbers were not large, however, and foreign situation reporting was only one, and not necessarily the best rewarded, of the many duties of embassy officers involved in observing diplomatic protocol, socializing with other diplomats, and attending to the trivia of commercial and consular relations. There was no secret agent intelligence network at the time, since espionage had never been seriously conducted by the United States except in time of war.

In 1939 the entire State Department in Washington had only about 1,000 people working in it, of which about half were administrative. Considerably fewer served abroad. In Washington, as overseas, State had no separate intelligence organization or activity as such prior to the end of the war in 1945. Secretary

Hull, in general, thought of his organization as a "Department of Peace" and left plans and preparations for meeting the military thrusts of the time to the Department of War, which he correctly anticipated would run things if hostilities broke out.

In November 1940 State set up a new unit labeled functionally as an "intelligence" section under the name "Division of Foreign Activity Correlation." It was small—total personnel numbered 18 in 1943—and it concentrated on extracting information about foreigners from the Passport and Visa units and interviewing foreign political leaders and foreign-born citizens visiting the Department. As Dean Acheson, an Assistant Secretary of State in 1941, later said, the State Department as a whole was "unequipped" for appraisals of foreign capabilities and intentions based on painstaking correlation of intelligence. In fact, he observed, the Foreign Service establishment collected intelligence abroad with the same techniques John Quincy Adams used in Russia or Benjamin Franklin in France, only differing in employing the typewriter and telegraph to transmit reports. What was reported was reviewed only by desk and supervisory officers in the line of command, not by special intelligence analysts. It was an amateurish system depending almost exclusively on the experience and intuitions of the Foreign Service officers abroad and those at senior levels in the Department. It was oblivious to claims of a special professional skill inherent in intelligence work. Sherman Kent, an outstanding intelligence analyst and historian of intelligence doctrines, stressed in *Strategic Intelligence for World Policy* that the task of selecting and analyzing strategic evidence relating to issues of peace and war is "a specialty of the very highest order" quite different from line duty in either the diplomatic or military service. He rightly considered both State and the military departments hopelessly unprepared to carry out strategic intelligence analysis. If this was true in 1946 when Kent was making his observations, one can imagine what the situation was like in 1941.

## Army and Navy: Military Collection and Evaluation

Except for the brilliance of their cryptanalytic work on Japanese diplomatic and military communications, the War Department, which then contained the Army Air Force, and the

Navy Department, were almost as inept as the State Department in dealing with foreign intelligence. They were better off only in the formal sense that they had specific units for collating and analyzing information from attaches abroad and from their intercept stations. The War Department's Military Intelligence Division (G-2) had 22 officers when war broke out in 1939. They had reached a total of nearly 500 men in Washington in December of 1941. At this rate of expansion, it was obvious few officers had any real intelligence experience.

Brigadier General Sherman Miles, who had become Chief of Intelligence in May 1940 after serving as Military Attache in London, testified at the Pearl Harbor inquiry that his unit was almost wholly preoccupied with "anti-subversive precautions," i.e., counterintelligence measures to protect U.S. Army facilities against sabotage. He also controlled the military attaches abroad, of which there were 60 by 1940. But the Army had no paid agents abroad and little access to information beyond local gossip picked up, as General Marshall later said, over after-dinner coffee cups.

The Navy was perhaps just a bit more sophisticated about the need for foreign intelligence, since its ships visited many ports across the seas, but it was equally unprepared structurally and intellectually for dealing with the tasks at hand. In mid-1940 the Office of Naval Intelligence (ONI) was still in a state of disorganization due to the rapid rotation of officers at a time when the pressure on officers in the Navy was to get assigned to sea duty. As late as mid-1941 the ONI had only 150 officers and civilian analysts in Washington, most of whom were new to the job. Captain T. S. Wilkinson, the third officer to head ONI in 1941 alone, took over on October 15th—with virtually no previous intelligence experience.

Like General Miles, Wilkinson felt his Domestic Branch for counterintelligence and prevention of subversion or sabotage was critically important. His Foreign Branch collected basic information on foreign countries, especially navies, but the ONI was expressly forbidden in 1941 to undertake any comprehensive "evaluation" of the significance of the reports. This function was reserved for the more prestigious War Plans Division of the Navy Department, headed by the higher ranking and more imperious Rear Admiral R. K. Turner.

The Navy was better represented abroad than the Army, having in the 1940-1941 period about 130 officers posted as attaches and observers in foreign capitals and at principal foreign ports. The information collected was restricted mainly, however, to technical data about ports and navies and was not much more helpful in divining foreign plans and intentions than was that collected by the Army or State Department personnel abroad.

Most of what the ONI got from all sources went straight to Admiral Turner who recast it as he saw it in relation to war plans to send to fleet units. He was aided in this process by snippets of information from Embassy reporting passed along through Captain R. E. Schuirmann, the Navy's perceptive special liaison officer with access at the senior working level in the State Department. The State Department did not divulge U.S. policy views or negotiating positions or outgoing diplomatic messages to the Navy, or to the War Department, any more than the Navy and War Department confided in the State Department details of their strategic war plans. Policymakers, like intelligence officers, worked in bureaucratic compartments largely unaware of what was going on in any area other than their own.

This structure of foreign information agencies working in separate parts of the Washington forest and doing their poor best to comprehend what was going on abroad constituted the foreign intelligence establishment of the day. In view of the general fragmentation of decision-making, the absence of a common data base and the lack of any centralized evaluation of foreign events, frustration with the system expressed at the time by President Roosevelt, and later remarked on by General Marshall, General Dwight D. Eisenhower, and Dean Acheson, is entirely understandable.

## Code Breaking: No Game for Gentlemen

The one bright spot in the whole chaotic picture of prewar intelligence was in the contribution made to policy officials by a breakthrough in intercepting and reading Japanese foreign diplomatic and military messages sent, mostly by radio, to other capitals or naval units at sea. Cryptanalysis, the science of deciphering or decoding messages deliberately scrambled for transmission, is several hundred years old, but it came into first-line prominence in the age of worldwide cable and radio networks. In World War I reading enemy messages, as the British were able to do, was important to success. As World War II approached, its value was magnified many times over. The British were successful again in the preliminary phase of World War II in 1939-1941, but the United States in this respect also had a valuable contribution to make from its own work in cryptanalysis.

In the early 1920s the State Department, the Army, and the Navy had operated a very successful joint "Black Chamber" for decoding foreign cablegrams borrowed from cooperative overseas telegraph companies or intercepted electronically. This interagency facility was closed down in 1929 on the grounds, later said by then Secretary of State Henry Stimson to be, that "gentlemen do not read each other's mail." This was the time of the equally idealistic Kellogg-Briand Pact "outlawing war" as an instrument of foreign policy—a declaration with no enforcement sanctions.

By 1939 it was painfully clear that non-gentlemen were in charge of affairs in large parts of the world. The U.S. Army and Navy, never having doubted this fact, were plugging away with the slender resources allotted them to read as many international messages as they could. By 1940 the two military services had something on the order of 750 personnel assigned to intercept and read radio signals. Most of these were radio technicians, but a few were skilled cryptanalysts and linquists. Indeed, with the singular good fortune that allowed the United States to find leaders like George Marshall and Dwight Eisenhower in the long-neglected armed forces when the military crisis came, the American government in 1940-1941 benefited from having some authentic geniuses in cryptanalysis available when they were most needed.

The Navy was concentrating on Japanese codes and ciphers, achieving some initial success in breaking them in 1939 and 1940. Then William F. Friedman, relatively little-known civilian Chief Cryptanalyst of the Army's Signal Intelligence Service, and his close associate, Frank B. Rowlett, broke Japan's top-level PURPLE diplomatic code in August 1940. Eventually, by the time of Pearl Harbor, the Army and Navy were deciphering reams of Japanese messages. The translations of these messages were christened collectively MAGIC, a marvellously appropriate code word for the few who knew what it meant. Both signal intercept services, though small and little-known or respected in their own combat-oriented organizations, were providing General Marshall, President Roosevelt, and a few top Army and Navy officers with astonishingly relevant intercepted intelligence about Japanese and, indirectly, German military activities, as well as some glimpses of diplomatic policies.

This extraordinary achievement proved of enormous value throughout World War II, but in the early period it was never exploited effectively, in part because it was distributed only to the very top officials and nowhere synthesized skillfully with diplomatic reporting and other data about foreign affairs available in Washington. Of the three main tasks of an intelligence system—1) collection of information, 2) evaluation or analysis of the data for meaning and relevance to decision-making, and 3) appropriate dissemination of findings to permit exploitation by policy and action authorities—only the first was fairly successful. As Roberta Wohlstetter pointed out in her book, *Pearl Harbor, Warning and Decision*, there was a plethora of data on the probability of Japanese attack but nobody sorted out the meaningful "signals" from the irrelevant and confusing "noise" to piece together the impending danger. As a result, Pearl Harbor will go down in history as a disaster for the United States rather than the intelligence triumph it might have been.

## The Non-barking Watchdog: The Joint Intelligence Committee

One feeble effort was made to coordinate these efforts a little better in the military context. This occurred late in 1941, too late to help at the time of Pearl Harbor. In 1939 President Roosevelt took over personally, as Commander in Chief, the supervision of the somewhat desultory deliberations of the Joint Army-Navy Board, which had existed for many years to insure "cooperation and coordination" of all "joint action of the Army and Navy relative to national defense." In 1940 and 1941 it began to develop some coherent plans on munitions procurement and aviation development in the two services. It was not a staff agency but simply a committee capable only of making interservice recommendations. It was, nevertheless, in 1941 the only rudimentary high command the nation had, and it decided to make a stab, at least in principle, at providing an intelligence base to underpin its deliberations. General Marshall, Chief of Staff of the Army, and the capable Chief of Naval Operations, Admiral Harold R. (Betty) Stark, ordered the establishment of a Joint Intelligence Committee (JIC) as a central information group serving the Joint Board. The order was approved on October 1, 1941, setting up the Joint Army Navy Intelligence Committee. Army G-2 and ONI wrangled over procedures and office space with their service colleagues for weeks, however, and the first, somewhat sterile administration meeting of the JIC took place on December 3, 1941—too little and much too late. If the Joint Board and the JIC constituted the watchdog of the nation's military security, as it seemed to on paper, its significance was a little like the non-barking dog in one of Sherlock Holmes' famous cases; the intelligence watchdog was not yet ready to bark when the blow fell.

## Counterintelligence: The FBI

A different kind of interagency intelligence committee had been set up earlier, the Intelligence Coordinating Committee, established in mid-1939 and publicly announced September 6, 1939. Its range of vision was limited. The mission of this Committee was to work out coordinated programs in the Army's Military Intelligence Division, the Navy's ONI, and the Justice Department's Federal Bureau of Investigation (FBI) for all investigation of foreign espionage and sabotage in the United States.

J. Edgar Hoover, the power-hungry head of the FBI and its only chief from 1924 until his death in 1972, thus became the first civilian official to become involved in intelligence. Perhaps it was partly his influence, although it was certainly also a reflection of official and public fears of German and Japanese threats to internal security, that led General Miles and the several Navy captains who headed the ONI in the 1939-1941 period to emphasize counterintelligence so much, to some extent at the expense of collecting and analyzing positive foreign intelligence about events outside the United States.

Hoover had long benefited from a highly developed instinct for bureaucratic longevity and a knack for generating favorable publicity about FBI achievements. He and his G-men were most famous for gangbusting in the Al Capone and John Dillinger days of the 1920s and 1930s, but Hoover made his name early as a stern opponent and investigator of Communist subversion and violence.

It was not surprising that President Roosevelt turned to Hoover in the late 1930s when he became concerned about subversive activities not only by Communists but by Fascists (Italian and German) who were believed—accurately—to wish to manipulate economic and political life in the United States in their own interests. According to Hoover, Roosevelt authorized him "confidentially" in September 1936 to begin counter-espionage investigations of all foreign subversive agents in this country. He was to work with the Army and Navy and consolidate in the FBI all information available in other parts of the government, including the State Department.

Until then the FBI had been essentially a law enforcement agency, investigating individual cases of espionage as they occurred, but its authorization to exchange information, build files, and coordinate activities with the military agencies to foresee and forestall espionage and sabotage gave it primary responsibility in the civilian field. It received an appropriation of $50,000 for counterespionage investigations in 1938.

There was some resistance in State and Treasury to FBI authority at first, but the establishment of the interdepartmental Intelligence Coordinating Committee in 1939 nailed down Hoover's position in the domestic field. Ever aggressive, the FBI quickly began to yearn for a role in overseas intelligence operations. Hoover was always reluctant to share power, even in his own agency. In mid-1940 he asked for authority to set up a "Special Intelligence Service" to operate in the foreign field with a secret agent capability abroad, just as in the United States.

President Roosevelt made a typically pragmatic decision by dividing the field of espionage and counterespionage abroad among the FBI in the Western Hemisphere, the Navy in the

Pacific, and the Army in Europe, Africa, and the Panama Canal Zone. Oddly, Hawaii was the only area where "coverage of Japanese espionage" was a joint responsibility of the Army, Navy, and the FBI rather than exclusively the task of Hoover's men. It stayed that way until the Pearl Harbor attack, when there was enough blame for all three agencies.

The FBI moved out actively in South America and the Caribbean, establishing liaison with British clandestine intelligence stations in the Caribbean in particular, and obviously began to groom itself for the central role in nonmilitary intelligence across the board. It kept control of its special apparatus in Latin America throughout the war. Where the FBI failed was in getting permission to extend its agent network into other overseas areas. It was not the Army and Navy but another civilian agency, Donovan's new outfit, that preempted this field. Otherwise the United States might have combined all of its clandestine capabilities and the all-important responsibility for coordinating secret intelligence in a single body organized more or less along the lines of the KGB—the Soviet secret police organization that controls both domestic counterintelligence and foreign intelligence collection. In view of what hindsight tells us of the tyrannical, secretive manner in which Hoover ran the FBI in his later years, and the skill with which he intimidated Washington politicians with hints that any loose behavior of theirs might be recorded in the sacrosanct FBI files, it is a blessing that his attempt to establish an all-purpose, police-oriented intelligence system was sidetracked.

Probably it was Roosevelt's political instinct, in keeping with the constitutional doctrine of separation of powers, that made him avoid concentrating secret powers and overall intelligence responsibility in a single law enforcement agency. Something, in any case, caused events to take a quite different turn. As a result, domestic agent operations in the United States remained quite apart from the apparatus set up to collect and coordinate all foreign intelligence overseas.

## Intelligence Gifts from Britain

In the pre-World War II era, in mid-1941, an entirely new civilian intelligence agency entered the field to frustrate Hoover's ambitions. It was the short-lived Office of the

Coordinator of Information (COI), set up in July 1941, and subsequently in 1942 rechristened with the better-known name, the Office of Strategic Services (OSS). President Roosevelt deserves enormous credit for seeing the need at this early date for a revolutionary new concept in what was still peacetime—a civilian, central coordinating intelligence system. The credit for this vision must be shared, however, with Winston Churchill and a group of British officials who, for their own reasons, desperately wanted to help the United States create an effective intelligence system. They clearly saw the need for something better than the patchwork of bureaucratic bits and pieces that they observed with dismay in 1939 and 1940 as they sought to educate American officials about the crucial need to counter the German threat in Europe.

The motivating factor was that the British Government wanted to share its most sensitive intelligence—and it had much to share—with the United States, but share it in some way that would not allow careless handling to endanger good sources of information and also to insure it would be presented in an objective and integrated manner to high U.S. officials.

Churchill was certain the Americans would perceive their own danger and, in the fullness of time, come to the aid of beleaguered Britain if only the facts could be surfaced in Washington in an orderly and sensible way. To meet this need in part, the British tried to inspire the creation of a civilian-controlled central intelligence system in the image of their own. They conducted this ambitious covert political action in the United States so as to give their cousins across the Atlantic the best product of the British Joint Intelligence Committee and secret intelligence services machinery.

Churchill wanted Americans to face the strategic facts of life in their own (American) interests but also in time to save Great Britain, or at the very least the British fleet, from destruction. To this fact the United States in large part owed the concept of intelligence enunciated by Roosevelt in mid-1941, when the actual structure and competence of U.S. intelligence was abysmally inadequate.

The British had been casting about for some time as to how to come to grips with the problem of liaison with U.S. intelligence agencies. British military intelligence agencies were extremely well-informed about Europe, especially since they were recipients of signals intelligence and detailed clandestine agent reports from Europe, both provided by the quasi-independent, essentially civilian British intelligence organization known as the Secret Intelligence Service, or the MI-6. This was a secret agent intelligence agency tracing its origins back to the days of the first Queen Elizabeth and her great Secretary of State, Sir Francis Walsingham, when agents abroad, reporting in cipher or by safe hand, prepared England to meet and defeat the great challenge of that era, the attack of the Spanish Armada.

The label MI-6 was a cover designation suggesting a military section of the War Office staff. There was also an MI-5, the internal security service comparable to the FBI in the United States. In fact, the MI-6 was an independent civilian agency reporting directly to Cabinet and Crown, working under the very close policy supervision of the Foreign Office. This procedure came about as a result of a peculiarly British bureaucratic arrangement adopted in 1939 shortly after hostilities began, when it was imperative for foreign policy and military affairs to proceed on the same understanding and data base. Under this arrangement a distinguished senior Foreign Office official chaired an interagency coordinating group called the Joint Intelligence Committee, a subcommittee of the British Chiefs of Staff, the Army, Navy, and Air joint high command, through which the Prime Minister ran the war. By this interleaving of institutional interests and staffs, the British had created an integrated decision-making system and an intelligence organization to serve it.

In the entire wartime period beginning on November 5, 1939, the head of the MI-6, always referred to only as "C," was General Sir Stewart Menzies (pronounced "Mengiss"), a Guards Officer, a British clubman, and a friend of Winston Churchill's. He had direct access to the Prime Minister, which he exercised frequently after Churchill assumed that post in May 1940, but he worked very closely with the Foreign Office and the other Joint Intelligence Committee agencies to secure policy guidance and coordinate both activities and findings.

Menzies even earlier, when he was Deputy Chief of the MI-6, had been a key proponent of the British cryptanalysis staff which, under his personal sponsorship, in due time developed a machine—lovingly called the "Bomb"—that in 1940 began deciphering the German Enigma cipher machine. With the product of British cryptanalysis, called ULTRA, Menzies and the MI-6 had important chips to use in the British intelligence game. Because of the successful intelligence coordinating procedures and the fact that Great Britain was fighting for its very life, the British system worked much more smoothly, produced a great deal more intelligence, and fed it more directly into the policy chiefs in the Cabinet than the prewar U.S. intelligence agencies were able to do.

The MI-6 also had the full benefit of their agents reporting from the European continent and such important items of enemy order of battle as emerged from military, especially naval reconnaissance, radio-direction-finding, and mail censorship, which was carried out not only in Great Britain but in various colonies of the British Empire, especially Bermuda. British colonies in the Caribbean were particularly productive of information on German infiltration in South America, a matter of tremendous interest to the FBI.

Exchange of intelligence between the Americans and the British in the broad political sense of the word began as soon as war had broken out in Europe. During the "twilight war" from September 3, 1939 until May 10, 1940, Neville Chamberlain continued in office as Prime Minister despite wide disillusionment with his diplomatic surrender to Hitler at Munich and the sacrifice of Czechoslovakia, but he appointed a War Cabinet with Winston Churchill—its boldest member—as First Lord of the Admiralty. On September 11, 1939, Roosevelt sent Churchill a personal note referring gracefully to their single World War I contact when both were senior civilian officials in the respective U.S. and British navies, saying he was glad Churchill was back again in the Admiralty and inviting him to keep the President in touch personally with anything he ought to know about by sealed letters in the diplomatic pouch.

Churchill seized this opportunity with alacrity, sending, before the war was over, more than a thousand messages and receiving as many, mostly transmitted electronically. Churchill signed these messages "Naval Person" or, after he became Prime Minister in May 1940, "Former Naval Person" and addressed them to "POTUS." This acronym seemed to have the grandiose connotations Churchill always deliberately chose when he adopted code names for important projects, although in this case it simply stood for "President of the United States." Through this privileged channel passed the British views of the great dangers facing Britain and the rest of the world. After the fall of France and Churchill's assumption of leadership of Great Britain at the most desperate period of the war, Churchill came to look on this channel of communication as a lifeline to the New World on which he increasingly relied to counterbalance the overwhelming military power of Hitler's Germany in the Old World.

As soon as he took over the awesome responsibilities of Prime Minister, Churchill began casting about for institutional liaison devices through which he could educate the top ranks of the U.S. Government on the strategic issues of the time as he saw them. His chosen instrument was a Canadian, William Stephenson, whom he assigned to New York in June of 1940, not only as the MI-6's man in the United States but also as the Prime Minister's "personal representative" for building a secret resistance capability that could survive even the fall of England.

Even earlier, in April 1940, while he was still technically only in charge of the Navy, Churchill had taken a direct hand in the policy problem of intelligence liaison with the United States. In this kind of emergency evidently he felt he could and should approve special arrangements that bypassed then Prime Minister Chamberlain, whose political position was rapidly deteriorating. Churchill decided to pass to President Roosevelt personally much useful strategic intelligence, including ULTRA, intercepted German messages, and also inform him of evidence that Hitler's scientists had been successfully experimenting with atom-splitting, and were interested in acquiring "heavy water" facilities in Norway. The British already knew that Albert Einstein had alerted President Roosevelt in October 1939 to the staggering implications of atomic energy released in the form of a bomb.

It was remarkable that the civilian Cabinet minister in charge of the Navy, together with the MI-6, felt able to pass these sensitive intelligence reports to Roosevelt; it is even more amazing that the British intelligence establishment evidently never gave this information to appeasement-minded Prime

Minister Chamberlain nor told him of the special intelligence channel to Roosevelt that they set up.[2]

The man who was sent to the United States on this first mission in April 1940, and who was two months later assigned permanently as the MI-6's station chief, was an unusual character, a wealthy Canadian businessman with a keen concern for British Commonwealth security as well as many friendly connections in the United States. This representative of "C" in New York was referred to as "Little Bill" Stephenson, not only because he was slight in stature but to distinguish him from the much stockier "Big Bill" Donovan, who soon became his closest American confidant.

When Stephenson first visited Washington in April, he undertook to establish a channel for the secure passage of sensitive information by approaching the only civilian U.S. intelligence agency in existence at the time, the FBI. Stephenson made an appointment with J. Edgar Hoover through a mutual acquaintance, boxing champion Gene Tunney, rather than via official channels. Through other friends with access to the White House, he talked directly with Roosevelt about atomic bombs, about U.S.-British collaboration in cryptanalysis, and in particular about the British discovery of a German agent penetration of the U.S. Embassy in London, whereby even copies of the POTUS-Navy Person messages were being stolen. All of this information confirmed Roosevelt in his wish for the "closest possible marriage" with the MI-6, and he authorized liaison with the only secret intelligence instrument he had, the FBI, even concurring in Hoover's typically cautious stipulation that the State Department be left unaware of the arrangement.

Stephenson worked as best he could with Hoover, who was mainly interested in getting British information for the benefit of his own organization in its counterespionage work. Hoover was less interested in unraveling intelligence networks for the sake of strategically meaningful information about Germany than he was in finding spies and saboteurs in North America and arresting them. He also benefited greatly from close cooperation with British intelligence and police agencies in the British Caribbean and throughout Latin America, where German spies and political propagandists were very active. As for providing the President with an evaluation of strategic developments in the world, Hoover and the FBI were disappointing instruments for the British purpose. The FBI was happy to receive raw agent reports, censorship intercepts, and other pieces of what they considered "hard" information from the British, but it had, neither intellectually nor institutionally, any real capability for broad strategic analysis or estimates of future developments. It lived entirely in the world of counter-espionage investigations and the action-oriented gangbusting world of law enforcement.

Thus the FBI, particularly as reflected by the suspicious personality of its dogmatic chief, quickly proved unsatisfactory for the larger purposes Churchill had in mind in sending Stephenson to the United States. The British were able to secure tacit toleration from Hoover for their own extensive espionage, counterespionage, and covert propaganda activities throughout the Western Hemisphere; these were essential to protect the common security interests of the U.S. "arsenal of democracy" and the shipping lanes to Great Britain. This arrangement was indispensable. Stephenson was already on the lookout, however, for something better. He soon found his man, temperamentally totally different from and, personally, decidedly antagonistic toward J. Edgar Hoover. The man was William Donovan.

In some ways, Donovan was already in the intelligence business as a private citizen, a sort of one-man intelligence minister without portfolio. He was head of a successful Wall Street law firm with enough interest in international business to provide a rationale for his periodic travels to Europe's trouble spots throughout the 1930s. Personally he needed no excuse. His intellectual curiosity about world affairs was boundless. He wanted to be where the action was and to see for himself, two prime requirements of the natural intelligence officer. He was a much-decorated military hero of World War I, a Republican from Roosevelt's home state of New York, and by temperament a fighting Irishman. He was also a millionaire, a sophisticated patriot-nationalist, and an interventionist and activist in both national and international politics. Having had a first-hand look at Nazi Germany, Fascist Italy, the war in Abyssinia, and the proxy conflict in Spain, Donovan was psychologically prepared better than most for the shock of the conquest of Poland in 1939 and much of Western Europe in April and May 1940. By then he was 57 years old, a vigorous man with clear blue eyes, silvery gray hair, a burly build, and a quietly persuasive manner of speech.

Donovan had served as an Assistant Attorney General in the Justice Department for a time in the 1920s—when he learned to dislike the ambitious young Hoover—and had associated with national-level politicians and officials all his life, having run for Governor of New York in 1932. Frank Knox, owner of the *Chicago Daily News* and Republican vice presidential nominee in 1936, was a longtime close friend and admirer of Donovan. When Knox was brought into the Cabinet as Secretary of the Navy in June 1940 to give something of a national coalition aspect to FDR's administration, he was instrumental in Donovan's being sent to England as special envoy and observer for the President to size up the military and political situation there in the summer of 1940.

This step in itself testified not only to the grimness of the situation in Europe but to Roosevelt's consciousness of the inadequacy of his intelligence. From London he was receiving a steady barrage of pessimistic reports from the American Ambassador, Joseph P. Kennedy, predicting early British collapse or surrender. U.S. Army intelligence was taking a gloomy view of British military prospects, and both the Army and the Navy were reluctant to release arms to England that also were needed for the rapidly expanding U.S. armed forces. Roosevelt welcomed the idea of an independent review by a man who could report directly to him without bureaucratic hindrance or distortions.

It was a crucial mission and Stephenson grasped the significance immediately. Donovan set off July 14, 1940, by clipper flying boat via Lisbon on a "business" trip without prior notice to the U.S. Embassy, and returned in early August. He got a warm reception in England, was received by the King, by Churchill, and many other war leaders, as well as by the key men in England's intelligence system. From this visit flowed an exchange of secret information, not only intelligence but scientific and technical weapons developments, data which eventually helped a great deal in winning World War II. This collaborative effort was formalized in 1941 and was put into full gear as soon as the United State entered the war. This extraordinarily sensitive partnership, known to relatively few until quite recently, was a critical factor in strengthening the capabilities of both nations to permit the rapid codebreaking progress each made against Germany and Japan—achievements without which it is hard to see how the naval war and the air war could have been won by the British and American forces, especially in the crucial period of allied inferiority in 1941-1943.

Donovan came back to the United States early in August 1940 and reported to Roosevelt that the morale of Great Britian under Churchill was high, that it had enormous assets in its air force, its still secret radar defense net, its extraordinary intelligence yield from intercepting German military communications, and its newly formed irregular warfare teams under the Special Operations Executive (SOE) of the Ministry of Economic Warfare, which were being trained to encourage resistance behind enemy lines. He also reported that the British desperately needed U.S. arms and should receive them because Britain constituted the first line of American defense. He particularly urged the swap of U.S. destroyers for British Caribbean bases that, a few weeks later on September 4, 1940, linked American and British security together in an unmistakable way.

Correspondence of a candid, informal nature between the American and British leaders concerning this crucial reinforcement of England's naval defenses was handled through Stephenson, who was kept informed of developments by Donovan. As the British MI-6 station chief, Stephenson supervised all espionage, counterespionage, and signals intelligence work in the United States. He also was designated as the Prime Minister's personal representative for coordinating all other British secret recruiting and training activities in Canada and the United States for the new SOE irregulars—then largely amateur specialists in unconventional warfare and sometimes called the "Baker Street Irregulars."

The dapper Canadian, who spoke authoritatively for Churchill and easily worked his way into Roosevelt's confidence, set up in business as "British Passport Control Officer" in New York City and director of a new organization christened the British Security Coordination office (BSC). The BSC headquarters was in Room 3606, the International Building, at Rockefeller Center. Stephenson's job included responsibility for protecting munitions being manufactured in the Western Hemisphere and shipped to England—from sabotage and from successful interdiction at sea. He exchanged intelligence for this purpose with the FBI, giving J. Edgar Hoover many of his saboteur leads.

Primarily, however, Stephenson's job was to see that Americans of influence inside and outside the government correctly understood the situation in Europe after the fall of France and clearly saw the need to help keep England from going under. This was a covert political task, supplementary to the work of the diplomats in the British Embassy. As Churchill wrote to Lord Lothian, his Ambassador to Washington, "If we go down, Hitler has a very good chance of conquering the world." Stephenson was personally briefed by Churchill for his mission to the United States and was given his own cryptonym —INTREPID—a good description of both men. Both the United States and England owe much to the good work of Stephenson, but his greatest contribution probably was in recognizing the talents of Donovan.

Without question "Little Bill" inspired Donovan and Roosevelt to take the step of setting up the unprecedented post of Coordinator of Information in July 1941. By that time Stephenson knew full well how inadequate and chaotic Roosevelt's intelligence support was. The handsomest gift of all from Britain via Stephenson was the concept of a central, coordinated intelligence system. This idea, once articulated, could not be destroyed. It survived the war and eventually formed the core concept of a peacetime intelligence system under a Central Intelligence Agency.

## The Beginnings of a Central Intelligence System

A year elapsed between Donovan's first full exposure to the riches of British intelligence in July 1940 and the formalization of his charter to begin the effort to create a central intelligence system for the United States. In this period, due in great part to the superiority of its exploitation of the ULTRA ciphers and electronic signals analysis, Great Britain's meager but brilliantly led Royal Air Force withstood the full fury of German air attack and by September 1940 forced Hitler to give up the battle for control of Britain's air space, on which his plans for invasion across the English Channel depended. Although damaging city-busting raids at night continued, the real Battle of Britain had been won, and Hitler increasingly turned his attention to preparing a massive surprise assault on the Soviet Union on the other front.

By November 1940 Roosevelt had won his unprecedented election to a third term as President, and American sympathies increasingly turned to the courageous, beleaguered British. Churchill was pumping his views and a lot of information on the war directly into the White House for Roosevelt's benefit. The President gradually moved U.S. policy toward the concept favored by his Army and Navy advisers: all aid to Great Britain short of war. The Lend-Lease bill was passed on March 11, 1941, evidently based on Roosevelt's own invention of the idea that he brilliantly explained to the American people at a press conference in December 1940, evoking the analogy of "loaning" a garden hose to put out a fire in a neighbor's house. Secret joint military planning meetings with the British (termed ABC-1) were held in Washington from January 29 to March 27, 1941, to sort out common defense measures and strategy "should the United States be compelled to resort to war." On May 27, 1941, Roosevelt gave one of his most effective radio fireside chats, charging that Hitler aimed at domination of the world and had brought the war to the edge of the Western Hemisphere by his submarine warfare. The President committed the United States to use armed patrols "to insure delivery of the needed supplies to Britain." He then declared an unlimited national emergency.

In this period Donovan continued to consult closely with Stephenson and took an extensive trip to Europe and the Mediterranean for Roosevelt with Churchill's blessing. He visited British intelligence installations again, including Bermuda, the vital electronic and mail intercept site astride the air and shipping lanes, and visited the Balkans to observe the chances of German attack there and to encourage Yugoslav resistance— resistance that delayed the German attack on the Soviet Union and forced Hitler to fight "General Winter" as well as the Russians on the outskirts of Moscow at the end of 1941.

In all these matters Stephenson assisted Donovan, sometimes accompanying him and advising him on intelligence tasks and techniques. He cabled to Churchill after Donovan's first trip in the summer of 1940 that Donovan was "doing much to combat defeatist attitude Washington." When Donovan made his second personal reconnaissance of Britain and the Mediterranean theater of war from December 1940 until March of 1941, Stephenson cabled Churchill: "Impossible overemphasize importance of Donovan mission. He can play a great and perhaps vital role. It may not be consistent with orthodox diplomacy nor confined to its channels...."[3]

Stephenson had his own man, a young RAF attache named Roald Dahl, with personal access to the President both at the White House and Hyde Park. Stephenson and Donovan also kept in close touch with Ernest Cuneo, a young White House lawyer who served as the President's "special liaison officer," and took him to England with them when they all met Churchill at 10 Downing Street in the middle of a night as, dressed in his air-raid "jumpsuit," he was working on military problems until dawn.

When Donovan went to the Eastern Mediterranean on his second trip, Stephenson allegedly arranged for British Naval Intelligence to advise the Commander in Chief of the Mediterranean Fleet: "We can achieve more through Donovan than any other individual... He can be trusted to represent our needs in the right quarters and in the right way in USA...."[4] Stephenson already had cabled Churchill: "I have been attempting to maneuver Donovan into job of coordinating all United States intelligence."

Upon Donovan's return to Washington from his Balkan trip on the 18th of March 1941, he fully justified British confidence. He made a public radio address on March 25, stating his views on "national defense, an essential part of which is our policy of aid to Great Britain." He said, "We have no choice as to whether or not we will be attacked. That choice is Hitler's: and he has already made it... not for Europe alone, but for Africa, Asia and the world. Our only choice is to decide whether we will resist it." It was at this time, at the very end of March, that

Stephenson reported that President Roosevelt endorsed the idea of some kind of central intelligence machinery. He wrote: "Donovan saw President today and after long discussion wherein all points agreed, he accepted appointment coordination all forms intelligence including offensive operations. He ... will be responsible only repeat only to President."[5]

If Roosevelt had made up his mind this early, he delayed putting it into execution for several weeks, undoubtedly knowing that bureaucratic opposition would be intense, and wanting the Army and Navy to go along gracefully with the proposal. His decision to move on establishing an institutional role for central intelligence probably came after reading Donovan's reports on his trip. Donovan had written Frank Knox on March 27, 1941, summarizing his observations on his Balkan journey and reporting on the British system of central coordination and processing intelligence for the use of high officials in the United Kingdom.[6] On April 26, he wrote for Knox the first paper—some four pages—specifically dealing with creation of a central intelligence system for the United States. In it he described the British system and listed the basic principles that he thought should guide a similar U.S. organization: control by the President, access to secret funds, and, without taking over the existing duties of the intelligence agencies, sole charge of intelligence collection abroad. The new institution would interpret all intelligence for the President. In this paper Donovan also discussed the function of propaganda and subversive activities abroad.

The President's response to this was to request Stimson, Knox, and Attorney General Robert Jackson to work with Donovan on a proposal for a U.S. service for coordinating strategic information. Donovan thereupon submitted a "Memorandum of Establishment of Service of Strategic Information," dated June 10, 1941. Key passages read:

> Strategy, without information upon which it can rely, is helpless. Likewise, information is useless unless it is intelligently directed to the strategic purpose. Modern warfare depends upon the economic base—on the supply of raw materials, on the capacity and performance of the industrial plant, on the scope of agricultural production and upon the character and efficiency of communications. Strategic reserves will determine the strength of the attack and the resistance of the defense....
>
> Although we are facing imminent peril, we are lacking in effective service for analyzing, comprehending, and appraising such information as we might

obtain, (or in some cases have obtained), relative to the intention of potential enemies and the limit of the economic and military resources of those enemies. Critical analysis of this information is as presently important for our supply program as if we were actually engaged in armed conflict...it is essential that we set up a central enemy intelligence organization which would itself collect either directly or through existing departments of government, at home and abroad, pertinent information concerning potential enemies....

The basic purpose of this Service of Strategic information is to constitute a means by which the President, as Commander-in-Chief, and his Strategic Board would have available accurate and complete enemy intelligence reports upon which military operational decisions could be based.[7]

It was just at this time that the British Director of Naval Intelligence, Rear Admiral John Godfrey, was in Washington consulting on the establishment of a permanent British Joint Staff Mission attached to the British Embassy and designated by the cover name of Advisers to the Supply Council. Godfrey was accompanied by his personal assistant, Lieutenant Commander Ian Fleming, whose romantic fictional spy stories about 007, James Bond, were to distort American conceptions of intelligence many years later. They both urged coordinated intelligence machinery in Washington and coordination between Washington and London. Godfrey did not feel he made any progress with the FBI or the Army and Navy. Through friends of Stephenson, he wangled an invitation to the White House and spoke his piece privately to the President about the importance of having one "intelligence security boss, not three or four." Ian Fleming also gave Donovan a detailed memorandum on what we would not call intelligence requirements that the British wanted the United States to satisfy by querying its diplomatic and consular posts in "Axis or Axis-occupied territories" on such things as state of morale and bombing targets.[8]

In any case Roosevelt received Donovan at the White House on June 18 and discussed his suggestions, which had included descriptions of secret paramilitary activities like the British irregulars, whose training Donovan had studied with care. Finally the President asked him to accept the role of "Coordinator of Information," told him he would have the rank of major general, and would be responsible for covert offensive action behind enemy lines as well as collection and analysis of intelligence.⁹ Although Donovan wanted a combat role for himself in the event of war, he accepted the President's offer.

A "Military Order," dated June 25, 1941, was drafted establishing the "position of Coordinator of Defense Intelligence" to operate "under the direction and supervision of the President" and designating Donovan as "Coordinator of Strategic Information." The key clause in this document granted Donovan

> Authority to collect and analyze information and data, military or otherwise, which may bear upon national defense strategy; to interpret and correlate such strategic information and data, and to make it available to the President and to such other officials as the President may determine, and to carry out, when requested by the President, such supplementary activities as may facilitate the securing of strategic information not now available to the government.¹⁰

This document was faulty in not specifying any institutional home for Donovan, but by referring to him as "Donovan, U.S. Army," it presumably would have placed him somewhere in the War Department, where there already was a G-2 Division of the General Staff with somewhat similar functions.

This June 25 document is seldom cited and seems to have no official standing.¹¹ It is evidently a draft that was then amended to provide the text for a second Presidential order that soon appeared, dated July 11, 1941, in the form of a Presidential Directive from the White House printed in the *Federal Register*. It is less sloppily drafted than the first and must be considered the charter document for the civilian forerunner of the OSS. It is *in toto* the embodiment of the concept of central intelligence as conceived in 1941:

### DESIGNATING A COORDINATOR OF INFORMATION

By virtue of the authority vested in me as President of the United States and as Commander in Chief of the Army and Navy of the United States, it is ordered as follows:
1. There is hereby established the position of Coordinator of Information, with authority to collect and analyze all information and data, which may bear upon national security; to correlate such information and data, and to make such information and data available to the President and to such departments and officials of the Government as the President may determine; and to carry out, when requested by the President, such supplementary activities as may

facilitate the securing of information important for national security not now available to the Government.

2. The several departments and agencies of the Government shall make available to the Coordinator of Information all such information and data relating to national security as the Coordinator, with the approval of the President, may from time to time request.

3. The Coordinator of Information may appoint such committees, consisting of appropriate representatives of the various departments and agencies of the Government, as he may deem necessary to assist him in the performance of his functions.

4. Nothing in the duties and responsibilities of the Coordinator of Information shall in any way interfere with or impair the duties and responsibilities of the regular military and naval advisors of the President as Commander in Chief of the Army and Navy.

5. Within the limits of such funds as may be allocated to the Coordinator of Information by the President, the Coordinator may employ necessary personnel and make provision for the necessary supplies, facilities, and services.

6. William J. Donovan is hereby designated as Coordinator of Information.

(Signed)

THE WHITE HOUSE ........................... Franklin D. Roosevelt
July 11, 1941

The sentence that reads: "collect and analyze all information and data" is significant and certainly reflected the spirit of "all source" intelligence that animated Donovan, Allen Welsh Dulles, the OSS, and the CIA. The word "correlate" is prominent in both documents, and it carried down into the CIA charter to indicate that the unique quality of a central intelligence agency is to put together in a meaningful pattern all information available from any source.

The order emphasized the authority and responsibility of the President in strategic intelligence and the importance of passing centrally correlated and analyzed information directly to the President and his immediate policy advisers. There was no reference to Donovan's belonging to the "U.S. Army" in this directive, and in fact he did not get his promised rank of major general for a long time.

The order also invented the phrase "national security" that has lived on to the present, explaining the rationale for much intelligence activity and serving also as a vague pretext for almost anything a President wanted done. The independent status of the office of the Coordinator of Information, outside any Cabinet Department, gave it wide freedom of action but also guaranteed it ample bureaucratic opposition from intelligence elements within old-line Cabinet Departments. The term "coordinator" itself implied voluntary cooperation, not dictation to other agencies. This unusual status in what came to be called "The Executive Offices of the President" left the new agency somewhat exposed to the abuse of its authority by any particularly imperious President. The elastic clause about carrying out "supplementary activities" when requested by the President was designed to cover a multitude of secret actions and hence was capable of covering a multitude of sins.

It was all there, a Presidential prescription for filling the compelling need for central intelligence in a charter that, if properly read, called for clandestine collection of intelligence, analysis of intelligence from all sources, and "supplementary activities," which were understood to include secret or covert actions to frustrate Nazi Germany's control of Europe.[12]

This tripartite assignment of functions meant that there would no doubt be enormous difficulty in controlling an organization with such irregular, secret duties within the framework of a free society. This 1941 solution was determined by the pressures on Roosevelt to prepare for the war that lay just ahead. The confusion inevitably surrounding the creation of any new instrument of government was compounded by uncertainty as to just what a central intelligence organization should do, and this confusion about the several roles of intelligence has persisted down to this day. Nevertheless, the basic concept was so sound and so clearly articulated in this first U.S. central intelligence charter that it survived intact the trials and troubles of the next 40 years.

The irony is that this tremendously useful new U.S. instrument of government might never have come into being if it had not been urged upon the United States by the British and fashioned after the British intelligence system. In helping to create an effective U.S. central intelligence system, British leaders were in effect carrying out a covert political action—one they believed was not only essential for Great Britain but also extremely important for the United States. They were right. It was a classic example of the best kind of covert action, one that immensely benefited both nations.

*Chapter Two*

# OSS: "Wild Bill's" Band of Secret Warriors

It was easy enough for Roosevelt to provide a charter, empower Donovan to start an agency, and receive authorization to spend several millions of largely unvouchered dollars.¹ Still, it was not easy for Donovan to acquire the staff he needed, find office space for them, get them paid either as civil or military personnel, and impart some sense of specific duties to his fledgling outfit. Army and Navy intelligence, the FBI, and the State Department inevitably resisted what they viewed as encroachment on their domains, and the Bureau of the Budget watchdogs were reluctant to release funds under the rather vague description of duties in the Donovan charter.

"Wild Bill" deserves his sobriquet mainly for two reasons. First, he permitted the "wildest," loosest kind of administrative and procedural chaos to develop while he concentrated on recruiting talent wherever he could find it—in universities, businesses, law firms, in the armed services, at Georgetown cocktail parties, in fact, anywhere he happened to meet or hear about bright and eager men and women who wanted to help. His immediate lieutenants and their assistants were all at work on the same task, and it was a long time before any systematic method of structuring the polyglot staff complement was worked out. Donovan really did not care. He counted on some able young men from his law firm in New York to straighten out the worst administrative messes, arguing that the record would justify his agency if it was good and excuse all waste and confusion. If the agency was a failure, the United States would probably lose the war and the bookkeeping would not matter. In this approach he was probably right.

In any case, Donovan did manage during the war to create a legend about his work, and that of the OSS conveying overtones of glamour, innovation, and daring. This infuriated the regular bureaucrats but created a cult of romanticism about intelligence that persisted and helped win popular support for continuation of an intelligence organization. It also, of course, created the myths about intelligence—the cloak-and-dagger exploits—that have made it so hard to persuade the aficionados of spy fiction that the heart of intelligence work consists of properly evaluated information from all sources, however collected.

The second way in which Donovan deserved the term "Wild" was his own personal fascination with bravery and derring-do. He empathized most with the men behind enemy lines. He was constantly traveling to faraway theaters of war to be as near them as possible, and he left to his subordinates the more humdrum business of processing secret intelligence reports in Washington and preparing analytical studies for the President or the Joint Chiefs of Staff (JCS).

Fortunately Donovan had good sense about choosing subordinates. Some were undoubtedly freaks, but the quotient of talent was high and for the most part it rose to the top of the agency. One of Donovan's greatest achievements was setting in motion a train of events that drew to him and to intelligence work a host of able men and women who imparted to intellectual life in the foreign field some of the verve and drive that New Deal lawyers and political scientists had given to domestic affairs under Roosevelt in the 1930s.

Thomas G. (Tommy) Corcoran, Washington's durable political lawyer and an early New Deal "brain-truster" from Harvard Law School, says that his greatest contribution to government in his long career was helping infiltrate smart young Harvard Law School products into every agency of government. He felt the United States needed to develop a highly educated, highly motivated public service corps that had not existed before Roosevelt's time. Donovan did much the same for career experts in international affairs by collecting in one place a galaxy of experience and ability the likes of which even the State Department had never seen.* Many of these later drifted away, but a core remained to create a tradition and eventually to take key jobs in a mature intelligence system of the kind the United States required for coping with twentieth century problems.

## Research and Analysis

One of the first things Donovan did was to consult Archibald MacLeish, the intellectual and poet who was the Librarian of Congress. MacLeish pointed out that a mine of data was in the Library in books, magazines, newspapers, and maps, if it could be exploited by research scholars familiar with such sources. He offered the facilities of the Library of Congress and suggested some scholars who might be willing to help. In fact, many new employees of the COI and later the OSS went to work initially in an annex of the Library because it was the only place they could sit and be usefully employed in reading, pending completion of their security clearances. Eventually Donovan got some space for most of his scholars in an old apartment house at 23rd and E Streets, N.W., an annex of the State Department, which became the habitat of nearly 2,000 research analysts with an astonishing array of foreign-area expertise. Soon his empire spilled over into the complex of red brick and gray stone buildings originally belonging to the National Institutes of Health, plus several dreary World War II temporary gray frame buildings back of the old Heurich Brewery at the end of Rock Creek Drive along the Potomac. All of these finally constituted the main institutional home of the OSS referred to by the single address of 2430 E Street, N.W.

---

*McGeorge Bundy, President of the Ford Foundation and formerly President John F. Kennedy's Special Assistant for National Security, has described this aspect of the OSS in an essay published in 1964: "It is a curious fact of academic history that the first great center of area studies in the United States was not located in any university, but in Washington, during the Second World War, in the Office of Strategic Services. In very large measure the area study programs developed in American universities in the years after the war were manned, directed, or stimulated by graduates of the OSS—a remarkable institution, half cops-and-robbers and half faculty meeting." See *Dimensions of Diplomacy*, Edgar A. G. Johnson, Editor (Baltimore: John Hopkins Press, 1964) pp. 2-3.

Virtually the first recruits to the new outfit in town were two extraordinarily able and industrious scholars, James Phinney Baxter, President of Williams College, and William Langer, Professor of European History at Harvard.[2] Baxter stayed a relatively short time and Langer became Chief of the Research and Analysis Branch, a job he held throughout the war and that he drew upon for experience when he was brought back in 1950 to set up the CIA's Office of National Estimates. As an outstanding historian of Bismarck's Germany, he was especially qualified to analyze the situation and prospects for the German effort to subjugate all of West Eurasia and the Mediterranean. He brought in many notable scholars to assist him, including Sherman Kent from Yale, another European historian who later also served as Director of the CIA's Office of National Estimates. For a time the group of scholars plugging away in the Library of Congress or at 23rd and E Streets was about all there was to Donovan's COI office.

The gradual collection in this office of a body of distinguished research people pleased Donovan mightily and impressed others to whom he described his brainy "professors." It did not impress the State Department much, since even then the Foreign Service was dedicated to the proposition that the experience and intuition of ambassadors and Foreign Service officers was the best possible basis for policymaking and that systematic research was sometimes useful but not an essential ingredient for understanding foreign affairs. This general view, though not held by the more farsighted Foreign Service officers, is deeply imbedded in the State Department to this day. The two viewpoints are in many ways alien to one another. Only the gifted among both professions see the enrichment of foreign policy and diplomacy that can derive from genuine cooperation between Foreign Service specialists and intelligence specialists.

Sumner Welles was then Under Secretary of State, Roosevelt's closest contact in Cordell Hull's rather inert State Department, and he undertook to work in reasonable harmony with the COI and later with the OSS. He reached an understanding with Donovan, on August 10, 1941, conceding to the new agency responsibility for the collection of economic information and other related data overseas and levying on it a requirement for reports and studies on foreign countries of foreign policy interest.[3] This coverage was not to include Latin America, where not only J. Edgar Hoover but also Nelson Rockefeller, Coordinator of Inter-American Affairs, were already active.

The collaboration was, however, always something of a one-way street. The COI and the OSS were always in the role of supplicant for information from diplomatic cable traffic, which was doled out sparingly and with restrictions on dissemination outside the State Department. Nobody thought of the new intelligence agency as a partner in foreign policymaking or even as a central intelligence authority, but rather as a somewhat superfluous service agency that occasionally provided interesting and useful secret reports or analytical studies.

Nelson Rockefeller had operated his Latin American fiefdom quasi-independently of State for almost a year, but greeted Donovan's outfit cordially in 1941 since it provided him with useful research papers on Latin America and shared his enthusiasm for anti-Nazi psychological warfare. Both were preempted from secret intelligence collection and counterespionage operations in Latin America because the FBI had earlier won this prerogative; and Hoover defended it fiercely throughout the war, relying heavily on his British intelligence connections to demonstrate his skills in the area. Neither the COI nor the OSS ever budged the FBI on this issue.

## Espionage

The biggest hurdle for the OSS to get over was the establishment of primary responsibility for espionage in other parts of the world where the Army and Navy theoretically had jurisdiction. It took several months to iron out the difficulties with State, Army, and Navy, but by September 1941 Donovan won the privilege of monopolizing clandestine "undercover" intelligence collection. The support of broadminded civilian leaders like Frank Knox and Henry Stimson undoubtedly assisted Donovan in nailing down this function for the COI.

After the fall of France in June of 1940 the United States maintained diplomatic relations with Vichy France to observe developments in the German occupation zone, an area where Great Britain was excluded. Churchill approved of this policy, though many patriotic Americans excoriated the State Department for continuing relations with the Petain government. The benefits became apparent only much later, when the military landing in French-controlled North Africa was eased by secret negotiations with French authorities—negotiations that would have been impossible except for the intelligence links forged under cover of the diplomatic ties maintained with Vichy.

The United States was technically still neutral in 1940 and down until December 1941. Admiral William Leahy, a trusted friend of Roosevelt's, was made Ambassador to the Petain government at the end of 1940 and reached his post in January 1941. His military attache was Colonel Robert Schow, who joined the CIA's clandestine operational element after the end of the war. By the spring of 1941 Schow was getting secret intelligence from anti-German officers of the French Army. A great deal more freedom of action for Americans was possible, however, in unoccupied French North Africa, where anti-German sentiment was also strong.

The intelligence opportunities there were exploited by a gifted Foreign Service career office, Robert Murphy, who subsequently served in many important politico-military posts and continued his interest in the intelligence process. Later he was a member of the President's high-level Intelligence Oversight Board. In this prewar period Murphy was first Counsellor of the Embassy of France and then was sent on a special diplomatic mission to French North Africa. In February 1941 he negotiated an economic agreement with Vichy France's Governor of North Africa whereby the United States would continue to trade with the area if food control officers could be posted in Algeria, Morocco, and Tunisia to observe the shipments and see that they did not go to Nazi Germany. In the spring Murphy was assigned as U.S. Consul in Algiers and posts for 12 Vice-Consuls were authorized under the designation "food control officers."

These were the first official clandestine intelligence jobs approved by the State Department. In fact Murphy and his "twelve disciples" were mainly intended by Washington to collect secret intelligence on North Africa and France. The Army and Navy scoured their lists for twelve men with solid language and area backgrounds to fill these posts. They were found and were sent to North Africa in June 1941. For the first time in this era Americans listed as diplomatic officials found themselves competing for scraps of information in the cafes and casinos with foreign diplomats and assorted spies of all countries. Within a few weeks these "vice-consuls" were sending descriptive reporting to Washington responsive to the requirements for information left with Donovan and Roosevelt by Ian Fleming during his visit to Washington in June 1941.

One of the vice-consuls was former U.S. Marine Colonel William A. Eddy, assigned under Naval Attache cover to Tangiers—the only Arabic-speaking officer with a background in intelligence. He was a combination scholar-soldier-spy of the new breed Donovan was looking for, a Dartmouth professor, a university president (Hobart and William Smith Colleges), born in Syria, and fluent in French and Arabic. He had returned to military duty early in 1941 to serve in the Naval Attache's office in Cairo and readily agreed to transfer to Tangiers, an international "free zone" alive with spies. Later in the war he served as Minister to Saudi Arabia and was chief of intelligence in the State Department in 1946-1947. In effect, in 1941 Eddy was creating, in cooperation with Murphy, what was to become the first and one of the OSS's best espionage nets, made up of clever amateurs converted from civilian roles as businessman, banker, wine merchant, lawyer, librarian, and anthropology professor. Of such were COI and OSS intelligence officers created.[4]

The State Department was characteristically uneasy about this clandestine role, and it was not really clear exactly for whom they were working, although the Army and Navy valued the information they sent in. It was probably only because the United States was not yet at war that the Army and Navy agreed in the fall of 1941 to shift responsibility for clandestine collection by civilians abroad to the new civilian organization being set up by Donovan. In September 1941 the chiefs of Army and Navy intelligence yielded responsibility for this function to Donovan. The memorandum for the Secretary of War from General Sherman Miles, dated September 5, 1941, and approved by Chief of Staff George Marshall the next day, explained the move:

MEMORANDUM FOR THE CHIEF OF STAFF:

Subject: Undercover Intelligence Service

1. The military and naval intelligence services have gone into the field of undercover intelligence to a limited extent. In view of the appointment of the Coordinator of Information and the work which is understood the President desires him to undertake, it is believed that the undercover intelligence of the two services should be consolidated under the Coordinator of Information. The reasons for this are that an undercover intelligence service is much more effective if under one head rather than three, and that a civilian agency, such as the Coordinator of Information, has distinct advantage over any military or naval agency in the administration of such a service.[5]

Donovan sent a copy of this memorandum under cover of a note to the President, dated October 10, indicating he had assumed the clandestine intelligence function as a result of agreement with the Army and Navy intelligence services.[6] The COI operation in theory now had responsibility for two main central intelligence functions, clandestine collection and intelligence analysis.

Donovan, drawing largely on British professional and technical guidance, began collecting staff and establishing training programs for additional overseas operational elements. Of course, all this was only the beginning in the building of a real intelligence machine, but the job had been recognized as necessary and the central tasks assigned.

## Other Elements

At this early stage one of the obstacles to establishing greater clarity about roles and missions of the new organization was its entanglement in radio propaganda. In keeping with his activist concept of the COI mission, Donovan expended a great deal of his energy in first setting up and then quarreling over a radio news branch headed by the well-known playwright, Robert E. Sherwood, a close friend and admirer of the President. Donovan and Sherwood never did see eye-to-eye and each was strong-minded in pursuit of his own objectives. Donovan leaned toward psychological warfare to mislead and disturb the enemy, whereas Sherwood thought more in terms of providing useful supplementary information to the news media at home and abroad. Sherwood set up business with his branch in New York City near the U.S. communications industry networks to which he could pass news stories about the war in Europe. It never was really an integral part of the COI machinery in Washington and was split off from it formally in the spring of 1942 with a certain amount of hard feelings mixed with mutual relief. Sherwood's group became a main element in the Office of War Information (OWI), which operated under the leadership of the great radio commentator Elmer Davis. It devoted itself to straight news, leaving with the COI the embryonic function of covert psychological warfare—an element that figured importantly in most thinking about central intelligence from then on despite the fact that the COI and the OSS were able to do little with it.

The early days of the COI also saw the establishment of the Visual Presentation Branch with some extraordinarily talented artists and design specialists from the world of publications and advertising. Most of them drifted off to other places, particularly to the Pentagon where the demand for visual gimmicks was insatiable once the U.S. war effort began running full tilt. Some of them built for the Joint Chiefs the deluxe command centers with glass walls, graphic displays, sliding panels, and control communications lashups that became the hallmark of U.S. military headquarters the world over. A pilot model briefing room was designed and built for the COI but it soon became apparent after U.S. entry in the war that the big action in this field would be at the Pentagon, not at 2430 E Street.

Nevertheless, after Visual Presentations broke up at the time of the transfer of Sherwood's outfit to the OWI, some of the design people stayed on in the COI and the OSS. They helped establish the tradition that exists down to this day in the CIA that a presentation staff should assist the scholars so that intelligence reports could be well-designed, with photographs and other illustrations as needed, and be accompanied by superior maps of the areas described. Especially effective work was done on maps. Langer's Research and Analysis Branch established a Geographic and Cartographic Division that distinguished itself by topographic analysis and the presentation of geographic data on maps and relief models. Top officials in Washington were in due course astounded by erudite government reports in the language of Harvard, presented in *Reader's Digest-Life* style. The maps, the topographic models, and, in particular, some five-foot floating globes—supported on hidden ballbearings—brought distinction as well as occasional envy to the new central intelligence agency.

## Office of Coordinator of Information, 1941

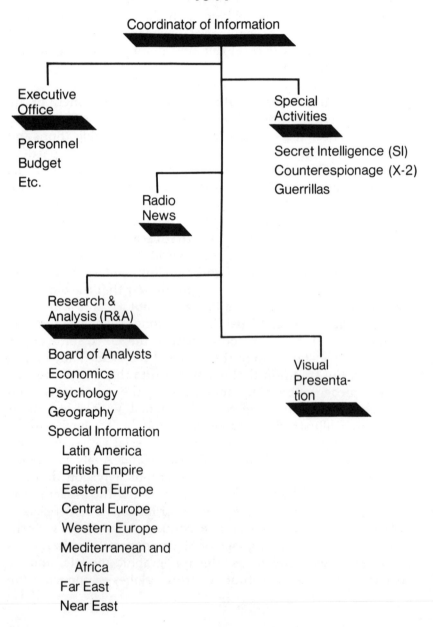

Coordinator of Information

Executive Office

Personnel
Budget
Etc.

Special Activities

Secret Intelligence (SI)
Counterespionage (X-2)
Guerrillas

Radio News

Research & Analysis (R&A)

Board of Analysts
Economics
Psychology
Geography
Special Information
   Latin America
   British Empire
   Eastern Europe
   Central Europe
   Western Europe
   Mediterranean and
     Africa
   Far East
   Near East

Visual Presentation

With some scholars in residence, a dozen men in North Africa, a training program for agents and "guerrillas," and some expansive ideas, Donovan was theoretically in business on December 7, 1941. In fact he had been able to achieve nothing by that time that could in any way have forestalled the Pearl Harbor attack disaster. The best that can be said is that the Pearl Harbor attack illustrated the significance of correlating intelligence data and evaluating it for the President and his immediate advisers. This lesson was not brought home, however, even to the officials who suffered most from the lack of good intelligence, until the full-scale postwar investigation revealed what had happened, what was known, and what went wrong when the Japanese attacked.[7] In Washington after December 7, 1941, the existing intelligence agencies, like all others associated with what was usually termed "the war effort," simply expanded rapidly on an emergency basis.

Donovan, from the beginnings of the COI, had very much in mind irregular paramilitary forays behind enemy lines along the lines of the British Special Operations Executive (SOE) guerrilla team concept. His Special Activities Branch was identified on the early COI organization charts as being responsible not only for secret intelligence collection and counterespionage, but also for "guerrillas." Evidently, after Pearl Harbor, Donovan came quickly to the conclusion that his new civilian agency had to be militarized if it was to be effective, especially in a paramilitary role. Whatever other reasons there may have been, the whole personnel management problem and logistic preparations for overseas activities of all kinds would have become impossible unless Donovan could keep his military personnel, grant deferments to essential civilians, and claim priorities for transportation and supplies. With the organization of the United States Joint Chiefs of Staff as the primary instrument of planning and advising on strategic policy, it would have been absurd to collect and report intelligence information only to the President without also making the effort useful to the Joint Chiefs.

Speedily the American military leaders (Marshall, Admiral Ernest J. King, and General Henry H. (Hap) Arnold) became the driving bureaucratic command element for every aspect of military action. They organized their staffs to work in harness with the better-established British Chiefs of Staff committees. The U.S. JCS conferred regularly on a weekly basis with Washington representatives of the British Chiefs of Staff in an international committee structure known as the Combined Chiefs of Staff. It had a Combined Intelligence Committee in it, and this perforce required the U.S. Joint Intelligence Committee to pull itself together belatedly to try to analyze threats to U.S. and British forces.[8] Whereas the British, particularly in their intelligence system, were geared to Foreign Office deliberations, the U.S. State Department for the most part continued to act as a Department of Peace, semi-immobilized, while the War Department took over for the duration of hostilities. In these circumstances Donovan and his men were locked in by the military mold in which the nation's efforts increasingly were cast. The only solution was to join the system, not to try to remake it in the rush of military pressures. By March 1942 Donovan told Roosevelt that it was necessary for COI to convert into a quasi-military organization reporting to the U.S. JCS as well as to the President.

Everything was channeled into the war effort and Donovan's new intelligence outfit was obliged to conform. From being truly central, coordinating, and analytical as originally intended, the COI became subordinated to military goals and organizations, while becoming mainly operations-oriented. The language of Donovan's note on converting the COI into a quasi-military agency shows not only the extent to which the Army and Navy now had the leading role in Washington decision-making but also shows how eager Donovan was to become part of the fighting force.

MEMORANDUM FOR THE PRESIDENT:[9]
FROM: William J. Donovan                                          March 30, 1942

There has been submitted to you by the Joint Chiefs of Staff a proposed order which would bring more closely together the Office of the Joint Chiefs of Staff and our own agency. They have told me that this matter has been taken up with Harry Hopkins for submission to you.

I hope you will approve the order. It exactly conforms to your original directive to me, both in name and function—but which was finally modified at the insistence of the Army and Navy. The present proposal comes at their instance. The services now seem to have confidence in our organization and feel that we have in motion certain instrumentalities of war useful to them. For these reasons, and in order more closely to integrate with the armed forces the various elements that we have been developing, they recommend the signing of th order.

On March 16th (my memorandum No. 334) briefly tried to describe to you how our principal units supplement and support one another. I think it essential that both Chiefs of Staff, under your direction as Commander-in-Chief, should have these services at their disposal. There would then be welded into one fighting force every essential element in modern warfare. You will note that they have even provided for the Commandos.

I am glad to concur in the recommendation of the Joint Chiefs of Staff, because I believe this is a sensible and necessary step toward the most effective use of all modern war weapons.

(Signed)
William J. Donovan

Within a few weeks after this memorandum went to the President, a reasonably amiable bureaucratic arrangement was worked out with the Bureau of the Budget, the President's managerial experts, and the Army and Navy establishment. The result was a cryptic rephrasing of the basic charter in a new Presidential Order.

This document was issued June 13, 1942, as a Military Order. It was brief and rather noncommittal. Nowhere was the responsibility for a national or Presidential level of analysis mentioned; this level, for the duration, was largely subsumed by the Joint Chiefs. The new name, Office of Strategic Services, harked back to Donovan's original proposal but the duties henceforth during the war would obviously depend on what the Joint Chiefs "required."

MILITARY ORDER[10]
Office of Strategic Services

By virtue of the authority vested in me as President of the United States and as Commander-in-Chief of the Army and Navy of the United States, it is ordered as follows:

1. The office of Coordinator of Information, established by Order of July 11, 1941, exclusive of the foreign information activities transferred to the Office of War Information by Executive Order of June 13, 1942, shall hereafter be known as the Office of Strategic Services, and is hereby transferred to the jurisdiction of the United States Joint Chiefs of Staff.

2. The Office of Strategic Services shall perform the following duties:
  a. Collect and analyze such strategic information as may be required by the United States Joint Chiefs of Staff.
  b. Plan and operate such special services as may be directed by the United States Joint Chiefs of Staff.

3. At the head of the Office of Strategic Services shall be a director of Strategic Services who shall be appointed by the President and who shall

perform his duties under the direction and supervision of the United States Joint Chiefs of Staff.

    4. William J. Donovan is hereby appointed as Director of Strategic Services.

    5. The Order of July 11, 1941 is hereby revoked.

| | |
|---|---|
| The White House | Franklin D. Roosevelt |
| June 13, 1942 | Commander-in-Chief |

In some ways the new OSS went on its way much as Donovan originally conceived it. Its civilian spirit was never lost and it remained an innovative, maverick kind of organization wherein sergeants supervised officers, civilians supervised both, and a combination of loose discipline and enormous talents won the OSS a unique reputation, on the whole rather admired if occasionally denigrated. The organization evolved during the war, but essentially it simply fleshed out the outline of 1941 with greatly expanded emphasis on the paramilitary action elements. (See chart on p. 73 for basic structure toward the end of the war.)[11]

As it developed the OSS grew in size, reaching a total strength of about 13,000, including Washington headquarters and overseas staffs.[12] Thus a semi-civilian agency with a broad latitude to dabble in intelligence analysis of foreign developments of interest at the national level took on shape and character alongside a clandestine collection apparatus and a multifaceted and rapidly proliferating paramilitary and psychological warfare service.

## Perspective

My personal view of this new creation in the American political process was, naturally, colored by the way in which my life became entangled with it. It is hard to recreate the mood of the war years but I recall vividly the sense of challenge, of danger, of exultant dedication to new experience, and of fascination with the realities of international power. After returning to Harvard from England in 1940 an interventionist, I went about the business of graduate training for a life of academic research and teaching. By good fortune I was chosen in 1941 as one of eight young scholars selected on a country-wide basis each year to become a Junior Fellow in Harvard's Society of Fellows.

# Office of Strategic Services
# 1945

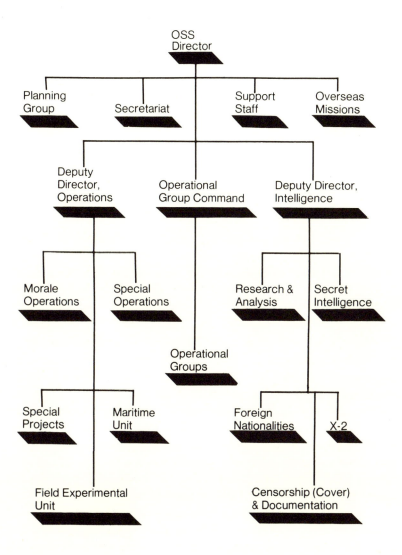

This appointment, to a three-year term, involved undertaking some piece of original research, attending any courses in the University of interest, and coming to dinner once a week for an evening's discussion with other Junior Fellows (in my year they included American historian Arthur Schlesinger, Jr., and McGeorge Bundy, who later was Harvard's Provost, President Kennedy's Assistant for National Security, and President of the Ford Foundation) and the Senior Fellows (they included former Harvard President Abbott Lawrence Lowell, philosopher Alfred North Whitehead, and the brilliant historian Crane Brinton). The stipend was so good, for those leaner academic days, that I was able to get married on June 4, 1941, just as plans for Donovan's new intelligence agency were firming up far removed from Harvard Yard. Not only was my eye fixed on academia, but in truth I had never heard of any American intelligence agency, let alone the new one of Donovan's.

The attack on Pearl Harbor swept away those controversies and uncertainties over political and international aims which until that time had been as devisive as the student controversies of the late 1960s and early 1970s were to be. Hitler's attack on Russia in June 1941 and Japan's attack on the United States in December brought nearly every one together under Roosevelt's leadership. By the spring of 1942 people were leaving Cambridge in droves. The idea of national service was suddenly paramount among what had been a rather irreverent generation of students. When a Harvard professor with an amateur's passion for cryptanalysis convinced me that the Navy needed me for cryptanalytic work, I left for Washington on leave of absence from the University, to which I never returned. The search for manpower was already so intense that the Navy promised my wife a job as cryptanalyst too if I would come. We stored our things and headed for the nation's capital without knowing what our position or salary would be.

A new way of life opened up to us during the next six months' duty (August 1942—April 1943) at the Nebraska Avenue Navy Annex where we worked on breaking Japanese Navy codes, after the Battle of Midway Island had shown beyond question that superior information wins battles. I learned a little Japanese and became fairly skilled at "recovering additives," a menial but essential component of this process of cryptanalysis.

The trouble was that the Navy was haphazard in its forced expansion, and was trying to mechanize the code-breaking process rather than develop new young civilian specialists. The Watch Officers in charge seemed to me impossibly rigid in attention to rank and shipboard procedure in managing this unorthodox shore activity on Nebraska Avenue. Where I sat, we never saw any real Navy officers but only hastily mobilized Reserve Lieutenants and Commanders who had been quick to leave their civilian posts to become erstaz officers. Their attention to the privileges due them under naval etiquette was phenomenal, something I seldom observed when I later got to know career Navy officers.

In any case, I resigned, intending to enlist in the Army, but allowed myself to be signed up for the OSS, which I had heard about from friends from Harvard who turned up at Washington parties talking about a new organization that wanted people for research and writing. In June 1943 I reported to 2430 E Street, already qualified as a civil service employee of very junior rank, and already aware that the drudgery of collecting intelligence through signals analysis could contribute something extremely important to the war effort. I am grateful for having started at the collection end of intelligence, having learned the hard way how much human effort and how much managerial skill is involved at every stage of discovering facts and bringing them to bear on government decision-making.

## The Current Intelligence Staff

By mid-1943 the OSS was sufficiently shaken down so that I went directly into a spot in the agency where I felt useful and where I was able to observe a lot of OSS activity from a central vantage point. It was an incredibly lucky assignment for me, due to no foreknowledge or foresight on my part. Without doubt the Harvard connection was the entering wedge. Donald McKay, French history professor at Harvard, interviewed me on the recommendation of mutual Harvard friends. He was a member of the Board of Analysts whom Bill Langer, by then Chief of Research and Analysis (R&A), relied on for quality control and substantive estimates to guide the work of his whole staff, then quite sizeable. McKay sent me to S. Everett Gleason, an Amherst professor with Harvard training, an extremely able man with a flair for bureaucratic management, who was then head of the Office of Current Intelligence in the R&A Branch. With him at the time were two staff members of my vintage from Cambridge, Arthur Schlesinger, Jr. and Carl Schorske, who had been a graduate student of Langer's and eventually became a distinguished professor of European history.

I went to work there and, as time went by and my colleagues moved on to other posts, I ended up in 1944 as Chief of Current Intelligence myself, which job I held until the end of the war and the end of the OSS on October 1, 1945. Due to the war, the guidance of academic friends, and bureaucratic happenstance, I monitored a fascinating flow of intelligence and a wide range of intelligence activities. The curse of becoming immersed in intelligence about foreign affairs is that the problems never end; there are new, fascinating vistas at every turn, and it is never possible to insure that enough of the information provided is actually used by decision-makers to permit anyone involved to relax. The work is inherently addictive.

Current Intelligence was structurally a component of R&A. Its task was to goad the patient researchers in the analytical divisions to take time off from preparing long descriptive research papers on their specialties to write short snappy articles on trends that they thought needed to be called to the attention of the Joint Chiefs or the President in our daily or periodic reports. It was also functionally an analytical service staff for the Deputy Director for Intelligence, Brigadier General John Magruder, who supervised not only the work of research and analysis but also of clandestine intelligence collection. Our staff occupied office space adjacent to Magruder's office.

Magruder, a gentle, hard-working man from a distinguished old Virginia military family, was a career officer who had served in Army intelligence with enough distinction to be given the assignment of heading a U.S. military assistance mission to China before Pearl Harbor. He devoted his wartime career to trying to make harmonious sense out of the efforts of the secret intelligence, counterespionage, and analytical components of the OSS.

Donovan trusted Magruder completely, and allowed him to supervise and rationalize these parts of the agency while Donovan himself concentrated on the paramilitary side of the OSS. Magruder used to swear about the fact that Donovan prided himself on all "his professors" but showed inadequate inclination to find ways to use them profitably or even to listen to them when he already had his mind made up. It was Magruder who tried to shake loose Secret Intelligence (SI) information from its tight security controls so that it could be distributed via the Current Intelligence staff to Donovan's "professors" in R&A where it could be systematically analyzed. He also pried cables out of the State Department so his intelligence collectors and analysts would have good background understanding of foreign policy issues. The Current Intelligence staff was the go-between with State for him in handling this cable traffic. Finally, Magruder wanted daily, weekly, and *ad hoc* analytical reports written briefly, and in polished style so they would make an impression in Joint Chiefs' circles, in the State Department, or at the White House. Donovan, of course, wanted all of this done; Magruder saw that it was done. As the staff link in carrying out all these functions, Magruder leaned heavily upon Langer's Current Intelligence Office. My job was to meet these requirements.

Aside from being convenient for Magruder's frequent consultation, Current Intelligence was housed in the Central Building of 2430 E Street, because it was the custodial staff for the war room or situation room, the product of one of Donovan's early brainstorms. His Visual Presentations artists had started to create the fanciest briefing center in town but eased back on the revolving stages and special carpeting when it became clear after Pearl Harbor that the COI would not be able to attract the real VIPs from the White House and Pentagon, where inevitably even grander war rooms were built. For these reasons I inherited the situation room along with my job in Current Intelligence and for two years had a desk in this elegant space, twice as impressive as any other in the OSS. The room was designed by Eero Saarinen, the brilliant architect of Finnish extraction, who had provided in makeshift quarters a beautifully decorated, air-conditioned briefing room complete with three layers of sliding map panels, a huge, fluted natural wood column as room divider, and a modest briefing theater. We had one of those 5-foot revolving globes (with a lucite quadrant for measuring air distances) that had been created for Roosevelt, Churchill, and the Joint Chiefs; what I had was the first model, a real beauty. Because we stored secret State cables, SI reports, and magnificent rubber and plastic topographic models, and because Donovan and Magruder wanted to impress visitors with our early morning oral briefings for senior OSS officials, we had a uniformed guard at the door to admit people by name only.

A more liberal education in handling intelligence at the top of government was nowhere to be obtained. We prepared the OSS written contributions for the *JIC Weekly Summary*, the nearest thing to an interagency intelligence report that existed in those days. I went to meetings of the working committee that cleared this text for publication under the somewhat negligent auspices of the Joint Intelligence Committee of the JCS. The highest authority in the field with whom I ever dealt directly was Colonel Ludwell Lee Montague, a learned, courtly Virginian who served as the Army's Executive Secretary of the JIC and whose word was law. The editor of the *Weekly Summary* was a former English professor, Colonel Bowie Millican, who was profoundly grateful to get some literate articles on politics and economics to grace his collection of Army and Navy prose.

I was constantly told that the OSS's economic and political analysis added immensely to the readability of this pitifully limited survey at the "SECRET" level of classification. Part of my early education was learning that this highest level interagency magazine did not contain any very sensitive intelligence material, that the OSS reserved its hottest SI reports from the field for special memos to the President and the Joint Chiefs, that our OSS writing did not either much influence or reflect the technical military intelligence papers prepared by G-2 and ONI for the Joint Planners and Joint Chiefs. Neither the *JIC Weekly Summary* nor any component of the OSS ever used signals intelligence in its reporting. I knew from Navy experience this source was essential for authoritative all-source analysis, and it was a serious limitation that the OSS had only minimal exposure to intercepts.

To tell the truth, I suspect that more than half of our current intelligence came from the news ticker tapes that clattered away down the hall in our quarters. We clipped interesting stories from the news services for display on bulletin boards. Senior officers dropped in to read these quite often, usually—but not always—lingering to look over the classified reports we kept out on reading tables at the back of our briefing room.

I quickly learned that controlling the newsbreaks, whatever the source, is the best entree to the great men, who like to be up to date even more than they like to be well briefed. I believe my staff, never very large, did some useful work. Probably our most important task was putting in clear language with adequate analysis many reports from Allen Dulles, the OSS Chief in Switzerland, who had good access to secret agents inside the German government and who managed to arrange in the spring of 1945 the early surrender of all German forces in Italy. He also reported on the July 1944 plot that very nearly succeeded in assassinating Hitler, although no one in Washington did anything to help the conspirators or exploit the resistance elements thus revealed. Magruder used to hold Donovan at bay with difficulty while we made sense out of a Dulles message full of transmission garbles and ambiguous phrases that needed to be placed in context.

After Arthur Schlesinger, Jr. went to Europe, Gleason to a staff responsible for liaison with the Joint Chiefs, and Schorske back to head a research unit in the main element of R&A, I ran this operation with the aid of several Radcliffe girls who wrote well and helped organize the morning briefings for the OSS brass; an experienced daily intelligence summary editor on detail, Maurice Ragsdale, from *Reader's Digest*; a gifted writer, Edward Downes, who became an outstanding music critic after the war; Leonard Meeker, a lawyer, who later became legal advisor to the Secretary of State; and an energetic writer and staff liaison genius, Merritt Ruddock, who excelled at getting information from other components of Magruder's domain and who after the war served a time in the CIA.

My most perspicacious move was the selection of Dr. R. Jack Smith, an English professor from Williams College, who backstopped me in digging out current intelligence items and drafting longer analytical papers that we called current intelligence studies. Jack Smith, who later was in charge of current intelligence reporting in the CIA, was instrumental in luring me into the CIA in 1949, and much later replaced me as the CIA's Deputy Director for Intelligence.

## Intelligence Collection and Analysis

At the dogged insistence of John Magruder, many OSS reports were filtered through the evaluative and drafting mechanism of my staff so that we could meld together agent data from the field and analytical comment or interpretation from Bill Langer's other experts. It was rudimentary intelligence analysis, but it helped win the OSS a reputation for thoughtful, reliable intelligence output. The Current Intelligence material supplemented in a conspicuous way the bulk of more routine field reporting, passed directly to the State Department and the military agencies, and the mass of economic and geographic writing emanating from R&A experts, which were mainly contributions to country surveys compiled in collaboration with the Army and Navy. The Joint Army-Navy Intelligence Surveys (JANIS) became the principal interagency effort in intelligence. They contained compilations of detailed basic intelligence about different regions of the world. Such intelligence had been nearly completely unknown prior to the war but was urgently needed to prepare for landings and cope with occupation duties.

It is now clear to me that the OSS work in research, analysis, trend forecasting, and current reporting fell far below the mark in quantity and quality compared to the kind that would have been most useful. Access to all the sources was simply lacking. Coordination and central analysis were concepts honored in the breach rather than in the observance. The perennial policymaker liked the intelligence that happened to come to his attention, but most of the intelligence product was self-generated, aimed in the dark, and to a great extent ignored. This hard lesson from the pioneer days taught me that central intelligence is always vulnerable to neglect and ignorance of its true function, which was to provide an objective underpinning for policy.

Yet part of the legacy of the OSS was established beyond doubt: scholars did have something to contribute in the way of evaluating the secrets discovered by spies. Donovan's and Magruder's professors and amateur agent handlers established traditions and a cult of achievement in espionage and intelligence analysis that guaranteed that good intelligence input into decision-making at the national level could be made if high-caliber people could be put to work and if policymakers would pay attention.

The chart of the OSS branches under General Magruder (p. 73) is largely self-explanatory. The R&A of the COI days continued its work in the OSS but with more sophistication and greater understanding of the relationship of analysis to national strategy and policy as made by the President, the JCS, and the State Department. OSS scholars never even got their hands on all of the incoming intelligence data, and their reports generally provided useful background information rather than national estimates tailored to throw light on the tough questions before policy officials. R&A's connection with the JCS and the White House was too remote to permit the necessary intellectual give-and-take at top command and staff levels. The JCS did not really use the military intelligence agencies in that way either, looking on them instead as a kind of reference service for data rather than professional judgments. There was no effective coordination of interagency research and analysis except in the JANIS studies—compilations of basic geographical intelligence materials on individual countries. The bright dream of 1941 that visualized correlating and evaluating intelligence for the President remained precisely that.

Another part of the intelligence side, the SI work, got under way in earnest in May 1944 when Donovan finally insisted that the British intelligence agencies recognize that the elaborate training programs that they had helped the COI and the OSS devise had by then surely prepared a few American agents and agent handlers to begin their jobs on the Continent. Up until then espionage reports passed out in Washington by the OSS were mainly from British MI-6 sources. By late 1943 and 1944, however, an OSS intelligence collection net had gradually developed throughout the world. It mainly used Americans of foreign extraction and foreigners already disposed to help the enemies of the German or Japanese occupation authorities. It helped, of course, that OSS officers usually had plenty of money to use. The OSS agent roster contained all kinds—good, bad, and indifferent—but in many places they performed heroically.

The star of the show was unquestionably the urbane Allen Dulles, who had left the OSS office in New York to slip across the French border into Switzerland on the very day the TORCH landings in North Africa closed the border to Americans. He set up in business in Berne in a flat in a picturesque building at Herrengasse 23 under very thin diplomatic cover as "Special Assistant to the U.S. Minister." Neutral Switzerland was a natural focal point for secret intrigues and secret information. A group of disaffected Germans, the most daring of whom was Hans Gisevius, a German intelligence officer, soon found their way to Dulles and kept him informed of what was going on in Nazi Germany—even inside the German intelligence agencies—in remarkable depth. Foreign office documents, military attache cables, and descriptions of plotting by anti-Hitler forces flowed to Switzerland and thence by scrambled radiophone to Washington's OSS Headquarters. It was magnificent stuff and brought great credit to Donovan and his men.

Other intelligence collectors were less successful, even infamous. As Stewart Alsop reported, some of the OSS amateurs "lived in a dream world of cloaks and masks and daggers" in which they romanticized their own roles so conspicuously that they could not expect to succeed.[13] However that may be, in an eager, somewhat frenetic effort, Donovan put his men in the field and set up the first large-scale professional U.S. espionage network ever to operate abroad. To a great extent, however, collection work became mixed up with the quite different behind-the-lines work of the OSS's covert paramilitary action teams. Espionage agents often ended up in contact with internal political or guerrilla resistance forces, and paramilitary teams often ended up sending back useful intelligence, particularly tactical military data. It is virtually impossible for two such similar secret activities to take place in the same area without overlapping. It is the most persuasive argument for keeping clandestine collection and covert action programs under central control in one agency.

Another branch under General Magruder was called "X-2," a name deliberately chosen to conceal the fact that it was the counterintelligence-counterespionage arm of the OSS. It collected information on foreign governments' intelligence operations and tried to penetrate hostile espionage or sabotage organizations in order to counter their efforts. Drawing initially on overseas personnel of the Bureau of Narcotics, the X-2 gradually accumulated from its work and from exchange with other U.S. and friendly agencies, especially from British MI-5 and MI-6, a basic "name-check" file of dossiers on all individuals who had been reported by anyone to be engaged in espionage.

Whether the counterespionage file was a simple card file, as it was initially, or a vast computerized research bank, as it became in the CIA, it is impossible to conduct any foreign intelligence collection or to analyze hostile intentions toward the United States without building such a set of records. Continuity and comprehensiveness is the mark of counterintelligence data. It is impossible to tell in advance when a nickname, an acquaintance, a snapshot, a physical blemish, or a job record will provide the missing clue to an identity that makes other evidence fall into place. All is grist for the espionage mill. Patience, thoroughness, skepticism, and tireless review of data are the marks of a good counterintelligence officer. Donovan selected James Murphy, a quiet, competent Washington lawyer (who had been his law clerk) to head the X-2, which ended up with about 700 employees. An OSS employee named James Angleton, the son of an American businessman who had been resident in Italy before the war, became an expert in this recondite field at an early stage of his career when he was fresh out of Yale and more interested in poetry than international affairs. Eventually he became "Mr. Counterespionage" at the CIA. For many years, he poured over reports on the activities of hostile intelligence services, particularly the Soviet KGB and the intelligence services in other Communist states, to counter their efforts by alerting their targets. In no other area is continuity in pursuit of secret information so indispensable. His service ended abruptly when he himself became the target of adverse, albeit erroneous, newspaper criticism published at the end of December 1974.

Another element on the OSS organization chart, the Foreign Nationalities Branch, headed by DeWitt Poole, a distinguished diplomat and educator, marked an innovation in intelligence gathering that was to have a long history—overt collection of useful data about foreign areas voluntarily provided by U.S. citizens and foreigners. The information was given on the understanding that their furnishing it was kept confidential. With Europe closed off during the war, these sources proved valuable for analytical writing and planning of both clandestine and military operations. They also provided leads to many individuals who volunteered for secret work with the OSS in regions with which they were familiar. Basically, however, the function was simply overt information collection, a task central to any national intelligence group. It was preferable to collect needed data in this manner rather than risk agent lives in searching for the same information abroad. This function was preserved in the work of "domestic contacts" units that through the years served the CIA by collecting overt information from U.S. businessmen, scientists, and travelers who wanted to help their government without its being known that they had passed along data procured in the normal conduct of their business or travels abroad.

There is some sentiment today that U.S. citizens, especially journalists, ought to have as little contact with the CIA and other intelligence agencies as possible lest they be in some way "contaminated" by secrecy. This attitude was not present in the patriotic surge of feeling during World War II, and much useful information came into the OSS through the Foreign Nationalities staff.

The remaining OSS unit under the Deputy Director for Intelligence was Censorship and Documents (C&D), sometimes more accurately known as Cover and Documentation. This group collected from radio broadcasts and from censored mail as much information as could be found about security control systems employed in Axis-occupied territory. The group also gradually developed the technique of forging documents that would pass as authentic when used by American agents in hostile areas. Passports, labor permits, identity cards of all kinds, draft cards, travel permits, ration coupons, photographs, postmarks, etc. were all part of that field of research and the kind of identifying material that agents had to be supplied with to provide them "cover" excuses in denied areas. Special papers and printing presses, official stamps and signatures were produced in quantity. "Pocket litter" like match books, cigarette packs, and personal mail all had to be just right. Sometimes they were successful; sometimes they failed. It is an exacting service eternally posing new challenges as control techniques change. It is everywhere an indispensable part of secret operations of any kind, and yet it benefits from being in touch with the flow of incidental data that passes through a large analytical research staff. The modern CIA name is "Technical Services" and it embraces this documentation activity, combined with other specialities like developing disguises, manufacturing concealed electronic listening devices, and even doing laboratory analysis on the kind of poisons that might be used by secret agents themselves in extreme danger, or perhaps employed against them by opposing intelligence forces. It is essential for such a unit to be in the forefront of research on such materials. Technical services were to grow in complexity and skills, but the basic tradition was established in C&D, which had some of its laboratories beyond a locked door in Central Building leading to the basement under Magruder's offices and my own.

Altogether these five branches—Research and Analysis, the Foreign Nationalities Branch, Secret Intelligence, X-2, and C&D—constituted what, in my view, were the main intelligence components of the OSS. These branches certainly had grave limitations on their capabilities and did not always cooperate as well as they might have with one another or with other agencies. Foreign Nationalities was easy enough for R&A to work with. The SI people, however, were extremely secretive, as might be expected, and I had to sweat blood with their Washington Reporting Board to get reports out of them to show to area experts in R&A or to incorporate into current studies. I never to my recollection got any information from X-2, and I certainly knew nothing of the details of C&D work at that time nor even for sure exactly what went on in the basement under me. Yet, in a pinch, Magruder always insisted on the OSS units working together as a bureaucratic entity, fighting with Donovan for orderly procedure and for sophisticated intelligence reporting, drawing on all the resources in the branches under his supervision.

## Covert Action Elements in the OSS

While there was nothing illegal, immoral, or even particularly secretive about the task of Washington reporting and analysis, it took place behind the security fence at the OSS and relatively few people ever learned about the achievements of Magruder, Langer, and company. Ironically, eventually nearly everybody in Washington heard something about the more dramatic, action-oriented elements that undertook daring missions to aid resistance efforts in Europe, the Far East, and Southeast Asia.

In December of 1941, the COI's Special Activities section, which then handled secret intelligence collection as well as guerrilla operations, split, in part to enable better cooperation with the British whose parallel organizations (SOE and MI-6) were handled by two different cabinet ministers. While intelligence collection remained on the Intelligence side already discussed, a Special Operations side (SO) now had the primary mission of training and infiltrating teams to conduct sabotage and organize and support guerrilla forces and resistance groups. The SO teams operated in all areas except the Central Pacific, where they were unneeded in the naval and air operations of Admiral Chester Nimitz, and in the Southwest Pacific, where General Douglas MacArthur insisted on running his own intelligence and covert paramilitary show. The SO teams were small, usually three to five men, designed to parachute in at night and establish continuous contact with local resistance forces, maintain clandestine radio communications with U.S. support bases and OSS Headquarters, and arrange for air drops of military supplies and equipment to guerrilla units. The Maritime Unit developed plans and equipment for clandestine small boat or submarine landings on coastal areas. The Special Projects and Field Experimental units were small spinoffs from the main SO staff. They were set up late in the war to concentrate on developing field equipment or for devising ways to attack special targets such as the German rocket (V-2) program.

A section called Morale Operations (MO) was the residual staff of psychological warriors left over when straight radio news handling went into OWI early in 1942. It experimented with "black" documents such a fake local newspapers or forged military orders intended to confuse the troops. They used agents to spread anti-German rumors behind the lines, and they operated several "black" radios broadcasting to the Continent without attribution of U.S. affiliation. MO may have done some good, but their achievements were intangible, and most OSS people thought it was one of Donovan's wildest follies.

There was another larger spinoff from the main SO elements toward the end of 1944. The Operational Group (OG) Command trained, deployed, and commanded larger U.S. commando or ranger teams of relatively heavily armed troops with foreign language training who fought as integrated groups—platoons of 30 to 40 men—alongside local guerrilla or resistance forces. These OGs were especially useful when German forces were retreating in Italy and France. They were more combat-oriented, as distinct from liaison-oriented, than the SO teams, but they did essentially the same job when once in place behind enemy lines. They were experts at sabotage and, along with local resistance fighters, did a great deal to disrupt German transport and logistics in the last year of the war in Europe.

In all, counting both SO teams and OGs, around 1,500 men were infiltrated into enemy territory. They were covertly introduced but scarcely clandestine; they made a splash once they arrived if they possibly could. They established cordial contacts with British and French irregular military teams and became renowned for their dash, vigor, and courage. Their practical assistance to U.S. military forces as they advanced in Europe won the respect of U.S. military leaders.

General Donovan clearly envied these men and often boasted of their exploits. The first American to parachute into France arrived by Christmas 1943. The cream of the paramilitary crop were the joint U.S.-British teams, organized largely under British auspices under a secret allied plan with the code name JEDBURGH. Donovan gave top priority to his men assigned to JEDBURGH teams, or "Jeds" as they became known. The teams usually consisted of a U.S. or a British officer, plus a French or other European national, and a radio operator. William E. Colby, later Director of the CIA from 1973 until 1976, was a Jed officer in France and survived to lead a 30-man OG of Norwegian-Americans into Norway in March 1945. Donovan got as close to his paramilitary support bases as possible, as often as possible, visiting theaters of war to get first-hand reports and meet operational officers going in or out. He kept close track of the "theater desks" and "country desk" at Headquarters that kept supplies and communications moving.

One of Donovan's lasting achievements for central intelligence was securing the right of independent encrypted radio and cable communications with all of his field units. This was sound in principle, essential for clandestine intelligence collection operations, and an indispensable precedent for building up the magnificent professional staff of communications operators, which later gave the CIA the advantage of prompt, secure links to the field with regular staff communications or clandestine radio nets that neither the State Department nor the military agencies could rival. Still, the OSS might not easily have preserved this right to separate communications if a few prestigious Army commanders had not been impressed with the paramilitary operations conducted by the OSS units in support of advancing military forces in the European theater of war. Here, as in so many areas, the OSS liaison with British operational commando teams, participation in their rigorous training, and in their actual infiltrations paid off.

The heavy concentration on planning for and deploying SO, Jed, and OG units put an enormous strain on the overseas theater staffs of the OSS. Much of the wartime action took place in Algiers, Cairo, London, New Delhi, and Chungking, where the OSS sections in various relationships with U.S. military commands tried to oversee all the work of OSS men deployed abroad. Only in Nimitz's and MacArthur's territory was OSS unable to establish some role to play. In addition, the OSS set up independent stations, as intelligence outposts came to be called universally in the CIA days, in the few countries able to maintain their neutrality during the war. These were Sweden, Switzerland, Turkey, Spain, Portugal, and the International Zone of Tangiers. The OSS stations in these countries reported directly to Washington although each came under the general supervision of the geographically appropriate OSS theater command.

## The TORCH Operation

The first important OSS covert action operation overseas took place in North Africa, where the COI had inherited its embryonic operational net of intelligence collectors—the Vice-Consuls under Bob Murphy and Bill Eddy. After the Army and Navy transferred all responsibility for clandestine operations to Donovan in September 1941, Eddy in Tangiers became in effect the first COI/OSS station chief, in this case operating under Naval Attache cover. Once the United States entered the war, the intelligence operation in North Africa became vital. After it became apparent that the only landing U.S. and British armed forces could make in 1942 would be in Africa, not a cross-Channel attack in France, every scrap of local information from the target area was in demand. It was this demand that also first gave the scholars at the Library of Congress and on 23rd Street an urgent task to do—scrape up by every means possible facts about landing beaches, terrain, and armed forces in North Africa. In their generally poor state of intelligence readiness, the Army and Navy willingly accepted both clandestine agent reports and data gleaned from books and magazines and soon were planning the TORCH landings that finally took place November 8, 1942.

It is most revealing about real-life intelligence operations that what began as an information collection program in North Africa inexorably became, under military pressure, a covert action project. Donovan recognized immediately in the fall of 1941 that his handful of men under cover in what was technically still neutral territory in the unoccupied French colonies were a unique asset for influencing the French armed forced in North Africa as well as for spying on their dispositions and intentions. It also became clear very quickly to the OSS operators that a majority of the French Army was more sympathetic toward the United States than toward Germany and would cooperate with Americans if they had an opportunity to assist in liberating France.

The British were in a less favorable situation because the British Navy attack on the French Navy and French Navy bases in 1940 had caused the expulsion of all British nationals, including all diplomats, from French North Africa. Hence the secret intelligence collection burden fell mainly on COI/OSS.

The OSS also had clandestine contacts with sources in the French army that could be exploited when it became urgent to insure an unopposed landing. The Allied invading forces wanted to fight the Germans, not the French. How to arrange this was the problem.

Fortunately, when the requirement shifted from collecting intelligence to using it to influence events in a direction favorable to U.S. policy, the fledging COI/OSS operation met the test. Murphy and Eddy were swept into the intricate political maneuvering and debates over precisely which French generals could be trusted to support the United States. Much of 1942 was spent arguing about which military and political leaders—Arab and French—should be given money. All of this was new to the United States—the evolution of clandestine collection into opportunities for covert action to assist U.S. strategic policy. The President, Donovan, the JCS, and the British argued endlessly over these options and settled almost nothing before the TORCH landing took place. Yet the debate over what the OSS should do brought attention to the OSS's assets at a very early date—when, in fact, there was little else to rely on.

As a result the OSS net was called into action in September 1942 to try to ease the way for the military move a few weeks later. Murphy and Eddy had been shuttling between their posts and Washington and London all summer. They finally convinced Roosevelt and many of his advisers that their contacts with a group around General Henri Giraud would be helpful. Murphy was then assigned directly to General Dwight Eisenhower in London as "political advisor" in charge of coordinating OSS activities in support of TORCH. On October 22, Eisenhower's deputy, General Mark Clark, made a secret rendezvous, traveling by submarine to a point off the French African coast where his party boarded small boats and then waded ashore to meet Bob Murphy and one of the Vice-Consuls, Ridgeway Knight, who had been educated in France and had traveled the region as a wine merchant. Knight later served as U.S. Ambassador in Syria and several European countries.

The American military men met Giraud's representatives, headed by French Army General Charles Mast, who made some impossible demands but held out hope of a friendly reception for American troops. In fact Giraud did finally escape secretly from Vichy France and joined Eisenhower in Gibraltar November 7, hours before the landings. He was of little help at such a late date and remained so adamant about wanting top command of the invasion forces that he was an embarrassment to Eisenhower. Nevertheless the OSS contacts in the underground French Army did go into action in Morocco. Unfortunately they did not have adequate coordination with the assault forces, which landed on the wrong beach and encountered stiff resistance. Murphy and Mark Clark finally were able to make a deal with the politically opportunistic but astute Vichy Admiral, Jean Darlan, who stopped the fighting in return for the post of French High Commissioner in North Africa, Giraud receiving the lesser post of Commander of Military Forces.

This essay into secret political negotiations and encouragement of resistance groups, while far from a brilliant success, put OSS into the big time as far as American military leaders in Europe were concerned and insured Donovan the support of both Roosevelt and Eisenhower. Even at this early stage, high-level interest in operations of a paramilitary and political action character already had begun to overshadow the achievements of intelligence collection. As far as analysis goes, the OSS was writing studies and reports on Giraud, Darlan, Charles de Gaulle, and the whole gamut of policy issues involved in North Africa, but there is little evidence that these intelligence reports had much effect on the policies that actually were adopted. There certainly was no feedback on what intelligence evidence or analysis might have been useful at the policy level. Most decisions seem to have been taken by Roosevelt on the basis of advice from Eisenhower and Marshall as to what military needs dictated. Certainly this was the basis for justifying the deal with Darlan, which the State Department and many other analysts in Washington found unsavory from any point of view other than military expediency.

This whole TORCH episode showed that secret intelligence was valuable but also showed how difficult it was to get intelligence properly coordinated and used at the policy level. In addition, it demonstrated that good adventure stories about secret submarine rendezvous and underground resistance could easily dominate impressions of the OSS's work, tending to blot out recognition of the vital but less dramatic job of setting up the clandestine net overseas that provides the information making political and paramilitary action possible. As for the analytical studies, officials read them for current interest but seldom, as far as I could tell, used them as a basis for their decisions.

Because of the reputation won in North Africa, the OSS was welcomed, along with British and French intelligence agencies, into the European military commands partly as clandestine intelligence collectors but also as paramilitary operators with sabotage and resistance capabilities. When the Mediterranean Theater moved its General Headquarters to Italy, near Naples, the OSS transferred most of its theater operations from Algiers to Caserta, where OSS elements were designated the 2677 Provisional Regiment. The militarization of the OSS in this area was virtually complete, although the spirit remained unconventional, irregular, and innovative. Enormous quantities of arms, supplies, and equipment were delivered to resistance groups in the Balkans and Western Europe as a result of British and the OSS paramilitary teams and clandestine communications channels. The day-to-day contributions to military command components from the OSS clandestine and paramilitary operations paved the way for overall acceptance of the upstart organization in Europe.

## Worldwide Theater Operations

Other OSS theater operations took on a character somewhat similar to the North African operations. As a matter of fact, the first overseas mission headquarters set up abroad had been the COI office in London, established in November 1941. When Eisenhower and his staff came to London, it was OSS London that set up the working relationship that led to the participation of the OSS elements in the Mediterranean theater of operations. The primary task of OSS London was to establish an effective liaison with the several British intelligence services whose interest had helped lay the groundwork for the creation of the COI. The British agencies in London continued to cooperate closely with COI/OSS; under their tutelage most American intelligence officers received their training for collection and paramilitary action assignments in Europe. Because of their prior entry in the field, British services customarily took the OSS into a kind of junior partnership that evolved into an equal-share enterprise by the end of the war. In Cairo and sometimes in other British-dominated theaters of war, it is true the OSS officers had a hard time making their way against the suspicions of their competence held by more experienced British field intelligence operatives. In London, however, under Colonel David K. E. Bruce, who took command of the OSS mission in London in April 1943 as it was getting into high gear, excellent rapport with the British was the rule.

Bruce's mission came to include elements of every branch of the OSS, including Research and Analysis, becoming thus a facsimile of Washington headquarters, with each element working in liaison with the appropriate British agency. By mid-1944 there were over 2,000 employees assigned to OSS London, making it the largest overseas mission. Research and Analysis specialists were found very useful in the London headquarters, especially in compiling economic studies that provided much of the material that eventually went into air target folders. In London, as elsewhere, however, the main emphasis in the work and virtually all of the praise received related to the paramilitary exploits of the Jeds and the OGs who were cooperating with British, French, and local guerrillas in disrupting German rail communications, sabotaging munitions plants, and harassing the German military and security forces. Some very effective OSS clandestine agent nets were also operated on the Continent from London, but their reporting was largely military and blended in with the reports of successful harassment of German units by paramilitary action. As the war went on, OSS London followed Allied Forces Headquarters into France and in time into Germany, where the OSS units continued to be accepted as useful service elements for U.S. military commanders although very few really knew exactly what OSS was doing. Russell Forgan, a New York banker, succeeded Bruce in the last period of the war and managed the European effort until the end of the OSS and the dissolution of this extraordinary collection of talents.

The OSS also made a substantial investment in supporting U.S. military forces in the India-Burma and China areas. These too became renowned by stories through the grapevine of OSS activities, particularly in Burma, and here too the main thrust of operations and all of the knowledge that seeped out were mainly about covert paramilitary action behind the Japanese lines. General Joseph W. (Vinegar Joe) Stilwell, the senior U.S. Army man in India-Burma, accepted the first detachment of 20 COI men late in the spring of 1942. These expanded in numbers and became OSS Detachment 101, which infiltrated the quasi-autonomous tribal area of Burma near the intersection of the borders of Burma, China, and Thailand to work with an army of nearly 10,000 local Kachin tribesmen in harassing actions against the Japanese and in flank-protection scout operations that led the way to the recapture of Myitkyina airfield and the opening of the Ledo Road. At its peak, Detachment 101, by then under the command of Colonel (later General) W. Ray Peers, had more than 500 Americans directing Kachin operations through OSS liaison officers with 138 working clandestine radio sets.

The OSS also was remarkably successful in setting up and maintaining a clandestine agent net in Thailand with the total complicity of the Thai authorities right under the noses of Japanese occupation forces. Two thoroughly Caucasian American OSS officers managed to stay under cover in Bangkok "safehouses" provided by anti-Japanese Thai officials for a year and one-half after they were infiltrated by sea in January 1944. They wirelessed out to OSS Ceylon or OSS Kunming intelligence on the Japanese provided by the Thai and they operated agent teams in different parts of the country that were able to rescue a number of downed Allied airmen. Numerous covert air flights in and out of Thailand were carried out without discovery. The main story from Bangkok, however, was the remarkable achievement in covert political liaison with the local Thai rulers who were looking toward the independence of Thailand after the expulsion of the Japanese occupiers. The OSS legacy in Southeast Asia provided a solid foundation for subsequent CIA activities in the region.

The OSS got into China belatedly on April 15, 1943, when Donovan negotiated a tripartite collaboration with a U.S. Navy Group already well established in China under Captain (later Admiral) M. E. Miles, and Chungking's national intelligence and police service under General Tai Li. Little was accomplished under this SACO (Sino-American Cooperative Organization) because of the markedly different operating procedures and interests of Tai Li's internal security-oriented outfit and the two competitive U.S. groups. The foot in the door in China eventually led, however, to a large OSS effort in support of "Flying Tiger" General Claire Chennault's 14th U.S. Air Force in Kunming. Set up April 26, 1944, this joint Air Force-OSS "Resources Technical Staff" sent out numerous air warning, weather, and tactical intelligence teams to operate behind Japanese lines in China. The intelligence thus derived was very useful to Chennault's staff for planning air attacks on Japanese units in China and on ships off the China coast.

OSS China, designated Detachment 202 in December of 1943, sent teams into Indochina, where OSS officers were in touch with Ho Chi Minh before the Japanese surrender there, and supplied five members of the 17-man "Dixie Mission" established at Chinese Communist force headquarters in Yenan, North China, on July 24, 1944, under Colonel David Barrett and Foreign Service officer John Service.

The OSS reporting on the guerrilla capabilities of Chinese Communist forces and the political aspirations of Ho Chi Minh's Vietnamese independence movement made unique contributions to knowledge of these regions and was widely distributed in Washington. The operations that acquired the information, however, propelled the OSS into the political arena, since the policy question of supporting indigenous Vietnamese paramilitary forces against the wishes of the French was a red-hot issue, as was the question of working directly with the Chinese Communists who were already virtually at war with the Nationalist Chinese government.

The OSS managed to keep the confidence of U.S. China Theater Commander General Albert C. Wedemeyer, who was determined to maintain an objective intelligence view of the situation on the ground, regardless of overall policy restraints that might be imposed from Washington. However, the story of U.S. intelligence efforts in China during the war is a sorry one, with U.S. agencies and Chinese agencies working at cross-purposes and with objective reporting on China caught up in bitter political controversies between partisans of Chiang Kai-shek and his critics. Many reputations and careers eventually were destroyed as a result of the China conflict, as the whole country erupted into civil war.

Some of the issues at stake are still unsettled. It is clear that a political setback for the U.S. occurred in China and that neither American foreign policy nor intelligence gathering and analysis procedures were able to cope with the situation. Perhaps the American impact was bound to be minimal. From the point of view of intelligence processes, however, the story of the OSS in China mainly serves to prove that neither the structure, the performance, nor the common understanding of the function of strategic intelligence lived up to the words in the 1941 COI charter. This was true across the board, but it was graphically demonstrated in China, where objective intelligence correlation and evaluation were sorely needed but were not accomplished in a way that might have helped the United States in better decision-making on a crucial strategic issue that still plagues U.S. policy.

## The Legacy

One public legacy from the OSS was an overemphasis on the benefits of covert paramilitary operations behind enemy lines. This doctrine reflected a rather unique wartime experience, with the fairly friendly reception accorded Allied troops landing in North Africa and with the all-out cooperation of organized resistance groups in Western Europe. The doctrine proved less applicable, though relevant, to the problems of Asian guerrilla movements, but here too, in Southeast Asia and China, victorious U.S. air and naval forces in the Pacific created a general climate in which eventually most of the resistance efforts seemed valuable. The benefits of covert paramilitary action in peacetime tended to be favorably regarded on the basis of a romantic recollection of these wartime experiences of the OSS. The totally different strategic situation in the 1960s and 1970s proved less congenial than wartime to large-scale guerrilla efforts by U.S. intelligence agencies. In this later period the OSS legacy turned out to be, at best, a mixed blessing, and in some cases a disaster.

The most valuable OSS legacy that endured was Donovan's belief in the value of bringing able people from all walks of life into intelligence work. He lifted intelligence out of its military rut, where it had little prestige and little dynamism, and made it a career for adventurous, broad-minded civilians. This tradition carried down to the CIA, which regularly recruited some of the most able graduates from U.S. universities to learn the intelligence business from the cadre of OSS veterans who stayed on in public service.

Donovan was constantly on the lookout for new staff employees and did not care a bit how they were fitted into an appropriate status in the OSS table of organization. He was the OSS's leading public relations representative, always buoyant about what his outfit could do. As in all secret intelligence agencies, the OSS quickly adopted codewords and cryptonyms for subjects, places, people, projects, and operations. In our cable traffic Donovan was known as "109," and when any OSS unit learned that "109" would visit, spirits automatically lifted. Donovan eventually got his two stars and when he strode into my briefing room with a chest full of combat ribbons and decorations, including his World War I Medal of Honor, everyone felt that here was a genuine leader.

Besides the OSS officers already mentioned, quite a few of the men he chose are likely to be remembered today for their distinction. Among them were Colonel Edward Buxton, the competent chief administrative officer whose title was Assistant Director, a prominent Republican textile manufacturer who came to the East Building to try to keep the lid on the 2430 E Street complex while Donovan was in his office, as well as to straighten problems out when he was off on his innumerable trips; Louis Ream, former executive in U.S. Steel, who gathered together an astonishing hoard of military equipment and supplies and showed genius in readying them for instant dispatch behind enemy lines; Atherton Richards, wealthy pineapple king from Hawaii, who tried with little help from Donovan to introduce concepts of organization and management into the sprawling OSS complex; and John O'Gara, who was borrowed from Macy's department store in New York to create some semblance of system in the OSS's hastily improvised personnel structure and became the first Inspector General of OSS. Two sons of J. P. Morgan graced OSS, Junius in Finance (appropriately enough) and Henry in Censorship and

Documents. For a time the President's son, James Roosevelt, was Donovan's liaison officer for dealing with other agencies.

In R&A in Washington and abroad were scholars such as economists Edward Mason, Charles Hitch, Emile Despres, and Walt W. Rostow; Russian studies expert Geroid Robinson from Columbia; China experts John K. Fairbank and Martin Wilbur; Japanologist Burton Fahs, Southeast Asia anthropologist Cora DuBois, African specialist Ralph Bunche, who became prominent later as U.N. Under Secretary General, British historian Conyers Read from the University of Pennsylvania, historian Hajo Holborn from Yale, and some who went on to prominence in academic life such as John E. Sawyer, Franklin Ford, H. Stuart Hughes of the Chief Justice's family, and Carl Kaysen. The political cast of mind of this super-faculty of university pundits in R&A was generally moderately liberal, although its ranks did include some prominent scholars from the left such as Latin Americanist Maurice Halperin and Herbert Marcuse in R&A's German section.

The SI Branch had many distinguished alumni including William Casey, who managed espionage penetration operations against Germany from the London OSS headquarters, and later held many high official posts such as Under Secretary of State for Economic Affairs and President of the Export-Import Bank in the 1970s. He came out of retirement in 1981 to be Reagan's Director of Central Intelligence. There were also in SI Arthur Goldberg, Supreme Court Justice, and Whitney Shepherdson, a Harvard lawyer who was a leader in New York's Council on Foreign Relations, as well as the young Richard Helms, Director of CIA from 1966 to 1973. The SO complex was supervised by Colonel Preston Goodfellow, a former Hearst newspaper executive; as Deputy Director for Operations, he was General Magruder's opposite number in the organization. Besides Bill Colby in this field, there were men who had already earned distinction, such as SO Executive Officer William Vanderbilt, former Governor of Rhode Island, and many who became well known in later life, such as Hungarian-born economist Nicholas Deak, now president of one of the world's largest foreign currency exchange organizations, who served the OSS in Egypt, Italy, and Vietnam. The Vietnam team included at various times Frank White, later a

*Time-Life* film executive, at that time an OSS major who had become a confidant of Ho Chi Minh, and Lucien Conein, who later was the CIA's man in contact with the armed forces in Saigon during the hectic days of the military coup against President Ngo Dinh Diem.

The OSS mission in Greece included Thomas Karamessines, one of CIA's Deputies for Operations. Frank Wisner, CIA's first chief of covert action operations, a Wall Street lawyer from a wealthy Mississippi family, was successively OSS station chief in Istanbul and Bucharest. A clever writer from the *National Geograhic* named Beverley Bowie preceded Wisner in Rumania and wrote about his experiences in an irreverent book entitled *Operation Bughouse.*

Some very distinguished psychologists gathered together in the OSS to do research on the testing and assessment of men and women as suitable candidates for intelligence work, particularly clandestine assignments. Leaders in this new field were Dr. John W. Gardner, later a Cabinet officer and director of Common Cause, and Dr. (Colonel) Henry A. Murray of Harvard. Their work has been described in a pioneer book called *Assessment of Men*, published in 1948. Another psychologist, Walter Langer, a brother of Bill Langer, supervised the publication of an extraordinarily insightful personality profile of Adolf Hitler, published as a book many years later, which pointed the way to similar sketches of foreign leaders by the CIA's psychiatric staff.

The list of OSS men of note could go on and on. There is in existence an organization of Veterans of OSS, (VOSS) with a distinguished membership. Recently retired as President is John Howley, another one of the bright young lawyers in Donovan's law office who, like Otto C. Doering and Edward Putzell, were tapped at various times as loyal aides to assist "the Colonel" after he left New York to take on the COI and OSS assignment. Geoffrey Jones, a veteran of clandestine operations behind German lines in the south of France, is now President and I, a representative of R&A, am a Vice President.

Through all of these men the romantic legacy of the OSS lived on after World War II. The amazingly high quality of the veterans of the organization inadvertently did an excellent job of advertising about the OSS and central intelligence as a function. The Veterans of the OSS persisted through the period of trouble for CIA in demanding preservation of a good intelligence service. The appointment of Bill Casey, a past President of VOSS, as DCI justified in the minds of his fellow veterans the value of the legacy of the OSS for the CIA.

The action staff in the OSS, especially those in the overseas stations, benefited enormously from being celebrated in prose written by skillful and successful writers. The mythical aspects of the CIA took wings almost immediately after the end of the war when two able journalists, Corey Ford and Alistair MacBain, were given permission by Donovan to write a breezy suspense story called *Cloak and Dagger: The Secret Story of OSS*. It came out in 1945 with a "tribute" by General Donovan, printed as foreword, that began: "Now that the war is ended it is only fair to the men of the OSS, who have taken some of the gravest risks of the war, that their courage and devotion should be made known." In 1946 a slightly more substantial book by two first-class writers who had served in the OSS, Stewart Alsop and Tom Braden, was written under the title *Sub Rosa: The OSS and American Espionage*. Alsop and Braden had parachuted into France as JEDBURGH team members; they described the bravery and excitement of the OSS operational missions in stories that still read well and provide a good bit of the substance for later, more systematic books on OSS operations. The literature of the OSS revealed some of the frantic improvisation of OSS espionage and covert operations, but it invariably left an overwhelming impression of daring, unconventionality, and heroic achievement. While Alsop, at least, knew enough from his friends in R&A to include some indication of the central intelligence analysis function of the OSS, this part of the story seems inevitably humdrum in comparison to the derring-do.

The story of the research and analysis function of the OSS might not have survived at all if it had not been written about by the thoughtful historian, Sherman Kent. Kent stayed on in Washington for a short time after R&A was transferred to the State Department, before he returned to Yale. (He came back to Washington a number of years later to serve for 20 years in the CIA's Office of National Estimates.) His book of this period, *Strategic Intelligence For American World Policy*, finished in October

1948, provided a generation of intelligence officers with a rational model for their profession of collecting and analyzing information. [14] By the time the book came out the fledgling CIA was in existence and Kent uses terms that suggest he is describing the new organization. Actually he is reflecting on his experience in the OSS's R&A Branch and outlining an idealistic concept of the hard work of the intelligence analyst.

Since it does not really tell what went on in either the OSS or the CIA, Kent's book is an abstract treatment of a concept that had been articulated but never realized. Kent told me at the time that he had a hard time finding a publisher. There was no broad commercial success for *Strategic Intelligence* as compared with *Cloak and Dagger* or *Sub Rosa*. Nevertheless, the essence of the intelligence process had been captured on paper. As Kent put it, intelligence is "the kind of knowledge our state must possess regarding other states in order to assure itself that its cause will not suffer nor its undertakings fail because its statesmen and soldiers plan and act in ignorance. This is the knowledge upon which we base our high-level national policy toward the other states of the world." Furthermore, Kent observed what is to this day difficult to persuade people about, "some of this knowledge may be acquired through clandestine means, but the bulk of it must be had through unromantic open-and-above-board observation and research." These truths, too, were part of the legacy of the OSS, although they were nearly buried under the legends of cloaks and daggers and paramilitary operations.

*Chapter Three*

# Seeking National Security in the Postwar World 1945-1952

Ironically the new peacetime Central Intelligence Agency might not have ever gotten onto a sound footing if it had not been for three war-related factors that gave strong impetus to its creation: 1) the Congress made public the full story of the Pearl Harbor tragedy, an almost perfect model of disastrous handling of crucial strategic intelligence; 2) the Soviet Union violated its wartime understanding with Churchill and Roosevelt and seized political and military control in most of Eastern Europe between 1945 and 1948, while threatening to do the same in Greece, Turkey, Iran, Yugoslavia, Italy, and Berlin; and 3) the Soviet and Chinese Communists sponsored an attempt by North Korea in June 1950 to conquer all of Korea. This latter "incident" brought about a quasi-wartime situation that permitted the CIA to establish itself on sound footing.

To their credit, Donovan and General Magruder tried to do what they called laying the keel of such an organization more than a year before World War II ended in 1945. It reflects the long lead time in our system of government that Donovan's recommendations of 1944 did not become law until 1947. The CIA began to get the authority, the funds, and the staff to operate as a real central intelligence machine only under the impetus of the war in Korea in 1950. By 1953 the modern CIA was in being and operational.

I clearly remember Magruder conferring at length with Donovan and other senior OSS officials on a November 1944 memorandum to President Roosevelt. The actual drafting, I believe, was done by my former Current Intelligence Staff Chief Everett Gleason, who had moved to Donovan's staff for interagency liaison, and his friend and senior liaison officer, William M. McGovern, another professor who was OSS's principal link with the JCS. Gleason, a fine historian who later served with distinction in the National Security Council Staff and in the State Department's Historical Office, explained the main ideas to me as he went over the draft in the summer and fall of 1944. The proposal as Donovan approved it is tightly written and succinctly lays down the main ideas later embodied in the provisions of the National Security Act of 1947 that established the CIA. He left blank the places where a name for the new organization would appear, but if those blanks had been filled in with the words "Central Intelligence Agency" the document would have served perfectly well as a charter for the agency set up three years later. It read:[1]

18 November 1944

Pursuant to your note of 31 October 1944 I have given consideration to the organization of an intelligence service for the post-war period.

In the early days of the war, when the demands upon intelligence services were mainly in and for military operations, the OSS was placed under the direction of the JCS.

Once our enemies are defeated the demand will be equally pressing for information that will aid us in solving the problems of peace.

This will require two things:

1. That intelligence control be returned to the supervision of the President.

2. The establishment of a central authority reporting directly to you, with responsibility to frame intelligence objectives and to collect and coordinate the intelligence material required by the Executive Branch in planning and carrying out national policy and strategy.

I attach in the form of a draft directive (Tab A) the means by which I think this could be realized without difficulty or loss of time. You will note that coordination and centralization are placed at the policy level but operational intelligence (that pertaining primarily to Department action) remains within the existing agencies concerned. The creation of a central authority thus would not conflict with or limit necessary intelligence functions within the Army, Navy, Department of State and other agencies.

In accordance with your wish, this is set up as a permanent long-range plan. But you may want to consider whether this (or part of it) should be done now, by executive or legislative action. There are common-sense reasons why you may desire to lay the keel of the ship at once.

The immediate revision and coordination of our present intelligence system would effect substantial economies and aid in the more efficient and speedy termination of the war.

Information important to the national defense, being gathered now by certain Departments and agencies, is not being used to full advantage in the war. Coordination at the strategy level would prevent waste, and avoid the present confusion that leads to waste and unnecessary duplication.

Though in the midst of war, we are also in a period of transition which, before we are aware, will take us into the tumult of rehabilitation. An adequate and orderly intelligence system will contribute to informed decisions.

We have now in the Government the trained and specialized personnel needed for the task. This talent should not be dispersed.

William J. Donovan
Director

TAB A
Substantive Authority Necessary
in Establishment of a
Central Intelligence Service

In order to coordinate and centralize the policies and actions of the Government relating to intelligence:

1. There is established in the Executive Office of the President a central intelligence service, to be known as the _____, at the head of which shall be a Director appointed by the President. The Director shall discharge and perform his functions and duties under the direction and supervision of the President. Subject to the approval of the President, the Director may exercise his powers, authorities and duties through such officials or agencies and in such manner as he may determine.

2. There is established in the _____ an Advisory Board consisting of the Secretary of State, the Secretary of War, the Secretary of the Navy, and such other members as the President may subsequently appoint. The Board shall advise and assist the Director with respect to the formulation of basic policies and plans of the _____.

3. Subject to the direction and control of the President, and with any necessary advice and assistance from the other Departments and agencies of the Government, the _____ shall perform the following functions and duties:

   (a) Coordination of the functions of all intelligence agencies of the Government, and the establishment of such policies and objectives as will assure the integration of national intelligence efforts:

   (b) Collection either directly or through existing Government Departments and agencies, of pertinent information, including military, economic, political and scientific, concerning the capabilities, intentions and activities of foreign nations, with particular reference to the effect such matters may have upon the national security, policies and interests of the United States;

   (c) Final evaluation, synthesis and dissemination within the Government of the intelligence required to enable the Government to determine policies with respect to national planning and security in peace and war, and the advancement of broad national policy;

    (d) Procurement, training and supervision of its intelligence personnel;

    (e) Subsversive operations abroad;

    (f) Determination of policies for and coordination of facilities essential to the collection of information under subparagraph "(b)" hereof; and

    (g) Such other functions and duties relating to intelligence as the President from time to time may direct.

4. The _____ shall have no police or law-enforcement functions, either at home or abroad.

5. Subject to Paragraph 3 hereof, existing intelligence agencies within the Government shall collect, evaluate, synthesize and disseminate departmental operating intelligence, herein defined as intelligence required by such agencies in the actual performance of their functions and duties.

6. The Director shall be authorized to call upon Departments and agencies of the Government to furnish appropriate specialists for such supervisory and functional positions within the _____ as may be required.

7. All Government Departments and agencies shall make available to the Director such intelligence material as the Director, with the approval of the President, from time to time may request.

8. The _____ shall operate under an independent budget.

9. In time of war or unlimited national emergency, all programs of the _____ in areas of actual or projected military operations shall be coordinated with military plans and shall be subject to the approval of the Joint Chiefs of Staff. Parts of such programs which are to be executed in a theater of military operations shall be subject to the control of the Theater Commander.

10. Within the limits of such funds as may be made available to the _____, the Director may employ necessary personnel and make provision for necessary supplies, facilities and services. The Director shall be assigned, upon the approval of the President, such military and naval personnel as may be required in the performance of the functions and duties of the _____. The Director may provide for the internal organization and management of the _____ in such manner as he may determine.

Washington's cheerful mood of 1944, engendered by the rapid collapse of German resistance in France, was punctured by the surprise Ardennes offensive of December that set U.S. forces back on their heels. An overly pessimistic view then set in about the necessity for a costly, long drawn-out battle to bring the German and Japanese armies to surrender. Probably this new mood accounts for the slipshod way in which Donovan's memorandum was handled. Roosevelt sent it to the JCS for comments. While there was a great deal of support for the idea at the senior working level—for example in the JCS's hard-pressed Joint Intelligence Staff that was working on its own intelligence plan in the fall of 1944, as was the State Department— the general bureaucratic reaction to the recommendation for an agency with a strong coordinating role and direct responsibility to the President was almost automatically hostile. Part of this hostility was no doubt due to dislike of Donovan himself.

J. Edgar Hoover, who had his own plan for the FBI to control all overseas intelligence, bitterly opposed the idea and probably leaked the proposal to the press. Journalist Walter Trohan's articles appeared in the *Chicago Tribune* and the *Washington Times Herald* in February 1945, denouncing the proposed "all-powerful intelligence service" as a New Deal "super spy" organization "to spy on the postwar world and to pry into the lives of citizens at home." The articles also denounced the JCS plan for a national intelligence authority. Roosevelt was forced to put the matter on the back burner for a time and did not take it up again until April 5, only a week before his death, when he asked Donovan to try to get a consensus of the chiefs of intelligence and internal security units in the various Cabinet Departments on the establishment of a central intelligence agency. This task, probably impossible anyway, got nowhere. The Cabinet members who replied were all opposed. With Roosevelt's death the first, indispensable prerequisite of a true central intelligence system also perished—Presidential understanding of the concept and the Chief Executive's trust in the man who would put the concept into practice.

It was natural that President Harry S. Truman could not address himself immediately to the peacetime intelligence issue and that he would require time and experience in the White House before he grasped the urgency of the need for central intelligence handling. Before Truman reached this stage, Nazi Germany had surrendered, the world's first atomic bombs fell on Japan, and hostilities ended everywhere. In the rush to tidy up administrative matters, the Bureau of the Budget, directed by Harold D. Smith, which had always been unhappy with Donovan's unconventional style, strongly urged prompt abolition of OSS. Smith argued that the State Department should provide high-level intelligence support to the President and that no other central intelligence operation was needed. Truman agreed and issued an Executive Order, dated September 20, and effective October 1, 1945, putting an end to OSS and to Donovan's dream.[2]

## EXECUTIVE ORDER 9621
## TERMINATION OF THE OFFICE OF STRATEGIC SERVICES AND DISPOSITION OF ITS FUNCTIONS

By virtue of the authority vested in me by the Constitution and Statutes, including Title I of the First War Powers Act, 1941, and as President of the United States and Commander in Chief of the Army and the Navy, it is hereby ordered as follows:

1. There are transferred to and consolidated in an Interim Research and Intelligence Service, which is hereby established in the Department of State, (a) the functions of the Research and Analysis Branch and of the Presentation Branch of the Office of Strategic Services (provided for by the Military Order of June 13, 1942), excluding such functions performed within the countries of Germany and Austria, and (b) those other functions of the Office of Strategic Services (hereinafter referred to as the Office) which relate to the functions of the said Branches transferred by this paragraph. The functions of the Director of Strategic Services and of the United States Joint Chiefs of Staff, relating to the functions transferred to the Service by this paragraph, are transferred to the Secretary of State. The personnel, property, and records of the said Branches, except such thereof as is located in Germany and Austria, and to much of the other personnel, property and records of the Office and of the funds of the Office as the Director of the Bureau of the Budget shall determine to relate primarily to the functions transferred by this paragraph, are transferred to the said Service. Military personnel now on duty in connection with the activities transferred by this paragraph may, subject to applicable law and to the extent mutually agreeable to the Secretary of State and to the Secretary of War or the Secretary of the Navy, as the case may be, continue on such duty in the Department of State.

2. The Interim Research and Intelligence Service shall be abolished as of the close of business December 31, 1945, and the Secretary of State shall provide for winding up its affairs. Pending such abolition, (a) the Secretary of State may transfer from the said Service to such agencies of the Department of State as he shall designate any function of the Service, (b) the Secretary may curtail the activities carried on by the Service, (c) the head of the Service, who shall be designated by the Secretary, shall be responsible to the Secretary or to such other officer of the Department of State as the Secretary shall direct, and (d) the Service shall, except as otherwise provided in this order, be administered as an organizational entity in the Department of State.

3. All functions of the Office not transferred by paragraph 1 of this order, together with all personnel, records, property, and funds of the Office not so transferred, are transferred to the Department of War; and the Office, including the Office of the Director of Strategic Services, is terminated. The functions of the Director of Strategic Services, and of the United States Joint Chiefs of Staff, relating to the functions transferred by this paragraph, are transferred to the Secretary of War. Naval personnel on duty with the Office in connection with the activities transferred by this paragraph may, subject to applicable law and to the extent mutually agreeable to the Secretary of War and the Secretary of the Navy, continue on such duty in the Department of War. The Secretary of War shall, whenever he deems it compatible with the national interests, discontinue any activity transferred by this paragraph and wind up all affairs relating thereto.

4. Such further measures and dispositions as may be determined by the Director of the Bureau of the Budget to be necessary to effectuate the transfer or redistribution of functions provided for in this order shall be carried out in such manner as the Director may direct and by such agencies as he may designate.

5. All provisions of prior orders of the President which are in conflict with this order are amended accordingly.

6. This order shall, except as otherwise specifically provided, be effective as of the opening of business October 1, 1945.

The White House  HARRY S. TRUMAN
September 20, 1945

The obscure administrative prose of this order transferred R&A, with its small Visual Presentations staff of artists, to the State Department and transferred to the Secretary of War the SI Branch and X-2, plus whatever else was left over after demobilization. Since the paramilitary services of OSS phased out rapidly, what Army got was an independent organization (called SSU—the Strategic Services Unit) containing espionage and counterespionage elements. Truman's Order was a "Solomon's solution," dividing the baby in half.

Bill Langer took R&A to State to serve under a New York lawyer named Alfred McCormack, who had in the latter part of the war built up in the Army a rather efficient military evaluations group dealing mainly with signals intelligence. Initially 1,655 OSS personnel and their slots were given to State;[3] but many left during the postwar decampment from Washington, and State, which in no way wanted this intelligence burden thrust on it, only tried to get funds for 800 to 900 men. General Magruder took SI and X-2 and the other remnants to the Army where they remained in an ambiguous status for some time, although Magruder himself soon left in disgust because of military disinterest. Such was the inglorious end of OSS as a government entity.

## Perspective

My own perspective in this period reflects the uncertain status of central intelligence as a permanent career. Like most of the men and women who had more or less accidentally fallen in with OSS, I had not the slightest thought of staying in public service after the war. While Gleason's talk about perpetuating a central intelligence organization fascinated me, I felt no sense of obligation to do anything about it. My aim was to return to Harvard, where I still was on leave of absence. Instead, a rare opportunity for a young historian came along, and I stayed on in Washington another four years in a pursuit only collaterally related to intelligence.

At the end of the war, General Marshall and General Eisenhower authorized the preparation of official U.S. Army histories. Eisenhower said early in 1946 that he thought he must have done something right in winning the war and he wanted an objective, historical analysis of the lessons to be learned from this great national experience. He was determined these lessons be captured on paper as soon as possible; he said if the Army left the job to "a bunch of elderly colonels" it would take 25 years and probably not be sensitive to the national, as distinct from the Army, viewpoint. The proposition described to me was that the project start at the top with a study of what Marshall called his "command post," the Operations Division of the War Department General Staff that was responsible for all strategic planning and transmission of instructions to operational commands in theaters of war. It was agreed that civilian historians would be brought in to do the job and be given complete access to the classified files of the Joint Chiefs and the war plans element of the Operations Division.

No one outside the Pentagon had seen these documents, literally rooms full of secret and top secret papers, recording the strategic thinking and the managerial skills of our military leaders and their staffs. It was a rich harvest for any historian, and I eventually was given the job of chief historian for the Operations Division history. This assignment began early in 1946 and kept me busy until the summer of 1949. At first a year or two seemed all that would be required, but the files were so full of valuable raw materials that I not only wrote the volume Eisenhower wanted, *Washington Command Post*, but collected a staff that went on to complete some other volumes that, in time, became part of a 99-volume official history series, *The U.S. Army in World War II*.

Aside from its historical value, my study of military planning and strategic organization of forces was an unparalleled opportunity to see how our government worked in a time of great stress, from 1939 through 1945, and, in particular, to note how intelligence was used by strategic planners and policy-makers. I was able to interview almost all the general officers who held key command or staff roles in World War II, beginning with Eisenhower, who gave 100 percent support in getting me access to files seen only by a few senior Army officers. He also granted approval to publish the history despite the fact that nearly all materials cited remained under security controls.

In a sense these years were a diversion from active intelligence duty, but they gave me insights into national political and military problems at the command level that could hardly have been gained in any other way. This experience also provided a detached view of the way policymaking officials looked at intelligence as an input to their decision-making. It was not reassuring, being more a chronicle of missed opportunities and fuzzy thinking than a story of effective use of strategic intelligence. I remember a senior general telling me that the Army's G-2 division kept reorganizing, first lining itself up to studying things by geographical regions and then shifting to sections studying functionally defined subjects; he concluded "it was never worth a damn to a decision-maker either way!" A favorite wartime story, regrettably true, told how G-2 was so little geared into high-level strategic decisions that it was engaged in a colossal shuffle of office space when D-Day for the Normandy invasion came along; all of G-2's files were locked up sitting in safes in the halls waiting for moving crews when frantic requests for data on the landing zone situations began to descend on the hapless Army intelligence officers, who hardly knew each others' phone numbers, let alone what was in the files.

I discovered that the military services, too, like OSS, had leaned heavily on British skills for their triumphs in intelligence, especially in the signals intercept field, but that they had imperfectly understood how the British coordinated intelligence at the national level, inserting estimative judgments based on intelligence evidence at the very top of the command structure. Perhaps more than anything else it was the awareness of how little these concepts had sunk in that caused me to take up a career in intelligence work in 1949.

## A Pseudo-Central Intelligence System: 1946-1947

What passed for central intelligence machinery in this period was essentially a facade of centrality covering up the usual departmental fragmentation and inefficiency. Donovan and Magruder had lost their argument over institutionalizing a peacetime OSS. The many bitter bureaucratic struggles of that day are pointless to recount now. President Truman expected the State Department to take the lead in organizing central intelligence, but it never organized its own house to do so. As a result, in the end the plan that was most influential was a compromise pushed forward by the Navy, which was more afraid of domination by the Army than anything else. Ferdinand Eberstadt, a banker and friend of Navy Secretary James Forrestal, directed a study on defense integration and policy-making. That part of the Navy report that dealt with centralization of intelligence was authored by Rear Admiral Sidney Souers, a St. Louis businessman who had become Deputy Chief of Naval Intelligence. This Navy plan sought a central structure strong enough to prevent any other agency from dominating everything but weak enough to present no threat to Navy's control of its own affairs. The Navy argued that a complete merger of the various intelligence services was not feasible since each department required intelligence peculiar to itself. However, the plan recommended that a central intelligence agency should be established, reporting to a National Security Council, for coordinating the production of intelligence.

The one thing that Army, Navy, State, and the FBI agreed on was that they did not want a strong central agency controlling their collection programs. Admiral Ernest J. King, an efficient but narrowly partisan military man, voiced a fear that has always been present; King told Navy Secretary Forrestal he "questioned whether such an agency could be considered consistent with our ideas of government."[4] Truman himself repeatedly said, more with reference to the FBI, that "this country wanted no Gestapo under any guise or for any reason."[5] These expressions of doubt are legitimate concerns, but they all served as bars to necessary centralization of intelligence tasks. The fact is that it is possible to introduce checks and balances that render central intelligence accountable to our constitutional government; it is not possible for the government to cope with the problems that beset it abroad without an efficient, coordinated central intelligence system.

The numerous studies and recommendations in 1945 were further adjusted in a paper prepared by the JCS's Joint Intelligence Staff, which, according to Ludwell Montague, very much craved some central national coordinating process. Truman approved this JCS/JIC compromise plan as the first of a series of interim intelligence structures he created before finally turning to an effective coordinating agency.

The President set up by Presidential Directive, on January 22, 1946, a National Intelligence Authority (NIA) comprised of the Secretaries of State, War, and Navy along with the President's personal representative, Admiral William D. Leahy. These departmental czars, with a watchful eye from the White House, were responsible for the work of an organization to be known as the Central Intelligence Group (CIG). Both funds and staff were to come from the departments that retained autonomy over their own intelligence services. The CIG was expected to reassemble some analysts to process intelligence from the various agencies, with a staff originally planned to number only 80.[6] Rear Admiral Souers took over as head of the new CIG for a term limited at his own insistence to six months. He later became a White House Assistant to Truman, dealing with intelligence and national security affairs.[7]

Lieutenant General Hoyt Vandenberg of the Air Force succeeded Souers as Director of the CIG in June 1946 and served until May 1947, when he turned the agency over to Rear Admiral Roscoe Hillenkoetter. Vandenberg was a nephew of the great Senator; this connection, as well as his military rank, gave the CIG a certain protection. Vandenberg's contribution to central intelligence otherwise was mainly in raising the sights on personnel ceilings, aiming at ten times Souers' modest proposal of a total strength of 80 in research and analysis. An Office of Reports and Estimates (ORE) was formed in August 1946 and began to produce a current intelligence daily summary of foreign events and conduct a certain amount of economic and scientific research. As its size and competence increased, this new research and analysis facility added some interesting paper to the flow of reports from other agencies that arrived at the desks of the President and other decision-making officials. It cannot honestly be said that it coordinated either intelligence activities or intelligence judgments; these were guarded closely by Army, Navy, Air Force, State, and the FBI. When attempts were made to prepare agreed national estimates on the basis of intelligence available to all, the coordination process was interminable, dissents were the rule rather than the exception, and every policymaking official took his own agency's intelligence appreciations along to the White House to argue his case. The prewar chaos was largely recreated with only a little more lip service to central coordination.

Under Souers and Vandenberg the CIG did get back an independent clandestine collection capability, the old SSU, which still had several field stations operating on a skeleton basis. A cadre of OSS operators had done what they could to keep in business. Dick Helms, for example, was able to stay on in Germany trying to preserve some of Allen Dulles' operational assets. Philip Horton, an early OSS hand, was station chief in France, Alfred Ulmer in Austria, Jim Angleton in Italy, and James Kellis in China.[8] The SSU, at home and abroad, was redesignated the Office of Special Operations (OSO) and brought with it to CIG the functions of espionage and counterespionage, although these activities were both highly compartmented from ORE's analysts. The voluntary overt collection of information from domestic sources (which—as the Foreign Nationalities Branch in OSS—had proved useful) was incorporated in the Domestic Contact Service that has carried on until today; and the staff of what was later called the Foreign Broadcast Information Service (FBIS) was transferred to the central agency as one of a number of so-called services of common concern. By June 1946 the CIG staff amounted to about 1,800, of which one-third were overseas with OSO. In Washington another 400 people worked in OSO and some 600 were in administrative and support duties. That left only about 200 for analysis and reporting.[9]

The expansion under Vandenberg made the agency a little bigger than before but not much better. It was filled largely with military men who did not want to leave the service at the end of the war but were not in great demand in the military services. The quality was mediocre. Vandenberg had his eye on a top command job in the U.S. Air Force and stayed on in CIG for only one year. In keeping with the rotational practice normal among the military services, it was the Navy's turn again to appoint a director. When Hillenkoetter took over, in the spring of 1947, the CIG was a disorganized assembly of parts, not a working machine. It was by then slated to have a legislative foundation to replace the 1946 Presidential Directive, an unprecedented move that would primarily establish the central intelligence function.

The structure of strategic intelligence at the national level in this 1946-1947 period was only marginally improved over pre-World War II conditions and that was mainly because there were more people involved. State had a small intelligence staff and there was in CIG a central clandestine collection unit and a central analytical intelligence staff, albeit one with little authority to capture policy-level attention. The picture in early 1947 looked like the chart on the following page.

## Creation of CIA

Unfortunately, CIG did not really begin to meet the need for a central intelligence organization. For a year and a half, until the creation of the CIA by the National Security Act of July 1947, the argument—confederation vs. centralization of intelligence activity—continued, this time within the larger debate over the unification of the armed forces. The NIA and CIG had been set up by executive directive to meet the President's needs and now Donovan and Allen Dulles, among others, argued the case for providing a legislative basis for a permanent civilian intelligence agency.[10] This was done, finally, in the 1947 Act, almost as a by-product of reorganizing the military agencies and the State-Army-Navy procedures for handling political and military problems at the strategic level. The operative language in the Act that set up the Central Intelligence Agency under a National Security Council closely conformed to the concept of Donovan's original 1941 charter

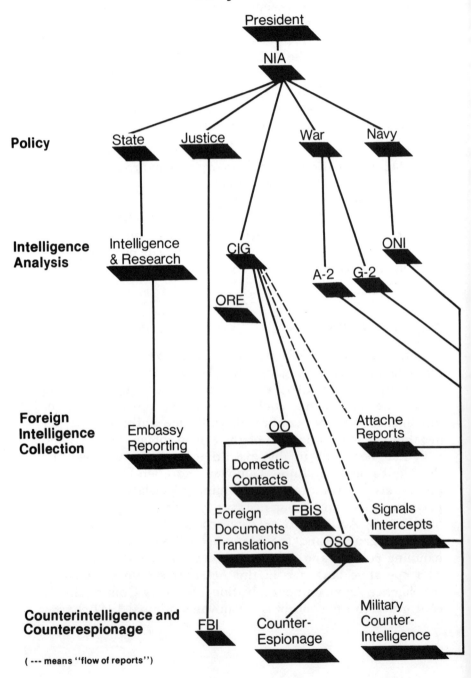

*Seeking National Security in the Postwar World*

and his November 1944 memorandum to President Roosevelt.*

One of the truly creative innovations in American Government in our time was the establishment of this National Security Council (NSC) under the chairmanship of the President, with the Secretary of State and the Secretary of Defense as key members. A crucial element in this structure was that the Joint Chiefs of Staff reported directly to the NSC on military policy and the Central Intelligence Agency was to report directly to the NSC on foreign situations, trends, threats, and opportunities. Truman considered the building of the NSC system one of his great accomplishments.

The Act gave the CIA a line of command to the NSC because the NSC was presided over by the President himself. Since the duties of the Cabinet officials designated as members of the NSC could only be advisory, in that they simply shared in the Chief Executive's power, the effect was to give the CIA the direct channel to the President that the advocates of central intelligence had always sought. Section 101 of the National Security Act established the National Security Council and provided that:

The function of the Council shall be to advise the President with respect to the integration of domestic, foreign, and military policies relating to the national security so as to enable the military services and the other departments and agencies of the Government to cooperate more effectively in matters involving the national security.

At last it was to be recognized that peacetime problems could not be dealt with by a separate department of peace and an isolated department of war, but should be examined as political-military issues.

Section 102 of the Act dealt specifically with the establishment of the Central Intelligence Agency. There was an extraordinary amount of prose devoted to defining the status and pay of a commissioned officer of the armed services if he

---

*Larry Houston, who served many years as CIA's General Counsel, and his principal associate, John Warner, were the CIG staff officers mainly responsible for drafting legislation for the new CIA. Walter Pforzheimer, CIG's Legislative Counsel, was CIG's representative on Capitol Hill working to facilitate the passage of this part of the National Security Act. The three of them for many years have been primary sources for the early history of CIA. Pforzheimer, in addition, is a well-known rare book collector and probably the world's outstanding expert on the published literature of intelligence.

should become Director of the CIA, but the crucial provisions of the law were quite succinct. Section 102 (a) said:

There is hereby established under the National Security Council a Central Intelligence Agency with a Director of Central Intelligence, who shall be the head thereof. The Director shall be appointed by the President, by and with the advice and consent of the Senate, from among the commissioned officers of the armed services or from among individuals in civilian life.

Section 102 (c) gave the Director of Central Intelligence (DCI) discretionary authority to fire employees when "necessary or advisable in the interests of the United States" without regard for the normal civil service procedures—a prerogative vital to a serious central intelligence operating agency.

Finally Section 102 (d) assigned functions to the new agency, not mentioning either espionage or counterespionage, that were tacitly covered under the "common concern" clause in subparagraph (4) as follows:

(d) For the purpose of coordinating the intelligence activities of the several Government departments and agencies in the interest of national security, it shall be the duty of the Agency, under the direction of the National Security Council—
(1) to advise the National Security Council in matters concerning such intelligence activities of the Government departments and agencies as relate to national security;
(2) to make recommendations to the National Security Council for the coordination of such intelligence activities of the departments and agencies of the Government as relate to the national security;
(3) to correlate and evaluate intelligence relating to the national security, and provide for the appropriate dissemination of such intelligence within the Government using where appropriate existing agencies and facilities: Provided, That the Agency shall have no police, subpoena, law-enforcement powers, or internal-security functions: Provided further, That the departments and other agencies of the Government shall continue to collect, evaluate, correlate, and disseminate departmental intelligence: And provided further, That the Director of Central Intelligence shall be responsible for protecting intelligence sources and methods from unauthorized disclosure;
(4) to perform, for the benefit of the existing intelligence agencies, such additional services of common concern as the National Security Council determines can be more efficiently accomplished centrally;
(5) to perform such other functions and duties related to intelligence affecting the national security as the National Security Council may from time to time direct.
(e) To the extent recommended by the National Security Council and approved by the President, such intelligence of the departments and agencies

of the Government, except as hereinafter provided, relating to the national security shall be open to the inspection of the Director of Central Intelligence, and such intelligence as relates to the national security and is possessed by such departments and other agencies of the Government, except as hereinafter provided, shall be made available to the Director of Central Intelligence for correlation, evaluation, and dissemination: Provided, however, That upon the written request of the Director of Central Intelligence, the Director of the Federal Bureau of Investigation shall make available to the Director of Central Intelligence such information for correlation, evaluation, and dissemination as may be essential to the national security.

Except for the reference to the FBI's requirement that material from their files be provided only upon written request—a concession to J. Edgar Hoover's independence and fanatic protection of his files—the authority of the new CIA was clearly established. The Director of Central Intelligence was to have access to all intelligence relating to national security, including military intelligence and signals intelligence. The concept was clear that the new CIA was not intended to be a supplicant pleading for information from the older agencies but instead a central coordinator and a central evaluator.

With the prohibition against "policy, subpoena, law enforcement power, or internal security functions" and the assignment of legal responsibility "for protecting intelligence sources and methods from unauthorized disclosures," the provisions of the National Security Act of 1947 gave the CIA a charter that has served it well for nearly 35 years. It was a tribute to the foresight of the handful of men around Roosevelt and Donovan in the turbulent era of the early 1940s that this central intelligence concept was finally written into law. The CIA formally came into existence September 18, 1947.

## Covert Action

Unfortunately, the reorganized intelligence machinery received a workable charter just as one of its weaker Directors took office. Rear Admiral Hillenkoetter did not have the rank, the prestige with his fellow officers, or the political clout with civilian officials to lead the CIA into high-gear performance. His agency was still full of people detailed from other agencies, mainly Army, Navy, and Air Force, and many of them lacked the professional education or experience to do a first-class job.

While the CIA's clandestine intelligence collection and intelligence analysis were proceeding in a rather desultory way, a new element entered the central intelligence picture. It was covert psychological and political action. This function was fated to play a crucial role in coloring perceptions of the CIA, but it was not one sought by the agency.[11] The CIA entered into covert action operations under pressure from leading U.S. officials of the day to support basic U.S. foreign policy. In the light of Josef Stalin's activities in Central Europe and Berlin in 1947 and 1948, there was great pressure by many thoughtful, patriotic men to find ways to forestall Soviet use of local Communists or nearby military forces to intimidate and dominate the governments of Western Europe.

The officials who argued that the United States had to fight back covertly against widespread political subversive efforts sponsored by the Soviet Union in Germany, France, and Italy in 1947 and 1948 were Secretary of State George C. Marshall, probably the most distinguished statesman to emerge from World War II, Secretary of War Robert Patterson, Secretary of Defense James Forrestal, and George Kennan, then Director of the State Department's Policy Planning Staff. President Truman concurred in their recommendations, and every subsequent President of the United States endorsed the wisdom of trying to frustrate Soviet—or other Communist—subversive political activities by giving covert assistance to those who would oppose Communist aims.

It is hard now to remember how menacing the Soviet encroachments appeared. In February 1948 the Communist coup in Czechoslovakia succeeded and then in March the popular and well-known Foreign Minister, Jan Masaryk, jumped—or most probably was pushed—from a window to his death. The shock in the United States was tremendous. I remember the moment because friends told me the Czech coup was the reason one of my Harvard advisers, a distinguished Professor of American Literature, jumped to his death from the top of a Boston hotel. He had been an advocate of Soviet Communism for many years.

The brutality of Stalin's actions in Europe horrified American observers. Many American officials, such as General Lucius Clay, Commander of U.S. Forces in Europe, anticipated an outright military attack on Berlin and Western Europe. It was common in Washington to hear predictions that war would come whenever the Soviet Union succeeded in manufacturing an atomic bomb, thus neutralizing the only U.S. weapon that could stop the massive ground forces Stalin kept poised along what Churchill christened the iron curtain.

The U.S. strategic response was the Kennan strategy of containment, which reasoned that the Soviet police state would "mellow" and its outward thrusts for dominion would diminish, if the USSR's external aggression did not pay off. Hence the Marshall Plan was adopted to give economic incentives to the threatened states of Western Europe, and a substantial American military force remained in place to provide security. Between economic assistance and military protection, a middle zone of low-intensity conflict short of war arose. This was the zone in which the U.S. would use covert political and psychological efforts to counter Soviet influence, supplementing U.S. diplomatic efforts by assisting moderate, non-Communist groups.

Opinion in 1948 in Washington was that this effort to stabilize Western Europe against the threat of Soviet assaults on Italy, France, and Germany would fail unless Soviet support of local Communist parties could be exposed and countered. To expose the threat of subversive takeover from within, intelligence was needed about the USSR, its intelligence system, Communist Party ideology and tactics, and the inroads they had made into Western European political, labor, cultural, and journalistic circles. To counter these inroads, non-Communist political parties had to be provided with information about Soviet efforts so they could win electoral support. Newspaper stories, radio broadcasts, and political pamphlets had to be written, disseminated, and financed to let the public know the dangers of the situation.

With respect to Italy in particular, which had an election scheduled for April 1948, Americans with knowledge of Italy, especially Americans with family connections or religious ties to the Catholic hierarchy, were sought to carry a message to Italian voters that association with the United States would save Italy whereas Communist rule would destroy it. The methods employed were psychological and political. Mainly they involved teaching American electoral techniques to

Western Europe and providing money for local political groups to organize, counter Communist propaganda, and get out the vote. From the viewpoint of U.S. officials, the aim was entirely democratic—in the tradition of our own often hard-fought state elections—totally for the good of the country concerned as well as for the benefit of U.S. interests in Western Europe.

The weakest point in Western Europe in the bleak winter of 1947-1948 was undoubtedly Italy. It is symbolic that the very first numbered document issued by the new National Security Council on November 14, 1947, was NSC 1/1, a Top Secret report entitled *"The Position of the United States with Respect to Italy."** The political perils of Italy were reexamined in very similar terms a few weeks later in NSC 1/2, February 10, 1948, and once more in a companion study, NSC 1/3, on March 8, drafted very shortly before the April 18th Italian general election.[12] These papers show that it was very much feared that the Communist Party of Italy would defeat the moderate, center, and right parties that supported parliamentary government and a Western strategic alignment. The Democratic Party leader, Alcide De Gasperi, then Prime Minister, and Pope Pius XII showed extreme anxiety lest the parliamentary parties be decisively outvoted as a consequence of Communist strength, discipline, and militancy. The discussion, recommendations, and conclusions of all three NSC 1 studies were virtually identical in tone and substance, reflecting the temper of the times perfectly. Key passages from the conclusion of NSC 1/2 read:

> The United States should make full use of its political, economic and if necessary, military power in such manner as may be found most effective to assist in preventing Italy from falling under the domination of the USSR either through external armed attack or through Soviet-dominated Communist movements within Italy, so long as the legally elected Government of Italy evidences a determination to oppose such Communist aggression.

In addition to shipping large quantities of wheat and other essential commodities to Italy as part of an extensive economic

---

*It is worth noting that in this early period under Truman, the Executive Secretary of the NSC, Sidney Souers, merely informed the NSC members that the Secretary of State would submit the report to the President with a notation that the report's conclusions were an expression of the Council's advice to Truman. There is no trace here of the independent power exercised by later Assistants to the President for National Security Affairs.

aid program and assisting the feeble Italian armed forces with equipment, supplies, and technical advice, NSC 1/2 called for

> Actively combatting Communist propaganda in Italy by an effective U.S. information program and by all other practicable means....

What these other means were is spelled out in the conclusions of NSC 1/3 as follows:

> Between now and the April elections in Italy, the United States should as a matter of priority immediately undertake further measures designed to prevent the Communists from winning participation in the government....

Measures ordered into effect included the following:

> Urge key members of Congress to announce immediately that the attitude of the American people is such that they would never support economic assistance to Italy if its government included parties inimical to the United States....
>
> Immediately initiate in this country, and encourage in Great Britain and France, a campaign of speeches by government officials and private individuals, including labor leaders, and a letter-writing campaign by private citizens, regarding the political issues in Italy.

NSC 1/3 also proposed that, in the event of Communist electoral victories in Italy, the United States should, among other things:

> Provide military equipment and supplies to Italy only if such equipment and supplies are received by anti-Communist elements and are not permitted to fall into Communist hands.
>
> Continue efforts, by all feasible means ... to detach the Italian Left-wing socialists from the Communists.
>
> Continue to assist the Christian Democrats and other selected anti-Communist parties....

To carry out these formally approved policies of the U.S. Government, certain covert steps were taken in addition to the many overt ones listed. The omissions indicated by three or four dots in the State Department's published version of these NSC papers indicate exactly where "all feasible means" to prevent the Communist from winning the April election edged over into covert action of a kind that the Embassy diplomats could not engage in directly. These kinds of financial and technical assistance to the Christian Democrats and other non-

Communist parties, as well as the efforts to split off Socialists from the united front group dominated by the Communists, had to be covert. Italian party leaders could not afford to let Communists obtain evidence that they were supported by foreigners because it would blunt public anger at the Communist Party for its own financial and policy dependence on the Soviet Union. Hence CIA got the job of passing money and giving the technical help needed to get out the vote and win the election.

These covert action programs in Italy were viewed simply as part of diplomatic and military policy. George Kennan, Director of the State Department's Policy Planning Staff, took an active role in support of all aspects of implementing the Italian policy outlined in the NSC 1 series. His view, never belligerent from the military viewpoint though firmly in favor of containing further Soviet advances in Europe, is very revealing. On March 15 he cabled:

> ... I suspect that many of the European Communists, partially victims of their own propaganda, are excited by recent successes and by prospect of seizing rich prizes in western Europe. On the other hand, the savage abruptness and cynical unconcern for appearances of recent action in Czechoslovakia leads me to feel that Kremlin leaders must be driven by sense of extreme urgency.... As far as Europe is concerned, Italy is obviously key point. If Communists were to win election there our whole position in Mediterranean, and possibly in western Europe as well, would probably be undermined.[13]

The very first meeting of the NSC on December 19, 1947, had approved NSC 4, on "Coordination of Foreign Intelligence Information Measures." This document directed the Secretary of State to coordinate anti-Communist information activities. NSC 4/A, a Top Secret annex, instructed the DCI, despite some reluctance on his part and that of his legal counsel, to carry out covert psychological warfare in pursuit of NSC 4 aims. NSC 4/A was thus the first official charter for covert activity by any U.S. agency since the close of World War II. A Special Procedures Group was set up in OSO in December. This group was the one that worked on the election in Italy.

The results of covert action in Italy, along with diplomatic and economic efforts, were viewed by policy officials as an enormous success, relieving some of the great anxiety felt by Kennan and his colleagues. The parliamentary parties triumphed at the polls.

In May of 1948, Kennan advocated the formal creation of a permanent covert political action capability. The CIA was authorized to assume this function in June in NSC 10/2. Its activities were plainly intended to include paramilitary operations as well as political and economic warfare. A covert action staff thus was officially added to the CIA's roster and it soon was named the Office of Policy Coordination (OPC), in effect replacing the Special Procedures Group. From the beginning the OPC element was headed by Frank Wisner, the former OSS station chief in Rumania.

Indicative of the thought at the time, OPC was totally separate administratively from the CIA intelligence collectors in OSO, as well as from the CIA intelligence analysts in ORE. While OPC's budget and personnel slots were lumped in with the secret funds voted for the CIA within the military budget each year, policy guidance and specific instructions to the Director of OPC came from State and Defense and bypassed the Director of the CIA completely. Naturally the initial staff was small; in 1949 there were only 300 employees altogether, including clerical and administrative staff. The men who set it up thought covert action would be approved only on an occasional basis when a crisis was at hand that normal diplomacy and military measures could not cope with, as was the case in Italy in 1948.[14]

The National Security Act of 1947 had said nothing about psychological warfare, covert action, or any secret operations; but a carefully controlled, limited program of anti-Communist activity was being discussed at the time of its passage by senior government officials.[15] Like clandestine collection operations, covert action operations were not mentioned in the law. An elastic, catch-all clause was included, referring to the CIA's performance of "such other functions and duties related to intelligence affecting the national security as the National Security Council may from time to time direct" and this clause was later cited as giving authority for covert actions. Clark Clifford, later Chairman of the President's Foreign Intelligence Advisory Board and also Secretary of Defense under President Lyndon Johnson, said in 1975 he considered covert action authorized by this elastic clause.[16]

When OPC was formally set up in the CIA, the NSC 10/2 directive authorized the CIA's continued conduct of covert activities as worked out in a consultation and review procedure with a special "10/2" panel of State and Defense officials.[17] The CIA was to be an instrument of policy, not an instigator. It was instructed to propose specific information programs and other political action that would negate Communist efforts to expand Soviet political influence in Western Europe. These projects were discussed in the 10/2 panel by the OPC director who was designated by the Secretary of State. Frank Wisner, who held the position, proceeded to carry out the projects under the authority of the NSC when State and Defense did not object. The CIA director undoubtedly knew what OPC was doing, but he was not in the command chain. It was a haphazard system and the marvel is that it worked as well as it did from June 1948 until October 23, 1951, when a new NSC directive was issued.

By this time the CIA was firmly in business as a covert political staff. State and Defense guidance was indeed very general, and the responsibility appeared to belong to CIA for meeting the Soviet challenge in those secret "back alley" battles. The operations themselves, or at least the foreign policy program within which they were carried out, were remarkably successful. CIA got a lot of credit, which it only partly deserved, and much later was to get most of the blame when covert action programs got out of hand—blame that also largely belonged to the policymakers, not to the instrument of covert action, the CIA.

## Perspective

In the spring of 1949 I was concluding my Army history, considering a college teaching job, and inquiring of friends who had stayed in intelligence what had happened to the kind of work that had intrigued me in OSS. By then the encroachments by Soviet military forces, intelligence agents, and Moscow-trained Communist party members in Eastern Europe and the Mideast were alarming. The Chinese Communists were clearly winning control of mainland China, the political freedom of Czechoslovakia had ended, and the Berlin blockade had electrified the West. It seemed to me a little pallid to go back to university life, and some of my old friends urged me to stay in government in an intelligence job.

The determining factor, I suppose, was my friendship with Jack Smith who had left OSS's Current Intelligence Staff after my departure. He went back to teaching for a while but found the lure of public service and international affairs too insistent. In mid-1949 he was in charge of current intelligence in the CIA's ORE, and he urged me to sign up somewhere in the shop, which was slowly expanding its staff. Jack arranged for me to interview one of the truly professional intelligence officers in the business, Ludwell Lee Montague, who, as Colonel, had tried to make integrated interagency intelligence work in the Joint Intelligence Staff during the war. He had become a complete convert to the concept of an independent civilian agency coordinating and introducing more scholarly methods into the work of the military services and the State Department. While our wartime acquaintance was slight, our experience and interests matched in a number of ways. There were not a great many men in the CIA of that day for whom I wanted to work, but I had a great respect for Montague's intellectual integrity, analytical skill, and dedication to improving the quality of national decision-making.

Most of ORE was organized in regional divisions, mirroring the State Department. The Chief was Theodore Babbitt, an amiable official who tried desperately to placate State, Army, Navy, and Air Force and seldom won a bureaucratic battle. For a few important papers that ORE tried to prepare as national estimates for the NSC, Babbitt relied totally on a group of three men comprising ORE's Global Survey Division. The Chief was Montague; his principal assistant was DeForest Van Slyck, a genial, breezy gentleman with a penetrating mind and quick wit who had been an Air Force briefing officer for General Hap Arnold during the war. Both of these men devoted the rest of their active careers to the CIA's Office of National Estimates. The third man, William Reitzel, left at this time for a career in research and teaching. Montague offered me this third slot in the Global Survey Division. It was an elevated enough post in terms of the then rather parsimonious Civil Service pay system and, as far as I could tell, would call for extremely interesting research and analysis of strategic factors affecting U.S. security on a worldwide basis. I took it, reporting for duty in the early summer of 1949.

It was a lot like coming home to OSS again, although the horizons had expanded and the resources of the CIA were more commensurate with the tasks of central intelligence. My job in this period was mainly drafting a monthly report of four or five printed pages with a fancy cover page and the resounding title of "Estimate of the World Situation." Being the new boy, I scouted up news items from Jack Smith's current intelligence daily summary and from the desk analysts in the ORE regional research divisions. Mostly I simply wrote down analytical comments based on my reading of the newspapers and periodical literature, adding items from the research analysts wherever possible. These I had to clear with the analysts, and of course Montague and Van Slyck signed off on the whole report before it went on its way to its prestigious audience in the White House and other Cabinet Departments.

James Lay, a close friend of Montague, was first Deputy Executive Secretary and then Executive Secretary in the new NSC organization, and he cheerfully received my contribution each month, which as far as I could tell was the only regular contribution of ORE to deliberations at the policy level. I doubt that anyone paid much attention to it. DCI Hillenkoetter gave no sign of interest in my report as long as this monthly response to the only requirement for an "evaluation" levied on CIA by the NSC got delivered on time. Montague said everyone was happy with my writing because I used some new phrases and concepts for describing trends and broke some of the cliches that had come into use in the previous months, something that tends to happen to any periodically issued report.

I had plenty to write about because the Chinese Communists took over all of the mainland; North Korea began to make menacing preparations for war; Stalin continued his campaign to destroy Tito; and the USSR exploded its first atomic bomb in September 1949, some years ahead of military intelligence predictions.

It is hard to believe that the slight papers wrapping up world trends that I prepared did much good. Indeed the weightier estimates on Soviet military strength and Soviet, Chinese Communist, and North Korean intentions, which Montague and Van Slyck argued over with their hardheaded opposite numbers from State and the military services, seemed to have little impact. At this stage the CIA estimates still were long in the preparation, too noncommittal as a result of the effort to get agreement, and, in other cases, too studded with service-biased dissenting footnotes and, always, too little read by the policymaking officials.

Montague, at this time, however, was making an input on behalf of the CIA to the great NSC 68 policy study of worldwide strategic difficulties confronting the United States in the spring of 1950. Paul Nitze chaired the study group that produced this paper on the Soviet threat. After the Korean war broke out the NSC 68 recommendations were adopted, committing U.S. military procurement and planning firmly to the strategy of containment. Its approval also caused appropriations for defense to increase from $15 billion a year in fiscal year 1950 to about $50 billion a year.[18] This kind of close intelligence support to the NSC staff was a model of what the CIA should have been doing, but it was virtually the personal enterprise of one man.

Montague also was conspiring with Lay and others to put teeth into the requirement that the CIA pull together coherent estimates on pressing foreign threats. As an institution, however, the CIA was not geared into the working machinery at the top level of government. It is symptomatic that when Truman called the NSC together in June 1950 to deal with the first real crisis of this era, Hillenkoetter was not present. CIA had written some warnings about the possibility of a North Korean attack before it occurred, but they were insufficiently emphatic to capture the NSC audience they should have reached. The CIA was criticized, somewhat unjustly, as having failed to forecast the outbreak of hostilities in Asia, and nearly everybody in the Executive Branch suddenly decided something drastic had to be done about central intelligence; war once again gave impetus toward achievement of an effective intelligence collection and analytical system.

## The Bedell Smith Reforms: 1950-1953

The new wave of reform that struck the CIA caused a solid year of turbulence but began to show constructive results immediately. As a first step, ORE did something to meet the demands of the Korean War that it should have done years before; it organized an all-source research and estimates center where signals intelligence, still a voluminous information source, especially on Soviet economic and military data, could be studied in depth by analysts at their own desks with other source files at their fingertips.

The new central intelligence analysis staff in ORE had cracked the signals barrier, something OSS had never been able to do. When I started working in the CIA in 1949, however, communications intelligence was kept behind closed doors. Cleared analysts had to visit this area periodically to keep up to date. The hold on access to intercepted material was still very tight in deference to the views of the military services, reflecting World War II experience when signals information was kept out of regular military communications channels and was virtually unavailable to all but the top commanders and the most senior civilians in government. Security argues in this direction, of course, but an enlightened attitude required the development of procedures that would permit intelligence analysts to make full use of the data and provide their findings to decision-makers at all levels. A former Navy signals intelligence officer, Knight McMahan, was in charge of handling signals files in ORE, and he did his best with the archaic and restrictive rules for using this lucrative source.

When hostilities broke out in Korea everyone wanted better intelligence fast, so ORE conspired to get more clearances and more space and organize a staff able to get at all-source data. It was agreed that I would be chief of a new analytical staff of some sort in this center; but the plan scarcely got off the ground before bigger changes occurred. Nevertheless the principle prevailed, and one of the forward-looking features of the CIA research and analysis from then on was that every major unit was cleared to use all sources and had a center where everything could be filed. This was the single most significant step taken to insure that compartmentation of signals intelligence would not again contribute to a Pearl Harbor disaster.

The best thing that happened to the CIA in those years occurred next—the advent of General Walter Bedell (Beetle) Smith as Director. When Truman appointed him to replace Hillenkoetter in October 1950, Smith approached the job with determination. He was a shrewd, dynamic man with broad experience and absolutely no tolerance for fools. It was often said he was the most even-tempered man in the world—he was always angry. Beetle, as his friends called him, was a man with no more than a high school education, who had enlisted in World War I and worked his way up through the ranks in the Regular Army. He had an intimidating personality and was a perfectionist. Largely self-educated, he had a photographic memory, encyclopedic knowledge, and shrewd judgment about people and ideas.

Beetle became Secretary of the General Staff under General Marshall in 1942, a crushing job of managerial planning and supervision that he performed with dogged perseverance. Marshall released him to be Chief of Staff and administrative *alter ego* to Eisenhower when Eisenhower went to London in 1942 and he backed up Eisenhower in this role throughout the European war. He was named Ambassador to the USSR just after the war, an experience that gave him some perceptiveness about working with Russians that stood him in good stead in dealing with intelligence experts on the Soviet Union. The intense pressures of his career resulted in surgery for stomach ulcers in the summer of 1950. Because of his illness Smith had lost about 40 pounds; when I first saw him at a CIA conference table, he weighed about 135 pounds. Yet it was plain that this frail figure carried both political and professional weight.

As soon as his health permitted, Smith accepted Truman's appointment. For the first time since Donovan, central intelligence was in the hands of a man with vision and drive, a man with the prestige persuasive to military commanders, ambassadors, and Congressmen, and, finally, a man who had the full support of a President who wanted action.

The link between Presidential authority and central intelligence is, for good or ill, crucial. Under Truman and Smith, as with Roosevelt and Donovan, trust and confidence made great strides possible. With the 1947 charter behind him—supplemented by the CIA Act of 1949—Smith took charge. He moved rapidly and effectively.

The CIA that Smith inherited was organized along functional lines with rather loose managerial supervision at the top and a tenuous connection with other intelligence agencies through an Intelligence Advisory Committee (IAC), made up of the chiefs of all the individual intelligence units in Cabinet Departments. The FBI participated actively only in discussions or preparation of papers with a bearing on U.S. internal security, while the Atomic Energy Commission interested itself only in Soviet atomic energy data. All of the agencies used the IAC to prevent estimates being written contrary to their individual departmental policies, rather than to issue coordinated requirements for intelligence collection or to produce good, analytical reports. The JCS representatives from the Joint Intelligence Committee were particularly difficult because they were preparing their own papers that reached the Secretary of Defense and the President through military channels. Until the arrival of Smith the DCIs did not have the clout to get agreed joint papers forward in a timely and effective fashion. The first estimate on the USSR that the new central intelligence machinery tried to produce took two years to finish, from March 1946 to March 1948.[19]

In these circumstances, the CIA devoted most of its analytical effort to publishing current intelligence in a daily report for the President, imaginatively nicknamed the "Daily," which Truman read and seemed satisfied with, although he continued to receive separate State and military reports too. It also began in 1949 to pay special attention to scientific and technological developments of strategic significance and set up a special analytical office for this purpose.

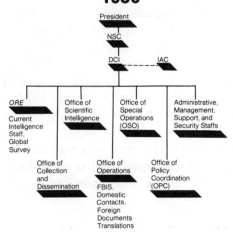

It was a very sensible organization. It simply did not work very well in carrying out the assigned functions.

The first thing Smith did was to pick his first-line assistants as if he were picking troop commanders in the field. He wanted the best and he got them. In November 1950 he approached Bill Langer, the OSS's R&A chief who was preparing for publication a powerful two-volume account of U.S. moves from isolation to war, 1939-1941, co-authored with Everett Gleason, my first chief in OSS's current intelligence staff. Smith insisted, with President Truman's support, that Langer organize the Office of National Estimates (ONE) as the highest level analytical and estimative body in the CIA, which meant in the entire U.S. Government. Beetle pressured Harvard into granting Langer a year's leave of absence and Langer was forced to fly to Washington immediately, leaving his family to follow. It was Langer's return that disrupted my career, agreeably. Langer, after long discussions with Smith on the organization of the office, asked me to become the first Estimates Staff Chief under him in the new office.

It was clear that Smith believed that all intelligence activities should be tightly coordinated so as to permit the preparation of authoritative interagency estimates based on all sources of information and evaluated by impartial experts. He considered this to be the first priority for the CIA and he backed Langer completely in insuring that good papers were written laying out the evidence and various probable courses of action for the benefit of the President. He insisted that the military agencies and State participate constructively. He read the National Intelligence Estimates carefully and he insured that they were presented to Truman without contrary briefings being given him by other agencies as so often had happened before. If other agencies disagreed with these estimates, they were entitled to state their dissents in footnotes to the agreed text. In this vital respect the CIA began to work the way it had been hoped it would. The NSC itself began to become a more systematic planning and decision-making body and the CIA began providing not only useful decision-making current data but the best evidentially-based answers to the strategic questions that could be hammered out by all the experts under the scholarly guidance of Bill Langer. Quick and authoritative papers were demanded by Smith. Langer and his colleagues provided them. The CIA had finally achieved full responsibility for analysis and forward estimating.

The second great man Smith brought back to the intelligence profession was Allen Dulles. Although in private law practice, Dulles had kept his Washington connections alive and was often called on for informal as well as formal advice on intelligence issues. He had participated with William H. Jackson and Matthias F. Correa in an NSC study in 1948 that lambasted the CIA as then constituted for failure to draft authoritative national estimates and failure to coordinate intelligence activities of other agencies. Much of the same kind of criticism was incorporated in the Hoover Commission study of the CIA in early 1949 and in an NSC study (NSC 50) of July 1949, so Smith turned to Dulles and Jackson to carry out the recommendations. Jackson became general administrative officer for the reorganization, with the title of Deputy Director of Central Intelligence, and served 10 months in this capacity.

Dulles also accepted Smith's bid but found to his dismay that Smith was unwilling to proceed at once with integration of OSO and OPC, the clandestine collection and covert action offices, as the Dulles, Jackson, Correa report had recommended. Dulles nonetheless took on the arduous task of reducing the clandestine and covert activities to some semblance of order, accepting an assignment on January 2, 1951, as a Deputy Director responsible for both OPC and OSO. While Smith and Dulles never really hit it off too well personally, they respected each other's skills. Dulles stayed on duty in CIA for 10 tumultuous years, moving up to replace Jackson as Deputy Director after Jackson left. In due course, when Eisenhower took office as President in 1953 and Allen's older brother, Foster, became Secretary of State, he became the first professional intelligence officer to be Director of Central Intelligence. No other man left such a mark on the Agency.

One managerial problem of consequence was solved immediately by Smith. As soon as he took office he simply stated that he would take over the administrative responsibility for and control over OPC covert action operations. Thus Defense and State would exert policy guidance through the DCI rather than deal directly with Frank Wisner, the OPC Chief. The new arrangement was accepted formally by State, Defense, and the Joint Chiefs on October 12, 1950. Smith delegated some of the job of coordinating OPC and OSO operations to Dulles, whom he designated as Deputy Director for Plans in January 1951. Thus Smith brought covert action into a clean line-of-command position in the Agency and, through Dulles, kept an eye on these units' activities. By 1952 Smith accepted the logic of Dulles' position on the awkwardness and frequent embarrassment of having separate OPC and OSO units doing secret work in the same place at the same time, competing for resources and personnel. In August 1952 he formally set up what came to be called the Directorate of Plans, usually referred to as the DDP, in which the two were combined.

Gradually the two offices, OPC and OSO, began to coordinate activities at least to the point of not competing for the services of the same agents by offering higher wages and better privileges. In time some individuals in the field began to perform dual functions, collecting information and maintaining covert political relations and often using the same sources for both purposes. The merger did not really become effective across the board until Dulles became DCI, but in its Directorate of Plans the CIA already, by the end of the Smith reform era, had consolidated the clandestine and covert functional tasks sufficiently for the generic term "clandestine services" to come into use to describe the two operational elements of the agency assigned to duty under the DDP. When in August 1952 the old OSO and OPC merged into a complex semi-geographical, semi-functional structure, the intelligence collectors retained, psychologically and bureaucratically, a separate identity from the operators—the covert action specialists. The general character of the initial merger was reflected in the fact that the Deputy Director for Plans was Frank Wisner of OPC, while his second in command, with a newly created title of Chief of Operations (COPS), was Richard Helms of OSO. Over time the lines gradually blurred as the supervisory echelons of the clandestine services were required to handle both espionage and covert action cases.

Smith made a somewhat similar move to regularize the intelligence analysis group by appointing a Deputy Director for Intelligence (DDI). At first Smith expected Langer to play this role, but Langer wanted no part of the administrative headaches involved in deciding what to do with those parts of ORE he did not want in his new National Estimates office. Later Smith picked an outsider, a young lawyer, to take this job, but his choice, Loftus Becker, stayed only a short time. He was succeeded in 1952 by a Harvard Law School professor, Robert Amory, a clever and articulate Bostonian from a distinguished family who had good Eisenhower Republican connections. He joined the CIA in the Smith era, but served through the Dulles decade, leaving the CIA early in 1962.

It is characteristic that the group of offices under the DDI's supervision did not really have a formal designation until the term Directorate came into general use in the early 1960s. Nevertheless, the loose congeries of units that, alongside ONE in the national estimates field, did analytical research and writing, constituted an interrelated analytical services cluster comparable to the clandestine services cluster. The DDI component by January 1952 included an economic and geographical research office (ORR), a scientific research office (OSI), and a large current intelligence reporting office (OCI). These units and ONE were supported by a reference and library unit then called the Office of Collection and Dissemination (OCD) that later became the CIA's Central Reference Service— a complex, computerized library of classified intelligence materials. This included, eventually, a community-wide service element of enormous usefulness, a biographic register of foreign, non-military personalities. The collection of overt foreign information from domestic contacts continued to be a DDI responsibility as did the translation of foreign broadcasts and foreign documents.

Finally, to provide support services for personnel handling, finance, and logistics, a third element was established, a Directorate of Administration (DDA), for a time called Directorate of Support (DDS). It handled routine administrative work, but it mainly was occupied with the complex work of supporting clandestine or covert operations overseas. Providing money, supplies, weapons, and technical equipment to secret agents is a complex, time-consuming task, and this support mechanism soon became quite large, with a goodly number of its staff serving overseas as part of clandestine station staffs. One of its most vital tasks was providing secure communications to overseas stations, and this job was done so superlatively under a gifted retired General, Harold (Mac) McClelland, that the CIA communications personnel came eventually to provide the communications service for many entire embassies as well as the CIA station personnel, using separate code and cipher systems for State and the CIA.

The organization of the CIA by the end of 1952 had a fairly tight structure, although in many cases individual offices retained a great deal of autonomy under the general supervision of the new, functional Deputy Directors invented by Beetle Smith. The biggest change was in the style of operation, with Smith dominating the other intelligence agencies in an unprecedented way. The Intelligence Advisory Committee, later to become the U.S. Intelligence Board (USIB), became much more cooperative and constructive, more advisory and less obstructive. As with all institutions, progress was uneven, depending greatly on the personality and managerial skill of the men involved. Nevertheless, Smith imposed a pattern reflecting the missions actually assigned the CIA, and the pattern remained virtually unchanged for 20 years. The structure looked like the chart on the following page.

During the Korean war period so many demands for information services and covert action were levied on the CIA that it grew by leaps and bounds. Suddenly, money was no limitation and staff accumulated rapidly. The cluster of offices under the DDI reached a personnel strength total of about 3,000 by 1953. The OPC grew from 302 in 1949 to 2,812 plus 3,142 overseas contract employees in 1952. The OSO staffs also grew, though less spectacularly, so that the clandestine services became by far the largest component in the agency. The Administration offices all grew in proportion to the other components that they had to service. As the CIA shot to around the 10,000 level, an enormous bureaucratic upheaval inevitably occurred. Jobs were taken on at virtually anybody's behest. The CIA attracted many of the most talented men and women from universities, law firms, political organizations, and military service. The OSS aura returned, at least in part, as well as some of the confusion.

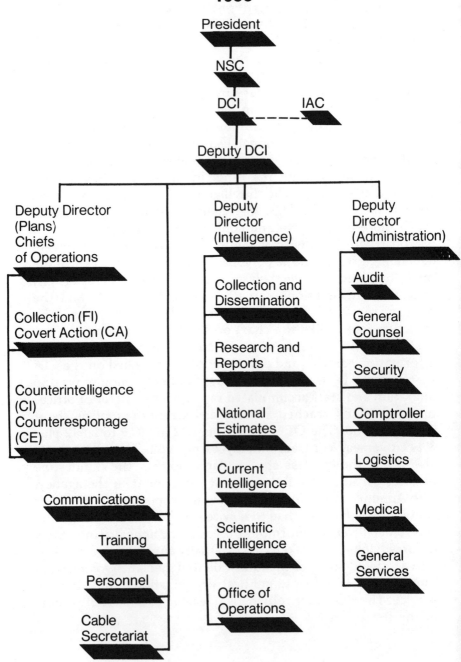

Gradually, a true central intelligence structure was put together with an enormously able staff. By the time Allen Dulles took over as DCI in February 1953, the material resources were in hand and the opportunity was present for most of the work Donovan had visualized so long before. Again, it took a war situation to bring it about—the Korean incident—but since President Truman and the Congress did not treat this incident legally as a war, the CIA had its chance in what was, technically, peacetime to function with a large staff, a virtually unlimited budget, and a cadre of seasoned leaders who undertook to make the CIA into a going concern.

The Bedell Smith reforms in three short years fulfilled the conditions needed for a central agency to become strong and effective. It did. The basic pattern for the next two decades had been established by the beginning of 1953, when Eisenhower shifted Smith over to the State Department to become Under Secretary of State to make room for the great brother act of the 1950s: Foster Dulles at State conducting conventional diplomacy to create an alliance system to contain Soviet and Chinese Communism; Allen Dulles at the CIA collecting and analyzing intelligence and carrying out secret political actions to support the basic U.S. containment policy.

The object was to get nations to refuse to cooperate with Moscow or Peking and, if feasible, to get them to cooperate with Washington. The patterns of international thrust and parry in this decade were complex but were all related to containment and alliance building. Fundamentally, the leaders and the citizens of the United States in that period perceived an undeclared Cold War taking place. U.S. military strength, massive economic assistance, and diplomatic assurances were thrown into the struggle in a vast semicircle of alliances around the periphery of the Eurasian continent to strengthen resistance to outright Soviet or Chinese thrusts to expand their sphere of control.

In this conflict leaders of the United States and its allies considered a major threat to be the Soviet practice of sending secret political agents to work with local Communist parties to create economic and political chaos, to buy off or intimidate non-Communist political leaders, and to dominate electoral processes by infusions of money, propaganda, and technical advice for favored candidates. To discover the exact dimensions of Communist activity in all the countries of the world and to counter and negate Communist political gains were two main tasks entrusted to the new CIA.

It was not widely expected that it would be possible to "roll back" Communist control in Eastern Europe, but it was considered imperative to prevent the spread of Communist control outside the sphere of influence it had already established in 1950. At that time no one questioned the morality of using the CIA to conduct this covert part of the strategic contest—a contest so basic that it continues today, although in modified context.

This, then, was the charge laid on the CIA by Congress and the White House. Allen Dulles buoyantly and vigorously mobilized to meet it. His institutional resources gradually became effective in supporting him with reliable, clandestinely collected information, both from espionage and counter-espionage, with scholarly analysis of all-source data, and, finally, in selected cases and areas, with political action schemes to neutralize Communist political thrusts. There was an idealism and an urgency in all this that gave meaning to the lives of a generation of CIA officers and their many colleagues in other agencies in the U.S. intelligence community. This was the central intelligence system I grew up in and worked for in virtually every sphere of its far-flung activities.

*Chapter Four*

# Building an Intelligence System

The CIA that Walter Bedell Smith and Allen Welsh Dulles fashioned in the 1950s carried out its mission in a romantic atmosphere of adventure that no amount of disclaimer could deflate. Of course at least one-half of the CIA's staff members, a number that ultimately peaked at about 18,000, were engaged in clerical, secretarial, and routine administrative duties normally about as exciting as dishwashing. It made no difference; exceptionally bright men and women fresh from high school or college flocked to take jobs no different from those in the Pentagon or other civil service organizations, performed their duties with a sense of excitement because the work often dealt with important events and glamorous faraway places, and, even more, because they had a chance, in due course, of being sent to some exotic foreign locale to do their typing and filing and perform their fiscal, logistic, and communications chores.

Some of these CIA employees got involved in real cloak-and-dagger work in time. But that did not matter. Such was the mystique of the CIA that when any employee refused to disclose the precise nature of his work or, indeed, for whom he worked other than "for the U.S. Government," people assumed that the employee was deeply involved in dangerous undercover deeds. Not 5 percent of the CIA's employees ever had any significant contact with this world of spy fiction, and most of the agency employees had absolutely no first-hand knowledge of any activity more hazardous than driving to work each morning. Yet the mystique was there in the 1950s. Allen Dulles loved it, helped create it, and in many ways embodied it.

Some of the aura that grew up around the CIA in those days accounted for a certain dash and daring in the performance of all kinds of duties, from routine to politically sensitive. Later on, however, this very climate of mystery created suspicion in the public mind that the CIA might be performing wild deeds on its own, and it certainly obscured the fact that the CIA's main job of collecting and analyzing information had to be done for the good of the nation.

## National Estimates

My career in this era was in many ways a microcosmic reflection of the whole of the CIA. I was 32 years old in 1950 when Bill Langer appeared in the South Building in the very rooms where my OSS career began. Langer had a firm mandate to create a system for making national estimates suitable for DCI Smith to use to advise the President and stem the disorderly flood of advice based on military and diplomatic hopes or fears.

Langer told me Smith suggested an office of about 1,000 people to do this job. I told him it was quality that was needed and recommended he start off with about 30 men whose names I supplied. We could add men of stature from outside if they could be recruited. My suggestion was a top ceiling of 50, with every man a broadly qualified intelligence officer and all capable of writing a review of evidence and a summary of critical findings on a very broad strategic plane. Langer sided with me and in fact I think the Office of National Estimates never exceeded 100 staff members in its two decades of existence.

The structure was simple. We organized an Estimates Staff of intelligence officers, of which I would be Chief. In addition, we established a National Estimates Board, with Langer as Chairman, to review papers drafted in the Estimates Staff and to negotiate with State, Army, Navy, and Air Force on their concurrence. Langer was magnificent at this. He did his homework; he fought for objectivity, and he brooked no nonsense from Foreign Service and military officers regardless of their rank. He simply overrode all unreasonable opposition. With Smith's prestige behind him at the final review level, Langer was able to do this. I can see him now, at the head of the table, saying in his inimitable nasal twang, "Now, General, those are just a lot of words, and I want to get at the heart of this problem by saying flatly...." By force of personality and intellect he created a new genre of intelligence reporting, the coordinated National Intelligence Estimate (NIE). It was much needed.

My senior colleagues in the old Global Survey Division, Ludwell Montague and Deforest Van Slyck, became National Estimates Board members, providing the professional core that Langer needed at that level while we were trying to organize the new office. Montague personally shepherded through an *ad hoc* coordination process the first six short, snappy, estimative papers that Smith wanted on the precise threats facing the United States in the light of Soviet and Chinese support of the Korean War. Professor Ray Sontag from the University of California, an outstanding German historian, and Professor Calvin Hoover, a Soviet economy expert from Duke University—an OSS hand rare in having worked on secret intelligence collection instead of analysis—joined the Board. James Cooley, an exceptionally gifted, meticulous draftsman, came into the group to stay for 20 years. General Clarence Huebner, just back from Seventh Army Command in the occupation forces in Germany, was the first of a series of hand-picked elder statemen from the armed services who served over the years on the Board. An effort was made to have a flag rank officer from the Army, Navy, and Air Force always on duty. Some of them stayed on a long time and contributed much to the sophistication of estimates dealing with the technical aspects of weaponry, which theretofore had been virtually a monopoly of the armed services. U.S. Army General Harold R. Bull, who had been operations chief (G-3) under Eisenhower in Europe during World War II, was in my view the outstanding contributor in the early 1950s to the Board's objectivity and skill in handling evidence on military subjects, as U.S. Air Force General Earl Barnes was in the late 1950s and the 1960s.

Finally, Langer brought on to his Board as his Deputy and— after January 1952—his successor, an old colleague from OSS,

Yale Professor Sherman Kent, whose just published book on strategic intelligence made him the outstanding academic expert on a new profession. I had known Kent for a long time. His personal candor and charm made him a cherished colleague and his amazingly colorful and imaginative profanity was an asset in any tense negotiating session on an intelligence estimate. I remember his talking with me in late 1950 as to whether the contribution he could make justified his giving up his post at Yale to serve as Langer's Deputy on the National Estimates Board. We sat in one of the bare little offices in the old South Building looking at each other across a scarred old wooden desk inherited from OSS, and I told him that so few people in the new CIA knew what inteligence analysis was all about and such threatening situations existed in the world that he was needed. I do not know whether this influenced him but he came, stayed, and built the National Intelligence Estimates into a significant element in decision-making.

I myself spent a great part of the year trying to reduce the procedures for drafting NIEs to an orderly set of instructions that would insure cooperation and contributive efforts by State and the military agencies while also maintaining CIA control of the content and the intellectual integrity of the final document. In this I was enormously aided by Paul Borel, one of the great selfless managerial experts of the CIA who devoted a long career to making the institution work. In this process we were both lucky to have the help of one of the most efficient women in the world, Frances Douglas, who had been executive secretary to Bill Langer in OSS and returned with him to set up ONE. Fran was made Administrative Officer for the whole office and handled—with the help of a very small number of first-class secretaries and clerical employees—all of the support activities. Paul and I persuaded Langer to adopt a pay scale that allowed us some flexibility in setting the pay level to fit talent and experience rather than age and time in service.

The rest of my time was spent working with the Estimates Staff members preparing drafts of NIEs for Board review and interagency coordination clearance. At first I tried to assign tasks on a one-man-one-estimate basis, but it turned out as might have been expected that some of the staff officers could not write to please Langer and the Board, while others were ineffective in defending their conclusions before the Board.

Abbott Smith, a genial, dignified, ex-professor and a serious amateur musician, knowledgeable about British and Commonwealth affairs, was one of the most effective members of the staff. He succeeded Sherman Kent as Director of ONE about 20 years later. In 1950 he wrote estimative prose beautifully and argued patiently and persuasively. So did Willard Matthias, a generalist with a good background in European affairs, who stayed in ONE all his career and served a number of years on the Board. The only staff member younger than I was Robert Komer, a quick draftsman and a vigorous debater; he was then, as now, sometimes brash and abrasive in discussion, but Langer supported me in maintaining that analytical skill was more important than congenial manner. Komer later moved to the White House NSC Staff, where his enthusiasm and other qualities suited Lyndon Johnson, and he served in Vietnam as ambassador in charge of rural development programs in that important but thankless and ultimately unsuccessful job.

I myself drafted what I believe was the first comprehensive though very brief estimate of Soviet strategic intentions, and I adopted the practice of reviewing all drafts before they were submitted to the Board so that time would not be wasted drafting and redrafting in committee. My taking personal charge of the technical drafting problems and insisting that Board members concentrate on substantive suggestions was congenial to Langer but undoubtedly trying to distinguished Board members like Sontag. Perhaps I was idealistic, but I was trying to create an intelligence process and product I thought was essential to our government, and I imagine I was pretty rude to the older men on the Board who often seemed interminably verbose, infatuated with their own prose, and likely to be carried away by ideas that could not be supported by evidence. My reputation was quickly established as a fierce defender of the drafts prepared by my analytical intelligence officers and determined to fight for them through Board and interagency discussion without fundamental change. I suspect many colleagues were pleased when I went overseas in October 1951, after about one year in ONE.

## Intelligence Liaison

My understanding of the intelligence world increased immensely in this period when I succeeded in getting assigned to the CIA contingent in London, serving there until November 1953. The assignment was something of an accident. Beetle Smith decided to integrate the CIA activities overseas in major posts by assigning what he called Senior Representatives of the Director of the CIA. This meant the warring factions of OPC and OSO would have a local umpire in addition to the station chief, who often tended to get embroiled in the struggles. Smith appointed General Lucian Truscott to manage the mammoth German station and a suave, old-school Virginia gentleman, retired Brigadier General Thomas Betts, to be Senior Representative in London. Betts was one of the few professional military officers with a long career in intelligence. He had the good judgment to see that exchanging our new intelligence product—the NIE—with the British, in return for their Joint Intelligence Committee appreciations on the same subject, would be mutually beneficial. Betts asked for a staff officer from the new ONE to explain what we were doing to the British and to find out what was going on in the more mature British system.

When the message from London reached Washington, I immediately asked Langer to let me leave ONE, which had pretty well shaken down to the pattern of activities it maintained for 20 years, and establish this new job in London. It would give us the benefits of seeing how the evidence on common strategic problems looked from the viewpoint of another nation, a close ally with similar but separate interests. I thought ONE and the CIA would benefit and I would learn much from the British process. I believe I was right; the exchange of "finished"—i.e., evaluated and analyzed—reports with London continues to this day as does an informal liaison exchange system on the analytical level. At its peak, it kept 18 CIA analysts busy in London comparing notes with their counterparts in economic intelligence, scientific intelligence, and general strategic analysis. The link is still strong and valuable today. The foresight of Smith, Langer, and Betts paid off handsomely.

My real awakening in London was the discovery of how much we still benefited from formal liaison exchanges of intelligence with Great Britain, over and beyond the give and take of analytical papers. Tom Betts was an easygoing boss, perfectly willing to let me do whatever I wanted, and he gave me free rein to help other CIA components in London. I was also lucky in having taken one of the best of the ONE secretaries, Barbara Ewen, whose looks and southern accent devastated the young Englishmen I dealt with. She ran the office, handled the paperwork, and managed my program to maximum benefit.

This fact I mention not only to show why I had so much spare time in London, but to make a general point about secretaries, especially those dealing with the sensitive and sometimes delicate matters of intelligence handling and intelligence exchange. It can be serious if they make a slip in talking with high-ranking officials, especially foreign officials, by referring to specific intelligence items they may not be supposed to know about. My good fortune has been in having the help of extremely competent women. To all of them—most of them grossly underpaid for the responsibilities they carried—I am much indebted, especially to my OSS secretary Penny Wright, my first CIA secretary Marcelle Raczkowski, to Barb Ewen, to Rosie Sarson in Taiwan, and to Dolores Unick, my last CIA secretary, who went to Germany with me. These encomiums are also due to Thayal Hall, my secretary in the State Department in 1969-1973. All of these able women were actually research assistants, managerial backups for my administrative chores, and personal representatives with the outside world.

With such support from Barb Ewen in London, I got around, not ony with all kinds of British intelligence officials, but also with the CIA liaison staff in Great Britain. The wartime partnership was still paying off handsomely. The British, recognizing the importance of keeping the United States actively engaged in an effort to contain Soviet disruptive thrusts, were extraordinarily open and cooperative with Americans in intelligence matters. They provided not only most of their highest-level joint intelligence estimates but also supplied the station chief in London with most of their clandestine intelligence MI-6 reports. The station chief was not very communicative with me in accordance with clandestine tradition, but my OSS background, my acquaintance with senior U.S. military men I had interviewed while writing the Army history, and my entree to high-level British officials made me *persona grata* with his staff, particularly his deputy, who cooperated closely with me with the chief's tacit acquiescence. I learned a lot from this collaboration.

One of the CIA's most closely guarded secrets is that its own espionage efforts have been supplemented greatly in both numbers and importance by contributions from the intelligence services of friendly allies. Much of this intelligence is circulated in Washington as standard CIA Information Reports so that few know the difference. Of course a vast amount of reporting from foreign governments was not disseminated outside the CIA because it was unreliable or of little interest. Even this material has helped, however, to guide the CIA's own collection staffs.

Some of the material thus exchanged with liaison services was from intercepted electronic signal messages. Eventually most of this material was worked into the reporting system of the National Security Agency, the consolidated cryptanalysis and signals intercept facility set up in 1950 to manage the signals intelligence work of the military services. The contribution from this source has been enormous over the years and still is. Here, too, many Washington recipients of intercepted messages do not realize they are reading traffic that would not be available except for good liaison relations with allies. On the periphery of the Soviet Union and China, communications and other electronic (radar, missile telemetry, etc.) intercept bases provided unique data from remote regions.

The importance of these bases rose and fell with technological and political changes over the years, but it is fair to say that the CIA's official intelligence liaison in this field netted more reliable material for Washington analysts and intelligence processors than any other source. Many allies have contributed to U.S. security in this way. In particular, West German and the Nationalist Chinese efforts, exploiting native language abilities and regional expertise, have greatly assisted the success of the U.S. signals processing machine and thus created a solid fund of knowledge on which analysts could draw in making their all-source studies of defense and foreign policy issues. It was in London, the hub of the closest intelligence exchange in all history, that I perceived very early what vast benefits our allies provided in the way of good intelligence. Without them, the alliance system itself could not function effectively; U.S. citizens will understand and value our foreign friends better if they know this simple fact.

In Great Britain these extensive liaison arrangements were supplemented by equally crucial exchanges in the counter-espionage and counterintelligence field—also important in liaisons with many other allies with good internal security services—and by a unique system of sharing the burden of monitoring and translating foreign broadcasts. While this latter work is overt intelligence collection, it is a technically complex and costly undertaking. By roughly dividing the world between them and exchanging the materials recorded, the United States and Great Britain have always saved themselves a great deal of money and trouble and continue to do so.

It was most educational for me to have the opportunity to look at global intelligence problems from the viewpoint of this liaison link between the two most productive mature intelligence systems in the world. One lesson I learned from the British: there is no way to be on top of intelligence problems unless you collect much more extensively than any cost-accounting approach would justify and then rely on the wisdom and experience of analysts to sift out the small percentage of vital information that needs to be passed to the top of the government. You might think you could do without most of what is collected; but in intelligence, in fact, as in ore mining, there is no way to get the nuggets without taking the whole ore-bearing compound. Once at a cocktail party in London in 1952 or 1953 I heard this point made succinctly by Sir Kenneth W.D. Strong, the hawk-faced patrician Englishman who had served as Eisenhower's G-2 in the Allied Forces in Europe in World War II and stayed on to be the dominant personality in British intelligence for about 25 years.* He observed that "an intelligence official simply has to be temperamentally adjusted

---

*He wrote two reflective books on his career in intelligence, *Intelligence at the Top* (1968) and *Men of Intelligence* (1970).

to the fact that 95 percent of his organization's total effort is utterly wasted, although it is all necessary to get the 5 percent that is useful to policymaking." A young man there said in dismay, "General Strong, surely you are exaggerating the percentage of wasted effort?" Strong drew himself up to his considerable height and somewhat histrionically proclaimed, "Perhaps I should reconsider; yes, on second thought, I would say 97 percent is useless effort, but our national safety depends on finding the 3 percent!" It is not a bad formula.

## Covert Political Action

During my London tour I also discovered something of the character of the psychological and political warfare thinking going on in the CIA. Two men I knew well were in London for OPC, then still rather separate from the old-line OSO forces under the station chief. These men had a separate status in the U.S. Embassy very similar to my own. We were under the general supervision of Betts, we had diplomatic passports, and we generally kept some distance from the larger contingent involved in exchange of espionage and counterespionage reports. This was easy, since the station chief and his deputy had their bailiwick down the street in a separate building, as did the U.S. military personnel who, in still another building, maintained the very close U.S.-U.K. liaison in the signals field under only the most general cognizance of General Betts. At any rate I discovered some interesting things from my friends.

In addition to channeling funds and information to non-Communist political parties, newspapers, labor unions, church groups, and writers throughout Western Europe, Frank Wisner's OPC had undertaken to see that accurate news and political analysis reached not only Western Europe but Eastern Europe, where populations under the Soviet thumb were yearning for greater freedom. The instrument used to keep alive some knowledge of what was going on in open societies was Radio Free Europe. It was formed by the CIA, which ran it and its companion broadcasting service, Radio Liberty—which reported news for the benefit of Soviet listeners in the USSR itself—for 20 years. Staffed primarily by refugees from the countries to which programs were beamed, these radios have been able to get hard news into the regions behind the iron curtain, bringing subtle psychological pressures to bear on dictatorial governments to temper their control methods. The CIA organized this effort at the request of U.S. Government officials because it was thought the broadcasts would be more effective if their connection with the U.S. Government could be concealed.

Although it is hard to measure the influence of psychological weapons like Radio Free Europe and Radio Liberty, they both certainly won many regular listeners. The leaders of the Soviet Union have clearly feared the impact of ideas from outside on their society; they have spent millions and millions to jam these broadcasts, pausing only intermittently in brief periods of "peaceful coexistence" and then resuming the jamming. At their peak, these radio broadcast efforts cost about $30 million a year and employed several thousand uniquely qualified analysts and linguists. The effort was so clearly aimed at freedom of information and amelioration of Communist restraints on civil liberties that the U.S. Congress finally, in 1973, established a public board to manage these instruments of political action. CIA gladly shed its responsibility since the operations had become too large and had operated too long to be genuinely covert. The transfer from covert to overt U.S. sponsorship sets a pattern for what ought to happen to CIA projects when they become too well known to be secret but are still useful supports for U.S. policy. Radio Free Europe and Radio Liberty are public evidence of CIA covert action projects that were successful, served liberal democratic purposes, and never became the center of controversy as so many paramilitary projects did.

It was exciting to see the early evolution of covert action and psychological warfare activities in Europe in the early 1950s. Many other lesser projects were funded and pursued, many of them quite small-scale. Many international labor and youth movements benefited by having the CIA help non-Communist members oppose heavy-handed Communist efforts to seize control of all organs of mass opinion. Europeans made the major effort, but CIA support with money and information about Communist activities played a crucial part in preserving the multi-party political systems of Western Europe.

In my view, the CIA especially deserves credit for

encouraging left-wing intellectuals to find a democratic alternative in non-Communist organizations and enterprises. The Congress of Cultural Freedom, a genuine liberal intellectual movement in Europe, would never have got going without CIA help, and a number of first-class magazines of political commentary, such as *Encounter* and *Der Monat*, would not have been able to survive financially without CIA funds. Without CIA help, emigre groups from the USSR and Eastern Europe could not have published in translation the many documents they received from their old countries. This includes some of the celebrated Soviet *samizdat* protest literature describing life behind the iron curtain.

These U.S. projects seldom involved direct U.S. control but simply insured through the intellectual influence of capable political action officers that honest non-Communist ideas were being presented. European opinion makers, supported by the CIA directly or indirectly and often without their knowledge, created the free political climate in Western Europe in the 1950s. Without the countless covert political action projects of the CIA, they could not have done so. Similar projects in nearly every country where Communist agents have tried to penetrate and subvert local governments account for the vast majority of the hundreds and hundreds of covert action projects carried out by the CIA over the years.

The whole field of covert action has been tarnished by the large and unsuccessful paramilitary projects of the later years, particularly the Bay of Pigs disaster. Nevertheless, as I learned early in London, most CIA covert action is small-scale, neither violent nor illegal, plainly authorized by NSC directives, and, on the whole, rather successful in energizing local political groups to build their own parliamentary parties, free labor unions, and independent opinion media.

For good or ill, the European experience of the late 1950s and the Asian experience of the Korean War and the Quemoy Islands crisis created a strong tide in Washington in favor of CIA covert action. Whereas the European effort was largely political and information-oriented, the Asian effort in the early 1950s was mostly paramilitary. When the Nationalist Chinese retreated to the island of Taiwan in 1949 they left behind many thousands of troops, especially in the remote mountainous regions of Southwest China. The CIA was authorized, indeed urged, to build up agent nets and aircraft and small-boat fleets to support paramilitary efforts to impede the Chinese fighting in Korea by preventing Communist consolidation of its control over all of mainland China. The Nationalist Chinese forces under Chiang Kai-shek assisted these U.S. efforts in every way possible. It was in the Asian field that these OSS skills were recreated—lingering on into the Vietnam war era. The U.S. military was enthusiastic about anything that would ease the pressures in Korea and supplied capable military officers to work with the CIA in the paramilitary field.

As a result of the burgeoning political effort in Europe and the skyrocketing paramilitary programs in Asia, CIA's covert action arm grew by leaps and bounds. The OPC staff expanded to several thousands, its budget from about $5 million in 1949 to $82 million in 1952.[1] The sums of money grew even larger as costs mounted and they accounted for the largest part of the CIA budget down until the 1970s, which saw the divestiture of the big radio projects and the collapse of the last big paramilitary efforts in Laos.

It was probably this covert action responsibility, imperfectly understood by the State and Defense staffs that urged it, which accounted for the proliferation of the CIA stations. From seven overseas posts, largely left over from OSS, the CIA had placed OPC personnel in 47 overseas stations by 1952.[2] Of course the demand for information was insatiable, and intelligence collection staffs proliferated as well, along with the units needed to support both OSO and OPC. The enthusiasm in Washington for covert action of all kinds was reflected in a series of new directives, each broader than the last. In 1955 the NSC revised the control procedures in a new covert action directive labeled NSC 5412, and thenceforth covert action projects were reviewed formally by the "5412" or "Special Group," which varied in name and composition over the years, becoming the "303 Committee" under President Kennedy and the "40 Committee" under President Richard M. Nixon. Always, however, the NSC directives provided that a senior State official, a senior Defense official, the Chairman of the JCS, and a White House representative of the NSC proper approve projects on behalf of the President. Through the years primary influence in these matters gradually came to lodge with the Assistant to the President for National Security Affairs—the job held in the 1960s and 1970s successively by McGeorge Bundy, Walt Rostow, and Henry Kissinger.

In the early 1950s two major covert action projects were undertaken, with enthusiastic support from State and everyone else, in which political action merged into paramilitary action, blurring the distinction, much to the subsequent disadvantage of the CIA. In 1953, while I was still in London, a covert operation so successful that it became widely known all over the world was carried out in Iran. The Shah, then very young, had been driven out of Iran by his left-leaning Premier, Mohammed Mossadegh, whose support came from the local Communist (Tudeh) Party and from the Soviet Union. The CIA mounted a modest effort under a skillful clandestine services officer who flew into Iran, hired enough street demonstrators to intimidate those working for Mossadegh, instructed Iranian military men loyal to the Shah how to take over the local radio station, and paved the way for the Shah's triumphal return.

The trouble with this seemingly brilliant success was, as the officer in charge would testify, that the CIA did not have to do very much to topple Mossadegh, who was an eccentric and weak political figure. It took relatively little effort to restore the traditional ruler to his throne once he and his military supporters recovered their nerve and took advantage of U.S. help. It did not prove that the CIA could topple governments and place rulers in power; it was a unique case of supplying just the right bit of marginal assistance in the right way at the right time. Such is the nature of covert political action.

About a year later, in mid-1954, the legend of the CIA's invincibility was confirmed in the minds of many by a covert action project in Guatemala that inched one step further toward paramilitary intervention. President Arbenz Guzman had expropriated the holdings of the powerful U.S.-owned United Fruit Company and was discovered by the CIA to be about to receive a boatload of Czechoslovakian arms. This fact, publicized by the State Department on May 17, touched off a six-week crisis in which a rival Guatemalan political leader, Castillo Armas, launched a desultory invasion of Guatemala supported by three P-47 fighter planes of World War II vintage flying from friendly Nicaraguan territory. The aircraft were provided by the CIA and flown by soldier-of-fortune pilots recruited by the CIA. The U.S. Ambassador, John E. Peurifoy, was in charge of the operation and President Eisenhower had personally approved it on assurance from Allen Dulles that it would succeed in getting rid of a left-leaning dictator within the precincts of what was still considered a viable Monroe Doctrine. There was not much fighting, but the P-47s created a lot of excitement, and support for Arbenz Guzman crumbled. A junta took over, made an accommodation with Castillo Armas, and he became president in early July.

The stories about the CIA's prowess in toppling regimes increased in volume. In truth these were the only two political actions that resulted in a change of regime undertaken in the entire Dulles era; the only other attempt on a similar scale was to overthrow President Sukarno in Indonesia in 1958, and this failed. It made no difference that the two successes were unique cases and required little use of force, succeeding mainly because of shrewd exploitation of favorable local political circumstances. The mystique of the CIA's secret power was well established by the tales from Teheran and Guatemala City.

In the fifties these covert actions were perceived as great victories for democratic societies over Soviet moves to establish Communist dictatorships. Public and Congressional sentiment at the time wholly supported the CIA's use of covert techniques to oppose similar Soviet activities. The tragedy is that the concept of what the CIA was intended to be eventually became gravely distorted by the image projected as a result of the Iranian and Guatemalan capers. These covert political actions were justified at the time but the romantic misconceptions as to the role and capabilities of the CIA which they gave rise to were disastrous.

## Perspective

After a two-year tour, at the end of 1953 I turned over my post in London, coveted by many of my old colleagues, and returned to Washington. When I got back to Headquarters, still assigned to ONE, Sherman Kent was Director and Bill Langer had returned to Harvard. I wanted to work directly with the new DDI, Bob Amory, but he had appointed a capable ONE staff member, William Bundy, as his special assistant. Bill was the son-in-law of Dean Acheson, Truman's accomplished Secretary of State, then under heavy fire from the master anti-Communist demagogue, Senator Joseph McCarthy. In mid 1953 McCarthy attacked Bundy for having contributed funds to the legal defense of Alger Hiss. Dulles and Amory successfully defended Bundy, thus saving the career of a fine public servant who went on to be Assistant Secretary in both the Defense and State Departments. They also showed that stout resistance could rout McCarthy and protect the CIA.

Since I did not really want the administrative burden of the Estimates Staff job again and certainly had no wish to have Bundy moved from the DDI's office, I requested and was given an assignment as Estimates Staff officer in charge of Soviet estimates. Having worked on many British estimates on this subject, I set out to reorganize and update the concept of the basic Agency National Intelligence Estimate (NIE) on Soviet capabilities and intentions. I felt strongly that this intelligence problem was the key one in national policymaking and that the NIE ought to be the last word on the subject, dealing with military aspects of Soviet strength so authoritatively that the U.S. military services could not disregard it. As I remember, the first Soviet NIE I had worked on in 1950 was only about 25 pages in length and rather given to broad generalizations. I undertook to strengthen the 1954 NIE with selected facts and significant figures on the USSR to buttress the conclusions reached so that they would carry conviction at the top reaches of our government. I followed the same presentational technique in analyzing the political and economic structure of the USSR, as well as its military forces and strategy. The length, as I recall, reached 75 to 100 printed pages, a behemoth for its day and one that set a pattern that has persisted. Other NIEs are often unread, but the CIA estimates on the USSR are fought over, read throughout the government, and in the main accepted by the President and the National Security Council as basic documents on which policy decisions rest. This at least was the case in the 1950s and 1960s, during which my formula became even more intensively applied and the total bulk of NIE coverage of the USSR came to be something more like 300 to

400 printed pages—too long, in my opinion, but too authoritative for the military intelligence agencies to ignore.

My good fortune during the year I worked on Soviet capabilities and intentions in 1954 was to have inherited a small staff of outstanding Soviet specialists who had come to ONE while I was away. They pulled the material together for me from State and Defense sources as well as from their own expertise based on the open literature available in the field. The Estimates Staff was organized according to geographical regions and three or four serious, full-time analysts of Soviet affairs were in residence at the end of 1953 when I came back to ONE. The chief of this small but extremely talented group was a brilliant Sovietologist, John Huizenga, who stayed in ONE for the rest of his career, becoming its fourth and last director in the 1970s.

I firmly believe in the Ludwell Montague—Beetle Smith concept of a small, capable unit with exclusive responsibility for making the difficult estimates in the light of evidence available from all sources with no vested interest in either foreign policy or military policy and no bias except toward establishing the truth as well as it can be perceived. I believe the ONE of my last year there (1954) was forthrightly dedicated to this process and an excellent example of what it could achieve.

## Drafting National Estimates

Of all the different duties devolving on the CIA as a result of the National Security Act's requirement that it "correlate and evaluate" national security intelligence, the preparation and dissemination of national estimates is the most difficult, the most sophisticated, and the most important. As the Pearl Harbor disaster showed, it is not enough for intelligence agencies to have in their possession bits and pieces of data. An analytical construct must be built, putting together these bits and pieces in a meaningful pattern and relating that pattern to the security or foreign interest of the United States.

Needless to say, the meaningful pattern does little good unless it is conveyed persuasively in timely fashion to policy officials with executive authority to act upon the intelligence provided them. Hence the National Security Act also called on the CIA to "Provide for the appropriate dissemination of ... intelligence within the Government."

The processes of collecting intelligence in all its variety are intricate but not too difficult to comprehend. The sifting out and accurate reporting of significant new items of incoming information are time-consuming and require experienced area analysts but are not, in their essence, inordinately difficult. What tends to be ill-understood and indifferently executed is the vital task of absorbing all of the incoming information and projecting from it a pattern or trend stretching forward in time beyond the frontiers of what can be clearly seen in currently available evidence. This task is what intelligence officers in the early CIA days decided to call "estimating," because the word itself conveys the concept of judgment needed to make calculations about potential developments not yet possible to foretell with certainty. A person can speak with reasonable certitude about the sun's rising at a certain time, but reservations and qualifications according to some scale of probability must be included in writing about most other events that might take place several years hence.

Estimates are careful descriptions of the likelihood that certain things will exist or occur in the future. National Intelligence Estimates are papers setting forth probable situations or occurrences that would make a major difference to our national security or our foreign policy. When the answers are clear to questions about the future, there is no need for an estimate. The easy questions are never asked. An estimate tries to reduce the inevitable degree of uncertainty to a minimum in making calculations about future situations. A National Intelligence Estimate tries to do this in making probability calculations about matters that national policymakers will have to take into account in deciding what the United States should do to be in a satisfactory posture to deal with the various situations that may exist at any given point in the future. It is not easy to make estimates that are well-calculated in terms of evidence and logic, carefully set forth with great objectivity, and plainly relevant to decision-making. It can never be done perfectly, but it will be done better if certain elements in the process are understood by producers of estimates and by the policy officials who use them.

Once it is appreciated that estimates are by definition projections of thought into the inherently unknowable, the next important thing to understand is that they must be tailored both for the purpose they are intended to serve and the audience they are intended to reach. Too many estimates are all-purpose documents, too complex and detailed for the busy President or the Cabinet Officer and too general for the staff briefing officer. At the bottom of this process, intelligence officers write for each other, for scholars and researchers outside the government who are cleared for consultation on specific subjects, and for working-level officials in the whole national security establishment in Washington. A certain amount of cross-fertilization among these groups takes place. It is a good thing. You cannot have too many viewpoints on an estimative problem. The most unconventional wisdom may supply the missing piece in the puzzle.

There need to be different types of estimative reports. A well-articulated estimates production schedule should include a group of monographs of a technical nature pinning down in detail the critical factors involved in specific estimative problems. Thus a monograph on submarine noise levels may need to be written in excruciating detail because it will give the best answers possible for various probabilities in anti-submarine warfare. Cost and incentive factors in Soviet agriculture are other monographic subjects that may be nearly incomprehensible to the average high-level official. Yet this problem needs to be dealt with, with estimates of best and worst cases and their consequences for the future, as well as the most probable evolution. These estimative monographs should be carefully drafted and widely circulated at the working level. There need not be word-for-word agreement, though substantial disagreements should be set out plainly in the papers. Estimative monographs should be available to interested officials but they ought to be written primarily as building-blocks for use in drafting more general estimates for a less specialized audience.

There are about 1,000 officers in the intelligence community and in the national security establishment who need a series of general estimates on the major problems confronting top-level decision-makers. What the total Soviet nuclear weapons strength is likely to be, what the Peking leadership will look like and think in the next few years, how the Arab-Israeli conflict will progress, how stable Yugoslavia will be in view of Tito's death; all these are topics on which there should be a considerable degree of common understanding among these opinion-setters in our national bureaucracy. What they need is carefully vetted data and skillful analysis—not total agreement.

National Intelligence Estimates drawing on the monographs, which I have described as the basic or bottom level of the process, should be prepared on about 50 to 100 subjects a year. They should summarize data and findings but should not be swamped with detail. They are to be read by officials who will try to carry the main conclusions in their minds—the most probable developments, the best and worst cases, and the far-out possibilities that might, just might, change all the dimensions of the basic strategic problem. These estimates should be persuasive and fully reasoned but not frustratingly technical. They need not be long. They should be read and understood by the President and the Cabinet officers but are intended for the officials whose opinions are frequent inputs to the policy papers or policy discussions of the Secretary or Assistant Secretary level. These are what have made up the bulk of NIEs over the years.

The third level of estimative papers should be careful summaries of the highlights and key findings in the whole range of National Intelligence Estimates just described. These summaries should go along with the estimates themselves and should be included in current intelligence summaries so as to alert all readers that the perceptions of the intelligence community have been reexamined, and perhaps redefined and significantly changed. It is to be hoped that the 250-odd staff briefers who cull information from all sorts of documents for their own Secretary or Assistant Secretaries would note the new or altered findings in these summaries and alert their top-level policymakers. Some of the top officials might then read the estimate referred to or even one or more detailed monographs bearing on problems for which they are responsible. In any case some estimative intelligence will filter up to the top.

It is unrealistic to expect the President, the Secretary of State, the Secretary of Defense, and other officials at Cabinet and sub-Cabinet level to read and absorb many long papers.

Although there have been and will be exceptions, important national intelligence estimates must be brought to their attention. Thus, I think the principal intelligence officers in State, Defense, and the estimative element in the CIA should routinely schedule formal oral briefings for top officials. They will be hard to arrange, but the impact on decision-makers thus made and the feedback to the intelligence community provided by questions is bound to be valuable. This level of communication at the very top completes the estimative process.

A few other things about making national estimates need to be said. First, objectivity is the only virtue that really counts in making judgments based on the available evidence, in developing arguments from varying viewpoints, and in presenting clearly mature reflections on the basic patterns and trends that can be perceived in world affairs. Estimates should be written in the full knowledge of all data and views from diplomatic and military officialdom, but should finally go forward as the best single integrated judgment of professional intelligence officers experienced and disciplined in making estimative judgments. Dissents and relevant best or worst cases should be clearly set forth.

This maximum objectivity, free from the bias of policy or operational responsibility, will be best achieved if there is an administrative fence around the estimative staffs. A staff or board or institute should be separated administratively—not in any sense intellectually—from operational elements of the government. It should be empowered to task collectors with requirements for data and to task research analysts anywhere inside or outside government for analytical reports, especially as contributions to the monographs that are the basic building blocks of the estimative process. The analysts working on estimates, and especially the intelligence officers supervising the whole process, should associate closely on a bureaucratic and intellectual plane with the policymakers who are users of intelligence. In this way they can discover what it is the policymakers need to know, while at the same time preserving the corporate professional identity that gives the makers of estimates a fiduciary responsibility to present the truth.

If a staff or board or institute concerned with national security and foreign affairs research has this responsibility for providing high-quality national intelligence estimative reporting to the government, it follows that the selection of the personnel is of critical importance. Everything should be done to stimulate high quality research, analysis, and estimates throughout the intelligence community. The very best experienced analysts from the CIA, State, Defense, and elsewhere should be selected for the estimative unit. Furthermore, personnel should rotate in and out of an estimates staff at approximately three to six year intervals so that the intelligence officers doing this kind of estimative work will periodically refresh their expertise in more specialized research and reporting. The estimates unit should not be a closed shop, but an interagency talent pool of highly qualified officers with solid roots in the intelligence research community where data and trend analysis is going on as the evidentiary foundation of the estimate process. Establishing and skillfully supervising this process governing the research, analysis, and estimates work of the intelligence community is, in my view, the most difficult and most important task of strategic intelligence.

This idealistic concept of how strategic estimates can be made and used is not likely to function perfectly. ONE in 1954 certainly did not do a perfect job, nor did ONE in the early 1960s when I supervised its work during my tour as DDI. Nevertheless, it did a highly creditable job that has never been done better anywhere. A band of talented intelligence officers made a substantial and valuable contribution to reason and intellectual integrity in the top reaches of government.

It is a tragedy, in my view, that ONE was abolished in 1973 in an effort to make NIEs more "responsive" to the needs of the NSC staff of Dr. Henry Kissinger, then occupying the dual role of Secretary of State and Assistant to the President for National Security Affairs. I think NIEs ought to be responsive to the evidence, not the policymaker; the policymaker should get answers to his questions, but he should not be in a position to bend them to support his views. Without the protection of a corporate structure like the Office of National Estimates, individual staff officers writing estimates cannot maintain the authority and integrity of the estimative process. I believe we did it about right in the 1950s and early 1960s.

## The Net Estimate

Since no subject related to intelligence is more important than the professional art of making estimates, this account of my experiences in the field is not complete without a description of a very special estimative process in which I participated during the latter part of 1954 when I was detailed to the Pentagon to assist in preparing a Net Estimate on the USSR. The several months I spent on this endeavor were extremely enlightening and, again, I am sorry that this experiment in intelligence processing ended after a few years and is imperfectly understood today. We prepared an excellent Net Estimate in 1954 and it had a marked influence on military strategy and policy—mainly because the President— Eisenhower—and his two top technical advisers in the matter, Dulles of the CIA and Admiral Arthur Radford, Chairman of the JCS, enthusiastically endorsed the project and paid attention to the findings.

The concept of a net estimate is basically a military one and it had evolved into a preliminary pilot project while I was in London. It was agreed at the NSC level to go all out on the 1954 effort. The concept is that while intelligence agencies are able to gauge enemy capabilities and intentions, these are most meaningful if weighed against an estimate of U.S. forces' capabilities and intentions. This latter estimate is prepared by planning and operations staffs of the JCS. If these two analytical processes are integrated intellectually and combined in one estimate of the probable balance of potential forces and the probable outcome of conflicts, this is a "net" evaluation or what in military tradition was called a "commander's estimate." The NSC under Eisenhower, who was familiar with this terminology, asked Dulles and Radford to prepare such a commander's estimate on the probable outcome of a war between the USSR and the United States.

In characteristic Washington procedure, Dulles delegated his responsibility to General Bull of the National Estimates Board, an experienced army operations staff chief with a fine analytical mind, and Bull chose me to go to the Pentagon and actually write the paper. Radford chose a brilliant but somewhat lackadaisical representative, Rear Admiral Thomas H. Robbins, who was quite content to let his staff assistants, some able young officers who intially had not a clue as to what we were supposed to do, take their lead from me.

I discovered what power there is in a military organization very quickly; with what amounted to a free-hand mandate from both Bull and Robbins, I could invoke Admiral Radford's authority over the military services and have things happen instantaneously. Early in planning the project, I decided we had to reduce the complex war-gaming of attack and defense forces to the then novel technique of computerized formulas. I discovered that I could preempt the time of the vast vacuum-tube computer then filling the basement of the Pentagon and I learned that the services had one really experienced war-gaming staff—outside of Washington. Consequently, I argued that we should use the computer and the war-gaming staff to make a computerized war-game for the first time part of what would then be the most ambitious Net Estimate yet written. On Friday this was cleared with Radford; on Monday the war-game experts were on hand and we went to work.

We made some interesting discoveries—among them that it was a pretty desperate move for the USSR to attack us with their substantially inferior long-range air force, that extensive U.S. radar tactical warning systems would make it impossible for surprise to be achieved in an all-out attack, and that the characteristics of defensive radar made it much more profitable to attack at low-level where "ground-clutter" returns confused the radar rather than at the high altitudes for which our bombers were designed. This last point, I believe, gave the main impetus for a revision of bombing tactics by the U.S. Air Force and helped it ready our aircraft and future aircraft design well in advance of the time when really effective ground-to-air Soviet missiles made it imperative for the United States to go to low-level attack.

With the war-game results and all of the latest NIE detailed estimates of Soviet capabilities at my fingertips, I wrote every word of that year's Net Estimate, cleared it with everybody, and prepared the text for an oral briefing on the findings, complete with visual aid charts, which Admiral Robbins presented at the White House. Eisenhower insisted that all top officials of the Defense Department attend this special briefing. Dulles and

Bull and I of course went along, the encomiums were great, and I believe we did demonstrate how useful a genuinely cooperative, interagency net estimate can be if the high command shows a real interest in it. The process was repeated for several years, without startling new findings, and the Net Estimate system eventually lapsed, although the term lingers on in various other contexts.

This Net Estimate and the NIEs of this 1950s era succeeded in reducing the Soviet military threat to the United States to reasonable proportions in the minds of war-planning staffs. The CIA probably never accomplished more of value to the nation than this quiet, little-remarked analytical feat.

It is hard to remember now that from about 1948 on, beginning with the Berlin Blockade and accelerating with the Korean War, Washington was inclined to expect a direct military assault by the Soviet Union and, later, by Communist China in Asia. Taiwan and Korea were the anticipated targets in Asia, whereas in Europe Soviet armies were expected to sweep across the North German plain to the Atlantic. The JCS in this period repeatedly estimated in their own papers that the USSR was bent on "world domination" and that the "time of greatest danger" of attack was two years hence. I believe this latter figure of speech died out about 1954.

In any case the ONE staff and Board members valiantly worked throughout the 1950s to moderate this black-and-white approach to estimates on the USSR, trying to suggest that an "ultimate" intention of "world domination" was not a sure indicator of specific near-term military action and that, on balance, the USSR would be unwise to resort to direct military attack to achieve its unquestioned purpose of increasing its political influence in Europe and the Mideast.

Most of the more moderate language describing, qualifying, and accurately quantifying the Soviet threat came from the CIA draftsmen, and had to be fought through up to the DDI and DCI decision levels. It was an educational process for all concerned, as we adjusted to a postwar world of ideological, economic, political, and military conflict. Gradually military intelligence officers and civilian analysts alike became more sophisticated, the short-of-war kind of conflict became better understood, and U.S. policy became based on strategic deterrence and politico-economic alliance-building as a way of containment. My own belief is that a handful of the CIA analysts and their chiefs served the country well in building this estimative foundation on which U.S. strategy and policy in its broad outlines rested for two decades. The ideas are familiar now, but they once were new and hard to sell.

## DDI Research and Analysis

One of the developments of Headquarters that had taken place while I was in London and during my year or so of work on NIEs and the Net Estimate was an expansion of tasks falling to research and current intelligence analysts in the DDI, outside ONE. Beetle Smith had apparently thought most such research and analysis would wither away, the responsibility for it reverting to State and Defense. He quickly discovered, as Allen Dulles had always believed, that the estimates process would not work unless accurate current intelligence analysis and skillful political, economic, military, and scientific research were done and that State and Defense were simply not geared or attuned to serve the CIA's national intelligence analysis and estimative needs. In other words, the CIA found out that, if it wanted intelligence research and analysis done in ways and at times suited to its needs, the Agency had to do it. I certainly found it invaluable to have political, economic, and scientific analysts close at hand to call on when I was working on Soviet estimates. All in all there were about 1,000 employees working in these fields in the mid-1950s under the general supervision of the DDI. They in turn used the services of another 2,000 or so in the overt collection services and in the central reference service—the classified data library of the CIA.

The DDI domain thus undertook more and more tasks, just as ORE had done before, because there was a demand not only for support of ONE but also for support of the planning elements in the clandestine services and, even more, a demand for high-quality current intelligence reporting in every agency of the NSC complex. A current intelligence daily report, weekly summaries of incoming intelligence at several levels of security classification, and numerous *ad hoc* reports on new trends and patterns in international affairs, in strategic forces and weapons, in economics—especially in the USSR and China—and in science and technology all received wide readership and a welcome reception as "services of common concern" to government agencies interested in foreign affairs.

My interest steadily grew in this analytical underpinning of the estimates process and I quickly discovered that timely, carefully evaluated current intelligence items provided the passport to the attention of senior officials like DDI Bob Amory and Allen Dulles. In particular, OCI, the Office of Current Intelligence, made a substantial impact because it developed a cadre of analysts who built up a great familiarity with all of the sources of data that came into the CIA. I remember that Van Slyck, my ORE and ONE colleague, said when we were planning to rely only on an austere number of analysts needed to draft estimates, "Who will read the cables every day?" It is true that thousands of items of information conceivably important in foreign affairs or national security reach Washington at all hours of the day and night. Knowledgeable analysts have to scan this vast outpouring of information, screen out the new and meaningful, and explicate each item with appropriate comment, putting the new data in context. This process is current intelligence analysis, the first-phase attack on the tide of data flowing in. Somebody had to do this job within the capabilities and frame of reference of any intelligence agency, and OCI did it for the CIA and for the rest of the intelligence community. OCI in time was able to operate on a systematic scale theretofore unprecedented. The OCI analysts tried to keep up with what everybody was reporting and tried to make sense out of it every day of every week of the year. Their knowledge in depth was formidable. Winnowing out the specific tidbits that the President might need or like to read gave a sense of purpose to what otherwise might seem an unending struggle to keep up with the flow of facts, figures, and reported views of foreign personalities. Once an analyst became accustomed to trying to know everything about his chosen field, however, he usually was hopelessly addicted to the search for the new and meaningful pattern or trend in the welter of incoming fragments.

One outsider who came into the CIA in the Smith era to organize the current intelligence shop was Huntington (Ting) Sheldon, who stayed on as Chief of Current Intelligence throughout the Dulles years and continued to work until retirement many years later as CIA's Senior SIGINT Officer, monitoring the relationship between the military signals intelligence agencies and the CIA. Sheldon wisely took on Knight McMahan as his Deputy and the two gradually brought into being the all-source research and analysis center that Knight and I had started to create in ORE just before Beetle Smith's arrival. Several hundred analysts, many of them with long experience in analyzing intelligence from their chosen area of expertise, were cleared for every security classification of material they might use, entry to the area was restricted by turnstile gates and policemen requiring picture-badge identification, and OCI began turning out a flood of the best written, most carefully analyzed intelligence reporting ever to hit Washington desks. It is a service to high-level officials that they invariably appreciate, and it is a way that all intelligence agencies use to capture the attention of the senior officials they want to serve. Policy makers do not always welcome something profound in the way of analysis, especially if it contradicts their own policy predilections, but most of them can be hooked with something new—especially if they get it before their peers in other agencies.

Sheldon was a genius at managing professionals with the analytical skills that made OCI's work outstanding. He had a shrewd sense of what would catch attention in the upward mobile chain of command, where at every level a fascinating tidbit of new intelligence gave entree to the next level. A lot of gamesmanship is involved in this process, and Sheldon was superb at it. He and McMahan set out to give first class service of this sort to everybody in town, and they made themselves indispensable. Both were tireless workers, managing a machine that gave 24-hour service of high quality. OCI made and still makes a great contribution to up-to-date knowledge in Washington.

Another gifted outsider, Professor Max Millikan, an economist from the Massachusetts Institute of Technology (MIT), organized almost all of the remaining DDI analysts into the Office of Research and Reports (ORR), which wrote in-depth studies on geographic characteristics of foreign areas, especially on foreign economic developments in the USSR and China. These analysts also prepared economic contributions to NIEs, a function that became increasingly important as cost and weapons production capabilities became crucial to long-range estimates of Soviet military strength. It was probably this economic expertise more than anything else that enabled CIA to get a handle on the military agencies and force them into effective coordination of substantive findings in NIEs.

Another contribution to this analytical research process came from the Office of Scientific Intelligence, a more specialized group of analysts who enabled the CIA to keep up with technical knowledge in the crucial field of atomic energy and—beginning in the mid-1950s—missile technology. The senior CIA officers in these fields assumed the leadership of interagency committees dealing with these special subjects, serving as "Mr. Nuclear Weapons" and "Mr. Guided Missiles" for the whole interagency intelligence system for many years. Otto Guthe, Edward Allen, and William Morell exercised similar roles in the economic and geographical fields. If OCI supplied the classified daily newspaper for Washington, the economic and scientific intelligence analysts provided the in-depth research volumes.

These and subsequent research and analysis shops in the CIA performed two important tasks beyond writing reports. First, the scientists and economists pioneered in developing techniques for detailed collection guidance in the form of requirements for the collection agencies, especially for the CIA's own clandestine operations stations overseas and for the military signals intercept units. General topical requirements are seldom much help to collectors in the field, but specifics as to where and how to find a particular fact or figure that would reveal a great deal to an analyst are often the key to a successful collection effort. This kind of work I later institutionalized in a DDI collection guidance staff that in some form or other is still trying to translate the broad topical interests of policymakers and intelligence analysts into the detailed requirements that an agent in the field or an electronics intercept station can zero in on to produce relevant data.

As the CIA moved into the photo-reconnaissance field in the 1950s, this extremely technical process of collection guidance paid off handsomely. The computerized guidance of reconnaissance satellites, a marvel of technology, is the product of the intellectual skills that were developed to link agent and signals collectors to the specific needs of analysts. No more important field of intelligence work exists nor one so imperfectly understood.

The second benefit derived from CIA's immersion in research in the economic and scientific areas was the contact built up with the university research world outside of government. Max Millikan went back to MIT in 1953 and established a consultancy relationship between the DDI scholars in CIA and the professors in the Center for International Studies (CENIS) at MIT. The CIA put substantial funds into the support of CENIS but this funding was later decried and discontinued. It is frustrating that the secrecy whch surrounds the CIA interferes with such research projects that, if they were entirely openly acknowledged, surely would be seen as a benefit for academic research and for the nation. I think links between our best intelligence analysts and the academic research people with expertise on subjects under study in Washington should be built up far more than has ever been possible because of fears that exchanging information and views with the CIA is somehow a corrupting process. In my view scholars inside and outside the government benefit from such consultation, and there is no need for outside scholars to become involved in any kind of clandestine activity or to accept and promulgate the CIA views.

In any case, despite the difficulties over the years, CIA economists and scientists especially, and, to a lesser extent CIA political scientists, have established intellectual ties that have enriched the scholarly content of U.S. strategic intelligence and also enabled university scholars to have access to a great deal of the information and analytical views of the CIA that would otherwise not be available to them. The CIA research and analysis shops deserve great credit for realizing from the first that a symbiotic relationship exists between scholars in government intelligence agencies and scholars elsewhere.

This respect for scholarship is one of the main distinguishing features that has given the CIA a marked superiority in intellectual quality over the Soviet KGB and other totalitarian intelligence agencies. A great deal more needs to be done to free this collaboration from the limitations that are properly imposed on contacts between clandestine operations officers and bona fide outside scholars. Much more has been done than is widely known to make the CIA's research available to the public, which after all pays for it, and to bring to intelligence analysts the information and judgments of experts in science, business, and all of the professions, in the wide reaches of U.S. society. Everyone gains in this process. The broad outlines of such rapport were established in the 1950s by the frank consultation with scholars that Beetle Smith and Allen Dulles sponsored.

To all of us in intelligence then, especially on the analytical side, the CIA seemed an integral part of our society, drawing on society's strengths and feeding back into the general pool of knowledge whatever the intelligence community could convey without jeopardy to its sources. This relationship has been tarnished in recent years by suspicions and fears engendered in the American intellectual community by exaggerated stories of the CIA's covert actions. If this confusion between the analytical and covert operational elements of the CIA can be cleared up, everyone in the United States will profit.

## Perspective: Headquarters, CIA, 1955-1957

My work on the Net Estimate permitted me to become better acquainted with Allen Dulles. My knowledge of his intelligence exploits went back to OSS days, and I sometimes sat in the back row of seats at meetings of the Intelligence Advisory Committee while its members, the chiefs of other intelligence staffs, reviewed NIEs with Smith and Dulles. The rule for staff officers in the back row, however, was never to speak unless spoken to. All this changed when I became the key draftsman of the Net Estimate, because I had to explain what I was doing not only to Kent and Amory but also to Dulles.

A further change in readiness of access to the DCI occurred when I opted to transfer from ONE to OCI, where many of my old colleagues from ORE days had settled in under Knight McMahan's gentle, scholarly guidance. Ting Sheldon was always on the lookout for salesmen of current intelligence and offered me a senior job in OCI that was tailored especially to my interests. I became Chief of the Sino-Soviet area analytical staff in OCI and served about three years as the CIA's senior analyst for current intelligence reports—as distinct from coordinated estimates—on everything having to do with the USSR, East Europe, the People's Republic of China, North Korea, and North Vietnam. My staff cranked out evaluations of new pieces of information for our daily and weekly summaries and, more important, prepared texts on significant new developments for Allen Dulles to present to the NSC when it met, as it did every week with regularity under the ex-military President Eisenhower. This time was one of rich learning for me about the use of intelligence to help the policymaker, the hardest part of the chain that links the collector, researcher, analyst, and estimator to the decision-maker.

I moved down the hill from ONE's loftier domain in South Building to the ramshackle World War II temporary building named "M"—which with "Q" next door housed the DDI elements outside of ONE. These buildings were the old OSS domain tucked in around the decrepit building of the Heurich brewery. I took nostalgic satisfaction in sitting down at my desk in the office occupied a few years earlier by Ted Babbitt, the unfortunate head of ORE in the Hillenkoetter times, and next door to where I labored on the "Monthly Estimate of the World Situation" for ORE's Global Survey Division in 1949 and early 1950. There was more satisfaction, however, in seeing that OCI was really an all-source shop, freely using signals intercepts along with the CIA agent reports, military attache reports, and the all-important Embassy reporting on foreign, political, and economic problems.

I took most pleasure, though, in my new job because of having persuaded OCI to look at the whole world of

Communist states from a single analytical viewpoint, that of my Sino-Soviet staff, so that we could detect similarities and, more significantly, differences among the various dictatorships that confronted us. This approach had long seemed to me to be a useful analytical tool, forcing Sovietologists and Sinologists to compare notes in detail rather than to think of the peoples they study simply as residents of two quite different parts of the world. The free world-Communist world conflict—perceived to be the key strategic issue confronting the United States—demanded, in my view, the application of rigorous common standards of political and economic analysis to all parts of this vast totalitarian empire, which I was certain could not be the monolith of which it was then fashionable to speak.

During my tenure in OCI, I designated a few analysts with detailed familiarity with Soviet political leaders, doctrines, and daily policy pronouncements to work alongside others who were equally knowledgeable about Mao's China. With a few East European and other Asian Communist specialists, they began an intensive search into the Sino-Soviet relationship that has not ended to this day. I insisted that they write nothing for current publication but instead devote themselves to becoming the greatest experts in the world concerning Communist states' behavior patterns.

This special research staff, elevated to high bureaucratic levels and expanded in size later on, was beginning cautiously to suggest the Sino-Soviet split as early as 1956, when the different Moscow and Peking reactions to disorders in Poland and Hungary were noted. This staff compiled the data that permitted the CIA to lead the way—against furious opposition elsewhere—in charting the strategic conflict between Soviet and Chinese styles of dictatorship and doctrine that was basic to the definitive split in 1960. On our understanding of this split, our global strategy has depended for the past 20 years. The 25-foot bookshelf of detailed studies that has been compiled on Communist leaders and doctrines is a virtually unknown but vital contribution that the CIA has made to the understanding of U.S. officials in many parts of the government on the fundamental character of these regimes.

My most exciting work in "M" Building was selecting and preparing current intelligence items for the DCI to consider for use at morning NSC meetings. Sheldon required the OCI analysts to labor long and hard to produce interesting material for Dulles, and the solid pieces of intelligence that got through to Dulles and Eisenhower made the whole process worthwhile. Once a week, usually late in the afternoon, Sheldon would take the suggested budget of NSC material up to the Headquarters suite on the hill, climbing the rickety wooden steps alongside South Building that led from the brewery area to what were the upper levels of the CIA—topographically as well as bureaucratically.

Allen Dulles was unquestionably the "Great White Case Officer" for all of the CIA, spending at least three-fourths of his time and energy, I would judge, on clandestine collection and covert action tasks. He loved the exoticism, the hint of danger, and the intellectual intricacy of overseas operations. I have heard him review the most detailed kind of clandestine arrangements with Dick Helms and other senior operations officers, chewing them out royally if he felt his own standards of tradecraft were not being employed. Dulles knew that the substantive analysis, reporting, and estimates business was a vital part of his responsibility, although he never became deeply involved in estimates work. I suppose he spent less than 5 percent of his efforts on the ONE effort, much to the chagrin of Sherm Kent and Bob Amory. The rest of his time Dulles devoted to current intelligence, special activities involving NSC work (the Net Estimate, for example), and preparation of speech material to use either publicly (rarely) or privately in his discussions with foreign dignitaries.

The OCI contingent, with Bob Amory and sometimes Sherm Kent in attendance, used to sit around in Dulles' office—sometimes on into the evening—on the day before NSC meetings while the boss read the draft texts. General C. Pearre Cabell, the Air Force officer who served as the Deputy Director of ICA and general administrator throughout Dulles' tour, also often sat in on these sessions. A point to note is that they all did their homework carefully because of the standard Eisenhower set at NSC meetings. Sheldon was shrewd enough to take his senior analysts along because they answered questions and defended judgments much more persuasively than any of the higher-ranking officials less familiar with the substantive evidence.

Dulles had a good feeling for current intelligence—he wanted brief, colorful, snappy items with dramatic quality. He often took a malicious delight in disregarding his higher-ranking advisers and siding with the junior analysts.

Because the Soviet Union or China was nearly always on the agenda for possible NSC reporting, I attended most of these briefing sessions and, if my items were selected for presentation, accompanied Dulles to the NSC meetings. This gave me an unexcelled opportunity to trade ideas and arguments with this man, whose memory of trends and people ran back to the Versailles peace conference after World War I. He was usually tired late in the day when he began to focus on what he would say at the next day's NSC meeting. He would ramble on about his thoughts and grumble about the material we offered, rejecting more than half of it. I can see him leaning back in his swivel chair, his steel-rimmed spectacles pushed up on his forehead so he could hold the papers he was reading about nine inches from his nose. His fingers were gnarled with gout, which plagued him, and his feet were often so painful that he wore carpet slippers in the office and propped his feet on the desk. We sat around in a circle like disciples, soaking up his remarks and explaining our suggestions. It was a very high-level, expensive seminar, but I learned more from it in three years of sitting in on this process than I ever did in any other educational forum.

Allen Dulles was no fool. He knew what policy problems were uppermost in Eisenhower's mind and in the thoughts of his brother, the Secretary of State. He wanted to use the CIA in every possible way to help them and, through them, the country. Good intelligence was one of the offerings he gave, though covert action in support of policy loomed much larger in his thinking and personal engagement of energies. I learned to respect this lively man very much. One of his firm beliefs was that open societies and honest intellectual inquiry would triumph over despotism and he insisted that the inscription in the marble entryway of the handsome new CIA building he constructed along the Potomac quote the Bible in saying: "And ye shall know the truth and the truth shall make you free."

He felt—more confidently than I did—that education would eventually mellow the Russians and that meanwhile it was the moral duty of our generation to contain the forceful expansion of any totalitarian regime so that free societies could survive. Allen Dulles was a patriot, world-citizen, and, in his own way, a scholar. It was a pleasure to work with him and for him.

The two Dulles brothers were really remarkably close, although they argued with one another on occasion in the best of family traditions. The case I remember best was at about this time when Foster sent over a speech for Allen to read; Allen asked me to critique it and then insisted that I go along with him to give Foster some rather major objections I had to one passage about the USSR. We sat at a small table in a private conference room next to the Secretary of State's office and went over the whole text. All went well until we got to the passage I had questioned, when Allen said brusquely that it had to be dropped or totally rewritten. Foster fired up and said, "I am the Secretary of State and it is my speech and I damned well will say it if I want to." Allen shot back, "My Soviet expert here says it is wrong, and I won't let you make a damned fool of yourself, Secretary of State or not!" I would have liked to disappear somehow, but was in the line of fire between the glaring Dulleses. Fortunately a few changes fixed things up to their mutual satisfaction, but it was a supreme test of diplomatic skill for me; it was also an example of how intelligence and policy interacted when it was all in the family!

It is not necessary to recall all of the interesting exchanges I had with this great man, whose flaw in excessive enthusiasm for clandestine operations for their own sake was far outweighed in my mind by his positive achievements in creating a dynamic, productive central intelligence system that really did enrich the policymaking process of our government. Dulles put the CIA on the map in Washington and abroad—perhaps too much so. Nevertheless he led it in its drive to collect and analyze whatever information Eisenhower and Foster Dulles and the Pentagon needed. He created a monument to himself not just in the building he constructed in Langley, Virginia, but, more important, in institutionalizing the whole process of secret intelligence at the center of government.

An example of the way the NSC briefing system worked comes to my memory from 1957, close to the end of my OCI tour. In mid-year our scientists and economists had begun to stumble onto evidence of an intricate sort that indicated Soviet testing of what we then called "earth satellite vehicles" with guided missiles that propelled them from central Russia (Tyuratam) to the Kamchatka peninsula. It was the dawn of the missile age, but the thinking in Washington was not really ready for it. I prepared a rather technical item giving the limited facts we knew on the test range activities; at the pre-NSC briefing Dulles resisted it, saying the President would never understand it—which meant he himself did not quite feel at home with the military and technical details involved. I argued vigorously but lost. We settled on presenting a description of Nikita Khrushchev's drastic reorganization of the Soviet bureaucracies dealing with economic production.

The next morning, as usual, I rode over to the White House in the limousine with him as he reviewed the revised texts. He fretted over some of the material, as was normal, and then said thoughtfully, "You really think that missile test business is important, don't you?" I only had time to nod before we alighted, went into the Cabinet Room near the oval office of the President, and began the briefing. The DCI always sat at the end of the long conference table next to the fireplace, while the President sat at the middle of the table with his back to the windows.

I sat in a chair along the wall next to the door to the hall, ready to place our visual aid charts on an easel by the fireplace and answer questions if they got too technical for the DCI. Since I later did this same job for John A. McCone, I have the scene well in mind. On this occasion in 1957 I was transfixed, however, when the DCI ended his briefing with the statement that some disturbing new evidence about Soviet weapons was available, which he would like Dr. Cline to present.

I sprang to my feet and looked at the grossly inadequate map showing economic regions of the USSR. With the bravado that comes from countless briefings, I swung my pointer to an area I hoped was within 500 miles of Tyuratam and briefly described the missile activity between there and Kamchatka. I said the experts thought the aim was to launch small earth satellite vehicles but of course the missiles had some potential as weapons.

Eisenhower took all this in thoughtfully, leaning forward to ask if the missiles could be fired as well from Kamchatka over the Pacific and whether, if so, they could reach the United States. Cursing my wholly inadequate map inwardly, I replied that theoretically they could reach Hawaii but not California, and that at the moment the range was set up the other way for other purposes. The President courteously thanked me and the NSC went on to other business. As far as I know this was the only time the subject ever came up at the NSC before Khrushchev electrified the world with "Sputnik I," the satellite launched to circle the world in October 1957. Dulles later told me he was exceedingly grateful that we had slipped that current intelligence item in when we did.

## Photographic Reconnaissance

At the time of its development I had only an inkling of one of the CIA's greatest achievements—the invention of the U-2 high-flying aircraft and the camera capable of taking pictures from 80,000 feet, pictures that would permit analysts to recognize objects on the ground with dimensions as small as 12 inches. It was the U-2 that pinned down with some precision in the course of time what was going on at Tyuratam and other military bases in the USSR. A photographic look at things from the air opened up a whole new era. This technical near-miracle revolutionized intelligence collection, eventually rivaling signals for producing voluminous details about foreign areas and reducing the burden on the secret agent enormously. It also gave the analyst historical depth in evidence, permitting researchers to identify lead-time traces in weapons development once new radars, missiles, aircraft, submarines, etc. had been discovered. The all-source research center where photographic signals, agent reports, and overt data files could be checked one against the other became more than ever the key to successful intelligence analysis.

The DDI had set up a small photo interpretation office in 1953, drawing on military specialists trained in the rudimentary air reconnaissance techniques of World War II. The leader of the group was Arthur Lundahl, a trained PI (photo-interpreter) and farsighted visionary, who constantly touted the potential of the picture that tells more than 10,000 words. He is one of the authentic heroes of post World War II intelligence technology. I called Art the super-salesman of photo interpretation. He started in with only about 20 photo experts and gradually built up a modern facility for the readout of U-2 and earth-satellite photography that employed about 1,200 people all told and constituted a crucial central element in most modern intelligence research and analysis. You cannot take pictures of what happens in the dark or under cover or what takes place inside somebody's head. For those things we still need agents or some other method of intelligence collection. Everything else, however, that is outside in the light of day lies open to inspection if a good enough camera can be put above it.

Lundahl's miracles of photo-interpretation were made possible by the parallel development of cameras, lenses, and special films for high-level photography. He worked with geniuses in American industry who, under contract, worked for the CIA to develop these photographic devices. At the same time another great contributor to the modern intelligence era, Richard Bissell, an economist with extensive administrative experience in government, who joined the CIA in 1954 as a Special Assistant to Dulles, was working on the platform to carry the camera over its targets above the reach of aircraft or antiaircraft fire. He engaged the services of an inventive aeronautical engineer at Lockheed Aircraft Company, Kelly Johnson, to hand build the U-2 in a separate little hangar called the "skunk works" in California.

The U-2 looked more like a kite built around a camera than an airplane; it was nearly all wing and its single jet engine made it shoot into the air like an arrow and soar higher than any other aircraft of its day. The need to keep the airframe light was so great that the plane landed on one set of tandem wheels rather than the normal pair and, when forward momentum was lost on landing, simply fell over on one of its long wingtips. Every landing was a crash landing, but the skids on the wingtips were built to take it. The wingspread was so wide and the airframe so light that the wings had to be held up by little "pogo" sticks on wheels that carried the wings down the runway until forward speed lifted the highly flexible wings and let the pogo sticks drop off on the ground. Such ingenuity made the U-2 a winner. It caught the Soviet Union unprepared. U-2s flew first in 1955 and flew over Soviet territory regularly from 1956 until 1960, when the Soviet military forces finally managed to down Gary Power's aircraft with a close explosion of an SA-2 antiaircraft guided missile.

Fortunately, Bissell had foreseen that countertechnology would one day catch up with the U-2 and had pioneered, with U.S. Air Force assistance, the development of even better camera systems and earth satellite vehicles capable of flying higher than the SA-2s. In 1961 the follow-on program became operational and soon the camera 90 miles or so high in space was able to send back the same level of photographic images that the U-2 had first captured in 1956. Since a satellite at about 100 miles altitude circles the earth every 90 minutes, it will, in the course of a week or two, traverse every part of the earth as the globe revolves beneath the satellite's path. Thus selective coverage of any target area on earth can be obtained.

While this quantum leap forward in technology won the CIA well-deserved kudos, and Bissell is an authentic hero of the intelligence profession for that reason, it also landed the CIA in the midst of a complex collatoration with the Air Force because the launching of every satellite required a military launch pad. As satellites and missiles became more complex and costly, the technological aspects sometimes seemed to overshadow the intelligence purposes and the mountains of film piling up required a whole new echelon of analysis and processing. Still, overhead reconnaissance and photo interpretation are here to stay. Modern intelligence analysis could not do without them, nor could arms control agreements and defense policies based on precise knowledge of the strategic weapons systems the USSR or China can deploy.

These technical collection achievements have since been broadened to include underwater reconnaissance. This fact came dramatically to the public's attention when the press broke the story of the U.S. attempts to retrieve a Soviet atomic submarine in the summer of 1974. By now, of course, the USSR has much the same reconnaissance capability as the United States, but the CIA put us first in the photographic imagery field by at least five years as a result of the brilliant work done in tandem by Art Lundahl's team and Dick Bissell's industrial engineers.

## Open Skies

My knowledge of all of this advanced technological planning was very limited while I was still in OCI, but I had one experience as an analyst that brought me very close to the open skies world that the U-2 foretold. In mid-1955 the President agreed to hold the first Summit Conference of Heads of Government of the USSR, Great Britain, France, and the United States. Dulles decided to send me along to Geneva as a member of the delegation so that an analyst could provide daily intelligence reports directly to the Secretary of State and to the President. I was there for about ten days, working day and night at the other end of the cable line to Washington. The conference lasted from July 18 to 23, produced the "spirit of Geneva," the first of the many detente periods in U.S.-Soviet relations, but produced little else in the way of concrete results. It gave me my first direct look at Khrushchev, Bulganin, Zhukov, Molotov, and the rest of the men I had been studying so intently for so long. I was only at arm's length from them whenever I went into the main conference hall to deliver a message to Foster Dulles.

I am always amazed when I remember the conference to realize that Eisenhower tried to achieve a diplomatic breakthrough on the basis of his foreknowledge of the U-2 by proposing an open skies mutual inspection pact based on aerial reconnaissance of each other's territory. In the eternal hopeful American spirit, he tried to make a gesture of good will and was sharply rebuffed by Khrushchev. I was standing outside the conference room when this extraordinary, farsighted proposal was made, and I learned from Ambassador Chip Bohlen, Eisenhower's interpreter at the session, as soon as they emerged, that the Russians called the open skies proposal nothing but an American espionage trick. I wonder if they ever regretted it in the next years as the U-2s began doing unilaterally over the USSR what Eisenhower had proposed they do on a reciprocal basis. It is ironic that the peace of the world now depends to a remarkable degree on the unilateral U.S. and Soviet technical means of monitoring arms agreements that evolved from this U-2 technology of 1955. In any case the balance of strategic nuclear power that protects U.S. security is guaranteed by U.S. intelligence efforts, based on the photographic techniques the CIA officers began working on 25 years ago.

## The CIA Overseas

After the first Summit adjourned with no agreement on anything consequential, a follow-up meeting of foreign ministers met in Geneva for several fruitless weeks, from October 27 to November 16, haggling over formulas for disarmament, German unification, and greater freedom of movement of peoples and information between Eastern and Western Europe. These subjects proved to be obdurate and they are still on the negotiating table today. In preparation for advising the President, I had organized a computerized index of data in the CIA files likely to be used in connection with agenda items in Geneva. It turned out to be of little use because nobody in the delegation ever asked the relevant questions, but since I was the only one who pretended to understand the computer file, I spent many weeks in Geneva purveying current intelligence and helping out on the State delegation whenever possible.

I operated in an open fashion, carrying my briefcase full of classified CIA reports around town as necessary, using an ordinary Geneva consulate car and chauffeur. I had done just the same during the Summit—when it was necessary to check in early each morning with Andrew Goodpaster at the villa where the President was staying to make my contribution to Eisenhower's morning briefing. What was impressive to me at that time was that I was shown pictures by the CIA station chief in Switzerland indicating that my opposite number on the Soviet side was General Serov, the head of the KGB, who arrived incognito and traveled around Geneva with bodyguards and bulletproof limousines. He was plainly playing the role of secret police chief, not intelligence analyst.

My presence in Europe resulted in requests from Headquarters for me to visit the CIA stations in Germany and Great Britain, to fill them in on the atmosphere and proceedings at Geneva. This was pleasant duty and, in Germany in particular, it brought me into contact with key officers from this important station, the biggest CIA operational complex in the world. As always, I discovered that clandestine services officers were similar in their concerns to analysts in Washington, often very bright and almost invariably full of useful detailed knowledge of the local situation that was simply not available in formal written reports to Washington. The more I learned about this operational milieu the more I felt this was an area of expertise that an all-round intelligence officer should be familiar with.

One fascinating episode opened my eyes to the world of agent debriefings. The Swiss station chief, a witty, urbane agent handler of many years, had one good clandestine source with contacts in the Soviet delegation. He debriefed his agent at length in a Geneva night club every night, then made a late, late meeting with me to pass on nuggets about Soviet reactions to the day's events at the conference. This enabled me to do the analyst's normal job on the spot, evaluating the raw material from the agent and condensing it into what was worth passing to the President or the Secretary of State. About 5 a.m. my current intelligence summary messages from Washington would come in and I would insert into the briefing for the President the items garnered from the agent a few hours earlier. This impressed everybody with our timeliness and was a great satisfaction to my audience, who did not know or mind that the system left me about three hours of sleep a night when the agent had something to report. This was probably a record for direct service of clandestine intelligence for high-level users.

When I finally got back to Washington, my ties with the clandestine services became closer than ever before, especially with Dick Helms, the career leader of the intelligence collectors. Dick and I began to exchange information and views on a regular basis. He handled several agents whose identity was very sensitive. He was pleased to be able to pass on their views to a DDI analyst whose discretion he could trust, and we developed a personal relationship of mutual respect and confidence that lasted throughout the years. Dick was the perfect model of the cool, well-informed professional manager of agent networks and case officers, the agent handlers of the CIA's stations. A case officer is the CIA officer, usually an American citizen, who maintains contact with the clandestine agents themselves, usually non-Americans, who provide the hard-to-get data that fills in the gaps of what cannot be obtained from overt sources or by technical means of collecting intelligence. Helms knew this arcane world, especially in Europe, better than anyone except Allen Dulles himself. I valued this link with the clandestine services environment because it enriched my understanding of agent reporting and enabled me to suggest priorities for collection. I served for a time in this period on the Intelligence Priorities Committee (IPC), an interagency group that met periodically to assign relative priorities to subjects and targets for the clandestine services. All of this experience built up in my mind the conviction, which has never changed, that an intellectual partnership between scholars and spies is the best formula for successful intelligence collection and evaluation.

## The Berlin Tunnel

A great undertaking of the mid-1950s in the CIA, costing millions of dollars and providing reams of factual information reports on the USSR, was the Berlin tunnel project. Its history is significant because it illustrates the way in which different intelligence functions overlap and supplement one another. Until the Soviet authorities in East Berlin stumbled onto the tunnel and sealed it off in April 1956, most of the communications between East Berlin and the USSR had been recorded for many months and sent back to CIA Headquarters for processing and analysis of their contents. The take was voluminous and very useful for Soviet analysts in the economic, scientific, military, and current intelligence research staffs in the CIA and elsewhere in the intelligence community.

This windfall came to us because a clandestine services unit in West Berlin had dreamed up the notion of tunneling under the border dividing the Soviet-controlled east sector of the city from the rest of Berlin. Careful clandestine operational techniques permitted this to be done without arousing the suspicions of the ubiquitous East German and Soviet guards. Access was gained to an unused building near the border, tools and equipment were spirited in at night, and a tunnel was dug through to emerge under the floor of another unused structure on the other side. Disposing of the dirt was a major enterprise in itself. You can imagine the ingenuity required to make all the necessary moves secretly, as well as the technical skills required from CIA's communications intelligence specialists to install banks of recorders and tap into East Germany's trunk cable lines inside the tunnel.

When the clandestine operations had pulled off the trick of preparing the site and the communications gear was installed, the task of translating and analyzing the messages thus intercepted was monumental. The DDP staffs involved turned to the DDI for assistance, and a joint operation on a closely compartmented basis went on for a long time to screen out the most meaningful data and distribute it to analytical units throughout Washington. The combination of the talents of the DDP spies, the communications technicians, and the DDI scholars provided one of the best examples of what modern centralized intelligence in the CIA could accomplish.

## Khrushchev's Secret Speech

One of the CIA's greatest coups of all time occurred in the spring of 1956, illustrating perfectly my point about this partnership. In February 1956 Khrushchev made his famous secret speech at the 20th Party Congress denouncing Stalin for his criminal cruelty and misgovernment. Gossip about it echoed through Eastern Europe and then worldwide. Dulles put the pressure on his collectors to get a copy of the speech—price no object. In the spring, in April as I remember, a copy of the speech was finally acquired through non-American intermediaries, at a very handsome price. It came back to Headquarters for study and Dulles insisted that Frank Wisner, Dick Helms, and Jim Angleton, the Chief of Counterintelligence and Counterespionage, who had played a role in getting the document, consult someone outside the clandestine services as to the authenticity and meaningfulness of the text they had bought. Probably because of my NSC briefings role and my contacts with Helms, Wisner decided to let me read and judge the precious document.

The denizens of the DDP lived on the other side of the Lincoln Memorial from the DDI elements of the CIA. Their home was in a dismal row of World War II temporary buildings labeled J, K, and L, now destroyed, but then stretching the whole length of the reflecting pool from 17th to 23rd Streets. There was not a great deal of intercourse between the two areas, mainly because of DDP clannishness and fierce tradecraft indoctrination in security. Occasionally representatives met, however, and I went down to the reflecting pool to give my views on the secret speech. I remember a solemn conclave chaired by Wisner with Angleton representing the DDP professionals' judgment on the speech. I was vastly outnumbered, but I was able to provide convincing, and most welcome, internal evidence that the text we had was an authentic account of what happened at the 20th Party Congress and that much of it was Khrushchev's own colorful prose. This made everyone happy.

Immediately, however, a disagreement surfaced. I made what I thought was an eloquent plea to make the speech public. I said that it would provide scholars and students interested in the Soviet Union invaluable insights into the real workings of Stalinist Russia. I also said it was a rare opportunity to have all the critical things we had said for years about the Soviet dictatorship confirmed by the principal leader of the Soviet Politburo. The world would be treated to the spectacle of a totalitarian nation indicted by its own leadership. To many amazement Wisner and Angleton demurred. Once we had agreed that the text was authentic, their operational minds began thinking about feeding selected bits of the text to specific audiences on which they wanted to have an impact. They kept saying they wanted to "exploit" the speech rather than simply let everybody read it. This was an example of the covert mind at work that, in this case, seemed excessively narrow and Byzantine. Jim Angleton much later admitted I was right, but that day he tried hard to keep his secret paper secret.

On this one I triumphed and what I consider an effective political action transpired, all the more successful for being open rather than covert. Some weeks later, on a Saturday, June 2, I was alone with Allen Dulles working on a speech that contained references to the USSR. Suddenly, in the way he often moved from one topic to a quite unrelated one, Dulles swung his chair around to look intently at me and said, "Wisner says you think we ought to release the secret Khrushchev speech." I related my reasons for thinking so, and the old man, with a twinkle in his eye, said, "By golly, I am going to make a policy decision!" He buzzed Wisner on the intercom box, told him he had given a lot of thought to the matter, and wanted to get the speech printed. Frank Wisner agreed, a little reluctantly but graciously, and Allen then phoned Foster Dulles at State to give him the same views he had given Wisner. Foster concurred, the speech was sent over to State and given directly to the *New York Times*, which printed the whole text on June 4, the following Monday.

This was one of the few examples of a genuine policy decision that I was involved in directly. It was an event of historic significance, documenting Stalinism as a fantastic political evil, forcing Khrushchev into a milder style of totalitarian control, and beginning the alienation between the Soviet leaders and Mao Tse-tung. Getting and publishing the secret speech let the whole world in on these momentous cracks in what was then seen as a Communist monolith.

## Around the World

In mid-1956 Dulles decided that he ought to visit all of this overseas stations that were in regions where his presence would not expose and endanger them. Fortunately he decided to take an analytical officer along to help him absorb what he learned on the trip and assist in writing up a report for follow-up action upon his return. He invited me to come along and then, to strengthen the analytical backup on what was essentially an operational trip, we added to the entourage a new young officer from ONE, James Billington, a student of Soviet history who stayed in the CIA only a short time and is now head of the Woodrow Wilson International Center for Scholars at the Smithsonian in Washington. This was a big break for me because Jim, being very junior, did most of the briefcase carrying and all of the complex changing of currencies day by day for our local expenditures. Dulles picked up local DDP men along the way to brief him on parts of the world he knew little about, but relied on his own knowledge of Europe. He said he had been getting around safely in Europe before most of us were born, which I guess was true. The point was that he intended to review operational programs but that he also was thinking of himself as chief analytical and estimative advisor to the President—hence my presence. In his own fashion Allen Dulles was combined collector, analyst, and policy-level Presidential adviser.

With a medical officer to keep the DCI's gout under control and the rest of us healthy, this odd complement made up the staff party. Mrs. Dulles, whose first name was Clover, a delightful, whimsical, perceptive woman, came along—making the inevitable socializing on the trip much more civilized because at most stops national leaders turned out with their wives and spared us the tedium of one long stag party after another.

The U.S. Air Force supplied a passenger-fitted cargo aircraft for the trip. This was just the beginning of the jet age, so we traveled in what was then the Cadillac of the air, a four-motored DC-6. The aircrew members assigned to this aircraft were charming and efficient. We spent 57 days aboard the plane or on the ground en route. Our adventures circled the world in a flight path well over 30,000 miles and were innumerable, partly due to the fact that the name of the principal traveler was not revealed in normal air communication channels—all advance arrangements being made through the CIA local stations, and many local U.S. military base commanders turned out to do the courtesies for an unknown sub-cabinet official and his party traveling under blackout communications orders. Of course, once Allen Dulles arrived in countries where heads of state and prime ministers started throwing formal state dinners for him, the press picked up what was happening and we made one of the most highly publicized clandestine expeditions ever made.

This trip revealed starkly how anomalous the CIA's role was. The DCI was head of an organization set up by law. He was assigned the open function of scholarly analysis of foreign affairs; he met foreign statesmen in his official role as one of the four or five most influential men around the President; yet he was chief of clandestine collection and covert action, which caused him to try to travel incognito under secret flight orders. Something has to give in an organization which attempts to combine such opposite kinds of activity, and what usually resulted was that truly clandestine practices were compromised while perfectly legal scholarly analysis was clothed in an atmosphere of secrecy that was unnecessary, frequently counterproductive, and in the long run damaging to the role of independent and objective evaluation for which the CIA was designed.

No one could be more charming than Allen Dulles. He was a great storyteller, a witty conversationalist, and a close observer of human beings. He had a dramatic flair that his "spymaster" image gave him a great deal of opportunity to display. When he was amused and threw back his handsome gray head to laugh, as he frequently did, he let out a booming, stagy Ho! Ho! Ho! that sounded like a department store Santa Claus. Listeners laughed at his laugh, if not always at his stories, and the combination of a sophisticated sense of humor and his stylized laugh to me represented much of the complexity of this great man.

It is not easy to live and travel with someone for two months without friction. We ended up with an affection for one another and a mutual respect in our quite different roles. Later Allen told me, and others, that he thought I was a good station chief. He may well have been exaggerating because he was generous with praise as well as criticism, and he undoubtedly thought — rightly—that I had learned a lot from him. Whatever the truth, I felt very close to Dulles until his death many years later, and I never saw him in later years without our reminiscing about this famous trip, unique in the annals of the CIA, until tears of laughter came to our eyes. We both knew such a secret yet flamboyant circuit of the globe by the U.S. Director of Central Intelligence could only have taken place in the Eisenhower era.

At that time, everywhere we stopped the great men flocked to meet the man who supplied the strategic intelligence on which U.S. containment and alliance-building efforts were based. There was no hesitation but, rather, much eagerness to deal with the CIA, then seen as an institutional bulwark of the Free World. I traveled a lot later with John McCone and on my own as Deputy Director for Intelligence and it was still a dignified and influential image that was projected abroad by CIA, but the romantic heyday was the Dulles era.

It was a whole new experience traveling in this pseudo-clandestine style with Dulles. Everywhere we went the time zone changes, complicated by various daylight saving schemes, tended to throw our schedules out of kilter. Dulles liked to make a grand arrival, modest-appearing but with style. He was a little vain about his appearance, especially when women were to be in the reception line at the foot of the aircraft landing steps. Our first semi-ceremonial stop was in Paris; the station chief and a senior clandestine services officer from Headquarters were confused about the time of arrival; they came out to the airport thinking they were 45 minutes early and were actually 15 minutes late. Dulles was crestfallen to find no reception party and quite angry. My first reaction was one of amusement, but Allen said something I have never forgotten. He hissed fiercely when he was really annoyed and he lectured us then severely in words something like this: "In clandestine operations success or failure, life or death, may depend on meticulous attention to detail and timing. No CIA officer should ever be late for a meeting or skip a single detail in carrying out instructions. The matters at hand may appear trivial, but Headquarters may have arranged things so that they are crucial without letting the operator know. Only perfection in performance is tolerable. If things can go wrong, they will, and every CIA officer should double-check and triple-check every detail of activity going on under his supervision."

It was not a bad point. The 15 minutes gap in the meeting at the airport meant nothing but a little embarrassment, but a CIA man overseas has to demand perfection at all times to establish patterns of behavior that may save him from disaster. I have passed this on many times, putting it as Dulles' law: Things will get fouled up if they can get fouled up, so triple-check every detail of every operation. Anyway, I warned my friends how steamed up the old man was, and they sent a cable to every other stop en route instructing all the CIA reception parties to be in place one hour in advance of expected time of arrival, just in case.

Another aspect of the clandestine environment struck me in Frankfurt, Germany, where we stayed some time to review the complex operations of this huge station, the stronghold of the remnants of OSS's overseas domain, and the place from which countless efforts were mounted to penetrate the iron curtain. We met in a standard "safehouse," the kind of quarters that could be rented under a false name and used to debrief agents or defectors. The local CIA security chief promptly unscrewed the mouthpiece on the telephones and removed the carbon disks that theoretically could be remotely activated to transmit signals out of the room. He also turned the water faucet on in the bathroom and set a radio to play quietly in the background —all to drown out any electronic bugging devices. These practices are standard tradecraft, but it was my first brush with the real thing.

I remember that the station demurred at my presence, in keeping with the accepted clandestine services doctrine that no one outside their own ranks should be told anything operational. Dulles promptly squashed this as nonsense, stating that I was there to help him remember important issues and that good liaison between senior DDP and DDI officers was profitable to both. This word, too, was flashed ahead to all of the stations, and I never afterwards during all my years in government intelligence work encountered any serious difficulty in getting information that I had any "need to know." In fact, later on, my problem became that I was known and trusted with sensitive information by so many colleagues in the clandestine services, in the signals intelligence agencies, in the photo reconnaissance business, and in the Foreign Service that I had to learn to discipline myself sternly to avoid blowing my friendly sources when I went into bureaucratic battle to try to remedy some deficiency they had told me about. It is the vital network of senior intelligence staff officers who understand each other and have confidence in one another's dedication to national problem-solving that makes our intelligence system work. When compartmentation of information prevents everyone from having an overall view, central intelligence breaks down and good decision-making at the policy level deteriorates.

As we progressed eastwards from Europe to Istanbul and Teheran, Pakistan, India, Thailand, Saigon, Singapore, Australia, the Philippines, Taiwan, South Korea, and Japan, the exotic East closed in on us. The temptation to tell colorful travelogue stories is great, but I will resist it; what I want to convey is that in most of the world outside the more familiar cultural confines of Western Europe, the processes of strategic decision-making are more personal and direct; people know that having good intelligence on potentially hostile developments is a source of great power. Throughout the periphery of Asia there was a tremendous fear of Russia and China—geopolitical and well as ideological adversaries—that made many nations look to the United States for friendship, aid, and leadership. The Dulles visits were received as precious signs of U.S. interest and U.S. friendliness toward the governments of the nations in which we stopped.

Power tends to be more realistically appreciated in countries where political stability is not well established, and the CIA represented great power. It was a little frightening and it persuaded me that the United States openly, and the CIA secretly, could not in any way avoid playing a significant role in these regions. Action or lack of it, the provision of intelligence or the withholding of it, open U.S. diplomatic, as well as covert CIA support, were life-and-death matters to many regimes. I felt that the CIA had to learn about these societies and find the economic and political strengths that would help these nations maintain the independence they wanted and become valuable allies of the United States. Intelligence had only a part of the job to do in these countries where economic assistance and military defense guarantees were vital, but the intelligence role had to be played well if U.S. policy as a whole was to succeed.

Our travel took place in 1956, a fateful year. It had begun with the Soviet denunciation of Stalin; it saw the seizure of the Suez Canal in July by Egypt, a bungled invasion of Egypt in October, and the brutal Soviet military crushing of the revolt in Hungary. The "spirit of Geneva" abruptly collapsed. No one we talked to expected anything but conflict and political instability in the years ahead. Most thought that Americans, with all their vagaries, were the best hope to deter war.

Allen Dulles believed in this role wholeheartedly and responded vigorously. The Secretary of State's worldwide alliance system was the international, legal embodiment of the U.S. commitment to these purposes. Economic aid and military advisory agreements were the main devices to carry forward U.S. programs. The CIA was the instrument for secret political counseling, for intelligence liaison, and for constructing a worldwide net of intelligence operations sensitive to every hostile thrust that might directly or indirectly affect the United States. This was the intelligence climate of the fabulous fifties.

*Chapter Five*

# The CIA in High Gear

Having spent several days in Hawaii at the end of Allen Dulles' 1956 trip helping him write up his recommendations and observations about the overseas stations we had visited, I was familiar with the main thrust of the DCI's instructions to the clandestine services for their upcoming year or so of work. I then began to formulate in my own mind the notion of broadening my intelligence experience with a tour in the field.

Although I always remained most interested and involved in the analytical aspects of intelligence, the rarefied atmosphere of clandestine work intrigued me. Understanding in depth the people and customs of another culture is one of the real challenges and one of the most satisfying achievements for a scholar. To live and work in a foreign country seemed the most stimulating thing I could do, and I made the rounds, putting my name up for an operational assignment.

In the CIA environment the words "station chief" carry some overtones that outsiders may not easily grasp. Whereas the atmosphere in the DDI elements was comparable to that of the faculty of a university, the DDP spirit was more an action-oriented one. To be a station chief in the intelligence business is to feel yourself in command of troops at the front, sizing up opportunities and dangers on the spot, taking risks as necessary to achieve the results Headquarters wants. A station chief does not suffer from lack of instructions from Washington, but when he dispatches an agent or approaches a foreign official to try to get him to take some political action in the U.S. interest, he is alone at the end of the line; he has the final authority—as well as the risk.

I am afraid the folklore about the farsightedness of station chiefs, who get their jobs done despite all the red tape and idiotic instructions from Headquarters, is an ineradicable part of the clandestine mythology. Perhaps, within reasonable bounds, it is a good thing, because there is difficult and important work to be done in the field with very little recognition or reward for success, except the respect and admiration of colleagues.

## To Taiwan

In any event, toward the end of the year, in 1957, I was offered a post as chief of station in Taiwan, the large island occupied by the Republic of China only about 90 miles from Communist-controlled mainland China. Taiwan has always been a base from which the U.S. Government has tried to find out what was going on in the People's Republic of China. Because the Government of the Republic of China has always been a close ally of the United States, and because the CIA work based on Taiwan has been conducted in close collaboration with the Chinese Government, it is no breach of security to say that I was the supervisor of the CIA intelligence work there for almost five years, from the time of my arrival in early 1958 until June 1962. In terms of my personal learning as well as professional interest, my work there was the most stimulating period of my career.

In part, the rewarding aspects of this assignment were due to the tremendous charm of living in the midst of a Chinese culture and making lifelong friends among the Chinese. Those who retreated from the mainland to Taiwan were the best educated and the most Western-oriented group ever to lead a Chinese society. They liked Americans, hankered after modern technology, yet retained the basic philosophic cast of classical Confucian China, with its strong emphasis on personal and family obligations. These Chinese could not accept Communism as a basis for running a country, and they have been trying now for more than three decades to build a society in Taiwan combining the best of East and West, the cultural and ethical style of Chinese society modified by American concepts of economic growth, free enterprise, and representative government. The 18 million Chinese now living in the Republic of China on Taiwan have succeeded to a remarkable degree in creating an Asian society with modern European-American technology and political institutions.

When the DDP, Frank Wisner, formally offered me the job in 1957, he said that he hoped I would take the standard training course for the CIA officers going overseas with the DDP. He told me that clandestine service officers were wedded to their doctrines, tradecraft rules, and occupational jargon, just as DDI analysts had their own style of working and speaking. I remember Frank's saying, reflectively, "I guess we are as proud of our professional standards as you are of yours." Wisner was right. There was a great deal to learn—not just to help me in my work but to enable me to communicate easily with the operations officers in my station, with other stations, and with the legions of staff officers in the DDP headquarters. Under an assumed name, I shifted into baggy military fatigue uniforms and retreated to the legendary training site in southern Virginia referred to as "the Farm."

This site is where an intensive course had been developed for supervisory personnel. The younger case officers took a much longer course, and some specialists trained for many months. A lot of the paramilitary routines—such as making night landings in small aircraft on a flare-marked grass strip to simulate an agent rendezvous in enemy territory in wartime—were rather irrelevant to my projected assignment. It was useful, however, to get a feel for the way case officers and agents are trained, and much of the tradecraft training on meeting agents, recording conversations, and handling sensitive documents was illuminating as to what is feasible and what is not.* Finally, I found it especially helpful to spend this time in constant contact with younger CIA trainees who were largely a highly motivated and extremely idealistic group.

---

*So much has been written in spy fiction and in often fanciful non-fiction about the techniques of clandestine or covert operations, called tradecraft by CIA, that it is unnecessary to elaborate here. Allen Dulles' *The Craft of Intelligence* (1963) and *The Secret Surrender* (1966) give some of the flavor of the authentic world of undercover operations. Most books on the subject of intelligence operations are garbage.

The learning process continued after I finished with training courses and began on-the-job training in Taiwan. My station was a large one and, mostly through liaison with our Chinese hosts, we collected intelligence in every conceivable way. I inherited a fleet of boats and airplanes that supported agent penetrations and airdrops and also collected the most sophisticated kinds of electronic signals and messages. As in England in my tour as liaison officer, I came to appreciate the enormous help that a reliable ally can give the United States in its intelligence collection. There was excellent cooperation with the authorities in the Republic of China, in part, I believe, because I was keenly interested in discovering all I could about Asia, quite apart from conducting intelligence operations.

## The Quemoy Crisis, August 1958

The period of my tour, at the end of the 1950s, turned out to be exciting. By the time I had got my feet on the ground the war in the Taiwan Straits for the islands of Quemoy and Matsu began—in August 1958. These very small islands are quite close to the mainland, and the Chinese regime in Peking began shelling them massively in an effort to crush the sizable Chinese Nationalist forces there. They undoubtedly also hoped to destroy morale in Taiwan, enabling them to take it over either by military force, political intrigue, or a mixture of both. I quickly found that Washington is an insatiable consumer of intelligence when a crisis occurs. There was a U.S. outpost on Quemoy, from which you could see the mainland quite clearly through binoculars, and it provided daily reports on the spirits of the Nationalist forces then under fire. As the senior U.S. intelligence officer in Taipei, I organized a small interagency committee of intelligence unit chiefs to maximize the productiveness of all reporting assets, and I began regular briefing of Ambassador Everett Drumright, with whom I had close rapport and from whom I received generous support throughout my tour. A CIA station chief has to be of real service to the Ambassador, the senior Embassy officers, and the various military components present in the area; in this way he can hope to obtain the understanding and cooperation he needs from them.

Somewhat to my chagrin, I found that my resolution to be a silent, secret operations officer was useless; as soon as hostilities broke out I received a series of high priority messages from Washington demanding "soonest" my analysis of the strategic nature of the conflict and my estimate of what the outcome would be. Allen Dulles, in a personal message, said he wanted a daily report to show the Secretary of State, giving the views of his own man in Taipei. This procedure in many areas has caused friction between the station chief and the local ambassador; however, I showed all my reports to Drumright and encouraged other U.S. intelligence units to send in their own views if they wanted to. It is not always easy to get a group of U.S. intelligence units to work in reasonable harmony under the Ambassador's authority. The key to success is in drawing on Headquarters and local CIA resources to help colleagues in their own work, thus creating a friendly climate for carrying out essential CIA tasks.

With some misgivings I tried out my new-found area expertise by making precise estimates of the staying power of the troops on Quemoy—more favorable estimates than most—and analyzing the Asian scene to suggest that it was in the interest of the United States to aid in the defense of Quemoy with logistic and noncombat military support so as to forestall a wider war. My own belief is that the successful defense of Quemoy by Chinese Nationalist forces, with an assist from the U.S. military advisers, provided the single decisive divergence of interests between the militant Mao regime and the more prudent Soviet Politburo that catalyzed all the other factors to produce the Sino-Soviet rift. If so, it was one of the most significant international events of the whole post-World War II era.

However that may be, Quemoy was defended, Chinese Communist Defense Minister Peng Te-huai was disgraced and later denounced as a traitor, and the government of Generalissimo Chiang Kai-shek on Taiwan gathered strength and morale from the episode. Mao kept an enormous number of troops along the coast opposite Taiwan for a long time but never again directly attacked Chiang's forces. I have a souvenir of the battle of Quemoy, a breech plate from an armor-piercing 153 mm shell that went through a bunker wall on the first day of the battle, throwing up fragments that scratched the face of the Defense Minister, Dr. Yu Ta-wei, who picked it up and later gave it to me. The interesting fact about the shell fragment, as Dr. Yu pointed out, is that it carried markings in the cyrillic alphabet indicating it had been made in Russia in 1941. The tides of international policies that brought this Soviet shell around the world to Quemoy, and thence to my desk, suggest the complexities that modern intelligence services have to unravel. Munitions markings is one of the ways by which quantitative and qualitative estimates of military weapons production are made.

## Station Operations

There is no need to describe my own station's operations in any detail nor would I be willing to do so lest still valuable sources and methods be exposed. It is important, however, to emphasize how little we knew about mainland China—in fact how little we know even now. A white face cannot get lost in a sea of Asian people, particularly not when the target territory is organized on rigid police state lines. For a time we sent off brave Chinese volunteers who were willing to be parachuted into remote areas of the mainland or infiltrated at night by rubber boats on uninhabited coastlines in an attempt to hide with old friends or family while they looked for information we wanted. These were heroic undertakings, some involving long flights in special aircraft over the Himalayas and up into northwest China, where we knew the USSR had built an atomic bomb test site and, we thought, was building a guided missile test range well out beyond the big uranium processing plant we knew the USSR had constructed in Lanchow.

The survivability of these agents was limited and we gradually turned to other intelligence techniques: the occasional traveler, the foreign diplomat, and, above all, the electronic and photographic collection platforms. It is a very stressful experience to sit in a radio shack perched on the high ground above Taipei, listening for clandestine radio signals from teams in Sinkiang; it was heartbreaking when after a time they came through with the prearranged coded signal that indicated the radio operator had been captured. Occasionally a useful item of information would get back from these sources, but they were usually low-level operations and scarcely cost-effective efforts.

By the end of the 1950s we had come to rely mostly on airplanes and intercepted electronic signals. We provided equipment to specially trained Chinese fliers and radio operators who took the terrible risks of overflying the mainland at low levels to record signals on the Chinese Communist radar and military weapons that were trying to shoot down our aircraft. These missions also caused some tense moments in the radio shack, but the electronic signals collection take was rich.

After the CIA's U-2 was shot down in the USSR in May 1960, we set in motion an arrangement for furnishing U-2s to the Republic of China Air Force and training their best pilots to fly them over the mainland, which was then defended with only a few of the S-2 missiles that had downed Powers' aircraft. We did not get approval until I went back personally to argue the case that we needed precise information on China's advanced weapons program in the remote northwest and probably had a few years of impunity in which to fly the U-2s. The Republic of China was delighted to take full responsibility, asking only for the equipment, and they already had splendid pilots willing to volunteer for such duty.

It surely can do no harm now to say that for a short period, before satellite photography became plentiful enough to cover Chinese targets as well as Soviet ones, most of our knowledge about Chinese Communist advanced weapons came from pictures taken by some of the bravest reconnaissance pilots I have ever known. One early mission, lasting many hours, brought back beautiful pictures of the missile test range everyone wanted to know about—demonstrating that Sino-Soviet work on very advanced technology had been going on but had been brought virtually to a standstill after the evacuation of Soviet technicians. These pictures were worth millions of dollars to us at the time, and our country owes a debt of gratitude to the air units that made such intelligence coups possible. Many of the fliers lost their lives on flights over the mainland, but when they got in trouble the Chinese pilots destroyed their airplanes and themselves rather than let the Communists learn anything from their capture.

One minor coup of the Taipei station while I was there was to participate with the Chinese Nationalists in the defection of a Chinese Communist Air Force pilot complete with MIG-15, the obsolete Soviet fighter plane that most mainland air units then flew. We had been dropping leaflets over the mainland for some time offering substantial rewards in gold for defectors who came out with military equipment or information. One day a young man who had been only a child when Mao's regime took power slipped away from his squadron when it flew through a cloud bank and headed east for Taiwan. He landed safely and settled down to live in the Republic of China with his reward. He was a modest young officer who said had never believed much of the Communist propaganda because he knew from his family that Mao's "great leap forward" was a failure and that food had been very short since 1960. He told us he had wanted to escape for a long time, but the aircraft he had flown never had enough fuel to reach Taiwan until this occasion, when a change of base was scheduled. The pilots did not have maps showing where Taiwan was, but he took a chance on finding it once he left the coast. His stories of the status of morale and training in the air force were good intelligence material and, despite its antiquity, the MIG-15 supplied some useful technical data.

One of my biggest headaches in Taiwan was keeping a weather eye on the main component of CIA's first established proprietary companies—the headquarters of the interlocking set of aviation enterprises that included Air America, Civil Air Transport (CAT), and Air Asia. The companies were built around the fleet of C-46 and C-47 cargo aircraft that were flown to Taiwan with the Chinese Nationalists. The fleet was gradually taken over financially by CIA to keep the pilots and aircraft available for clandestine or covert missions when these were needed. A fleet of DC-4s and DC-6s, the best transport aircraft of the pre-jet age, was gradually acquired, and eventually there were some Boeing 727s and one Convair 880.

One of the main tasks of the fleet was dropping supplies to the large Chinese Nationalist armies that fought on against the Communists in southwest China for a number of years before settling down semi-permanently in the wild China-Burma-Thailand border area. There some of them remain even now despite the discontinuation of U.S. support many years ago and the air evacuation of those willing to leave their jungle stronghold and settle down in Taiwan.

The CAT-Air America pilots and crews were true soldiers of fortune and accepted enormous risks on long, clandestine missions over hostile territory, such as flying missions under fire to make parachute drops at Dien Bien Phu in Vietnam for the French. These CIA-supported aviation companies had such a quantity of experienced ground and flight personnel that the U.S. Air Force eagerly contracted with them for transport services throughout the Far East.

Most valuable among the air proprietary assets in Taiwan was a maintenance and repair shop, originally housed in an old navy landing craft brought over from mainland China in 1949. With its well-trained Chinese repair crews it provided the best maintenance service anywhere in the Far East and was a regular money-maker, especially when hostilities in Vietnam picked up in the 1960s. These earnings were mainly used to offset losses in other categories of air activities. Whenever net profits accrued for the whole complex, the money was pumped back into the U.S. Air Force (in lieu of contract renegotiations) or to the U.S. Treasury.

This vast endeavor was so large that it had to be run from Headquarters, mainly under the eye of Larry Houston, the CIA's General Counsel. The local station chief was mainly useful as a channel for secret instructions to employees of the companies. I also occasionally had to intervene quietly to smooth out personnel employment policy problems, tax difficulties, and relations with various Chinese organizations that did not know about the U.S. connection. Eventually the Republic of China established its own passenger airline and this whole net was phased out—although it took the end of the Vietnam war in 1975 to bring about the last stage of the liquidation.

## Covert Action

One of the hardest things for outsiders to believe about the CIA covert action programs is that only a few are big, such as Radio Free Europe or the CAT-Air America complex, and even fewer are big paramilitary projects. Most covert action projects are small scale—getting pro-U.S. books printed or anti-USSR articles published in newspapers, or providing funds and briefings to youth and labor representatives attending international meetings likely to be exploited by professional Communist "agitprop" officials. These projects have few risks attached and often involve only small sums of money. Most would be hard to construe as illegal, let alone immoral. To provide an example of the more normal kind of covert action that CIA undertakes almost daily I can cite one project initiated in Taiwan during my tour there.

The Republic of China has long been an outstanding example of the successful use of U.S. economic assistance, especially in the field of agriculture. Its early land reform program, involving giving ownership of the land to the actual tillers and providing them with technical guidance on modern farming methods, is justly famous in developing countries. The use of miracle seeds and chemical fertilizers made Taiwan an economic showcase. Around 1960 or so, Washington came up with the idea of helping the Chinese Nationalists set up food-growing demonstration projects in Africa, the Mideast, and Latin America, where their techniques and their personnel were suited to the task of helping primitive agricultural societies.

Not only would this project be a genuine economic aid program and build prestige and political contacts for the Republic of China, it would also provide a demonstration of what Chinese people in a free enterprise system could accomplish at the very moment Mao's agricultural leap forward was producing famine on the mainland. This was the kind of imaginative political propaganda action that supported both U.S. policies and U.S. principles. The role of the CIA was to use its contacts in the prospective countries that would receive Chinese economic aid to explain the mutual benefits and get the enterprise going. It could have been an overt program except for the fact that acknowledged U.S. sponsorship would have caused some governments to shy away from it, and might have embrassed the Republic of China by making it appear it was forced to do the job by the United States.

By the time this project came along I had learned that the best way to obtain cooperation from Chinese officials was in quiet, off-the-record talks. This is good procedure in any country. In the Orient, where "face" is crucial, it is of paramount importance. At the time in Taiwan, as is still true today, the most farsighted political leader was Chiang Ching-kuo, the son of President Chiang Kai-shek; he has held an astonishing variety of posts in government and is now President of the Republic of China, but when I was in Taipei he had a general supervisory responsibility for most intelligence programs. I found that if an honest explanation of the mutual benefits of a program could be given privately to Chiang he would usually agree because of the emphasis he and his father both put on being a close and loyal ally of the United States. If he concurred, it was easy then to repeat the process with the appropriate key officials.

In this case, as in many others, Ching-kuo grasped the concept immediately and saw the benefits, as did Foreign Office and Agriculture policy officials. The program was organized by the Chinese with a minimum of help from the United States. In some regions it is still working and everyone has profited.

Partly because of successes like this one, the CIA continued to be pressed—and in some cases to press—for more and more ambitious covert action projects. One project involving support to Tibetan tribesmen resisting Chinese Communist control of their homeland resulted in a bonanza of valuable substantive intelligence. Peking eventually succeeded in establishing control of that remote mountain domain, but guerrilla resistance forces, on one occasion, recovered a mail sack full of secret Chinese papers reflecting on the poor state of morale in mainland China after the failure of the attack on Quemoy and the collapse of Mao's grandiose economic "great leap." These papers were eventually translated and released for use by scholars, who welcomed them greatly because of the scarcity of such evidence about conditions on the mainland; they never knew that the haul of documents was an accidental by-product of a paramilitary operation.

## The Indonesian Operation

The big CIA paramilitary project of the late 1950s was the effort to help a group of Indonesians overthrow their President, Sukarno. This case is the only major paramilitary undertaking I know of where covert action enthusiasts in the CIA took the initiative. Sukarno had proven increasingly dictatorial and inclined to favor both the huge Indonesian Communist Party and its sponsors in Peking. If the opposition forces had been able to gain control, Indonesia would have been spared much atrocious political and economic mismanagement by the arbitrary Sukarno and might have been spared the bloodbaths that occurred in the mid-1960s when the Indonesian Communists murdered many of the politically conservative leaders and tried to seize total control, an attempt that resulted in the widespread massacre of the Communists themselves. Still, the historical fact is that the CIA in 1958, with full authorization by the Eisenhower Administration, provided money and arms to the Indonesian rebels and the rebels failed.

A fundamental weakness in paramilitary covert action surfaced in this 1958 episode, although the lesson was not clearly perceived. The CIA aid followed the Guatemala example in that planes, in this case B-26s, flown by American pilots on contract to the CIA, began to make harassing raids intended to frighten Sukarno's military supporters into deserting him. They did not succeed, although the B-26 campaign was really too short-lived to be fully tested. One of the planes was shot down, and a pilot was captured and imprisoned. His identity was known to the Indonesians and his connection was traceable to CIA. The CIA immediately lost its enthusiasm for the venture; the State Department and White House realized their denials of U.S. responsibility would no longer be plausible as covert action required they must be. The rebellion was allowed to collapse. It was an ignominious failure in which Sukarno's power and his dislike of the United States were both reinforced.

The weak point in covert paramilitary action is that a single misfortune that reveals the CIA's connection makes it necessary for the United States either to abandon the cause completely or convert to a policy of overt military intervention. Because such paramilitary operations are generally kept secret for political reasons, when the CIA's cover is blown the usual U.S. response is to withdraw, leaving behind the friendly elements who had entrusted their lives to the U.S. enterprise. My station's role in the Indonesian fiasco was only indirect support, but I still remember my sorrow when our policy shifted from aiding the rebellion to placating Sukarno in order to obtain the release of our flier. The authorities in Washington evidently did not believe they could risk the political reaction to an exposure of their involvement; the operation showed how hard it was for a democratic society to play a secret paramilitary role in a civil war, regardless of what the political aims might be. Feasibility is a test that has to be rigidly applied in the planning phase of such operations.

## Entering the Kennedy Era

By the end of the Eisenhower Administration the CIA had reached a mature stage of development in collection, analysis, and covert action along lines advocated by Allen Dulles. In fact Dulles had so much made himself into the image of U.S. intelligence, and the CIA's activities insofar as they were known outside the agency were so fully accepted by officialdom and the public, that one of President Kennedy's first decisions after his election was to keep Allen Dulles at the helm at the CIA. Dulles' continuation in office largely reflected the good press the CIA enjoyed at the time and Eisenhower's confidence in his intelligence chief.

Eisenhower had been repeatedly pressed, however, to restrain Dulles from his over-involvement in clandestine operations and urge him to spend more time on coordination of interagency programs, budgets, and analytic findings. The usual recommendation was for a deputy to "run the CIA," while the DCI concentrated on broader issues. Eisenhower wisely recognized that Dulles was simply incapable of playing such a role.

Dulles hated bureaucratic wrangling and he loved clandestine operations. In order to maintain harmonious relations with the military agencies, Dulles kept Air Force General Cabell as his Deputy throughout his tenure. It was obvious that the intricate and detailed management of operations could not be turned over to Cabell, a nonprofessional. Instead Dulles worked directly with his DDP, first Wisner and, after Wisner's health broke down in the late 1950s, Dick Bissell, in managing covert action. In running clandestine collection, which did not usually present the same kind of policy difficulties or responsibilities, Dulles worked directly with Chief of Operations Dick Helms, or with the regional division chiefs, the senior satraps of the operations world who supervised the overseas stations.

In responding to criticisms of this managerial pattern, Eisenhower once said: "I'm not going to be able to change Allen ... I'd rather have Allen as my chief intelligence officer with his limitations than anyone else I know."[1] This judgment reflected Eisenhower's recognition that people determine patterns of bureaucratic behavior much more than directives and organization charts control people. He also was recognizing two fundamental facts: a President of the United States must have confidence in his intelligence chief, and there have been very few intelligence officers with broad understanding and experience from which to choose. Hence Kennedy took over a functionally and structurally mature CIA organized and operated in a pattern of behavior compatible with the instinct of Allen Dulles. It continued to look much like the CIA of Bedell Smith, and it continued to emphasize most strongly its covert action. More than half of the budget continued in this period and down into the second half of the 1960s to go to the DDP for clandestine and covert operations, not counting the substantial sums spent by the administrative office on supporting the clandestine services.[2] The organizational chart of Dulles' CIA at the beginning of the Kennedy Administration looked like the chart on p. 210.

## The Bay of Pigs and Assassination Planning

A great deal of documentation has been made public recently on the CIA operations against Fidel Castro's Cuba, as well as much testimony, often conflicting, by senior U.S. officials concerning efforts to get rid of Castro.[3] For this reason I intended to discuss only the highlights and the basic meaning of this first great disaster to befall the CIA at the end of the Allen Dulles era. I was stationed in the Far East at the time and, happily, was not involved with it. Still, I was aware of the broad outlines of what was going on and have learned a great deal more after the event.

In a sense, the Bay of Pigs invasion of 1961 represented the logical culmination of the trend toward increasing U.S. reliance on paramilitary operations conducted covertly by the CIA on the theory that the United States could plausibly deny responsibility for this kind of secret support to U.S. policy. The record is clear that both Eisenhower and Kennedy found the idea of a

Soviet-oriented Communist dictatorship close to U.S. territory extremely repugnant. After due deliberation, the Eisenhower administration in 1960 set up a CIA-run program for training hundreds of highly motivated anti-Castro Cuban refugees in guerrilla warfare. Vice President Nixon was a strong proponent of an active program to topple the Castro regime and Eisenhower, upon the advice of the NSC subcommittee responsible for reviewing covert action schemes, approved the Cuban paramilitary training project as a contingency plan—leaving its execution to be decided upon early in the new administration.

The CIA had advocated the "elimination of Fidel Castro" as early as December 1959, and the matter was discussed at Special Group meetings in January and March of 1960. At an NSC meeting on March 10, 1960 terminology was used suggesting that the assassination of Castro, his brother Raul, and Che Guevara was at least theoretically considered.[4] The idea of guerrilla operations was abandoned in November 1960. The anti-Castro Cubans were in fact organized into a Brigade that went into intensive preparations for an invasion by about 1,400 armed men in the Bay of Pigs landing area on Cuba's southwest coast. Allen Dulles endorsed the project repeatedly and the JCS concurred in it.

The project was the exclusive property of the DDP, with an assist from the Support Directorate, specifically from the Security Office Chief. Bob Amory, the DDI, was never officially consulted about the pros and cons of the Bay of Pigs landing and all estimates of probable success of the project were made by the DDP operators themselves, a remarkably unsound procedure. Dick Bissell, the DDP, and his covert action chief assistant Tracy Barnes, managed the project in Washington and issued detailed orders to the field echelons. The instructions to move against Castro were so explicit and the general atmosphere of urgency was so palpable that two very responsible officers, Bissell and longtime Chief of Security Sheffield Edwards, thought they had been authorized to plan Castro's assassination. Although it was an unprecedented act for the CIA, once the assumption was made that it was essential to get rid of Castro by assassination, it was not illogical to try to do it through the Mafia, since its former Havana gambling empire

# Central Intelligence Agency
# 1961

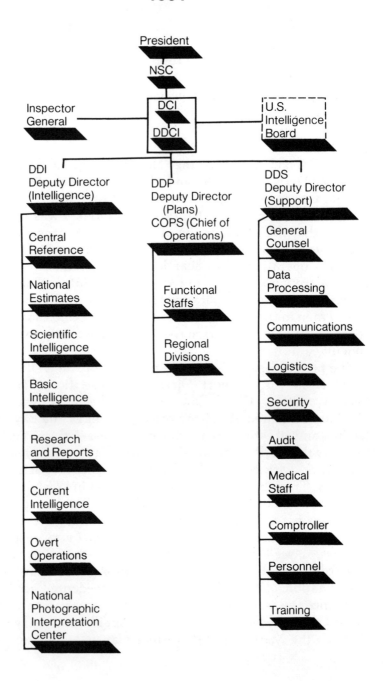

*The CIA in High Gear*

gave them some contacts to work with and since a gangland killing would be unlikely to be attributed to the U.S. Government. Whether President Eisenhower or Dulles or President Kennedy had actually intended to authorize Castro's murder is simply not clear from the records. I did not know anything about this assassination planning, although I clearly recall the animus against Castro manifested in every discussion of Cuba in this period at every level of government.

The CIA's becoming engaged in planning assassinations was not a momentary aberration on the part of the handful of men who were involved. In January 1961, when preparations for the Cuban Brigade were at a peak, Bissell ordered William Harvey, a veteran station chief, to set up a "standby capability" for what was called euphemistically "Executive Action," by which was plainly meant a capability for assassination of foreign leaders as a "last resort."[5] Harvey was a colorful figure, a former FBI man who carried a pistol at all times when posted abroad, something unique among the CIA officers. I am sure he believed that it was patriotic, even moral, to kill a foreign ruler when ordered to do so by his superiors for reasons of U.S. security. Many of the romantic so-called "cowboy" types of covert action officers would have accepted this proposition, and in 1960-1961 many officials outside the CIA would have subscribed to it as well. In any event, the responsible officers in the CIA, Harvey and Bissell, were convinced at the time that the White House had orally urged the creation of an assassination planning capability as a contingency precaution. The written record does not clearly demonstrate this to be either true or untrue.

My trips to Headquarters had become more frequent the longer I was stationed in Taiwan because I had become entangled in more and more projects of interest to the State Department as well as to the Defense Department, which was enthusiastic about signals and photo collection programs. As the new decade started off with a new President, I discovered that McGeorge Bundy and Arthur Schlesinger, Jr., my Harvard Society of Fellows contemporaries, were influential men in the White House and I visited them when I was in Washington to talk about China, Japan, and Southeast Asia.

Among my friends in Washington in the spring of 1961, Cuba was the topic of the day. In my recollection nobody in either the

Eisenhower or Kennedy Administrations doubted that it was crucial for strategic and domestic reasons to "get rid" of Castro. Arthur Schlesinger, Jr. tried to convince me and others that the Bay of Pigs operation was unwise because word of it had got around among journalists so widely that the official U.S. role could not be plausibly denied. In this he proved to be absolutely right. The prevailing mood, however, was that forceful action was essential; the untested, new, youthful Kennedy crowd felt very strongly that the United States had to show its dedication to political liberties and its firm opposition to the "wars of national liberation" that Khrushchev had declared in January 1961 to be the wave of the future.

My feeling is that Bissell, if he erred, made the mistake of being too logical. He had an elegant analytical style of reasoning, more suited to the world of economics or law than clandestine operations.* I heard Bissell describe and advocate the project for the Cuban refugee invasion, anticipating that success would be its own moral justification in view of Castro's iniquities. I can imagine Dick Bissell saying to himself, although he never mentioned it in my hearing, that it would be absurd to be willing to invade Cuba with 1,400 soldiers with certain prospects for numerous casualties and be unwilling to allow — indeed help—one of the Cubans to assassinate Castro, an act that might make the invasion unnecessary. Bissell certainly believed in the Bay of Pigs operation and knew that it had been set in motion by one (Republican) President and approved for execution by another (Democratic) President. He felt that the pressure to find means of "getting rid of Castro" was intense from both Eisenhower and Kennedy Administration officials.[6]

I suspect Dick Helms, who managed to maintain some personal distance from the Bay of Pigs project although he was aware of the same Presidential pressures, had the best retrospective feel for the nature of Presidential authorization of the various abortive assassination attempts. He agreed with Senator Charles Mathias (in 1975) that the situation was like Becket's murder in Canterbury cathedral when the King

---

*In 1969 Bissell gave a typically lucid, reasoned, thoughtful description of covert operations off-the-record to the New York Council on Foreign Relations. It appears, without his approval I am sure, as an appendix to Victor Marchetti's and John Marks' *The CIA and the Cult of Intelligence* (1974).

needed only to say "who will rid me of this man?" for the deed to be done. As Helms put it, the CIA operations chiefs like himself and Bissell felt that they were "hired out to keep those things," i.e., assassinations, "out of the Oval Office," but agreed that "some spark had been transmitted" from White House officials indicating that if Castro "disappeared from the scene they would not have been unhappy."[7]

I can confirm by my own general recollections of the climate of opinion in Washington in 1960, 1961, and 1962 that there was almost an obsession with Cuba on the part of policymakers and that the assassination of Castro by a Cuban might have been viewed as not very different in the benefits that would have accrued from the assassination of Hitler in 1944. The climate has changed, but elementary justice requires recognition of the fact that most Americans believe they were engaged in an undeclared war on many fronts to prevent the spread of dictatorial police states and that the consolidation of Castro's pro-Soviet rule in Cuba was the first breach in the wall of containment for more than 10 years.

The truth is that the CIA's experimentation with assassination was so out of the ordinary that none of the wild schemes developed by the senior DDP officials and the CIA technicians succeeded. No one was assassinated. The fact that assassination was planned and attempted shows more about the temper of the times than it does about the CIA.* It is highly questionable whether it is right in any circumstances for the leaders of a democratic society deliberately to assist assassination attempts against foreign leaders. Certainly our open society is more vulnerable to violence of this kind than are police states.

Certainly it is a disgrace that the CIA became involved in furtive moves to spark assassinations in the early 1960s. Such extreme measures should never be taken without explicit accountability; in all its actions the CIA must be only an instrument of policy and should not act independently. In the case of covert action of a political nature, even one that most Americans would be likely to favor it they knew about it, an

---

*The only other case where there is solid evidence of a CIA assasination effort was that of Lumumba in the Congo; it also was not successful. For discussions of these attempts see the Senate Select Committee's interim report on *Alleged Assassination Plots Involving Foreign Leaders*, published in November 1975.

inherently repugnant act like assassination should never be attempted unless duly constituted political authority is explicitly committed to some specific justification of the purpose that might override normal moral opposition to the means.

The Cuban Brigade landing at the Bay of Pigs, like the associated assassination planning, was a dismal failure. Here too, there was a vagueness about the extent of what was being approved rather than any doubt that the invasion itself was authorized. As Kennedy said later, there was plenty of blame to go around and many people shared in it. The truth is that as the project evolved it turned into an outright military operation with only the thinnest fiction that the United States was not responsible. It would have been much better, it is now easy to see, if the President had either canceled the operation despite all the security, political, and technical troubles that would have ensued, or approved sufficient U.S. backup support—especially air combat support—to make the operation a success. The Kennedy Administration was too inexperienced and the CIA involvement too far advanced for any penetrating review of the options to take place. The operation was discussed again and again and very formally approved at an NSC meeting April 4, 1961, with all the appropriate policy officials present. The President was in the chair, Dean Rusk and others from State, Robert McNamara and Paul Nitze from Defense, and several others including General Lyman Lemnitzer, Chairman of the JCS, William J. Fulbright of the Senate Foreign Relations Committee, and White House Assistant Arthur Schlesinger, Jr. were present. Dulles and Bissell described the landing plan and recommended it. Every man had an opportunity to speak. According to most accounts no one opposed the plans.[8] It is far from clear that all knew exactly what they were approving, a phenomenon not too unlikely in the rarefied atmosphere of the NSC meeting. As Kennedy later said, "The advice of every member of the Executive Branch brought in to advise was unanimous—and the advice was wrong."[9]

The Bay of Pigs invasion took place April 17 without having eliminated all of Castro's embryonic jet fighter force in advance, as had been planned and attempted. This fatal mistake was compounded by other military misadventures that could easily have been overcome with the full might of the U.S. armed forces behind the effort, but this support was denied. The inherent weakness of a major military battle being fought with only limited, covert U.S. support resulted in a dismal failure, despite the heroism of the fighting force and the covert supporting staff. The concept was faulty. The CIA had let itself be led into a big paramilitary covert operation without facing up to the hazards of trying to maintain secrecy or reckoning realistically the costs and alternatives in the event of failure.

Kennedy is said initially to have wanted to shatter the CIA into bits, but recognized that he had ultimate responsibility. He told reporters "victory has one hundred fathers and defeat is an orphan."[10] He accepted the blame but in future cases asked tough questions of the CIA, the JCS, and other agencies. Eventually he reached a clearer understanding of the CIA's capabilities and its inherent limitations than any President before or since. He did not despair as he surveyed the wreckage of his Cuban policy. He vowed in a public speech delivered April 20, 1961, "to intensify our efforts for a struggle in many ways more difficult than war, where disappointments will often accompany us," and to take serious notice of "the menace of external Communist intervention and domination in Cuba," facing up to "a relentless struggle in every corner of the globe that goes far beyond the clash of armies..."[11] Because of his views about the kind of world around him, Kennedy never really penalized the CIA; he merely set out to use it more effectively than before.

## The McCone Period

After a decent interval, to all appearances without vindictive feelings toward either Dulles or Bissell, Kennedy set out to restructure the high command at the CIA. For a brief period during 1962 and 1963 the CIA operated at its peak performance level in the way that its functional responsibilities called for, with greater emphasis on intelligence analysis and estimates and an attempt at greater circumspection and tighter control in covert action. The key to success was Kennedy's appointment of a new Director of Central Intelligence, John A. McCone, in November 1961. It was a bold move by Kennedy to pick McCone, an active Republican and a businessman turned government administrator, rather than someone with experience in intelligence. It turned out well.

The CIA needed a man with personal political stature to represent it at the highest levels in the White House and in Congress, especially in the dark days after the Bay of Pigs. McCone was an engineer who had made a fortune in construction and shipbuilding enterprises. He was well acquainted in private industry and, in addition, had earned respect as a public servant by working first as Under Secretary of the Air Force and later as Chairman of the Atomic Energy Commission. He had great energy and—above all—the inquiring, skeptical turn of mind of the good intelligence officers. He is the only DCI who ever took his role of providing substantive intelligence analysis and estimates to the President as his first priority job, and the only one who considered his duties as coordinating supervisor of the whole intelligence community to be a more important responsibility than the CIA's own clandestine and covert programs. Kennedy gave him a letter of instructions on January 16, 1962, designating him as the "government's principal foreign intelligence officer" with a charge to "assure the proper coordination, correlation, and evaluation of intelligence from all sources and its prompt dissemination . . . ." It also tasked him with "coordination and effective guidance of the total U.S. foreign intelligence effort."[12]

McCone tried to live up to this heavy responsibility and came closer to discharging it than anyone else. He hated being called a "spymaster," as he often was in press comments echoing the Dulles tradition. In collection efforts he took primary interest in the technical programs, especially the rapidly expanding satellite photo systems. Covert actions were small in scale and quietly carried out in this period and agent collection was recognized as a useful but intricate job best left to Dick Helms and his professional staff, provided they could answer McCone's occasional barrage of questions.

McCone spent by far the greatest part of his time on analytical intelligence, which he found endlessly fascinating, and management of all intelligence agency resources. His sharp, penetrating queries kept everyone in the CIA on his toes, and he had little patience with imprecision, inefficiency, or slowness in producing results. He demanded instant, full briefings on anything that caught his attention, and he absorbed more from complex briefings than any senior official I have ever worked with. He always did his homework, was anxious to learn, and, although strongminded, willing to adjust his opinions in the light of evidence and reasoned judgment.

In the agency his attitude was reflected in a widely repeated, true story: When a staff officer looked at a memo from McCone requesting a vast amount of information, he said in dismay, "I suppose you want it all tomorrow." Without blinking, McCone replied, "Not tomorrow, today—if I wanted it tomorrow, I would ask for it tomorrow." Actually he was reasonable about deadlines, but he demanded a lot of work, he delegated a lot of responsibility, and he expected prompt, full support from his deputies.

McCone took his time in making his key appointments. He chose entirely from the professional ranks, after checking carefully on careers and reputations. The high command of the agency by early 1962 was laid out as diagramed on the following page.

In addition, the officers relied upon a great deal by McCone were John Bross, an old DDP operator who skillfully and patiently handled interagency coordination problems, Lyman B. Kirkpatrick Jr., who played his managerial role as Executive Director very diligently, General Counsel Larry Houston, Sherman Kent of the DDI's Office of National Estimates, and Desmond Fitzgerald, who was the senior spokesman of the still numerous covert action specialists.*

McCone liked to get his principal subordinates together at 9 a.m. every day to listen to a short review of current intelligence and any pressing business of the day, then to acquaint us with his activities, ideas, and instructions. He was deadly serious most of the time, but he recounted his adventures at the White House level in detail with great skill, which frequently occasioned a little humor. He enjoyed the laughs if they did not

---

*One of this group, Lyman Kirkpatrick, has become the principal academic expositor of the organization and functions of U.S. intelligence. He left CIA in 1965 to take a position as professor at Brown University. In addition to teaching about the intelligence profession, he has written two solid books describing CIA and other intelligence agencies: *The Real CIA* (1968) and *The US Intelligence Community* (1973).

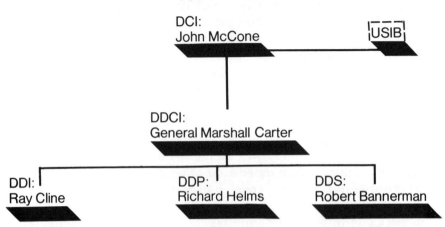

get in the way of dispatching the day's business. As I got to know him better, I learned that he had a warm and sentimental side beneath the stern Scots exterior, although it surfaced only from time to time and usually when we were away from the daily grind at an NSC meeting or on a foreign trip.

I had first met McCone in the Philippines at a Far East station chiefs' meeting convened by Bissell, still DDP until February 1962. I explained the rather complex set of operations then underway in Taipei and listened to the gossip about Headquarters. Shortly afterwards, in March 1962 as I recall, McCone called me to Washington to discuss Chinese policy problems and the management of the Directorate of Intelligence, a job that he offered to me before I returned to Taiwan. I made seven round trips across the Pacific in the next 11 weeks while I was disengaging from the Taipei station and picking up responsibility as DDI, and settled down happily as DDI at Bob Amory's desk on the seventh floor of the brand new Headquarters Building overlooking the Potomac in June of that year.

One compact I made with McCone was that he would consult me on DPP projects where an analytical DDI opinion might be helpful. As far as I know he observed this understanding with scrupulous care. The only important thing the DDP became involved in during that period that I did not know of was the continued planning of the assassination of Castro. It is hard for me to understand how this could have happened without McCone's being told, as he clearly was not until August 1963.[13]

McCone at all times expressed total disapproval of consideration of assassination as a CIA covert action, opposing it on both personal moral and political grounds. He never mentioned to me that the CIA had been involved in such planning, although he brought me thoroughly into his thinking on Operation MONGOOSE, the economic warfare and sabotage program approved by President Kennedy on November 30, 1961 and monitored personally by Robert F. Kennedy as a member of the Special Group (Augmented).[14] Other covert action projects were usually referred to the regular Special Group (McGeorge Bundy, Alexis Johnson of State, Roswell Gilpatric, Under Secretary of Defense, and the Chairman of the JCS), which was renamed the 303 Committee, replacing Eisenhower's 5412 Group.

McCone and I always spoke of MONGOOSE as a covert pressure program of economic harassment and individual acts of sabotage of factories or transportation—pretty strong stuff—but never explicitly involving assassination. When the subject came up at an August 10, 1962 Special Group (Augmented) meeting, McCone vigorously opposed it. The Special Group (Augmented) was disbanded after the Cuba missile crisis of October 1962, the anti-Castro caper gradually lost its steam, and CIA turned to more congenial tasks.

## Close-in Analytical Work with the White House

This sorry story of operational confusion and misguided covert efforts in the aftermath of the Bay of Pigs was obscured at the time by the fact that in other ways the CIA was working well under McCone and had won its way back into the good graces of the President. A main factor in restoring the CIA to a place of prestige and active participation in the policy process was the services it performed during the Cuba missile crisis of 1962. Largely through the good offices of McGeorge Bundy, whom I saw two or three times a week, the Directorate of Intelligence became directly engaged in trying to answer the questions confronting the President on strategic policy issues. McCone encouraged me to work as closely with the White House as possible, keeping him informed.

The story of the missile crisis is well known and I shall not repeat it.* The main thing to note is that the CIA coordinated a comprehensive interagency intelligence collection and analysis program aimed at discovering what kind of military weapons the USSR was sending to Castro in the summer and fall of 1962. The analysts did not believe Khrushchev would be so foolish as to send nuclear weapons to Cuba, where U.S. conventional military superiority gave Kennedy the upper hand. Khrushchev and his advisers badly miscalculated, thinking either that U.S. intelligence would not discover the missiles until they were installed, bringing the United States under a nuclear threat of considerable size, or that Kennedy would simply not have the nerve to face up to the challenge in an effective way. At the CIA, McCone was alone in believing that missiles were being installed, but the Agency never stopped its effort to find the facts, succeeding in doing so when a U-2 flew right over a medium-range missile site being constructed at San Cristobal near Havana on October 14, 1962.

The photo experts alerted me as to what they had found late in the afternoon of Monday, October 15, and my missile experts assured me we were seeing a major investment in nuclear missiles that would double the number of nuclear warheads the USSR could fire on the United States.

The first notice that the crisis was on went to Bundy at the NSC via a phone call from me on the evening of October 15. Simultaneously I insured that General Carter, Acting Director of Central Intelligence on that day in John McCone's absence, would alert all the intelligence and policy chiefs in the Pentagon that evening. My final call was to Roger Hilsman, the State Intelligence Bureau Chief, to inform him of the evidence of offensive missiles in Cuba and to ask him to tell Secretary Dean Rusk, which he did that same evening. The next day, October 16, I went with a few staff officers to show the photographs to McGeorge Bundy, Robert Kennedy, and a few other senior officials, and Bundy took them to the President.

An NSC group met formally later in the morning and subsequently constituted itself as the EXCOM (Executive

---

*A full account can be read in Graham T. Allison, *Essence of Decision* (1971), and Herbert Dinerstein, *The Making of a Missile Crisis: October 1962* (1976).

Committee of the NSC) that met to advise the President throughout the "Thirteen Days" in October described in Bobby Kennedy's book of that title. This intelligence performance was a unique example of interagency coordination and rapid response to the requirement for accurate intelligence on a crucial strategic issue. We got the critical evidence in time for the President to digest it in private, with only his closet advisers aware of what we had found. This is a luxury that permits policymakers to examine options thoroughly, ready their moves in secret, and act firmly to deal with the dangers that intelligence has uncovered.

Afterwards I asked both Bundy and Kennedy if they would tell me how much that single evaluated piece of photographic evidence was worth, and they each said it fully justified all that the CIA had cost the country in all its preceding years. A copy of the photograph of the San Cristobal site on October 14 is on my wall. It is to me a symbol of what can be accomplished by a coordinated team of spies, who reported Soviet military activity in the San Cristobal area, technical intelligence collectors, who brought back and interpreted the pictures, and scholars, who day by day during the crisis kept Kennedy and his NSC executive group fully informed about the exact nature and timing of this threat.

McCone sat in the EXCOM, the NSC policy group; I came in almost every day to give briefings, deliver intelligence reports, and—on the last day, October 22, 1962—help draft the President's speech opening up the situation to public knowledge. In these years McGeorge Bundy felt free to show the closely held Khrushchev-Kennedy correspondence not only to Ambassador Llewellyn Thompson for analysis and action on preparing responses but also to me, as Deputy Director (Intelligence) at the CIA, for vetting to garner any light it shed on Soviet policies and intentions. This sharing of diplomatic correspondence of the highest sensitivity with the CIA analytical component made it possible for me to guide intelligence output into matters directly germane to policy issues of the moment and also to pass along in a discreet way insights into Khrushchev's attitudes that my intelligence analysts needed to know. I cannot imagine a more intimate linking of intelligence in all functional categories with the highest level policy decision-making. From that time on until

Kennedy's death, McCone and I felt that we were on the first team at the White House and that we had ample opportunity to provide the services of which the mature CIA was capable.

One well-publicized espionage penetration of higher level Soviet officialdom provided the CIA and the military intelligence agencies with a mass of useful data in the early 1960s. Colonel Oleg Penkovskiy, a dissident official with access to secret publications of the Soviet military, scientific, and technological establishments, volunteered his services to the U.S. and British intelligence agencies. Many of the CIA's best agents have been volunteers or, in the CIA jargon, "walk-ins." Close cooperation between the two governments resulted in an effective exploitation of this spy in Moscow, and he copied and sent abroad thousands of pages of writings on the progress the USSR was making in military technology. The reports in Washington were originally restricted in distribution to a tiny list of cleared analysts,but the added dimension that these reports gave to U.S. understanding of Soviet military capabilities was extremely valuable. Things that were photographed or overheard were explained in Penkovskiy's stolen documents, as well as many things that would have been unknown altogether if this agent had not been such a prolific source. The information he had provided on types of Soviet missiles proved invaluable to U.S. intelligence analysts during the Cuba missile crisis of the summer and fall of 1962. This reporting may have been his undoing; somehow he was discovered, arrested on October 22, 1962, and a few months later was tried and shot. *The Penkovskiy Papers* consisting of materials he had forwarded to Washington provide an authentic record of the efforts of this man, the most successful CIA secret agent of the late Dulles-early McCone era.*

The other major strategic issue in the Kennedy era, aside from Cuba, was Southeast Asia. Here the CIA did not fare so well. McCone and I talked a lot about the U.S. involvement in Vietnam, and we both agreed in advising that intervention there would pay only if the United States was prepared to engage in a long, difficult process of nation-building in South

---

*\*The Penkovskiy Papers were published by Doubleday and Company, New York, in 1965.*

Vietnam to create the political and economic strength to resist a guerrilla war. The CIA's estimates and other analytical papers in the entire Kennedy-Johnson era were soberer and less optimistic than those of the Defense Department, particularly those of McNamara, who in September 1963 predicted victory by the end of 1965. Desmond Fitzgerald and I both tried to warn that an Asian guerrilla war was not to be easily won by conventional military forces and weapons, but the message did not get across very well. The Kennedy team also made a fateful mistake when they let Averell Harriman, Roger Hilsman (then Assistant Secretary for the Far East), and Ambassador Henry Cabot Lodge in Saigon encourage the Vietnamese armed forces to overthrow the strongest ruler Vietnam had found, President Ngo Dinh Diem. This State Department-supported coup resulted in the armed forces' murder of Diem on November 1, 1963, only a few weeks before Kennedy's own assassination. McCone and I and the local CIA station chief strongly opposed this course of action.

I remember once—in the Lyndon Johnson period—being asked by Bundy to have the CIA prepare an objective analysis of the results of the U.S. Air Force bombing of North Vietnam. He said, "Everyone agrees your analysts are the only honest guys in town, and we need to know the truth." A small group of analysts went to work making such evaluations. Over a period of time their work demonstrated that little progress was being made in slowing down the North Vietnamese infiltration of the South. The CIA was the bearer of bad tidings throughout the Vietnam war, and was not very happily received by any of the policymakers who tried to make the Vietnam intervention work. The intelligence was sound, but the policy was not firmly based on the evidence. The result was a tragedy for the United States and the peoples of Southeast Asia.

The one major change in the CIA's structure that McCone made was one I disapproved of. He felt strongly that the CIA, in order to compete with the Pentagon in the field of technical reconnaissance research and development, had to strengthen its scientific and technical resources. Accordingly, he created a new Directorate, Science and Technology. In order to give some warm bodies and an appearance of bulk to the Directorate, he took the scientific intelligence analytical staff from the DDI and turned it over to his new Deputy Director, a young scientist, Albert (Bud) Wheelon, who stayed only a short time before going back to industry. The result was, in my opinion, that the CIA advocacy of its own scientific collection techniques became mixed up with its objective analysis of all scientific and technical developments. The appearance of objectivity was hard to maintain when analysis and collection were supervised by the same staff. Without deprecating the excellent work of this Directorate, I have always felt it violated a cardinal rule of sound intelligence organization in allowing the same unit to conduct intelligence operations and then evaluate the results.

McCone was intent on emphasizing a new field, that of science and technology, but in fact he began weakening CIA's analytical voice when he fragmented the DDI domain in this way. Later, the estimates business was separated out from DDI, and this too left the CIA analytical and estimative front less united in dealing with other intelligence agencies and the consumers of intelligence. The substantive side of intelligence needs all the unity and balance it can achieve in order to have its voice heard in a policy world where clandestine operations and technical collection gadgetry always command attention and analytical judgment is often neglected. I think the DDI had its maximum impact under Kennedy, and a single and consolidated research and analysis facility should have remained in being as the center of CIA's efforts to bring reasoned judgment and objective evidence to the decision-makers.

After Lyndon Johnson became President, the White House style changed; and CIA had to change with it. We had invented a special publication for Jack Kennedy, called the President's Intelligence Checklist (PICL). It had a unique format and its contents were tailored for the President, giving him only the current intelligence we thought he would find interesting and useful and permitting ourselves comments and operational references that we would not have put in the regular Daily Intelligence Bulletin circulated to senior officers in every NSC agency. Kennedy liked a humorous item now and then, and we included one when it was germane.

We promptly changed format, style, and time of delivery to try to suit Johnson. He did not want to start off each day with intelligence as Kennedy had, but instead wanted a paper he could read in bed at night. We obliged by making the deadline for delivery 6 p.m., and we altered the presentation to make it a little more solemn. Maybe that was the trouble, but we had difficulty getting feedback from the President. Kennedy used to make comments and ask questions, usually filtered through Bundy but sometimes phoned directly to me, my Current Intelligence Chief, Jack Smith, or the longtime genius of the President's special daily intelligence report, Richard Lehman. I confess I was not always pleased when Kennedy called me up; he was usually angry about something he had read—more often than not in the newspaper rather than in our publications—and he always wanted categorical reassurance on some matter that sometimes was hard to give off the top of my head. I always felt in touch with White House concerns, however, and I nearly always accompanied McCone to NSC meetings, often giving the briefings on McCone's behalf. With Johnson the NSC became even more of a sometime thing than under Kennedy, and our insight into the President's needs became less clear.

McCone himself did not always operate on the same wave length with Johnson, and the CIA felt the lack of intimate contact. Johnson tended to operate in a Congressional rather than a Presidential mode, chewing things over with a few cronies—some of them not even in the government—and trying to "reason together" with them to work out a compromise of some kind. It was just not congenial to him to listen patiently to staff recommendations and make a decision on the basis of the evidence. He wanted to talk things over, but not with the experts in the CIA and the other staffs.

The NSC began its long decline in these years, being used more for show purposes than decision-making. As the Vietnam war became more worrisome, Johnson retreated more and more from orderly reviewing of evidence and systematic consultation. Kennedy had converted Eisenhower's methodical NSC process to a fast-break, executive task-force process, which worked well if the President really focused on the problem. Lyndon Johnson further narrowed the circle of participants in the NSC to the principals, whom he began to meet at a weekly luncheon—Dean Rusk, McNamara, and Bundy, who was replaced later by Walt Rostow. There were other groups; but this was the critical policy forum, and intelligence did not have a place at the table. Eventually Dick Helms, when he became DCI in 1966, was invited to the weekly luncheons; but at that time Johnson's mind was filled with only one problem, for which there was no good solution by then—how to get out of Vietnam without letting Hanoi take over the whole country. This same problem persisted into the Nixon era, when policymaking further narrowed its circle of full participants and all decisions were made by President Nixon and Henry Kissinger, Nixon's Assistant for National Security Affairs, who came to use the NCS apparatus and the intelligence community as his private staff rather than as supporting staff for the President.

## The DDI Domain

Under McCone's sympathetic guidance the entire intelligence analysis apparatus in CIA expanded its horizons and increased its competence. In Sherman Kent, Abbott Smith, John Huizenga, Willard Matthias, retired Air Force General Earl Barnes, and Ludwell Montague, of ONE, the DDI had a thoroughly professional, experienced estimative talent bank to rely on for interagency forecasts. The rules of procedure for NIEs had become somewhat cumbersome and the papers both slow to produce and lengthy to read. Nevertheless the intellectual quality was high, and the integrity of independent judgment could not be questioned. I sometimes intervened, in the interests of speed, to get specific responses to questions to which I knew the NSC urgently needed the answers. About 50 NIEs a year were brought out, and I believe that no man who read them all could say that he was not well informed about the key strategic issues of the day.

The Special National Intelligence Estimate (SNIE) became an art form much appreciated by the NSC because it was short and narrowly focused on specific issues facing the NSC; for example, what precisely Communist China would do in North Vietnam under various alternative U.S. courses of action. Because these SNIEs so often plainly reflected real planning alternatives being considered by the NSC, their circulation was extremely limited. On the whole, they were timely and intellectually sound. With the regular budget of NIEs on Soviet and Chinese Communist capabilities and intentions, plus a series of periodic NIE reviews of crucial conflict areas around the world such as Germany and the Mideast, the SNIEs provided an indispensable floor of common understanding of the world around us for the officials and staff officers who received and read them.

Beyond this the DDI had a first-rate Office of Current Intelligence headed by Jack Smith. In addition to putting out sophisticated daily and weekly summaries of important incoming intelligence items, the Current Intelligence staffs prepared quick appreciations of new situations to pass to Bundy for the President, prepared briefings for NSC meetings, although these were held with increasing irregularity, and prepared briefing materials for McCone and me to use when we presented CIA estimates to Congressional committees—as we did about once a month. We also used their materials to brief heads of state or other high officials when requested to do so by the White House or State Department.

An extraordinarily successful predictive analysis by the CIA enabled the United States to make a formal statement on the imminence of China's first nuclear explosion shortly before it occurred in October 1964. From photography of the test site in Northwest China and other bits of evidence on Peking's nuclear energy program, the CIA analysts and others in the intelligence community agreed on an estimate that the first explosion was at hand. The Secretary of State, Dean Rusk, felt that the psychological impact of this achievement on U.S. allies around the world would be minimized if he announced the event in advance, indicating that it was only an initial step for China in the long journey to becoming a major nuclear power in any way comparable to the United States or the Soviet Union. Rusk made the statement; the explosion occurred on schedule, and, as far as could be discovered, most governments did discount the event in advance in their own thinking.

In several round-the-world briefing trips in the McCone era, we kept the top defense and foreign policy officials of our allies up to date on Soviet and Chinese strength, as well as other pertinent strategic problems. The National Photographic Interpretation Center staff and the Current Intelligence staff collaborated in preparing the elegant presentations with charts, maps, and photographs in the old OSS tradition but, substantively, many times richer. Showing a detailed photograph of Moscow, Peking, or some remote advanced weapons sites to foreign political leaders invariably impressed them. These private meetings with NATO and other allied nations' leaders, the Australians and New Zealanders, for example, with Premier Sato of Japan in his favorite geisha house, and Premier Shastri at a secret meeting place in India, gave our friends around the world the feeling we knew what we were doing and cared what they thought. In nearly every case these substantive briefings stimulated discussions that provided insights into the thinking of these world leaders, a bonus benefit for intelligence analysts in Washington. This was intelligence performance at the height of its effectiveness.

None of these high-level secret briefings on national intelligence matters by the CIA ever caused unfortunate publicity. The one flap that did occur over a briefing, however, showed how little the U.S. press understood the U.S. intelligence process. At the end of 1963, just after Lyndon Johnson became President, I presented a briefing at the White House prepared by the economists in my Office of Research and Reports (ORR). This group, under the leadership of veteran analysts Otto Guthe, Ed Allen, Bill Morell, and Rush Greenslade, had developed professionally over the years to the point where it had files, experts, and intelligence information unique in the world. They also were beginning to cover so-called "free world" areas that nominally the State Department's Bureau of Intelligence and Research (INR) should have covered but did not because of lack of staff. In any case, ORR discovered at the end of 1963 that there had been severe agricultural shortfalls in the preceding year of a kind that periodically plagues the USSR. This crop failure brought Soviet economic growth almost to a halt that year—to less than 2 percent—and completely torpedoed Khrushchev's boasts of overtaking the U.S. economy.

President Johnson was delighted by this good news and instructed the CIA to release the data. We were already beginning to make such reports and statistics available to scholars after we had concealed or omitted the secret sources of the data, a process we called "sanitizing." This process was too slow for the President's purpose, however, so we were directed to pass the information to the press. The word soon spread among journalists and it was decided to hold the first press conference ever convened in the CIA Headquarters Building in Langley. It was the last, at least during my tenure in the CIA.

I presented essentially the same very sober economic data the President had seen and offered to let the CIA economists answer questions. Thirty or 40 journalists showed up and, I believe, grasped the significance of the economic facts being presented about the USSR. Very few straight news stories emerged, however. Many reporters wrote colorful stories about being escorted through the security barriers at Langley and being escorted to the bathrooms. The worst coverage though was in the *New York Times,* which even before the press conference printed the whole story as a front page, column one item attributing the story directly to the CIA and stating in effect that the CIA was conducting psychological warfare against the USSR by releasing dubious statistics on the economy. The reporter had called up a few good university economists who said, quite rightly since we had not yet shared the data with them, that they did not have the evidence to support the CIA findings. The *Times* treated these statements as an indication that the CIA was feeding false information to the press.

It was an incredible performance, revealing how unwilling this particular great newspaper was to acknowledge the contribution objective intelligence reporting could make to public understanding of foreign issues and how quick it was to attribute sinister motives to anything the CIA did. This attitude is a burden on the intelligence community that still makes it hard for the nation to benefit fully from our national intelligence machinery. The truth of the briefing to the press became obvious within a few weeks, but no correction of the initial sensational treatment ever appeared. It was a bitter experience. I briefed dozens of journalists individually throughout the period of my government service, giving them insights and information that were often reflected in stories they wrote. The press has always been eager for this assistance from the CIA officers around the world and always received every consideration because the Agency believed that accurate press treatment of international events supplements and simplifies the intelligence reporting task. Nevertheless, experience showed that newspaper management and the broadcast media harbored extravagant suspicions of the CIA as if it were solely dedicated to what they loved to call "dirty tricks," that is, covert action. This attitude called for sensationalizing all news about the CIA. It was no surprise when in the post-Watergate era the news media savaged intelligence so viciously that the resulting press and Congressional reaction threatened for a time to destroy the whole intelligence structure.

Meanwhile the other DDI components were doing some of their best work. The photo interpreters under Art Lundahl and the strategic military research analysts under Bruce Clark, a Current Intelligence officer, combined forces with the economists and scientists to provide the Office of National Estimates with evidentially-based judgments that were often sounder than those emanating from Defense and State. In particular, the CIA estimates and analytical reports on Vietnam provided an increasingly isolated light of reason and caution in an otherwise imprudent climate of opinion.

In this whole McCone period I benefited, as DDI, from the extraordinary diversity of research pursuits on the part of officers and staffs throughout the Agency. For example, one night late in 1962 when President Kennedy called me to ask about the possibility that Soviet missiles were being hidden in caves in Cuba, I checked with the ORR geographers and economists who had formed a task force on Cuba and found that some conscientious soul had prepared a card index on every known cave in Cuba, with indications of size of entrance and suitability for storage of weapons—which they were sometimes used for. When we plunked that file down on the conference table in the Cabinet Room at the White House the next morning and said only a very few missiles could possibly fit into or get through the entrances of these caves, the problem died right then. This is a case of serendipity in intelligence that is likely to occur when you have an adequate staff of well-indoctrinated analysts.

Close contacts with the reconnaissance and photo interpretation world also paid off. At the height of the Cuba missile crisis McCone and I persuaded Bobby Kennedy and several others to go down to our photo center—then in a decrepit old building in downtown Washington—to look at the negative images on the processed film through our excellent optical system. The prints that we used at the White House were never quite as clear as the film itself. After this exposure to the black arts of Lundahl's crew, neither Bobby nor anyone else ever questioned the analysis of the Soviet weapons in Cuba that we presented on numerous occasions to the little band of NSC Executive Committee officials gathered together by the President to deal with the missile crisis.

Just before Kennedy made his great speech on Cuba on October 22, 1962, I was instructed to send teams of senior analysts as briefers, with a kit of photographic evidence, to accompany special ambassadors to Ottawa, London, Paris, and Bonn to fill in the governments in these key capitals on the Soviet provocation and on our decisions. William Tidwell, chief reconnaissance targeting expert, Chester L. Cooper, the DDI deputy for NSC liaison, Sherman Kent, and Jack Smith went to these cities; at each place the photo kit was so persuasive our allies—even de Gaulle—fell immediately in line. Konrad Adenauer for a long time believed we had gone to the trouble to send a man under cover to brief him; I think we never convinced him Jack Smith could be a real name of a CIA officer! I myself went to the United Nations in New York shortly after Kennedy's speech to show the photographic evidence to friendly delegates and assist in the drafting of Adlai Stevenson's speech of accusation delivered in the Security Council—the one with the dramatic offer to wait till hell freezes over for an honest answer from the Soviet delegate about missiles in Cuba. There is a picture in Bobby Kennedy's book on Cuba, *Thirteen Days*, of this confrontation with the CIA briefing charts on an easel in the background.[15] Again our intelligence was never questioned in this, the proudest moment of DDI analysts.

Following McCone's lead in trying to emphasize substantive evidence and judgment at all levels, including the policymaking level of the NSC, the DDI often found itself involved in interagency problems related to the coordination of intelligence. A Special Deputy to the DCI was supposed to cope with interagency intelligence coordination. For the most part the incumbent could only smooth over agreements to disagree because the DCI had no executive control over the 80 percent of intelligence expenditures that went to units under the administrative control of the Secretary of Defense. CIA funds were concealed in the Defense budget, but the rest of the intelligence community got funds from regular items in the vast Defense budget; the exception was State's INR, which was funded—parsimoniously—in the regular State Department budget. Under McCone, John Bross was appointed to take this job with a fancy new functionally defined mission—National Intelligence Programs Evaluation (NIPE). The NIPE staff felt that the only way to get a grip on non-CIA intelligence programs was to evaluate them in terms of comparative contribution to overall analytical intelligence reporting. This could only be done by DDI analysts working with State and Defense analysts to review and critique all collection activities.

The main vehicle for interagency review was the subcommittee structure of the U.S. Intelligence Board (USIB). Guided missiles, atomic energy, signals intelligence, and numerous other specialized fields were assigned to subcommittees by USIB, and these groups worked pretty well in sorting out problems concerning the collection tasks to be levied on different agencies. The trouble was the USIB had to approve all recommendations and there was simply no way to get an intelligence agency represented on USIB to take on a task it did not consider as high in priority as its more parochial, departmental responsibilities—and no way to get such an agency to discontinue an activity it prized even though it was little regarded by others. The only real control in such matters is the budget, and the DCI did not control the budget.

Despite severe bureaucratic difficulties, Bross and his handful of colleagues accomplished some useful coordination of intelligence community efforts in this period. One effort that helped a great deal was to have assigned to Bross' staff a "China Coordinator"—for a long time one of the CIA's most judicious analysts, Harold Ford—to insure that adequate investments were being made in both collection and analysis on China, which always tended to be neglected in comparison to the USSR. Bross and McCone worked out a good, though complex, machinery for coordinating overhead reconnaissance programs and target selection, working mainly with the Air Force. While achievements in interagency coordination left a great deal to be desired, McCone and Bross laid the groundwork for the much more formal and elaborate attack on these problems by the much larger Intelligence Community Staff set up in the 1970s.

In attacking these managerial problems it was essential for the judgments to come mainly from experts who really knew which intelligence inputs were valuable, but it was also imperative to translate these judgments into cost and benefit calculations. In its own limited field the DDI took part in a pioneer effort of budget analysis along these lines. We only spent about $50 to $60 million a year in those days—a tiny fraction of the whole national intelligence budget. We did, however, try to relate program to function and function to cost in a budget presentation that policy officials could understand.

An economist, John Clarke, organized this work. He not only could manipulate the budget calculations effectively, but, more importantly, he cared about the true intelligence value of our effort. Clarke was so good that he became the CIA's Plans, Programs, and Budget Officer, later the CIA comptroller and, ultimately, comptroller on the Intelligence Community Staff responsible for preparing the whole intelligence community program budget. The combination of broad managerial ability and scholarly understanding of the purposes of intelligence collection is just as important as the combination of operational and analytical skills. Lacking tight program budget analysis and central budget control, collection almost inevitably overshadows analysis. Photographic satellites, signals collection equipment, and even human agents have a specificity and simplicity of purpose and often an operational glamor that wins support from professional budgeteers. Consequently most money goes for collecting information with not enough regard for whether the data are useful or whether analytical staffs are adequate to absorb and use the data.

Few of those broad managerial problems were solved in McCone's day, but they were defined. Many were aired at USIB but few resolved. The DCI's budget authority was simply not adequate. Thomas L. Hughes, now President of the Carnegie Endowment for International Peace, ran State's INR for most of the 1960s, and Air Force General Joseph Carroll represented the Defense Intelligence Agency (DIA) set up in October 1961.

They were both eminently reasonable men, but INR had little real support in State, as I discovered to my sorrow when I succeeded Hughes in that job, and DIA simply could not control the almost infinite number of Army, Navy, and Air intelligence units that were not interested in central guidance either from the DIA or the CIA. Good men need good organization, good procedures, good support from the top policy level of government to perform at peak efficiency. Despite the efforts of McCone and all of us, this ideal was never recognized.

In coping with the manifold duties of the DDI and keeping up with the energetic John McCone, the DDI needed good staff support at every level. In addition to the colleagues already mentioned, there were several in my own immediate office who reached out to handle jobs that I could not possibly have taken care of myself. Ting Sheldon became my deputy, specializing in handling sticky signals intelligence coordination problems involving Defense's National Security Agency (NSA), the principal collector, and the users of intelligence in the CIA, State, and Defense. He was so canny and farsighted in this intricate task that he was eventually given a unique title— Senior SIGINT Officer—and served the whole intelligence community in this capacity until his retirement. Most other administrative tasks were delegated to another deputy, Paul Borel, my partner in organizing the Office of National Estimates for Bill Langer in 1950. He took on automatic data processing and information handling for the CIA and the whole community, reorganized CIA's entire overt collection and central reference system, and acted as my surrogate in soothing down the innumerable DDI personnel and jurisdictional frictions that inevitably occur in an organization of 4 or 5 thousand people. With this kind of help, and the assistance of Chester Cooper, an exceedingly insightful ONE colleague who was my special deputy for covering the NSC front until McGeorge Bundy stole him for his own staff, I managed for four years to stay afloat in one of the most difficult and responsible jobs in Washington.

### The Raborn Interlude

The frustration of the men around Lyndon Johnson with Vietnam and the lessening interest in objective intelligence which was often distasteful to them because it promised no easy way out, made the CIA an increasingly painful place for senior officers to work, especially in the DDI. There was enormous responsibility, endless tasks to perform, but less and less sense of engagement and appreciation at the top. This feeling got to John McCone and he eventually left the CIA at the end of April 1965. His departure marked the end of a period of maximum effectiveness in the CIA's functional and structural maturity. The great importance for CIA of having as its Director a man with political vision, managerial talent, and independent stature, giving him ready access to the President, became starkly evident when the time of troubles for intelligence began a few years later.

When McCone departed, he said he had advised President Johnson that his successor could be found among three of his professional subordinates, Dick Helms (DDP), Lyman Kirkpatrick (Executive Director), and myself (DDI). The clandestine operations facility, the central managerial machinery, and the central research, analysis, and estimative facility were represented in this choice. In a characteristically Delphic manner President Johnson opted for an outsider as Director of Central Intelligence, with the position of the Deputy Directory (DDCI) going for the first time in more than a decade to a civilian professional intelligence officer rather than a military man. The choice for the general managerial DDCI job fell to the Chief of the clandestine services, Dick Helms. The choice for DCI was baffling. It was Vice Admiral William (Red) Raborn, an engaging retired naval officer who had absolutely no background in intelligence, who had distinguished himself as program manager for the Navy's vital Polaris submarine production program, who had retired to take a job in the aerospace industry, and who in no way sought the job of DCI or thought he was well qualified for it. He stayed only about a year, leaving the CIA Headquarters in June 1966.

Raborn was a likeable man, an understanding boss, and a patriot, who took the job at the CIA because Johnson told him he was needed. It was probably a mistake to select a man with so little experience in foreign affairs or intelligence work; in any case it was tragic that the White House paid very little attention to the CIA after he was appointed, and the beginning of a long slide downwards in prestige began. Raborn tried to learn what he needed to know to run the CIA and he did in fact learn a lot. In the increasingly frenzied atmosphere of the Vietnam crisis in Washington, however, time to learn was a luxury. It is impossible in any case to learn what you need to know about an arcane profession like intelligence in less than a couple of years and Raborn got only a year. I worked closely with the new DCI; he was an intelligent man and he applied himself vigorously to his task. It was unfair that he was placed in a job for which he was not well qualified—and was then promptly assailed from all quarters for not being qualified. I have nothing but sympathy for him. He did his best in a virtually impossible situation.

The new DCI received his baptism of fire promptly, in an incident illustrative of the Johnson era. Raborn had come on duty toward the end of April and I was the first to brief him, spending all one morning explaining DDI functions. All the senior CIA officers then went off to a farewell lunch for McCone and shortly afterwards I was called urgently to Raborn's office. I suspect he called me because he had not had much chance to get acquainted with Helms or indeed anyone else. Anyway I entered his office and heard over the telephone, which was amplified so others in the room could hear, President Johnson announcing that he had decided to send U.S. armed forces to the Dominican Republic to prevent a civil war, which had broken out there, from ending up with a Castro-oriented dictatorship. Johnson told Raborn; he did not consult him or ask for advice. Naturally the DCI said, "Aye, aye sir!"

We promptly put the Agency into action to provide rapid reporting on the Dominican crisis. One solid achievement of Raborn's was the creation at this time of an Agency-wide Operations Center staffed to deal with all aspects of intelligence on a 24-hour-a-day basis. We had already established such a center for DDI intelligence handling and liaison with Defense and State on research and analytical matters. Raborn insisted that the DDP and other operational elements in the agency put representatives in the Operations Center so that requests for action could be expeditiously handled and prompt receipt and disseminations of field reports assured. The system worked beautifully. At one point the CIA agent reports were coming into the Operations Center within 20 minutes after the information was available in the CIA station in Santo Domingo, and were being distributed electronically all over town before an hour had elapsed. The Operations Center is now a fixture of CIA Headquarters life, tying the Agency into the whole NSC interagency net in a way that is absolutely essential. Raborn convinced Dick Helms and Fitzgerald, who had taken his place as DDP, that the CIA had to break down compartmentation enough to develop this facility.

A high mark in collaboration between the DPP and the DDI was reached at this time. Fitzgerald and I had worked closely together while I was in Taipei and trusted each other completely. We adopted the habit of meeting weekly to discuss each other's preoccupations. This procedure was unprecedented and it was very effective. One specific consequence developed quickly. In running through the cast of contending political characters in the Dominican Republic, Fitzgerald mentioned to me that the most capable of them was former President Balaguer, then in exile in New York. I filed this away in my mind because I knew Fitzgerald had excellent political judgment.

A few days later an NSC meeting was called for Sunday morning at the White House. Raborn asked me to accompany him. When we arrived we found the meeting had been canceled because Johnson was in bed with a sore throat; nevertheless, when the President learned we were there, he asked us to come over to the mansion into the bedroom, where a steamer was going and the day's newspapers were flung all over the place. The always strenuous Johnson was plainly not very ill, he was bored and he was worried about the Dominican Republic. At his request I briefed him in detail on the most recent developments. He then said, plaintively, "How the hell can I get my troops out of this damned mess?" Admiral Raborn cheerfully observed, "Maybe Dr. Cline has a suggestion!" Put on the spot, I said that we could only withdraw when we got a non-Communist leader firmly ensconced. The President pricked up his ears and said, "Who?" I reviewed all the potential leaders, pointing out serious weaknesses in all and then, remembering my conversation with Fitzgerald, described Balaguer as the ablest of them all. Johnson reared up in bed, said, "That's it; that's our policy; get this guy in office down there!"

There was no point in trying to tell the animated President

that it was none of the DDI's business or that it might not be easily accomplished, so I simply said I would pass on the President's view to the appropriate people, particularly Secretary of State Rusk. Whether or not State and the CIA ever did anything specific to assist Balaguer, their approval probably helped in the process by which he did in fact go back and was reelected.

Johnson was less fortunate in his Vietnam policy decisions. One of the most touching yet disturbing scenes I remember was an NSC meeting, early in 1965, I believe, in which all Johnson's advisers urged greater U.S. intervention in Vietnam to prop up the Saigon regime and prevent total Communist control. Some there, the CIA representatives in particular, stressed the long hard job ahead and more than one adviser raised the question of whether the American people would support a long foreign military effort. Johnson flared up, saying, in effect, quit telling me what the American people will do—that is the President's political responsibility and all the NSC has to do is to tell the President what is good for the country. He was right of course, and the NSC did indeed unanimously and repeatedly recommend that U.S. interests would benefit from maintaining an independent, non-Communist South Vietnam. However, he was wrong in thinking the task could be done semi-secretly, without adequate consultation with Congress and persuasion of both Congress and the people. In the end he failed to organize sufficient political support at home to permit him to accomplish what he was trying to do.

Unfortunately, McNamara was saying publicly the war could be won quickly, and the State, Defense, and the CIA programs in Vietnam proliferated wildly and often conflicted with one another. Limited successes were canceled out, psychologically at least, by conspicuous failures. The CIA under Raborn put enormous effort into covert action and counterintelligence programs, but the scale of effort and the overall militarization of style and procedure frustrated nearly every endeavor. Fitzgerald very early lamented that nobody running the war seemed to understand Asians and that whenever the CIA developed a promising, hand-tailored operation involving perhaps 100 Vietnamese, the U.S. military command wanted to take it over, increase the size tenfold, and change a sensitive covert man-to-man effort into a battalion-size, mechanized, impersonal campaign.

The so-called "secret Laos Army" is a case in point. When I was still in Taiwan, the CIA sent a few paramilitary case officers experienced in working with Thai and Lao peoples to establish small teams of Meo highland tribesmen in Laos to harass Vietnamese infiltrators and collect intelligence on their relations with the local Pathet Lao insurgents. It took guns and guts and careful direction to do this. This initial effort was so successful and so inexpensive that the program expanded from a few hundred skilled and loyal troops to 30 or 40 thousand in the end. The forces did well until the final collapse in 1973. Long before then, however, the secret Meo army had become too big to be covert; it was used to fight, not primarily to conduct intelligence reconnaissance, and it brought notoriety and discredit to the CIA, which was doing a paramilitary job that diverted it from its more basic tasks. This was the operational story of the mid-60s. Much useful work was done, but the covert action pressures on the CIA distorted its overall effort, even as Vietnam was distorting the political life of the nation.

## Helms at the Helm, June 1966-February 1973

By the spring of 1966 I had become very discouraged with the Washington environment. The departure of McGeorge Bundy was a blow to me, second only to the earlier departure of McCone. Although Walt Rostow was and is a friend, I found the Johnson White House a less and less congenial institution as time went on. In any case, four years is about as long as anyone should hold a demanding job. I approached Dick Helms to request assignment abroad and shortly became Special Coordinator and Adviser to the Ambassador in the U.S. Embassy in Bonn. Stewart Alsop wrote, after I had gone, that I was "exiled" for having ridiculed Admiral Raborn. It is true that stories about his supposed ignorance of foreign countries circulated, but I was not the source. My heartfelt sympathy was with the Admiral for trying so hard to absorb an immense amount of facts and terminology flung at him all at once. Moreover, I did not view going to Europe as exile; it was a delight. The four years I spent in Germany were rewarding in every way.

A lifelong professional intelligence officer finally became DCI when Helms replaced Raborn in June of 1966. A Vietnam-obsessed President Johnson and a secretive President Nixon never gave Dick Helms much of a chance to be the kind of DCI that Dulles was for Eisenhower and McCone was for Kennedy. They both viewed Helms and the CIA primarily as an instrument for the execution of White House wishes by secret methods. They neither seemed to understand nor to care about the carefully structured functions of central intelligence as a whole, and increasingly under Nixon and his principal assistant, Dr. Kissinger, disregarded analytical intelligence except for what was convenient for use by Kissinger's own small personal staff in support of Nixon-Kissinger policies. Incoming intelligence was closely monitored and its distribution controlled by Kissinger's staff to keep it from embarrassing the White House, and the national estimates function fell into comparative disrepute and neglect. I doubt that any could have done better than Helms in these circumstances. One thing is clear, however; the CIA was deteriorating in its influence and its capability to influence policymaking by objective analysis long before the storms of press criticism and Congressional investigations hit.

## Perspective

There is little to tell about my four years in Germany and my four years in the State Department that adds further light to the story of the evolution of the CIA functions and skills. My aim is not to tell a personal story but the story of an institution and a political process. I worked closely with the American Ambassadors, George McGhee and Kenneth Rush, to insure that our many-sided collaboration with German government agencies worked profitably and without political embarrassment.* The station reported from many sources on the background and motivation of Soviet policy moves that produced the lowering of tension between Moscow and Bonn,

---

*One important operation in Germany during my tenure was the defection and clandestine exfiltration of an important KGB Colonel, Eugene Runge, who had lived the illegal agent's life in West Germany under an assumed name for 12 years, stealing vital secrets from the German foreign office and from NATO. For this story, see John Barron's *KGB* (1974), p. 145.

and to a lesser extent between Bonn and East Berlin. I left reluctantly in 1969 to become Director of the State Department's Bureau of Intelligence and Research.

When I arrived in INR in the State Department, there were only a few of the former OSS R&A officers who had transferred to State many years before still on duty. Most were long gone. The haughty Foreign Service officers in the regional bureaus of the State Department—little baronies running the daily business of the embassies—have never been enthusiastic about having a research and analysis unit in State. By drawing on younger Foreign Service officers with a flair for research, as well as a few outside recruits, INR has nevertheless been able to keep a small cadre of career intelligence specialists together and in the business of providing centralized analytical reviews of foreign developments. State's analytical intelligence staff earns its salt and represents State in dealings with the CIA, although it has never acquired the staff or authority to do all the useful work in foreign policy analysis that should be done by analysts free from the day-to-day trivia of diplomacy.

Unfortunately senior State officials have never vigorously supported INR because it competes for money and personnel with the Foreign Service-oriented embassies and country desks. By the time I occupied the job of Director of INR, from November 1969 to November 1973, the bureau had shrunk to between 300 and 350 employees, counting clerical staff. Some of the analysts in this period were excellent, but the uphill battle for budget was an enormous handicap. I discovered that the Director, although clothed in the rank and privileges of an Assistant Secretary of State, had to rely on his connections in the CIA and the White House to get things done and make an impact in high-level intelligence matters, mainly because by and large the rest of State officialdom still did not really value an independent analytical approach that sometimes threatened already established policy positions.

My final separation from the CIA in 1969 removed me from day-to-day dealings with central intelligence. Still I was a member of USIB for four years, until my resignation and retirement from government in November 1973. I saw Dick Helms and many of my other old colleagues frequently and anguished over what was happening to them under Kissinger and Nixon.

At State I respected and enjoyed working with Secretary William Rogers as well as three fine Under Secretaries, Elliot Richardson, Ambassador John Irvin, and Ambassador Kenneth Rush, all able men. I think the performance of INR was improved somewhat, especially in getting it more actively engaged in international economic intelligence analysis and linking it closely with the Secretary's office and the State Department Operations Center so as to provide timely, evaluated current intelligence analysis.

Nevertheless, the White House almost totally disregarded the State Department in the Nixon era, subordinating it to carrying out White House directives and keeping crucial policy information out of State hands, just as crucial intelligence was often suppressed to insure that only Nixon and Kissinger had the full body of information on which to make broad judgments. The whole interagency bureaucracy was emasculated to provide a monopoly of power for the White House.

In dismay over this whole process I resigned from the State Department in October 1973, especially annoyed with Kissinger's further monopolization of power by becoming Secretary of State while remaining as Assistant to the President for National Security Affairs. Kissinger's personal handling of the Arab-Israeli war crisis of October 1973 and the Saturday night massacre, when Nixon fired then Attorney General Elliot Richardson and the Watergate special investigator Archibald Cox, were also shocking to me. Finally, it seemed clear that the policy of placating enemies and betraying allies in the process of detente was in the end going to weaken and humiliate the United States. Subsequent events appear to me to have substantiated my views on all of these points.

For the past eight years I have followed closely as a private citizen and scholar what has happened to the CIA and the intelligence functions of the U.S. Government. Most of my remaining comments stem from my own observations, reinforced perhaps by my awareness of what a long, hard struggle was involved in creating a central intelligence system. For most of this period the U.S. intelligence system has been deteriorating visibly, and I have felt an obligation to draw on my experience to explain and support the need for the CIA and the central coordinating process that developed during my years in public service.

## The Schlesinger-Colby Interregnum

That system received a severe buffeting when Nixon summarily transferred Helms out of the CIA after the election of 1972. We now know it was because Helms had not been cooperative in Nixon's efforts to use the CIA to cover up White House complicity in the Watergate operation. In 1971 a relatively unknown economist in the Bureau of the Budget, James Schlesinger, made a very sensible study of central intelligence. For his pains he was made Director of Central Intelligence to try to carry out his own suggestions; he stayed in this job only from February to July 1973, when he was abruptly transferred to Defense. He made three important moves in this brief period—all wrong. All were designed to tighten White House control of the CIA as a secret instrument of operational utility. One was to abolish the Office of National Estimates, a move not effected until after his departure, but one decided upon very early by Kissinger and Schlesinger; the second was to retire summarily over 2,000 employees, most of them the oldest hands at the CIA, an act that brought morale to a new low; the third was to subordinate to the clandestine services the CIA's long-established overt collection system responsible for contacting U.S. citizens who wanted to pass to the government information learned abroad. The deinstitutionalization of the national estimates system, which thenceforth had as its main purpose writing estimates to order for the NSC staff, the abrupt dismissal of so many CIA officers, making it look as if something had been very wrong, and the reinforcement of the cloak-and-dagger image in connection with perfectly overt CIA functions in the United States—all these were retrograde steps for which the CIA has suffered since.

The job of DCI was then passed along to Bill Colby, the able clandestine services officer who had returned from Vietnam to be Executive Director of the CIA under Helms and subsequently Deputy Director for Plans (DDP) under

Schlesinger.* This move probably accounts for the survival of the CIA as an institution despite the blows it has received. Bill is a courageous, broad-minded intelligence officer, a man of total integrity and dedication to the public service. It was a handicap for him to be tagged as a covert action operator of many years and a prominent activist in Vietnam just when the CIA came under fire for its covert acts, but he handled himself with great responsibility and professional dignity in a very tough situation. The end of the Nixon era was a bad period for the whole federal bureaucracy; for Bill Colby, the end of the Watergate episode when the President left office in August 1974 was followed by a wave of press and Congressional criticism that occupied him fully until the end of 1975. Colby acquitted himself well in this period, but it was a no-win proposition.

In the light of the Watergate inquiry in mid-1973, at Schlesinger's request, Colby reviewed all of the CIA's operations over the past years, asking every CIA officer to identify anything irregular or questionably legal that the CIA had ever done. It is an index of the honesty of the CIA employees that 683 possible violations of directives or law were reported. The summary report on the matters was dubbed the "Family Jewels." Colby quietly changed procedures where he felt they were wrong, advised the Congressional oversight committee chairman in the Senate and House what he had done, and hoped for the best. Unfortunately the atmosphere of Washington in the aftermath of Nixon's downfall was hostile to any form of secrecy. The leaks began occurring, first from Congress to the press, and then from everywhere to the *New York Times* in particular, which set out to make a name for itself in investigative reporting in the Watergate style that won the *Washington Post* such kudos. Regrettably, Colby chose to reduce the administrative clout of counterintelligence within the CIA and forced veteran counterintelligence chief James Angleton to retire. The cynical denizens of Washington immediately deduced—erroneously—that Angleton was in charge of all the

---

*Colby explains in his book, *Honorable Men: My Life in the CIA*, that he changed "the meaningless, misleading euphemism 'Deputy Director for Plans' [to] Deputy Director of Operations" (DDO), a title he held for a few months until he became DCI on September 4, 1973.

activities treated as wrongdoings, and that he was being fired for that reason.

Both Houses of the Congress got into the act with official inquiries, and 1975 was virtually a lost year for the CIA. It took over a year for the tales of misdeeds, nearly all taken from the CIA's own "Family Jewels" report, to become public.

It is impossible to look at Schlesinger's short tour and Colby's defensive operation as anything but an interregnum in the serious intelligence activities of the CIA. The FBI, DIA, and NSA also came under attack and the entire intelligence community went into a holding pattern.

The basic structure of the U.S. intelligence machinery was essentially what it had been for many years, with a more prominent role assigned to intelligence community coordination and a less formal, less sytematic place given to national intelligence estimates. The analytical components were the traditional ones, though some reorganizing took place as a result of moving the National Photographic Interpretation Center to the Directorate of Science and Technology, the elimination of the Office of National Estimates, and the transfer of the domestic contact services to the clandestine services. The central organization in this period was along the lines of the chart on the following page.

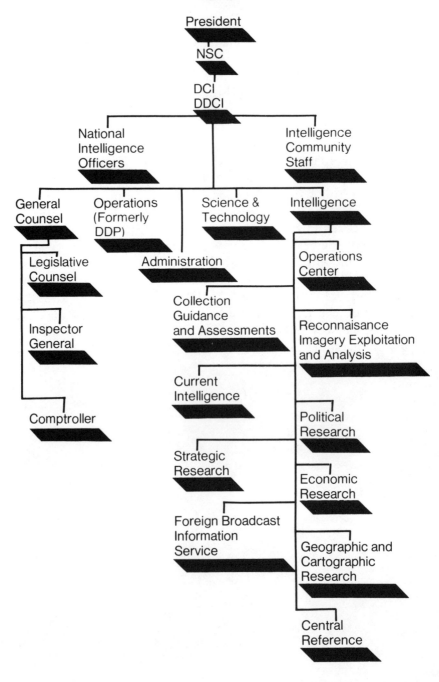

*Chapter Six*

# Time of Troubles

In some ways the CIA was only an incidental victim of the fever of intellectual and social change that swept through the country at the end of the 1960s and the early 1970s. It was catalyzed by the tragedy of the fruitless struggle in Southeast Asia that resulted in protest demonstrations against the government. This increasingly bitter and frustrated mood on the part of much of the public, especially the young, provoked President Nixon and his palace guard into progressive waves of anger, secretiveness, and vindictiveness.

Richard Nixon allowed the little band of ambitious opportunists who were his immediate advisers to adopt attitudes and political practices that constituted the gravest threat to representative government and open society that the United States has experienced. By June 1972, the tawdry, bungled, Watergate break-in brought the situation to a head; the Nixon inner circle set out to cover up their illegal action and, in doing so, nearly destroyed the political fabric of U.S. society. Nixon's resignation on August 4, 1974 marked the end of an era, and the following two years without a popularly elected President saw the CIA caught in the tide of paranoia and cynicism about public service built up during the Nixon-Watergate experience. Naturally the painstaking inquiry into the activities of the CIA, which has been doing business since 1947, turned up mistakes. This would be true of any government agency of a comparable size. Unfortunately, after nearly three decades of existence under provision of national legislation, the CIA still represented a mystery to most Congressmen and most citizens. The secrecy in which the CIA had enveloped its work, necessary to protect clandestine sources and intelligence methods but grossly excessive for the majority of the CIA employees and activities, backfired. In the post-Watergate climate, the nearly total lack of confidence in government institutions, combined with the heedless way in which the journalistic media and the Congress exposed the CIA to the public, nearly destroyed its effectiveness at home and abroad. It was going to take a long time to restore the confidence of the American people in the CIA despite its being an agency so essential to this nation's survival in a disorderly, often hostile international environment. Time and competent leadership over an extended period will be needed to restore the morale of intelligence officers, to reassure friendly foreign nations they can share secrets with the United States, and to rebuild the agent relationships that feed the central analytical intelligence machine in Washington.

The so-called CIA flap began when it emerged that one of the stumble-prone "plumbers" whom the Nixon White House hired to track down leaks and do other domestic political intelligence work for the 1972 election was a retired romantic clandestine operator of the CIA's earlier more expansive overseas period, Howard Hunt. I did not know Hunt, but he had the reputation of being something of a zealot. Despite his personal acquaintance with Richard Helms, then DCI, who was very tolerant of eccentrics and rather admired Hunt for having pseudonymously written a raft of spy novels, Hunt had been eased out of the CIA earlier.

With an unerring instinct for the machismo image adopted by many clandestine operators, the White House picked up Hunt and teamed him up with a similar eccentric, Gordon Liddy, a retired FBI employee. Only the Nixon palace guard could have selected such men for sensitive political ventures. Unfortunately Hunt used his White House connections to get the CIA to provide him an ill-fitting wig and voice-disguise device and, on another occasion, got the CIA to develop film for him that contained photographs of the building that the plumbers broke into in order to ransack the files of the psychiatrist of Daniel Ellsberg, the Pentagon Papers' source. While these things were done with the clear endorsement of the

White House, and the CIA support of Hunt was very quickly cut off, in retrospect the CIA should not have let itself be drawn into them at all. The CIA also prepared a psychological study of Ellsberg, a unique and unfortunate involvement in domestic affairs certainly outside the CIA's charter.

Then, it was revealed, Nixon had pressured Helms and his principal Deputy, General Vernon Walters, to have the CIA call the FBI off the track of the laundered money paid to the Watergate burglars. After a few days of ambiguity, the CIA decisively indicated that the CIA operations provided no grounds for diverting the FBI from the Watergate investigation. This unwillingness to cooperate in the White House cover-up was probably what cost Dick Helms his job five months later, after the 1972 election. Nevertheless, the episode raised suspicions—never confirmed—that the CIA had more to do with Watergate than had been surfaced.

In this atmosphere, attacking the CIA for a variety of reasons became more plausible for critics and profitable for journalists. At this point, in 1973 and 1974, the Senate and House Intelligence Subcommittees began to take closer notice of the CIA covert action, particularly in Chile, which was then under inquiry by separate Senate and House foreign relations subcommittees dealing with multinational corporations and inter-American affairs. It is now absolutely clear the CIA's covert action program in Chile in the 1970s was undertaken under express orders from President Nixon and his National Security Assistant, Dr. Kissinger. In fact, both the CIA and State were reluctant to become so deeply involved in what appeared to be an unfeasible program to keep President Salvador Allende out of office after he had won a plurality in the September 1970 election. At one point, the President and Dr. Kissinger even took matters out of the hands of the 40 Committee (the covert action review group) of the NSC and directed the CIA, much against its officers' judgment, to try to stage a military coup, a project which never came to anything. The CIA continued to provide large sums of money, evidently around $8 million, to support parliamentary opposition to the increasingly arbitrary and socially disruptive rule of Allende—especially to keep alive an opposition press. All of the CIA's efforts were unsuccessful. The military coup that overthrew

Allende on September 11, 1973 was not in any way under U.S. sponsorship or control, though it may well have been facilitated by U.S. anti-Allende pressures. In any case, a great deal of attention focused in 1974 on what the CIA had done covertly in Chile.

Ironically, the many U.S. covert action programs of earlier years had dwindled in number and scope at the end of the 1960s. Aside from the big paramilitary and counterintelligence operations supporting the U.S. military forces fighting in Laos and Vietnam, no big covert political action projects were then in operation. There were numerous, lesser, covert action projects of a psychological-cultural sort, but the last two major political interventions in foreign election processes had ended. After spending about $75 million over 20 years in Italy, to help save it from impending disaster in 1948 and to support the "opening-to-the-left" in the mid 1960s, the United States for reasons of political prudence and economy discontinued subsidies to Italian political parties. For similar reasons, the $3 million spent to support the progressive and popular Christian Democratic regime of Eduardo Frei in Chile in the early 1960s was phased out toward the end of his term; Frei could not succeed himself under the Chilean constitution, and it was the split between centrist rivals for his place that put Allende in office in 1970 with 36.3 percent of the Chilean vote. The USSR and Cuba quickly rallied to Allende, providing covert support in the form of money, arms, and political advice.

The advent of a Communist-supported political front in the Western Hemisphere in 1970 once again plunged CIA back into covert action on a massive scale—too massive to remain covert long. Nixon and Kissinger, beset by problems in Vietnam and the Mideast, quickly and inexpertly set out to win their strategic battles covertly. Money was pumped into Chile and once again invested in Italian politics, where Communist electoral gains had continued. The White House was using the CIA for what it conceived the CIA to be good for: fighting covert military campaigns in Southeast Asia and large-scale intervention in political elections in Chile and Italy. These efforts were the only big covert programs of the 1970s; they all came to grief. They also nearly destroyed the CIA.

I want to be clear about my position. I believe that small-scale selective, covert political action in countries of consequence in support of groups opposing dictatorship and outside domination by the USSR or Communist China is in the national interest of the United States. It should be, however, a quiet supplement to diplomacy, designed to elicit reliable intelligence as much as to pass on political guidance and funds when needed to groups wanting U.S. support. Almost every nation engages in this kind of secret political activity. The USSR invests much more systematically and heavily than the United States in such endeavors—including widespread political efforts to influence opinion and events in the United States. Intentionally or unintentionally, the United States influences foreign events by its action or by its inaction. It is too powerful to be neutral, and secret support of U.S. strategic and foreign policy aims is sensible in the interest of influencing events in the U.S. interest.

To achieve this goal, advice from professionals on covert intelligence work should be heeded on the key questions of feasibility, risk, and the possibility of withdrawal in the event of failure. I was in favor of the provision of covert support to the democratic opposition forces in Chile to help them survive in an increasingly polarized, brutal competition with revolutionary activists spurred on by the Cuban secret intelligence staffs working for Allende. I did not think it was feasible, however, to change the results of the elections by bribery *after* it had taken place and I thought it would probably be counterproductive to try. I certainly would have opposed the military coup excursions of Nixon's and Kissinger's Track II if I had known enough to speak up and had been given a voice in the matter.

There was plenty to criticize in this bizarre performance.[1] The more it surfaced, the more emboldened became the CIA's critics, who not only questioned specific areas where policy was thought to be wrong but wanted to shut down the whole covert action capability of the CIA. Indeed in some cases critics wanted to shut down the whole CIA on the grounds that secrecy is inherently immoral and incompatible with democracy. One of these anti-establishment critics in Congress took a decisive step in 1974 in surfacing the whole Chile story. Michael Harrington, member of the House of Representatives from Massachusetts and a legislator with an uncompromising passion for openness in government, borrowed the secret records of DCI William E. Colby's executive testimony to the House Armed Services intelligence subcommittee on Chilean operations, was outraged by the intervention in Chile, and wrote letters about it which found their way to the press. The fat was in the fire; CIA could not possibly defend itself publicly in so sensitive a matter where White House decisions were involved.

### The CIA Flap: What Went Wrong

As if the Chile affair were not enough, Seymour Hersh of the *New York Times* attracted worldwide attention at Christmastime, 1974, with an expose of the CIA. As usual, Washington and the news media proceeded to examine CIA's alleged misdeeds in true "Alice in Wonderland" style... sentence first, verdict afterwards, and little consideration was given as to how extensive questionable CIA activities might be or how much they were instigated by the White House.

The accusation was the "The Central Intelligence Agency, directly violating its charter, conducted a massive illegal domestic intelligence operation during the Nixon Administration against the anti-war movement and the other dissident groups in the United States..."[2] It was a very serious indictment, if true. The Presidential (Rockefeller Commission) and the Congressional (Church and Pike) inquiries have now sifted through the evidence and the facts are reasonably clear.

Illegal CIA activity was entirely in domestic fields, most of it where the White House had pushed the CIA into dubious enterprises, and these actions were not massive. Nevertheless a great deal of information emerged about specific CIA activities that the public had not known about before, and hostile critics found many of those activities objectionable. Some of them definitely reflected poor judgment by the CIA or White House officials. Defending itself against the charges of massive wrongdoing, the CIA provided its critics with other details to declaim against. This set up was virtually a no-win situation. No institution is totally without error and reasonable men may quarrel with the most conscientious of judgments, especially those made in a different international climate. Criticisms of CIA multiplied as the facts of its history became known for the first time.

CIA Director Colby released a long statement on January 15,

1975, in reply to the *New York Times* account. It began: "I flatly deny the charge." The story on Colby's denial was printed in the *New York Times* under a headline beginning, "Colby Admits . . ." Only a careful reader would note that what Colby admitted was a series of isolated acts, no one of which met all of the alleged charges. What Colby did was to make public most of the questionable past actions CIA officers themselves had pointed out. Little has emerged from news media or Congressional inquiries that was not already in the CIA's own "Family Jewels" report of 1973. Most of the activities mentioned were discontinued by Colby at that time.

There are legitimate arguments about the propriety and legality of the specific acts cited by Colby. I question a number of them. No stretch of the imagination turns them into the massive police-state activity initially conjured up. The CIA has never come close to being an American Gestapo. Yet the moral tone of much of the public criticism suggests this was a real danger.

The CIA's charter, the National Security Act of 1947, and related National Security Council Directives are in some areas vague. There are borderline responsibilities where foreign intelligence collection and counterespionage overlap FBI responsibility for internal security. One of the NSC Directives explicitly assigns responsibility for foreign intelligence collection and foreign counterintelligence and counterespionage to the CIA. The Security Act specifically gives the CIA responsibility for "other functions and duties related to intelligence affecting the national security as the National Security Council may from time to time direct." This last elastic clause leaves a lot of leeway for direct Presidential orders of any kind, since the President is head of the National Security Council. Finally, the DCI is directed by the Security Act to "be responsible for protecting intelligence sources and methods from unauthorized disclosure."

It is clear that the original *New York Times* story was based on the CIA's own inquiry into possibly dubious exercises of authority in the domestic field, as revealed some months earlier to Congressional oversight committees and released to the public in Colby's report of January 15. This may have been news, but it was scarcely balanced journalism. What the CIA did in conducting intelligence operations in the United States that has been criticized as beyond the margins of its legitimate functions can be outlined simply.

First, the CIA set up in its computerized information storage-retrieval system a special file with a name and organization reference index that included about 7,200 files on Americans associated in some way with anti-war or dissident groups, mostly supplied by the FBI in the form of requests for information about any foreign intelligence contacts of these individuals.

There are millions of names in the CIA files, and there are many thousands of American names among them that have turned up over the years in correspondence, routine administrative business, or intelligence reports. Most of the dissident names were entered in the CIA reference index because the FBI requested a check to determine whether or not the CIA had evidence that they were in contact with foreign intelligence agents or were receiving funding from foreign sources. In most of these so-called dossiers there was no other piece of paper except the initial query. The remainder of the material in the files were references to information reported from abroad citing evidence—not necessarily firm—that these individuals were thought to be in contact with foreign intelligence agents. The recording of these names was not a massive effort in terms of total CIA name reference files. The existence of a file did not indicate active CIA surveillance of any kind except in cases where a person was suspected of being in contact with foreign intelligence agents abroad. It was not illegal for the CIA to record foreign intelligence reports or to file and reference official queries about Americans suspected of working for foreign intelligence agencies. Whether or not the FBI acted legally or wisely in determining that someone was suspect and should be checked with the CIA is another matter. Some FBI internal security operations labelled counter intelligence against anti-war demonstrators were probably illegal and certainly politically ill-advised. Yet the U.S. Government was confronted with a climate of lawlessness among the protest organizers, and the FBI had a legal responsibility to prevent crime, including foreign agent espionage.

The CIA also spotted and established contact with foreigners in the United States to facilitate conducting clandestine operations abroad. This activity is in direct pursuit of the function of foreign espionage, which is assigned to the CIA by NSC Directive spelling out the intent of the National Security Act of 1947. The business of an agency responsible for espionage is to recruit spies, and one of the easiest places to do this is when they are here in the United States. It is not illegal to approach foreigners for this purpose, although reformers would like to outlaw the practice.

The CIA established cover positions in U.S. organizations for CIA officers to use for conducting clandestine operations abroad or for funding of such operations. Cover is essential for support of legitimate foreign intelligence operations. No illegal acts in the United States are involved. No domestic intelligence target is involved. Officers engaged in espionage abroad must have an apparently routine job and source of income. Unofficial American enterprises overseas provide the most natural cover. While some may disapprove of the secrecy inherent in cover arrangements, many patriotic Americans thought they should cooperate with the collection of information abroad. In some fields individual Americans already holding positions abroad were recruited by the CIA to collect information or disseminate views abroad in the interests of U.S. policy. It is difficult to see how U.S. intelligence can perform its assigned missions without the protection abroad of cover arranged by U.S. business firms and other organizations. This cover has included positions in cultural, educational, labor, and youth enterprises.

Gradually, under the pressure of news media protest the CIA has severed contacts with most of the people who work abroad in these fields. In mid-1976 the CIA announced that it would no longer recruit and employ any person regularly working in the field of U.S. journalism. This self-denial stems from the charge publicized initially by the magazine *Ramparts* in 1967, that the CIA used cover organizations and paid agents in them to corrupt the honest views of U.S. youth and infiltrate propagandistic misinformation into the American press. In fact the CIA used agents in these groups to collect information about Soviet propaganda efforts, to counter these efforts with objective information, and to sponsor the formation of U.S.-oriented organizations abroad. As far as the news media are concerned, the CIA has never tried deliberately to mislead them and, on occasion, cautioned writers to be wary of items planted abroad. The danger of "contamination" of the press by false information put out abroad by the CIA is greatly exaggerated. Competent editorial staffs are quite capable of checking for actual errors. Most contacts between the CIA and the media have been mutually beneficial news-gathering or news analysis exercises, helpful rather than harmful.

The CIA has systematically investigated the security of U.S. citizens under consideration for employment or for confidential cooperation with the CIA. This is the same kind of check conducted by the FBI, Civil Service Commission, etc. The CIA could not operate abroad or protect its methods without investigating the character and reliability of its employees and cooperating citizens. This is not illegal.

The CIA also contracted for analytical or manufacturing expertise, research, and development. Some of the great CIA technical achievements in electronic intercepts and photographic imagery are due to this collaboration among science, industry, and government. This is the same kind of contracting with private organizations done by Defense, State, A.I.D., H.E.W., and others. Secrecy is required to prevent unauthorized people from discovering intelligence methods. It would be ridiculous as well as very costly to the nation's security if the CIA were unable to obtain cooperation from U.S. experts in all research fields.

The CIA recruited and trained personnel for its headquarters and overseas operations. All government agencies conduct training. CIA conducts its training in secret so that some of its employees can operate overseas under cover. The object of this activity is to carry out a variety of functions within the CIA charter. The findings of the Rockefeller Commission confirmed that all of these above activities of the CIA were legal and proper.[3] No law or directive said the CIA should not operate in this manner in the domestic United States. It has to do so to carry out its authorized missions.

At this point we approach the borderline gray area of the CIA performance. For example, the CIA collected counterespionage information *abroad* on possible links between foreign governments or agents and U.S. dissidents; it specifically targeted, in its counterintelligence *abroad*, organizations or American individuals named by the FBI as suspected of illegal foreign contacts.

This activity, of a counterespionage nature, was authorized expressly by an NSC Directive. Explicit orders from the White House for this information were received. In many cases queries came from the FBI, the government agency that is charged with internal security functions. Solid evidence about American citizens working for foreign intelligence groups would have provided basis for criminal charges under the Espionage Act. Naturally the information and the operations carried out to obtain it had to be secret to permit collection of data foreign intelligence would try to hide. This secrecy also protects any American from injury by public revelation of reports that could not be substantiated. There was no other U.S. agency except the CIA to pursue this kind of inquiry overseas.

In this borderline gray area, where the CIA linked some of its work with FBI internal security investigations, the record becomes less favorable. Presidents Johnson and Nixon felt absolutely sure that the anti-war protestors were being financed from abroad. Both Hoover and Helms were persuaded to do things that in retrosepct seem unwise and probably illegal. First, the CIA employed Americans to join dissident groups in the United States so they would become attractive targets when they traveled abroad, where it was hoped they could obtain information on foreign intelligence activities and interests.

Fewer than 30 individuals were involved in this activity, and they were originally intended strictly as bait for foreign agents. Nevertheless, this procedure brought the CIA to the margins of an internal security penetration program. The CIA, in response to insistent demands from the White House for data on the dissidents, provided the FBI with reports on dissident group meetings collected as a by-product of these operations. There is a legitimate argument in favor of the CIA bait operations of this kind as an essential preliminary step for successful counterespionage abroad. In this sense these activities were not strictly in violation of the charter and no illegal acts occurred.

Nevertheless, secret penetrations of domestic American dissident organizations did take place in circumstances where it was impossible to avoid ambiguity as to the basic aims of the operations. It is easy to be wise after the event. Now it seems clear that the CIA should not have authorized these special penetration cases. The CIA knew it was in dangerous waters. The whole program for consolidating information on U.S. dissidents was organized into a special section, ultimately employing 52 people, disseminating reports to the White House. The unit responsible for what was codenamed operation CHAOS reported directly to Dick Helms, who handled it gingerly but clearly thought he had to comply in some fashion with direct orders from Johnson and Nixon. With hindsight he no doubt wishes he had refused the task.

The CIA also managed through its Security Office a short-term penetration of Washington area dissident organizations by approximately 12 agents to check reports that these groups threatened the security of the CIA personnel, installations, and files. Theoretically, at least, this action was justified by the CIA legal counsel under the National Security Act provision giving the Director of the CIA responsibility for protecting "intelligence sources and methods." This was a period of raids, file burnings, and "trashing" in American cities and universities. The CIA felt a special obligation to protect itself from what might be foreign-directed criminal activity.

Nevertheless this procedure also brought the CIA to the margins of an internal security program. Data on dissident groups were collected so the CIA could plan its own physical security precautions, and again some of it was disseminated outside the CIA. This operation certainly was not massive in scale and the effort continued for less than two years. The questionable activity was terminated when the Washington Metropolitan Police Department developed its own resources. Yet it was aimed at American dissident organizations in circumstances where it was impossible to avoid ambiguity as to basic aims. In this case, as in the previous penetration operation, the CIA should not have authorized the CIA security officers to mount these preventive-security penetrations. The agency should have relied on the FBI and other law enforcement agencies to protect it, despite the fact that J. Edgar Hoover was most uncooperative with the CIA. More important issues of the CIA's image and the public's confidence were at stake. The CIA again erred on the borderline between protecting its own security and becoming operationally involved in domestic internal security.

The CIA carried out a dozen break-and-enter operations of a counterintelligence nature against the homes of the CIA employees or ex-employees suspected of violating security regulations. These operations were illegal, although related to a legitimate counterintelligence function and the responsibility to protect intelligence sources and methods. The few cases hardly constitute a massive program, and the operations were targeted against the CIA officers, not against dissident groups. They took place in the United States, however, and involved law enforcement techniques. With the benefit of hindsight, these operations should not have been authorized without a judicial search warrant and assistance from law enforcement authorities.

The CIA tapped telephones where they suspected violations of security regulations by agency employees or thought other citizens were receiving intelligence information. There were 32 taps. Legitimate counterintelligence concerns led to these taps. The DCI had a responsibility for protecting intelligence sources and methods. The effort was not massive. Many of these taps were not illegal when they took place. The law has since changed, reflecting greater public emphasis on privacy rights. In the future, taps of this kind, in fact all intelligence taps, will have to be made only under judicial warrants. The Attorney General suggested to Congress a number of procedures to control the entire domestic intelligence field. The FBI, in particular, and the CIA will obviously have much more authoritative guidance in the future than it had in the past.

The CIA surveyed and opened selectively the mail of U.S. citizens to and from three important Communist countries in a program going back to 1953, when American contacts with those countries was quite unusual and when the United States was still in what amounted to an undeclared state of war in Korea. This mail intercept should probably have been done by the FBI, which did some interception of mail, if it were to be legal and in keeping with the CIA's charter. It did provide the CIA with leads for foreign intelligence collection through recruiting U.S. citizens with foreign contacts as agents. It also provided counterintelligence information about foreign efforts to recruit Americans as agents in the United States. The interest was in foreign connections. This mail intercept lasted a long time and, in its later years, was not properly and unambiguously cleared with higher authority. As in so many bureaucratic matters, a procedure of long standing seems to carry on under its own momentum without careful review of authorization. Opening mail in time of peace is clearly against the law, except under court order in pursuit of evidence on specific crimes. The operation was terminated in 1973. The CIA plainly committed an error in conducting this mail-intercept operation. Much mail was opened; this is the only protracted operation that has come to light that is categorically illegal.

After reviewing these areas of the CIA domestic activity that have been questioned, I can only say that the CIA was mainly guilty of vigorously pursuing espionage and counterespionage targets leading to foreign agents or information on foreign activity needed for U.S. security. It was in general following White House orders, perhaps too obediently, but not irresponsibly.

During all this flap too little attention was paid to the responsibility of the CIA to coordinate the activities of all the intelligence agencies and to insure that an integrated, objective body of evaluated analytic information is available to policy planners and decision-makers at the top of our government. It is now time to make sure that we have not fatally weakened this vital central intelligence function by sensationalizing past erroneous operational judgments. After all, for nearly 30 years the United States had the substantial benefit of high-quality strategic information from a highly professional intelligence service. The CIA has in no way ever remotely approached becoming an American Gestapo or KGB. If we ever destroy it, as we came close to doing in the early 1970s, the United States will be as naked and exposed in future international crises as it was when World War II came along. The price of such unreadiness in the last quarter of the 20th century would be a thousand times what it was at Pearl Harbor.

## President Ford's Reforms

The height of irresponsible criticism was reached at the end of the 1975. In 1976 public and Congressional understanding of intelligence began to grow and, as a result, belief in the essential soundness of our central intelligence system increased.

The House Select Committee investigating intelligence tangled itself so badly in procedural and security-classification snarls that it virtually self-destructed; its report appeared in the *Village Voice*, not in the halls of Congress, a fitting end to an effort that showed moments of brilliance and days of irresponsibility.[4] The Senate Select Committee wound up its hearings and issued a monumental report providing the data that refuted most of the more damaging charges against the CIA, including the Committee Chairman's own unfortunate speculation that the CIA might have been running wild like a "rogue elephant."[5]

In the meantime some excellent steps were taken to remedy the real errors and structural deficiencies of the intelligence community. The blue-ribbon panel Rockefeller Commission Report of June 1975, largely discounted by the hyper-suspicious investigative journalists, laid down some sound prescriptions for the future. For one thing, the Rockefeller group explained briefly but accurately how the Communist bloc intelligence forces, some 500,000 strong, would continue their activities even if the United States tried to get along without a competent, professional intelligence service.[6] The USSR and many other nations would go on collecting intelligence, particularly on the economic and technological advances on which every country's future strength depends. They would use that information to try covertly to influence economic, military, and political developments in other countries, especially in the United States, to their strategic advantage; the USSR, the People's Republic of China, and many other closed societies would continue to conceal within their own borders all those aspects of national policy and national behavior on which the future peace of the world hinges. The United States cannot afford to face this kind of international environment without knowing what is taking place.

The Rockefeller Commission members also made some important recommendations about the Director of Central Intelligence. They suggested that the Director of Central Intelligence have a principal deputy other than the military deputy responsible for "fostering relations with the military" and that this professional civilian deputy take over "day-to-day management duties"; this would free the Director for handling matters involving the intelligence community budget, broad policies governing all intelligence activities, and direct contact with the President and NSC officials. They also outlined a series of specific guidelines to protect the security of intelligence sources and method and yet plainly prohibit the kind of activities that had led to errors and misunderstandings in the past.

Finally, in what is perhaps the most pertinent comment in the whole Rockefeller Report, the members of this Commission recommended that careful attention be paid to selecting a person with independent stature for this crucial post of public service. They said:

Persons appointed to the position of Director of Central Intelligence should be individuals of stature, independence, and integrity. In making this appointment, consideration should be given to individuals from outside the career service of the CIA, although promotion from within should not be barred.

Another serious examination of intelligence problems was released to the public at about the same time by a Commission chaired by veteran Ambassador Robert Murphy. This group had spent three years examining the structure and process of foriegn policy, beginning long before the CIA flap. Its report included a thoughtful chapter on intelligence as an integral part of the decision-making process.[7]

The Murphy Commission members echoed the Rockefeller Report in many ways, including stressing the significance of independent stature for the chief intelligence officer of the nation. It went further than the Rockefeller Commission in urging that this officer should have regular and direct access to the President and have an "office in close proximity to the White House" in order to "meet his community-wide responsibilities as well as to function as the President's intelligence adviser."

This specific recommendation reflected the Murphy Commission's awareness that Nixon's near total inaccessibility and Kissinger's personal control of all intelligence in his dual capacity as Presidential Adviser for National Security Affairs and Secretary of State (1973-1975) was unsound; in the broader context of foreign policy structures, the Murphy Commission recommended that the Assistant for National Security Affairs "should normally in [the] future be performed by an individual with no other official responsibilities."

President Ford took this recommendation to heart and at the end of 1975 wisely separated the Secretary of State's role as foreign policy advocate from the job of honest broker of strategic intelligence that would be carried out by the Assistant for National Security Affairs. This restoration of a normal structure and political process in the NSC was a major step away from the Nixon overconcentration of power in the White House and toward a political process in which strategic intelligence can play a responsible part.

With this behind him, President Ford on February 18, 1976, issued a lengthy new Executive Order 11905 putting into effect a number of sound reforms of the intelligence community structure and procedure. It went about as far as is possible without legislation, and it was accompanied by proposed legislation amending the National Security Act of 1947 to make the provisions of the Executive Order permanent. It was a complex document, unquestionably representing significant steps in the right direction. This Executive Order was most meaningful because it elevated the position of the Director of Central Intelligence to a very high level in the White House, one in which he is unlikely again to be reduced by willful policy officials to silent acquiescence in practices, procedures, or intelligence judgments he considers fundamentally wrong.

This elevated status for the DCI was assured by his designation as Chairman of a three-man Committee on Foreign Intelligence (CFI) reporting to the NSC and hence to the President as Chairman of the NSC. The composition of this Committee was faulty in that no State Department representative was included, but sound in designating a Deputy Assistant to the President for National Security Affairs as a member and in designating the third member at the high level of a new Deputy Secretary of Defense for Intelligence. With the exception of the absence of a foreign policy member, this new CFI was well constituted to represent the interests of national security policymakers and the intelligence community at the highest levels of government. The CFI, and hence the DCI as chairman of this small executive-style committee, was specifically empowered to "control budget preparation and resource allocation for the National Foreign Intelligence Program." This authority enables the DCI, if he uses it properly, to enforce all other coordinating powers of the DCI.

With full Presidential support, which was implicit in the Ford Executive Order, the Director of Central Intelligence has the opportunity to rationalize, coordinate, and supervise in broad terms the entire intelligence collection and analysis program of the U.S. Government. In stressing the term "Foreign Intelligence," the Executive Order picked up a wise distinction made by the Murphy Commission that distanced the DCI and the CIA from internal security and law enforcement operations by the FBI, which are and ought to be controlled in a separate chain of command leading through the Attorney General to the President. This distinction should improve public understanding of the fact that the law enforcement duties of the FBI have nothing to do with CIA's intelligence mission.[8] Specific responsibilities and procedures for the FBI in its efforts to "detect and prevent espionage, sabotage, subversion, and other unlawful activities by or on behalf of foreign powers" were laid down in the order, with careful attention to the authority of the Attorney General to insure the legality of FBI operations and the limitation of its collection of foreign intelligence in the United States to occasions when it is requested by intelligence community officials.

The Executive Order also raised decisions on covert action by the United States in support of "national foreign policy objectives" and decisions governing "specific sensitive intelligence collection operations" to a new high level—that of the NSC. The 40 Committee, the last in that long line including the 5412 and the 303 Committee, was abolished and the kind of decision hitherto left to this secondary (Under Secretary) level of government will in the future be put squarely before a new five-man Operations Advisory Group (OAG) composed of the Assistant to the President for National Security Affairs, the Secretary of State, the Secretary of Defense, the Chairman of the JCS, and the DCI, with the Attorney General and the Director of the Office of Management and Budget as observers. Policy decisions of this kind in the future were to receive careful scrutiny at the Presidential level.

The President's Executive Order followed the patterns adopted by the Rockefeller Commission of specifying activities that are prohibited for intelligence agencies. Eleven concrete restrictions on intelligence collection were put into effect in this way, ending with the flat statement that "No employee of the United States Government shall engage in, or conspire to engage in, political assassination.
engage in, political assassination."

Finally, President Ford followed the prescription of both the Rockefeller and Murphy Commissions in strengthening provisions for outside oversight of intelligence organizations and their activities. The President's Foreign Intelligence Advisory Board (PFIAB), a part-time group of distinguished citizens interested in intelligence that had been counseling the Presidents since the 1950s, was continued in existence with a special group of three of its members constituted separately as the Intelligence Oversight Board (IOB). This new Board's responsibility was to review regularly reports by intelligence agencies' Inspectors General and General Counsels "concerning activities that raise questions of legality or propriety." By this provision, the internal inspection and review mechanisms were strengthened, and the chain of reporting responsibility carried right up to the Attorney General and the President, to whom periodic reports must be made.

Designation of three eminent Americans to this Oversight Board was made in an effort to set at rest reasonable anxieties about the future legality of intelligence activities insofar as Presidential action can do so. The members were Ambassador Robert Murphy himself, Leo Cherne—an international economist with an outstanding record in international rescue and civil liberties work, simultaneously appointed Chairman of the overall President's Foreign Intelligence Advisory Board—and Stephen Ailes, former Secretary of the Army. This executive oversight system was designed to prevent another quarter-century accumulation of improprieties like those listed in the "Family Jewels" report of 1973.

President Ford's appointment of George Bush, who served from January 30, 1976, to January 20, 1977, as the Director of Central Intelligence, reinforced this new intelligence structure. He had been a Member of Congress, a successful businessman, an Ambassador to the United Nations, and U.S. official representative in the People's Republic of China. He continued to be a highly respected political figure with presidential prospects. He believed in the vital importance of intelligence and set about to lift morale and efficiency in the intelligence community as well as to restore public confidence in the U.S. intelligence process. The CIA began to lift itself out of the despondency resulting from the assaults it endured throughout 1975 and to operate more normally to satisfy national intelligence needs. It is unfortunate that Bush had only a year in this post.

During that time however, he gave the 1976 reform program in the intelligence community real momentum. He did well in appointing E. Henry Knoche, an experienced analyst with a DDI background, to be the overall professional Deputy Director (DDCI) responsible for day-to-day management. Knoche helped Colby control the complex issues involved in liaison with the Church investigation. Bush also selected a competent senior military officer, Admiral Daniel J. Murphy, as his second Deputy responsible for supervising the Intelligence Community Staff in its efforts to coordinate all intelligence agencies in support of national intelligence programs.

CIA morale improved; Congressional and public confidence increased. The structure of the U.S. central intelligence system as Ford constituted it was as sound as it had ever been. The number of employees in the entire system shrank by about one-third from peak strength and the budget was also reduced in terms of real dollars by about the same amount as a result of inflation. A multi-billion dollar budget represents a lot of money to be spent without public knowledge of the breakdown of such expenditures, but the intelligence community is correct in resisting having the details of its expenditures made public. These still represent only a small part of our national defense expenditures, which are themselves running a little over 5 percent of our gross national product (GNP). The total national intelligence community budget works out at less than one-half of 1 percent of GNP—a bargain for a rich and powerful nation. It would be a bargain at twice the price. The question is whether we are able to staff it with qualified people and use it effectively.

The outlines of the national intelligence system, after President Ford's reforms, present a structure like the one following:

# Central Intelligence Agency
# 1976

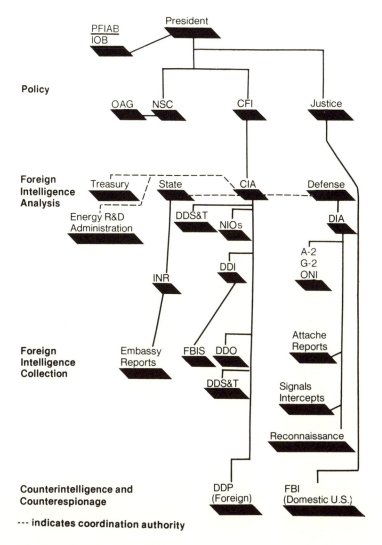

--- indicates coordination authority

This 1976 structure reflected the replacement of the corporate entity of the Office of National Estimates by a group of National Intelligence Officers, each responsible for a strategic area, reporting directly to the DCI. It retained the tripartite breakdown of functional directorates: 1. intelligence; 2. operations; and 3. science and technology. It is a schematic description of a mature central intelligence system developed after 35 years of experimentation and growth.

## The Carter-Mondale Era

Revelations, charges, and slanders about CIA continued to appear in the news media. At first they were accepted at face value, but in time it became clear to thoughtful citizens that efforts to torpedo the agency did not all spring from conscientious concern for civil liberties and that CIA had some merits.

Philip Agee, a CIA employee who resigned and then went to Cuba, instigated some of the most devastating assaults. He allegedly experienced a political conversion to Communism, definitely worked closely with Soviet and Cuban intelligence agents, and, in 1974, published a hostile book, *Inside the Company: CIA Diary*, about covert political operations in Latin America. He helped to organize *CounterSpy* and *Covert Action Information Bulletin*, two publications dedicated to exposing the names and addresses of CIA undercover officers stationed abroad. Two days before Christmas in 1975, Richard Welch, CIA station chief in Greece, was killed on his own doorstep after being identified by *CounterSpy* and later by a local Athenian newspaper.

Suddenly, all the media exposés bore some relationship to real people, and real activities of value to the U.S. Government in the conduct of foreign policy. Over a period of time, Agee's shrill attacks convinced Americans that the CIA could not be all bad if it had such enemies. Slowly, Congressional and public opinion began to turn around; people began to question the wisdom of harassing the CIA forever. Early in 1976, the attacks slackened off—but they did not cease entirely.

Presidential candidate Carter never understood these new attitudes; instead, he flailed away at what he labelled three national disgraces, "Watergate, Vietnam, and the CIA." He was elected in November of 1976, on the last tide of opinion that lumped the CIA with these other disasters. The President's Justice Department even assured Agee, who was expelled from Great Britain for endangering public order and national security, then denied residence in France and the Netherlands, that he was not guilty of a crime for which he would have been prosecuted in the United States.

The promising rise in morale and renewed effectiveness at the CIA seen under President Ford were soon neutralized by the Carter Administration. A novice in government, the President quickly fell under the influence of Vice President Mondale, whose Senate contacts and Washington experience were extremely helpful to Carter. Unhappily, Mondale's views on the CIA, formed during his tenure on Frank Church's Senate Investigating Committee, were quite negative. While he had no objection to intelligence analysis as a contribution to policymaking, he was extremely sensitive to the possibility that secret intelligence operations of any kind might impinge on American civil liberties. He deplored secrecy as an element in government and was flatly against any exercise of covert political capabilities to influence events abroad.

Mondale managed to have a number of liberal-left Democrats appointed to policymaking jobs in the Carter Administration. They shared his negative views concerning the CIA. One of them, his Senate staff aide David Aaron, was given the crucial position of Deputy Assistant to the President for National Security Affairs. There Aaron was able to monitor all CIA programs and to ensure that no unseemly clandestine proposals emerged from the intelligence community. His stewardship also virtually guaranteed that the CIA under Carter and Mondale would fail to rise above its 1976 level of performance.

How little Carter understood the intelligence problem quickly became apparent. First, he accepted the resignation of George Bush rather than try to persuade him, as a matter of public service, to continue his efforts at removing the CIA from the political arena. Bush probably could have been convinced to stay if Carter had appealed to his sense of patriotism, but the President did not ask. Instead, he decided to pay off a campaign debt to a New Frontier era lawyer who had been Jack Kennedy's favorite speech writer—Theodore C. (Ted) Sorensen. Unfortunately, Sorensen, who was not very interested in the CIA, accepted the post since it was the only top-level slot available. He belonged to the liberal-left wing of the Democratic Party, not the more conservative group fully supportive of intelligence. It turned out he had been a conscientious objector to military service, an attitude that did not qualify him, in conservative eyes, to lead a force involved in international covert strategic activities. The Senate inquiry on the Sorensen nomination promised to be so critical that Sorensen withdrew.

At that point, Carter took another look and nominated Admiral Stansfield Turner, a career naval officer with a reputation for brains and administrative innovation, who could not be faulted by Senator Henry Jackson or any of the other conservative Senators. Turner became DCI on March 9, 1977. He served out the rest of the Carter term, leaving the office to William Casey in January of 1981.

Turner had an excellent record but, in practice, he showed little of the skill in interpersonal relations necessary for an effective leader of the CIA's clandestine services or its analytical staff. He understood and managed technical intelligence operations efficiently, but photography and electronic signals could not reveal what was going on in men's minds. Espionage was desperately needed to fill gaps in our knowledge of foreign governments' intentions and the dangers to U.S. interests in complex revolutionary situations like Iran and the Caribbean. From his record as DCI, it is clear that Turner had little feeling for agent collection.

In addition, Admiral Turner brought in too many naval staff officers and tended to isolate himself from most of the professional CIA career intelligence specialists. Employees said he thought the CIA was like a battleship, with replacable crew members on call when needed. He seemed genuinely fearful of being outwitted by the old CIA hands, to whom he and Mondale attributed the defeat of Sorensen in the confirmation process.

Early in his term in office, Turner retired his able professional Deputy, Hank Knoche. He also agreed to the abrupt separation from duty of another 200 experienced clandestine staff officers and the abolition of an additional 600 unencumbered jobs in the covert action and espionage field. This was not an entirely unreasonable administrative move, but it was handled as a purge of senior operators. Turner lost the confidence of agency personnel and the public, too. He passed up the chance to follow the Bush style of winning the confidence of professionals and presenting their case to

Congress and the public. Congress was becoming increasingly concerned that in its attempt to eliminate the CIA's occasional mistakes, intelligence skill was being sacrificed as well. Turner was unable to reassure the lawmakers. Morale in the CIA plummeted again, never fully to recover under Carter's lackluster, strategically incoherent conduct of foreign policy.

There was little respect for our national leadership as a whole. Intelligence staffs continued to see official as well as public distrust of the intelligence agencies. The traditional pride felt by elite professionals and the sense of satisfaction they derived from unsung deeds in government service tended to melt away. Being used and appreciated kept the secret operations specialists going; when they were neither well used nor appreciated, their spirit flagged.

Foreign intelligence services, absolutely aghast at the flood of data revealed in the Church Committee inquiry, remained loath to share reports from their best clandestine sources for fear they would be compromised through leaks to the news media. Turner never appeared to have the sure hand of a Dulles or a McCone or, for that matter, a great deal of clout in the Carter Administration. The CIA went on in low gear.

The uncertain mood in Washington was reflected in many events of the Carter years. Admiral Turner said President Carter had asked him for assurances that the intelligence agencies would act strictly in accordance with the law and American values. Neither mentioned that the agencies should, above all, provide information needed for the security of the United States. President Carter's first legislative request related to intelligence was for a bill requiring a federal judge's warrant in order to use intrusive techniques (wire tapping and bugging) even when they were aimed at foreign intelligence operations.

The low regard for the CIA was revealed in November of 1977, when a former Director of Central Intelligence, Richard Helms, was fined, given a suspended prison sentence, and sternly rebuked by the court for failing to testify fully and responsively in 1973 about covert action in Chile. Helms' defense was that his loyalty to his Commander-in-Chief and his statutory obligation to prevent unauthorized disclosure of CIA secrets excused his misleading public testimony before the

Senate, but he did not contest the charges. He was, instead, obliged to listen to an emotional tongue-lashing by District Court Justice Barrington D. Parker, who told him, "You now stand before this court in disgrace and shame."[9] Only in the United States could such a thing happen!

Ironically, a little earlier in 1977, Soviet KGB Director Yuriy Andropov received an ovation from President Brezhnev and most of the Soviet Communist Politburo when he eulogized the intelligence agencies in the USSR for standing "guard over the security of the Soviet state and...social system." He quoted Lenin's remark that a "revolution is only worth anything when it knows how to defend itself."[10]

On January 24, 1978, President Carter issued Executive Order 12036, spelling out the administrative policies by which the U.S. intelligence agencies would be governed. It remained in effect into 1981. Carter retained most of the structure described in President Ford's Executive Order: they confirmed the DCI's authority and responsibility for central review and coordination of intelligence reporting, community budget, and assignment of collection tasks to the many different collection components of the whole intelligence system. An important symbolic provision of the Executive Order was retention (with new appointees) of the Intelligence Oversight Board to monitor activities possibly involving illegality or impropriety. This was in the face of Carter's decision, implemented earlier, to abolish the President's Foreign Intelligence Advisory Board, which had encouraged positive performance by the CIA and the other intelligence agencies.

Unfortunately, Executive Order 12036 went further into legal hairsplitting over definitions of functions of and restrictions on the intelligence agencies. In the 26-page document, 8 pages dealt with prohibited activities. The Attorney General was assigned broad powers to establish guidelines governing all of the intelligence agencies, especially the CIA and the FBI, in operations that might conceivably infringe upon the rights or the privacy of U.S. citizens and resident aliens. Compared with the positive tone of Ford's Executive Order, Carter's 12036 adopted a restrictive and punitive tone. This undoubtedly dampened the enthusiasm of agency officers anxious to do a good job but fearful that they might fall afoul of the complex prohibitions and definitions of forbidden activities.

The Carter-Mondale emphasis on restrictions of intelligence operations led to the passage of the Foreign Intelligence Surveillance Act of 1978, which in general required a court order for electronic monitoring of signals in the United States, even in national security cases. At about the same time, it became public knowledge that Soviet espionage in the United States was successfully penetrating the most carefully guarded CIA secrets about foreign surveillance. A young CIA intelligence watch officer, William Kampiles, was convicted of having sold a Russian agent an operations manual for an advanced U.S. photographic reconnaissance satellite system. At approximately the same time it was disclosed that two young Californians working for a contract manufacturer on CIA projects delivered data on a number of electronic and photographic reconnaissance systems to Soviet agent handlers.[11] These cases alarmed the public; journalists began to chastise the CIA because it could no longer protect its own most secret material. The pendulum was swinging back toward concern for national security.

Probably most influential in the spreading awareness of the fear that the handcuffing of the CIA might have gone too far was the knowledge of a steady buildup of new Soviet military weapons, including the SS-17, SS-18, and SS-19 missiles and a new supersonic bomber, the BACKFIRE. This growing Soviet military strength provided protection against American reprisal while the world witnessed a series of Soviet covert actions. Action by Cuban soldiers in Angola, Ethiopia, and Yemen increased Moscow's political and economic power. Vietnam became a formal ally of the USSR and provided facilities for Soviet military forces to resist the pressure of Communist China. Soviet troops moved into Afghanistan to prop up a shaky pro-Soviet regime there, while Iran slid into chaos—the Shah abandoned his throne and armies without any U.S. action on his behalf. Of course, the final indignity was a violently anti-American Islamic regime under Ayotollah Khomeini taking some 50 U.S. diplomats hostage in Iran and keeping them more than a year.

This is not the place to go into details about the tragedy that befell Iran and, indeed, the rest of the world in the latter half of the Carter term in office. The daily TV pictures of angry, fanatical mobs in Teheran shouting anti-American slogans must have convinced responsible citizens, who might not otherwise have paid such close attention, that a firmer foreign policy, a greater defense capability, and a more effective strategic intelligence apparatus were indispensable to the United States in the 1980s.

Certainly the CIA did not predict the revolution in Iran, did not inspire the Carter National Security Council to formulate sound strategic policies, and was not able to do anything to resolve the hostage crisis that frustrated this country from November of 1979 to January of 1981. In the circumstances, it is not clear just how the CIA could have done a better job. However, more people stopped carping at the CIA and started demanding better intelligence not only to keep track of the Soviet military buildup but also to cope with a kaleidoscopic pattern of geopolitical conflicts that raised the specter of Iranian-style anarchy and violence in other regions of the world.

By 1979, nearly everyone was complaining about shortcomings in foreign intelligence operations rather than about domestic transgressions. Senator Daniel P. Moynihan, a member of the Senate Intelligence Committee, observed that experienced middle-level and senior CIA officers were taking early retirement in unprecedented numbers. He noted that 400 had retired in 1977, 650 in 1978, and several hundred more early in 1979. *The National Review* of May 25, 1979, quoted him as concluding, "There is no intelligence agency of any kind in the United States today." President Carter himself complained about the quality of political intelligence he was receiving on complex situations like the one in Iran. The *U.S. News and World Report,* of May 7, 1979, spoke of "plummeting morale" in the CIA, and *The Wall Street Journal* of October 4, 1979, reported in a headline, "Experts Fear that U.S. Loses Espionage Battle with the Soviet Union." Columnist Hugh Sidey, an experienced and balanced Washington political commentator of many years' standing, wrote in *The Washington Star* of December 9, 1979, "Rising troubles show need to work the 'back alleys' again."

Eleven days later, *The New York Times*, which had done so much to launch the anti-CIA crusade, printed a column their editors had solicited from me arguing the case for "Rebuilding American Intelligence."

In 1980, President Carter (noisily) shifted foreign policy gears, saying that he had learned a lesson from the Soviet military occupation of Afghanistan—as if the study of Soviet policy had begun when he took office! In his State of the Union Message to Congress, January 23, 1980, Carter made the most balanced reference to intelligence to emerge from the White House during his tenure. Starting on a pejorative note, as always, he concluded by calling for more security controls of the kind he had deplored in the past and fewer restraints of the kind he had imposed:

> We also need clear and quick passage of a new charter to define clearly the legal authority and accountability of our intelligence agencies. We will guarantee that abuses do not recur, but we must tighten our controls on sensitive government information and we need to remove unwarranted restraints on America's ability to collect intelligence.

The end of the season of disenchantment with the CIA was indeed at hand although enthusiasm over the new charter mentioned by Carter in his message languished, until the Reagan Administration took office in 1981. Then, the White House and the CIA would be dealing with stalwart conservative Senator Barry Goldwater rather than liberal Democrat Senator Birch Bayh (who was not even reelected) as Chairman of the Senate Select Committee on Intelligence. A former senior CIA officer, John F. Blake, became Director of the Senate committee staff under Goldwater, going directly from the presidency of the non-profit Association of Former Intelligence Officers, an organization dedicated to a stronger, less hampered intelligence system. Of course, the plainest straw in the wind was the failure of Senator Frank Church, the investigative scourge of the U.S. intelligence community, to win reelection. Whatever other things voters may have wanted, they appear to have demanded a new agenda for the CIA.

*Chapter Seven*

# A New Beginning for Central Intelligence

When President Reagan took office in 1981, one of the key programs he initiated to strengthen the international strategic posture and credibility of the United States was rebuilding and revitalizing the national intelligence system, particularly the much criticized and grievously weakened Central Intelligence Agency. To reverse the tide of deterioration in intelligence capabilities that had flowed for most of the 1970s, the President drew on the advice and counsel of a former Director of the CIA, Vice President George Bush; to carry out the rebuilding program Reagan turned to a close friend, distinguished lawyer, and veteran of OSS clandestine operations, William Casey. An experienced public servant, Casey was head of the Security and Exchange Commission and the Export-Import Bank, and Under Secretary for Economic Affairs in the State Department in the Nixon-Ford era. He was a writer—author of a good book on the American Revolutionary War—and a skilled practitioner of the kind of politically oriented legal practice that flourished in Washington. More important, he was campaign staff director and chief transition planner for Reagan and, as a result, enjoyed the new President's complete personal trust, one of the prime requirements for a successful intelligence chief in the complex decision-making world of the American democratic political process.

His experience as an active intelligence officer dated back to World War II, when he headed the London office of OSS responsible for the espionage penetrations program against Hitler's Germany. (Casey's role is described in detail in a 1978 book entitled *Piercing the Reich* by Joseph Persico.) Much later, he served on President Ford's Foreign Intelligence Advisory Board, thus staying *au courant* with the fully developed CIA model that grew from the OSS origins. He was past president of the Veterans of OSS, a winner of that group's "Donovan Award" for outstanding public service, and a member of the Advisory Board of the National Intelligence Study Center.

Bill Casey encompassed the outlook, experience, and knowledge of the unique generation of Americans who had improvised a new central intelligence system to help win World War II and then watched it provide the underpinning of the strategic achievements of the "American Age" of world influence and security in the 1950s and 1960s. For him the timidity and defeatism of the Carter era were temporary aberrations understandable in the light of the U.S. withdrawal from Vietnam but in no way a guide for the future. Reagan feels the same way.

A quiet, unassuming man, Casey projected the image of an organizer and political thinker, in sharp contrast to the dashing OSS leader "Wild Bill" Donovan or the suave master spy, Allen W. Dulles. His style was unique, though it had something of the professional dedication of Dulles. In fact, Casey was most like the most skillful and successful of CIA's several leaders, businessman and public servant John McCone. Casey seemed to be the man who could in a time of international danger as menacing as World War II, bring alive the legacy of OSS.

Casey's mission was to work with a President who believed in strengthening United States defense forces and alliances with the association of democratic nations that had looked to Washington for strategic leadership for thirty years. The United States had to reach a common understanding with its allies to contain the influence of the Soviet Union and its satellites such as Cuba, North Korea, and East Germany.

Casey had two enormous advantages besides his own experience and ability. First, he came to the CIA at a time when the principle of accountability to Congress had been well established and practiced; this guaranteed constitutional procedures for dealing with intelligence tasks while providing security and thoughtful counsel to the intelligence community.

Second, Casey found that the ardor of Congress and the public restrictive charters circumscribing secret intelligence operations had cooled. These two advantages are worth examining in detail. They provided the elbow room the CIA needed to recharge its intellectual and operational batteries.

## Accountability: Congressional Oversight

The Ford reforms reflected in the Executive Order 11905 of February 18, 1976 prescribed remedies for most of the shortcomings in the intelligence community structure and performance record. They set up a chain of accountability through several lines of reporting to the President to insure that an agency necessarily operating in secrecy is not left in any doubt about the legality or propriety of its activities. There is a natural limit, however, to the confidence that the Congress and the public can feel in Presidential and Presidentially supervised checks on a secret intelligence system under the exclusive management of the Executive Branch of government. In our constitutional process, true accountability involves some checks and balances by the Congress to insure Executive Branch performance in keeping with laws devised by the element in our government most representative of popular attitudes. Nearly everyone who looked into the problem recommended some kind of joint committee of the Congress for intelligence oversight.

The House of Representatives was not able to wind up its inquiry into intelligence performance during the Ford Administration with any concrete House action, so it is not surprising that it was not able to join the Senate in setting up a joint committee. The Senate, recognizing that it might be a long while before the House acted on a joint committee, established a permanent committee of its own for intelligence oversight. It was set up as the Senate Select Committee on Intelligence on May 19, 1976. Subsequently, on July 14, 1977, the House Permanent Select Committee on Intelligence was formed with a similar responsibility to oversee the work of the intelligence agencies. This pointed the way to what is by far the most

# Directors and Deputy Directors of Central Intelligence

## Directors of Central Intelligence

RADM Sidney W. Souers, USNR
23 January 1946-10 June 1946

LTGEN Hoyt S. Vandenberg, USA
10 June 1946-1 May 1947

RADM Roscoe H. Hillenkoetter, USN
1 May 1947-7 October 1950

GEN Walter Bedell Smith, USA
7 October 1950-9 February 1953

The Honorable Allen W. Dulles*
26 February 1953-29 November 1961

The Honorable John A. McCone
29 November 1961-28 April 1965

VADM William F. Raborn, Jr., USN (Ret.) 28 April 1965-30 June 1966

The Honorable Richard Helms
30 June 1966-2 February 1973

The Honorable James R. Schlesinger
2 February 1973-2 July 1973

The Honorable William E. Colby
4 September 1973-30 January 1976

The Honorable George Bush
30 January 1976-20 January 1977

ADM Stansfield Turner, USN
9 March 1977-20 January 1981

The Honorable William J. Casey
28 January 1981

## Deputy Directors

Kingman Douglass*
2 March 1946-11 July 1946

BGEN Edwin K. Wright, USA
20 January 1947-9 March 1949

The Honorable William H. Jackson
7 October 1950-3 August 1951

The Honorable Allen W. Dulles
23 August 1951-26 February 1953

GEN Charles Pearre Cabell, USAF
23 April 1953-31 January 1962

LTGEN Marshall S. Carter, USA
3 April 1962-28 April 1965

The Honorable Richard Helms
28 April 1965-30 June 1966

VADM Rufus L. Taylor, USN
13 October 1966-31 January 1969

LTGEN Robert E. Cushman, Jr., USMC 7 May 1969-31 December 1971

LTGEN Vernon A. Walters, USA**
2 May 1972-7 July 1976

The Honorable E. Henry Knoche***
7 July 1976-31 July 1977

John F. Blake****
31 July 1977-10 February 1978

The Honorable Frank C. Carlucci
10 February 1978 -
5 February 1981

ADM Bobby R. Inman
12 February 1981 -

*Mr. Dulles served as Acting DCI from 9-26 February 1953

*Mr. Douglass served as Acting DDCI from 2 March-11 July 1946

**GEN Walters served as Acting DCI from 3 July 1973-3 September 1973

***Mr. Knoche served as Acting DCI from 20 January 1977-9 March 1977

****Mr. Blake served as Acting DDCI from 31 July 1977-10 February 1978.

practical solution yet proposed to the problem of reinsuring that the CIA and the other intelligence agencies will be accountable in a broad way not only to the President but to Congress. This system has helped a great deal to reassure the public that intelligence was being doubly monitored in a way that provided an Executive-Congressional check and balance system quite in keeping with our constitutional procedures. With separate Senate and House committees providing in effect a double check on Executive intelligence policies and on the performance of the CIA, the legal framework at long last had been put in place for effective Congressional oversight, a crucial part of the blueprint for the essential CIA that the nation needs.

When the Congress passed the National Security Act of 1947 setting up the CIA, there was a clear consensus on its part that a central intelligence system to collect and to "correlate and evaluate" information was needed. The brutal political methods by which Stalin (in 1946 and 1947) was seizing control of Central Europe while bringing military pressures to bear on Iran, Turkey, and Greece created the terms and the facts of the iron curtain and the cold war in these postwar years. In this climate the sense of need for an effective machinery to protect the nation against another Pearl Harbor was great. Little concern for extraordinary regulating, monitoring, or oversight procedures was registered.

In this atmosphere, and in the ensuing era from the Korean War in 1950 down to the Cuba missile crisis of 1962, the CIA became a vital part of the U.S. governing process without much public awareness or appreciation of its activities. Most Americans, including most Congressmen, were not very clear about what intelligence agencies actually were supposed to do and showed very little disposition to assert a right to know in detail about this part of our national security apparatus.

The National Security Act of 1947 made the CIA an independent agency. The main purpose in establishing the CIA was to insure that information related to national defense and foreign policy was gathered together, analyzed skillfully, and passed along in appropriate form to the makers of national policy on issues of national security. It was assumed, reasonably enough, that the best judges of how the CIA ought to perform would be the men who needed the service most. The President and his advisers on defense policy and foreign affairs oversee the work of all Executive Branch agencies, and the CIA was seen simply as another, albeit unusual, part of the array of agencies supervised by the President or his agents in carrying out the responsibilities of the President as Commander in Chief of military forces, principal manager of the foreign policy process, and the nation's Chief Executive.

The CIA and other intelligence agencies were thought by many Congressmen to deserve a unique freedom from restrictive oversight arrangements because of the inevitable secrecy in which much of their work had to be conducted if it was to be successful and because of the close association of intelligence activities in most minds with war, actual or "cold," in which the powers of the Commander in Chief are paramount for the safety of the nation.

Nevertheless, in keeping with the divided powers of government institutions in our open society, a system was evolved whereby the CIA came under Congressional scrutiny. The Constitution grants to the Congress sole power to collect money through taxation and appropriate it to "provide for the common defense and general welfare of the United States." The CIA from the beginning had to have money to pay staff, house them, and meet the operating costs of the complex business of gathering and coordinating intelligence from all sources and all agencies, including its own overseas staff. Beyond this, as the tensions of international conflicts grew, the CIA activities abroad in the fields of espionage, counterespionage, and covert political operations, at the time deemed to be of importance to U.S. national interests, became far-flung, complex, and expensive. Congress, because of its power of the purse, had to be consulted and it was in fact consulted on these matters. From the very beginning Congress was recognized to have the right, and as much opportunity as it requested, to oversee the CIA's work. Briefings of the Congress by the CIA for the purpose of facilitating this oversight and insuring that Congress was disposed favorably to vote the money for the CIA operations were conducted in accordance with special procedures adopted by the Congress itself. Prior to the Nixon Administration there was no history of the CIA holding back information requested by Congressional oversight subcommittee members authorized by the Congress to be briefed on CIA activities.

It was determined that the CIA, with its need for secrecy and strict internal discipline, partook more of the nature of a military agency then a normal Cabinet Department, and responsibility for legislation relating exclusively to the CIA was assigned to the Armed Services Committees in the Senate and House of Representatives. It was further determined that special CIA subcommittees of the Appropriations Committee of each House of the Congress had a need to know the purposes for which the Congress was voting money.

All of this was conventional enough, although it was unusual for budgets to be approved informally without an authorization bill. Two other special provisions of the Congress in carrying out its general legislative oversight responsibility deviated somewhat from the run-of-the-mill of Congressional business. First, very small subcommittees were set up in both Houses of the Congress under the Armed Services and Appropriations Committees to hold what amounted to hearings on intelligence programs with careful provision for secrecy about the proceedings, with no provision whatsoever for public hearings on the record, and with the CIA rather than the subcommittees keeping the record of the meetings in the interests of security of the information passed. The atmosphere surrounding these sessions was for many years informal and confidential. It is significant of the psychology of this procedure that CIA encounters with these subcommittees were usually called "briefings" rather than hearings. Congress appeared more interested in learning than in restricting or monitoring.

A second determination of how to handle this new and sensitive agency, which was considered to be doing essential tasks requiring absolute secrecy, was the decision to include the CIA appropriations under the Defense Department budgets without making it a line item. This procedure not only concealed the amount of money spent by the CIA from general Congressional or public scrutiny, but also made it possible for the Director of the CIA to be given authority (from 1949) to spend some of the funds within this budget as "unvouchered"— that is, accounted for only by the DCI's certificate of expenditure for confidential purposes and checked only by internal CIA audits rather than in the framework of the normal government accounting system.

Since it was clearly undesirable for foreign intelligence systems intent on penetrating the U.S. national security apparatus to have the benefit of a breakdown of programs and expenditures of U.S. organizations designed to counter their efforts, the Congress adopted the view that concealment in the Defense Department bill of the CIA's intelligence expenditures was appropriate and necessary. The CIA was unique in its dealings with the legislature, but these procedures were approved by the Congressional committee chairmen involved and without doubt reflected the opinion of the majority of the Congress during the 1950s and 1960s insofar as a coherent view existed.

The net effect of this oversight system was to have the small group of men in Congress assigned to the CIA subcommittees hold rather informal "briefing" sessions with the CIA, and then assure members of their parent committees in most general terms that the CIA programs were legitimate. If the special CIA appropriations subcommittees gave their sanction, the CIA appropriations were then buried in Defense appropriations so that neither the whole Senate nor the whole House of Representatives could get much of a handle on intelligence expenditures when they were voted on. This procedure certainly gave the CIA and the intelligence programs it sponsored an exceptionally privileged position in the legislative process. There was nothing furtive about it, however, and over the years the Congress repeatedly squelched bills to change the system.

Conventional wisdom from 1947 for about 25 years clearly held that intelligence needed these special safeguards and special procedures. Congress provided them and has employed them with only a little change down to the present time. In the mid-fifties and early sixties I learned something about the CIA briefing process for Congress and, when I was Deputy Director for Intelligence in the 1962-1966 period, participated directly in many of the briefings. They were serious efforts by the CIA to tell the Congressional members of the four CIA oversight subcommittees about important intelligence programs, especially when they cost a lot of money or when they might come to public notice in ways that would embarrass the Congressmen if they had not been forewarned. Subjects like the U-2 and satellite reconnaissance projects, the buildup of the Meo secret army under the CIA in Laos, and the U.S. intelligence capability generally, in every trouble spot of the world, were frequently discussed.

The key figures in my time were Senator Richard Russell and Congressman Carl Vinson, with other elder statesmen like Senators Carl Hayden, Stuart Symington, and Leverett Saltonstall directly involved. Later on, Senator John Stennis and Congressman Edward Hebert became key figures. Clarence Cannon and George Mahon, longtime Chairmen of the House Appropriations Committee, monitored the House subcommittees with close attention and often received special briefings. All of these men and the others associated with the CIA oversight had enormous prestige and much practical power in the Congressional committee system of the day. Their word was good with their colleagues. They were serious men, anxious to insure that the national security was well-protected. They asked many questions; they sometimes made suggestions. On the other hand, they did not see themselves as exercising anything more than the general legislative responsibility for intelligence activities that accrued to the Congress through its power of the purse. They did not often go into intricate detail, and they usually did not want to know the identities of sources or the nature of technical methodology. They were, in general, supportive rather than critical of what they learned and they learned all they wanted to know. They genuinely feared that they would inadvertently let slip secret data that would damage intelligence capabilities if they filled their minds with operational details.

This informal, limited, but on the whole reasonably effective oversight system lasted for many years. Occasionally the subcommittees of the foreign affairs committees of both Houses of Congress were given CIA substantive briefings. It is clear that uncoordinated Congressional subcommittees do not make a structured review group, nevertheless, the United States, within a 15-year period, built up the most comprehensive, competent intelligence system in the world, starting almost from scratch, and did it by common consent of the Executive Branch and the Congress, which agreed in thinking the need for it was overriding. No unauthorized disclosures of the CIA's secrets occurred in this period. Twenty or so key members of Congress knew what the general intelligence program was like and the money got voted. The intelligence community performed effectively in developing intelligence collection techniques, analyzing national security hazards objectively and—on the occasions when ordered to do so by the President—taking covert political or paramilitary action abroad to supplement American foreign diplomacy and military assistance programs.

It was this last function that proved to have in it the seeds of trouble. When there was a consensus in the nation and in the Congress on our national strategy of containment of the USSR and Communist China, almost any oversight system would have worked. But in the later sixties violent disagreements about Vietnam policies disrupted the fabric of public affairs in nearly every field of endeavor. Fundamental disputes arose over U.S. policies and were not easily resolved. These sometimes embraced the CIA's activities, particularly in foreign countries where the CIA had moved on a large scale into an action role, theoretically a "covert" action role, as in Vietnam and Laos, performing high visibility paramilitary tasks alongside its more conventional intelligence collection activities. Some of these programs, such as the training and direction of the Meo army, were not very covert in the real sense of the word. Many Congressmen were briefed, although some of those briefed have subsequently suffered convenient lapses of memory. Many newspapermen learned nearly everything about using the Meo hill tribesmen in attempts first to monitor and subsequently to interfere with the passage of North Vietnamese guerrillas and military supplies to South Vietnam along the Ho Chi Minh jungle trail. When the defense of South Vietnam from these North Vietnamese infiltrations was a popular cause, the Meo fighting tribesmen were much admired by those who knew about their raids against the invaders. Paramilitary operations by the Meo were carried out under the direct command of the U.S. Ambassadors to Laos, and the Defense Department enthusiastically supported the Meo operations because they provided much cheaper results than

U.S. military forces could give—a cost and manpower benefit ratio calculated at the time as about ten to one. It was also convenient for the administration that a Presidential order to the CIA on building up the Meo force could be carried out with a minimum of procedural red tape and no formal Congressional action. For a long time there were no demurrers from the oversight committees.

As long as nearly everyone believed in the Vietnam war, everyone approved of the Meo army and the somewhat similar paramilitary operations in Vietnam because they worked so well for the purpose intended and were extremely cost-efficient. The CIA's network of agents in touch with the fiercely independent tribesmen were the indispensable link in contacting, arming, training, and directing the Meo irregulars. Some Congressmen who later condemned it praised the Meo program lavishly at the time. I remember briefing at least a number of Congressmen on the Meo paramilitary structure in the course of general briefings of the oversight subcommittees and do not remember a single objection.

When public support for the whole Vietnam war waned, and especially when the Nixon White House became almost totally estranged from an increasingly suspicious Congress, questions were raised about this and other Vietnam-related covert operations. Some of them were legitimate questions about how such large paramilitary enterprises were approved and funded. Some were questions of principle. At the height of the Watergate revelations in 1973 and 1974, Nixon's many arbitrary abuses of the authority of U.S. agencies, including the CIA, and his resort to extremely secretive methods of governing in many fields gave rise to suspicions that vast misdeeds had occurred in the arch-agency of secret agencies, the CIA.

What emerged from the whole episode of press and Congressional investigation in 1975 and 1976 was that the Congressional oversight system of the fifties and sixties was no longer acceptable to the more inquiring and anti-establishment Congressmen of the seventies. It certainly would have been helpful if a Congressional oversight apparatus had existed that could promptly have helped to disprove suspicions in the minds of critics of the intelligence agencies and the President. As it was, the CIA suffered unfairly and grievously in its staff morale and its effectiveness in getting cooperation from foreigners in overseas operations. It turned out that the men in whom they had been confiding over the years as duly constituted oversight representatives of the Congress, particularly since the leaders such as Russell and Vinson had left Capitol Hill, could not stem the tide of fear and suspicion among their latter-day legislative colleagues, let alone in the minds of the press, the TV reporters, or the public.

In these circumstances a new oversight system clearly became essential. The first requirement of a good oversight structure is that it have the confidence of the Congress as a whole and yet permit the handling of sensitive information so that what is divulged to a Congressional committee will not leak to the press and public. Accountability to the elected representatives of the people is a fundamental concept in the American political process. The CIA has always been accountable to the President, but its relationship to Congress has been too vague and too little understood.

The Church and Pike Committees revealed both how difficult and how important it is to make good arrangements for protecting the security of sensitive information. There are few in Congress now who would deny that some secrecy in authorized intelligence work is required in the public interest and is not in contradiction to a democratic society just as secrecy in grand jury proceedings and privacy in internal revenue records are essential for the good of everyone involved and the country's political system as a whole. At times Americans talk as if everything secret is evil, but surely most reasonable men accept that it would be good to protect a secret about a weapon that is critical to the defense of the nation or a secret about an intelligence source capable of revealing and negating a foreign effort to overthrow a friendly government. Only the purist could argue that the obvious benefits of secret intelligence should be completely sacrificed on the altar of total openness in government operations.

The first need then is to have Congress maintain an oversight system with responsible Congressional leaders who can be consulted on very sensitive information involving the lives of men and the safety of the country against attack or subversion without running the risk of surfacing the information, the source, or the means by which the intelligence was provided. In other words, oversight should not work in a way that would break the provision of law in the National Security Act of 1947 requiring the protection of intelligence sources and methods.

The main responsibility in intelligence oversight is to approve the broad program and the budget for intelligence agencies, including the intelligence components of the Defense and State departments, as well as the FBI, and to review major intelligence proposals, especially for covert action. The membership in the oversight committees is broadly representative of both Houses of Congress since they must draw two members each from their respective Armed Services, Appropriations, Foreign Relations, and Judiciary committees. Each committee is likely to concentrate on things closest to its own legislative interests rather than aimlessly exploring everything across the board. Ideally, the House committee would mainly study the overall program and budget, with special reference to providing adequate intelligence support for defense purposes, in view of the Representatives' responsibility for initiating appropriations bills. The Senate committee concentrates on issues that plainly overlap with foreign policy, where the Senate has a clear though limited Constitutional responsibility to provide advice and give consent on making international treaties and appointing diplomatic representatives of the United States.

Obviously neither committee could be formally restricted in its sphere of investigations. Nevertheless subcommittee work reflects a greater division of labor than would a single joint committee. The main thing needed is for procedures to be adopted that will permit Congressional opinion to be brought to bear on overall policies and programs of the intelligence agencies, without stifling them completely through an overly cautious attitude or endangering their security by loose talk to other members of Congress or the press. Congress alone can decide how to organize itself for this purpose and the two Houses of Congress alone have the authority to discipline their own members or staff employees who hamstring intelligence programs by leaking information about them. On the whole the new Congressional oversight committees have achieved this kind of self-discipline and provided reasonably effective control.

Since most intelligence activities are in the field of collection and evaluation of data, Congressional oversight reviews will not be very controversial or difficult. In fact, the hard problem may be to get busy Congressmen who have genuine authority and prestige to spend enough time to do a good job on these matters. Insofar as oversight was lax in earlier years, it is because the Congressmen concerned were perfunctory or erratic in their performance of this duty.

Of course it will be equally important for the oversight apparatus of Congress to recognize from the outset that its members must leave the actual work of the agencies in all of its complex detail in the hands of the Executive Branch where it belongs according to the Constitution, and where the tasks can be undertaken by appropriately organized staff units accountable to, but not supervised in detail by, the Congress. Day-to-day management must remain in the hands of the Chief Executive and his appointees. Congressional oversight must be confined to policy review, program review, and budget approval and not be an attempt to take over or second-guess managerial and administrative decisions. These cannot be made practicably in committee, certainly not in the political atmosphere of a Congressional committee or subcommittee. The Congress has a hard enough time passing laws, and it experiences the greatest of difficulty in efficiently handling even those limited kinds of executive action it must take to manage its own housekeeping business.

Congress' valid concern ought to be to protect the national interest by monitoring performance sufficiently to be able to assure the whole Congress that intelligence programs and objectives are in conformity with the basic policies and principles of the country, whose voters they are elected to represent on such issues. Insofar as FBI activities concern domestic intelligence collection rather than law enforcement, the FBI should also report regularly to the intelligence committees. The aim would be to permit members of Congress to be advised and consulted—though not to be asked to give specific administrative approvals—on general directives and major decisions affecting the work of the several agencies.

With such a system, the members of the oversight committees could play a constructive role in giving the President and his Cabinet advisers a realistic feeling of what the attitudes of Members of Congress and their constituencies might be on critical matters. Everyone benefits from establishment of an atmosphere of bi-partisan cooperation in the public interest.

There is no way in our political system that the President can force the Congress to go along against its judgment on defense and foreign policy. There is also no way, except through the eventual drawing tight of the purse strings, by which the Congress can prevent the President from making a move in defense and foreign policy that he believes to be essential in the national interest. A better oversight system in Congress, with membership made up of the best and most respected leaders, would provide extremely useful counsel and guidance not only to the President but also to the CIA.

What is critical is that the Congress has adopted a procedure that encourages the President and the intelligence agencies to provide sensitive information in the expectation that procedures to prevent its leaking would be enforced in Congress as vigorously as they are in the Executive Branch. This should apply to all Congressional staff employees as well as to Executive agency employees.

There is probably no way to apply criminal sanctions to Congress or the press in view of constitutional guarantees of freedom of information and debate.* Nevertheless, where the public safety is at stake, the Houses of Congress are perfectly capable of disciplining their own members if need be, and they will do so if the members of Congress responsible for oversight stress the necessity of protecting intelligence sources and methods as well as reviewing intelligence programs and budgets. Fortunately the Senate and House oversight committees have emphasized this point strongly.

The sticky issue on which oversight proposals usually become controversial is the extent of advance knowledge a Congressional committee or committees should have concerning covert actions overseas. These actions are often

---

*The British Official Secrets Act, which provides penalties for anyone revealing state secrets, regardless of whether or not espionage is involved, is sometimes suggested as a model for similar U.S. legislation. It is often argued that a U.S. Official Secrets Act would be unconstitutional in view of the First Amendment.

controversial elements of key foreign policy or defense policy commitments. The CIA in these cases acts only as an instrument of policy—and it is not intelligence interests but the national strategy and diplomatic objectives at stake that determine the wisdom as well as the necessity of the covert action. All the CIA contributes to the policy decision is an opinion on the feasibility of accomplishing the mission covertly. It is inappropriate and counterproductive for the CIA or any other intelligence agency to try to explain these national policy decisions to Congress.

If a secret action by the CIA is about to be taken as a result of confidential instructions from the President or his duly authorized Cabinet representative, the oversight apparatus of the Congress must to be advised. If members of the committee or committees have reservations about the policy concept, they ought to be passed to representatives of the President as consultative or advisory opinions. It does not seem to me to be feasible for these members of Congress to exercise a veto. What they can do is warn the President that there might be objections in the Congress and among the electorate if the operation becomes public knowledge.

Members of Congress objecting to covert actions about which they were informed in their role in the oversight system should take the lead in discussing the matter carefully in an executive session with the Cabinet officer responsible, usually the Secretary of State and on occasion the Secretary of Defense, not primarily with the intelligence officers involved. Secrecy should be an absolute rule in such discussions. In any case, issues at stake here, where Congressional and Presidential roles and privileges in broad policymaking tend to meet or overlap, are not intelligence oversight problems; they are defense policy or foreign problems. Ample precedent exists for ironing out disagreement between White House and Congress in these policy areas.

Contention concerning covert action ought, however, to be separated clearly in everyone's mind from central intelligence problems. The CIA certainly ought not to be skewered by Congress for following Presidential orders pursuant to legal Presidential decisions governing foreign policy initiatives or defense force deployments and activities overseas. If covert paramilitary and political programs authorized for execution by the CIA are fully compartmented from other intelligence programs and dealt with in this separate procedural fashion, the bread-and-butter business of intelligence, which is vital, can proceed and these policy conflicts can be dealt with in a special context in keeping with Presidential and Congressional powers and responsibilities.

Few major covert action programs were proposed for a number of years for many reasons, one of which was the absurd requirement by Congress that members of eight separate committees be briefed in advance on any CIA action other than simple intelligence collection. This provision in the Hughes-Ryan Amendment passed into law as a rider to the Foreign Assistance Act of 1974, resulted in almost every important project so briefed leaking to the public immediately. President Ford wanted to provide covert aid to the non-Communist guerrilla forces in Angola in 1975, and he also was in favor of financial help to the center and right political parties in Italy at the same time. Both proposals were deliberately leaked by Congressmen or Congressional staff officers, and no substantial project was subsequently proposed. In June 1976 Congress approved the Clark Amendment to the Arms Export Control Act specifically prohibiting covert action in Angola. Covert action was incompatible with the Carter-Mondale philosophy, articulated clearly clearly by Mondale as explained in the introductory *Overview*, pages 17 and 18.

There obviously could be no real covert action under such a loose system. The result, of course, was near total atrophy of covert action skills and assets. In the last days of the Carter Administration, the Hughes-Ryan Amendment was revised. The CIA was thus less shackled as of the beginning of the Reagan era. If oversight procedures plainly isolate covert action proposals and deal with them secretly and responsibly, the country, the Congress, and the CIA will be much better off.

Finally, an intelligence oversight mechanism in Congress must deal with counterespionage, counterintelligence, and internal security. Where these problems are conducted overseas, the CIA is mainly responsible, along with the military counterintelligence services protecting their own forces and facilities. These activities should be reviewed in broad terms like any other intelligence program. At some point, however, intelligence about what enemy agents are trying to do abroad often melds into what they are trying to do in the United States in the way of espionage, subversion, or sabotage. These are illegal actions requiring internal security surveillance and—in the final stages—police action. These latter functions belong to the intelligence element of the FBI and the local police, clearly separated from the work of the CIA, as is now the case.

Nevertheless, the amassing of information about foreign agents by the FBI in pursuit of its domestic program is crucially interrelated with similar intelligence collection abroad, and the whole body of knowledge bears on general intelligence estimates of foreign capabilities and intentions. Just as this aspect of the FBI's work ought to be coordinated within the framework of the whole intelligence community, FBI intelligence programs in the internal security field generally ought to be reviewed by the same oversight authorities in Congress who oversee the CIA and the other agencies. Responsibility for the FBI budget can be shared with the committees handling the budget of the whole Justice Department.

It was the CIA's improper minor intrusions in the internal security field, under heavy pressure from President Johnson and President Nixon to find foreign connections of anti-war demonstrators, that got the CIA in the worst of its trouble in the late 1960s and early 1970s. Here effective Congressional oversight would have been a godsend and might have forestalled the necessity for the CIA to violate the spirit of its charter in trying to satisfy these two forceful Presidents. The gray area, where overseas counterespionage borders on and overlaps with domestic surveillance of enemy agents, must be more clearly delimited in Congressional minds as it has been in recent Executive Branch guidelines. Public confidence in intelligence activities impinging on the domestic scene requires the checks and balances aspects of Congressional oversight. Everybody wants to avoid anything approaching a Gestapo and the American people ought to be reassured on this point. With adequate Executive and Congressional guarantees against abuses, the CIA and other agencies can get the public support they need to do a good job of intelligence collection and evaluation and other tasks much less controversial than counterespionage and counterintelligence.

The larger objectives of restoring the confidence of the American people in the compatibility of a competent secret intelligence system with the demands of an open society can be met if Congress simply requires annual submission of a program budget. In it the Director of Central Intelligence should describe in general terms the functions and programs of each agency of the Executive Branch that collects, processes, or analyzes intelligence materials. Putting a budgetary fence around these activities would clarify the allocation of responsibility in a salutary way. The agencies themselves and the Congress would understand better where the taxpayers' dollars are going and for what.

There is no reason why, if Congress' creaky committee machinery makes it mandatory, the budget of each intelligence agency cannot also be reviewed by the various committees passing on the total budget of its parental Cabinet department, i.e., Defense, State, Justice. The detailed hearings on the intelligence aspects of the budget would always, however, be conducted in closed sessions by the intelligence oversight committees. The decisions made in these sessions would normally prevail when the Congress voted on a budget. Probably certain activities, like tactical air reconnaissance by the armed forces and law enforcement tasks of the FBI, would prove to be ambiguous as to whether they were really intelligence-related or integral to the operational mission of the unit concerned. The rule ought to be simply that, if the President and the Director of Central Intelligence determine that an activity is primarily related to national intelligence collection and analysis rather than to the operational responsibilities legally delegated to the Cabinet department, the intelligence program ought to include it; and in that case the intelligence oversight committees ought to review it and approve it.

Almost every agency of government collects intelligence for its own purposes, and some of these data are useful to central intelligence analysis and estimates experts. There should be no doubt of the availability of the data to the Director of Central Intelligence and his national intelligence system, but these primarily departmental activities should not be included in the intelligence program budget. For example, the Treasury

Department, the Justice Department's Drug Enforcement Agency, and the U.S. Postal Service generate a certain amount of useful information about foreign efforts to do things affecting the United States that are contrary to U.S. law and the national interest. These data certainly should be made available to the central intelligence mechanism. The general work of these agencies, however, should not be brought into the central intelligence budget or into the oversight purview lest the processes become cumbersome and ineffective.

One perennial question that arises is whether Congress ought to publish the intelligence budget as such or whether it should continue to be hidden in the huge Defense Department budget because this information is too revealing and too useful for foreign governments. There is a provision of the Constitution requiring that "a regular statement and account of the receipts and expenditures of all public money shall be published from time to time." Critics find the hidden CIA funds in violation of this requirement. In my view, a very broad program budget giving only the total of national intelligence expenditures could be published annually without giving more than marginal advantage to foreign intelligence agencies. Our society is so open that any sophisticated espionage organization can easily determine the general dimensions of the U.S. national intelligence program. While I wish we did not have to give the exact figures each year so that strategic planners in Moscow and Peking would know whether we were expanding or contracting our intelligence efforts, the marginal value of this information over and above what Soviet and other spies can now get is so small that it is less important than the gain in Congressional and public confidence in the accountability of our intelligence system that probably would come from publication of total budget costs. In the public media these are usually grossly exaggerated. If the Congress and the President can agree to go no further in breaking down into detail the total budget figures and the general description of intelligence functions, the net gain would justify public release of this information and tend to legitimate and regularize the work of Congressional oversight.

In addition to budget review and approval, the oversight apparatus in Congress also requests and studies periodic reports from the Director of Central Intelligence on activities of the intelligence agencies under his jurisdiction that may have crossed the border between foreign intelligence work and internal security. It should also request annual or semiannual reports from the Attorney General on activities of the FBI and any other national law-enforcement agencies producing national intelligence useful to the Director of Central Intelligence, with special reference to the FBI's conforming to laws and executive guidelines on legality of wiretaps, electronic listening devices, and surreptitious entry for search and seizure.

Since it now appears that judicial warrants will be required for the conduct of most electronic surveillance in the United States, it will be easy to draw up for Congressional oversight committee members a statistical report and a review of any borderline cases that come up. This procedure ought to serve to assure the Congress that no intelligence operation is conducted without due process of law and proper regard for civil rights of U.S. citizens. While it is clear that the CIA impinged on the rights of its own employees to privacy in a few cases where security of sources was thought to be at stake, in the future it should do so only with judicial warrants; the FBI should work within legal guidelines established by the Attorney General and made known to the Congressional oversight committee or committees. These procedures will eliminate the other two areas in which the CIA may have exceeded its charter authority, i.e., reporting on dissident organizations in the United States (Operation CHAOS) and mail opening. The former functions should strictly be left to the FBI under appropriate legal guidelines. The surveillance of mail should be conducted, if at all, only in grave emergencies and with notice given to the Congressional oversight committee or committees; the CIA would not be directly involved, though it might get the information if such operations are ever authorized in peacetime.

Lastly, the new oversight mechanism in Congress should act as a liaison channel for the passage of secret information of a substantive nature from the intelligence community to the Congress as a whole at appropriate levels of security classification. It is ridiculous for the United States to support a sophisticated research and analysis staff to study international issues for the benefit of the Executive Branch and to deny the findings of this analytical research system to the Congress. There is now an adequate procedure for handling secret information securely under the supervision of the oversight committees. The Director of Central Intelligence can consequently afford to make available to the Congress reports classified at the secrecy level required by their content. The Congress can use this information as is appropriate. A great deal of it could be made public if the Congress clearly established that the national intelligence agencies have an obligation to release all the reports they can without jeopardizing intelligence sources and methods. Opening up the rich resources of the CIA, State, and Defense to Congressional requests for briefing papers, as well as formal oral briefings, ought to elevate the level of dialogue between the Congress and the White House, facilitate the passage of sensible legislation relating to foreign affairs, and allow sound evidence to filter through the press and broadcast media to widen the knowledge of the citizenry. By its very existence, then, Congressional oversight of the kind here visualized is bound to aid in rendering government accountable and beneficial to the larger purposes of an open society.

The Senate and House committees, in operation since 1976 and 1977 respectively, have worked in close cooperation with the White House and the intelligence agencies. This aspect of conducting secret intelligence operations compatible with the procedures of a free society has been resolved about as well as it is ever likely to be. With a President who firmly believed in a strong intelligence service and with his own political party in a majority in the Senate, the oversight and accountability issue ought to have been laid to rest, at least for a time, under the Reagan Administration.

## The CIA Charter

The shifting mood in Washington on the role and respectability of intelligence agencies is most clearly revealed in the history of Congressional consideration of charter legislation for the CIA. Here, as in the case of legislative oversight, Reagan and Casey faced a much more hospitable prospect in working out reasonable arrangements with Congress than anyone could have predicted a few years previously.

The charter of the CIA, set forth in the National Security Act of 1947 and the CIA Act of 1949, served the agency and the country reasonably well for many years. While its description of duties and functions may have left some room for elasticity in interpretation and some ambiguity in uninformed readers' minds, the members of the National Security Council and the members of the early Congressional oversight committees knew exactly what the legislation meant and plainly wanted the CIA to conduct clandestine operations, including covert actions, without making it too explicit.

The sense of guilt about American use of power for international advantage, so pervasive during the Carter era, included an apologetic attitude toward the need to conduct secret intelligence activities and a desire to, as the saying went, "let it all hang out." The extremist civil liberties protagonists, who tended to argue that the Bill of Rights superseded the U.S. Constitution rather than supplementing it, sprang to the task of writing legislative shackles for the intelligence community.

Not surprisingly, Frank Church's 15-month inquiry into the sins of the CIA found that "the CIA's present charter, embodied in the National Security Act of 1947 ... is inadequate in a number of respects" and that "a clear statutory basis is needed for the Agency's conduct abroad of covert action, espionage, counterintelligence and foreign intelligence collection and for such counterespionage operations within the United States as the Agency may have to undertake as a result of the activities abroad."[1]

The Senate Select Committee on Intelligence, set up as a permanent committee on May 19, 1976, to oversee CIA in accordance with the Church committee's findings, had substantial assistance from Vice President Mondale and White House staff aides in producing a comprehensive proposed law reflecting the fears and fantasies of the most extreme critics of the CIA and the FBI. The result was S.2525, the National Intelligence Reorganization and Reform Act of 1978. It was a 263-page bill filled with complex definitions, multiple prohibitions and restraints, and elaborate provisions for herding the whole intelligence community into one vast bureaucratic corral, tended by a super-director of national intelligence (DNI vice DCI) and monitored by ten committees of Congress—Intelligence, Appropriations, Armed Services, Foreign Relations, and Judiciary in both Houses of Congress. The emphasis was on protecting civil liberties against an infinite variety of alleged wrongdoings by the CIA and the FBI.

The bill proposed to require 66 recurring periodic reports to Congress from the intelligence agencies, most of which related to the 92 pages of authorizations, procedures, and restrictions spelled out in Title I. The procedures for advance notification of covert action projects (which came to be called, coyly, "special activities"), as well as sensitive clandestine collection efforts, were especially onerous and seemed to intrude on constitutional prerogatives of the Presidency. They required prior notice of all foreign liaison arrangements, a particularly delicate aspect of clandestine operations. They also provided for the General Accounting Office of the Congress to audit confidential funds of a kind that had been provided secretly from the time of George Washington, who had personally supervised secret intelligence operations during the Revolutionary War.

This recording of intelligence operational detail seemed in contrast to the general's famous observations (made in 1777):

The necessity of procuring good Intelligence is apparent and need not be further urged. All that remains for me to add is, that you keep the whole matter as secret as possible. For upon secrecy, success depends in most Enterprises of the kind, and for want of it, they are generally defeated, however well planned and promising a favourable issue.[2]

A whirlwind of protest and criticism met this gargantuan bill during the course of hearings held over many months. The White House never objected to the proposed legislation, having been involved in its drafting, but was not enthusiastic about it. General Richard Stilwell, President of the Association of Former Intelligence Officers (AFIO), called S.2525 a potential "straightjacket." AFIO Legal Adviser John A. Warner, retired General Counsel in the CIA, called the bill "micro-management with a vengeance" and described some of its elaborate protective measures for civil rights as legislation to convey U.S. constitutional rights under the Fourth Amendment to Soviet Embassies, KGB officers, and other foreign intelligence agents.

Former DCIs Helms, Colby, and Bush all testified unfavorably.

Under this onslaught, the Senate Select Committee on Intelligence let S.2525 die with the 95th Congress and produced what some called the "son of S.2525," a bill introduced on March 25, 1980 as S.2284. It was a great deal shorter, only 171 pages, and drafted a little more tidily. It had a slightly more positive thrust but still contained a complex set of definitions and restrictions. Jack Blake, then President of AFIO, said that the revised bill, like its longer predecessor, would set many prohibitions into legislative granite and tend to shackle CIA rather than free it, as many people were then beginning to urge.[3]

As the steam ran out of the reform movement in Congress and international crises multiplied, enthusiasm for S.2284 languished as had its "parent" S.2525. The philosophy of Frank Church and Walter Mondale was more and more at odds with the changing public opinion on the issue of American intelligence.

In both of the bills presented by the Senate committee were some positive aspects approved by nearly all critics of the basic charter legislation. Three elements in S.2284 emerged as the only provisions likely to receive Congressional consent. They were: (1) a proposed modification of the Hughes-Ryan Amendment of 1974 eliminating the required briefing of seven (originally eight) committees on covert action, leaving the responsibility to review suggestions for such projects to the two select intelligence committees; (2) partial relief for intelligence agencies from provisions of the Freedom of Information Act (FOIA), eliminating the rigid legal obligation to answer all requests, even those of foreign intelligence agencies, for data that ought to be protected and would have required an enormous amount of "sanitizing" to meet the FOIA demands; and (3) imposition of criminal sanctions (up to $50,000 or ten years' imprisonment) for intentional unauthorized disclosure of the identities of intelligence agents.

During Carter's last year in office, the intelligence charter debate focussed on these changes in a way that was helpful rather than restrictive to the CIA. Senator Daniel P. Moynihan introduced the "Intelligence Reform Act of 1980," on January 24, which changed the Hughes-Ryan notification procedure to require reporting only to the two select committees, exempting certain categories of intelligence data from FOIA inquiry, and making it a crime to disclose agent identities (albeit with a penalty of only $5,000 or one year imprisonment). This pale shadow of S.2525 was only ten pages long; it supported efficient intelligence operations rather than concentrating on so-called abuses. Several identical bills were introduced in the House of Representatives, and the Chairman of the House Permanent Select Committee on Intelligence introduced a separate bill, H.R. 5615, on the protection of agent identities. The wheel had come nearly full circle.

Despite this legislative activity, none of these bills actually passed. President Carter's stunning defeat on November 4, 1980, demoralized the Democratic liberal reform element in the Senate, and the Republicans jubilantly awaited cues from the Reagan-Bush-Casey team preparing to take office.

One important action did take place at the end of the 96th Congress, however. That was the revision of the Hughes-Ryan Amendment on covert action briefing. Beginning in 1977, the two select committees had reported out an annual authorization bill for the intelligence community, although, in the interest of security, they had not been required to reveal the sums of money approved. This *pro forma* bill, which followed the normal Congressional pattern of authorizing expenditures before appropriating the money in separate legislation, was the vehicle for passage of the only important item that had been in the 1977-1980 parcel of proposals. The Intelligence Authorization Act for Fiscal Year 1981 (which became Public Law 96-450 in 1980) affirmed Congressional oversight authority and revised the Hughes-Ryan requirement. The President had only to notify two select committees on intelligence of proposed covert action, normally prior to initiation of the action but in "extra-ordinary circumstances" merely "in a timely fashion." This ended an era in which unwieldy and leak-prone procedures put CIA out of the international covert action business at the very time when international conflicts seemed to demand it as a supplement to U.S. foreign policy and military influence.

# Current Structure and Function of the U.S. Intelligence System

The battered intelligence agencies, luckily, were not subjected to any major reorganizations under the Carter regime. While designations of units and guidelines for tasks changed, a chart of the basic system of national intelligence under Admiral Turner looked much like the one under Bush except for the elimination of the President's Foreign Intelligence Advisory Board.*

One step in the right direction—backwards—was taken when the National Intelligence Officers were reconstituted as a corporate group (the National Intelligence Council) similar to the old Office of National Estimates (ONE), abolished in 1973. In early summer 1981, on the other hand, Casey brought the estimates-drafting process directly under the DCI's supervision and separated it administratively from the rest of the Directorate of Intelligence. National estimates had been clearly designated part of the research and analysis system under the DDI from the origin of ONE in 1950 until I left the DDI post in 1966. The estimates unit, whatever its name, can be better staffed and is less likely to become isolated in rigid in its views, if it is an integral part of the CIA analytical services. It would also be more likely, in my view, to be protected from White House political pressure.

Under the Turner system, the national estimates staff was symbolically separated from the other DDI offices by its identification as an intelligence community asset. A separate title for the DDI was invented for his special supervisory relationship to the National Intelligence Officers—Director of the National Foreign Assessments Center (NFAC). In this sense the National Intelligence Officers group was on a par with two other totally dedicated intelligence community assets: an element responsible to the DCI for "Resource Management" (mainly program and budget); and "Collection Tasking," the last, more elaborate incarnation of the small, knowledgeable DDI Intelligence Collection Guidance Staff I established in the

---

*See Chart 10, 1976, p. 267.

early 1960s. A sensible move during the Turner years was the return to the previous practice of subordinating to the DDI the analytical units studying scientific developments and weapons intelligence. This left the Directorate of Science and Technology in the business of developing technology for intelligence collection, collation of foreign broadcast and reconnaissance information, and processing it for dissemination. Casey has retained this structure.

The DCI command responsibilities bequeathed from Turner to Casey are illustrated on page 305, distinguishing units exclusively CIA managed, intelligence community staffs, and units with joint CIA and intelligence community responsibilities.

A simpler schematic reveals that the old structure persists if you understand that the National Foreign Assessment Center is a community name for the Directorate of Intelligence. The former U.S. Intelligence Board, advisory to the CIA on National Intelligence Estimates and other community policies, is now called National Foreign Intelligence Board (NFIB). It is still made up of chiefs of all the intelligence components of the community. (See DCI/CIA Organization, p. 306.)

The complexity of the system of interlocking and overlapping intelligence activities is apparent in this chart of the many agencies coordinated by the Director of Central Intelligence in 1981. (See The Intelligence Community, p. 307.)

Viewed from the top (the White House) down, the schematic outline of the current structure of the intelligence community places all functions in relation to the President. (See Direction, Supervision, and Coordination of National Intelligence, p. 308.)

A review of the structure of the U.S. central intelligence system as it existed when Bill Casey took office in 1981 shows a fundamental faithfulness to the structure that evolved out of OSS and earlier CIA experience. The fact that the intelligence community survived with main elements intact during the uncertain leadership of 1977-1981 makes it safe to predict a productive future for CIA and the supporting agencies subject to the DCI's coordination. Compared with the "guarded prognosis" of only a short while ago, the prospect for revival

# Director of Central Intelligence Command Responsibilities

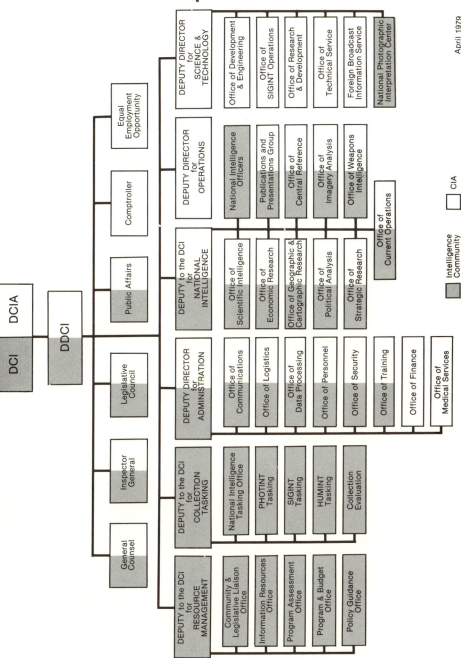

*The CIA Under Reagan, Bush and Casey*

A simpler schematic reveals that the old structure persists if you understand that the National Foreign Assessment Center is a community name for the Directorate of Intelligence. The former U.S. Intelligence Board, advisory to the CIA on National Intelligence Estimates and other community policies, is now called National Foreign Intelligence Board (NFIB). It is still made up of chiefs of all the intelligence components of the government.

## DCI/CIA ORGANIZATION

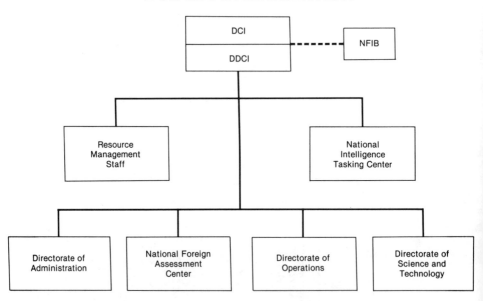

The complexity of the system of interlocking and overlapping intelligence activities is apparent in this chart of the many agencies coordinated by the Director of Central Intelligence in 1981.

## The Intelligence Community

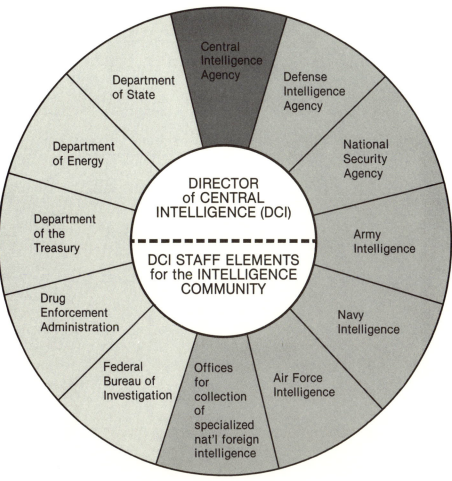

Viewed from the top (the White House) down, the schematic outline of the current structure of the intelligence community places all functions in relation to the President.

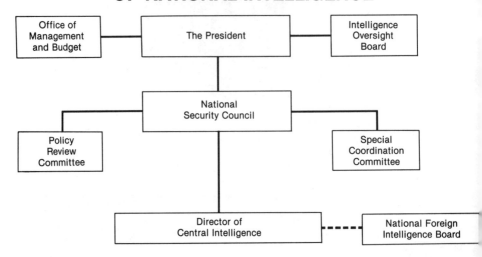

under management and policy formulation by the Reagan-Bush-Casey team is almost a miracle.*

## The Reagan Agenda

Casey chose as Deputy Director of Central Intelligence one of the outstanding intelligence professionals in the military service, Admiral Bobby R. Inman, then the skillful Director of the National Security Agency signals work. Inman had the background, experience, and talent to take over the meaningful machinery and run it efficiently, leaving Casey to work in his highly personal style on matters of his own choice. Casey began by concentrating on raising morale by identifying with the professional intelligence officers and following the Bush model of defending the competence of CIA and the need for its best performance across the board

He immediately set out to revitalize the clandestine services after an intensive study of the achievements of the overseas operations stations, many of which he visited during the first half of 1981. He emphasized close cooperation between the Operations Directorate and the Intelligence Directorate and undertook a variety of measures to increase the influence of the analytical research specialists in the world of academic expertise and "think-tank" research. Not only did he hope to enrich the intellectual resources of the intelligence community but also to return public confidence and respect for intelligence analysts to the level achieved during the Eisenhower and Kennedy years. All of these moves were healthy, although it would take time for them to bear fruit.

In the first months of the Casey incumbency the spirits of those in the intelligence community rose. Intelligence officers began to slough off the feeling of being pariahs—or even criminals—and to concentrate on rebuilding intelligence assets and capabilities. The leadership in the White House and in the intelligence community began to pay off in increased levels of innovation, incentive, and achievement.

---

*See my "guarded" analysis of the future of U.S. intelligence as of 1980, Chapter XVII, in the comprehensive volume prepared and published by the Hoover Institution, Stanford University, under the title *The United States in 1980*, edited by Peter Duignan and Alvin Rabushka, 1980.

The new team in Washington had prepared their case on intelligence well before the election. They were able to hit the deck running because of the mandate contained in a section of the Republican Party Platform that had been adopted at the Republican National Convention in Detroit in July of 1980:

National Intelligence

At a time of increasing danger, the U.S. intelligence community has lost much of its ability to supply the President, senior U.S. officials, and the Congress with accurate and timely analyses concerning fundamental threats to our nation's security. Morale and public confidence have been eroded and American citizens and friendly foreign intelligence services have become increasingly reluctant to cooperate with U.S. agencies. As a result of such problems, the U.S. intelligence community has incorrectly assessed critical foreign developments, as in Iran, and has, above all, underestimated the size and purpose of the Soviet Union's military efforts.

We believe that a strong national concensus has emerged on the need to make our intelligence community a reliable and productive instrument of national policy once again. In pursuing its objectives, the Soviet Union and its surrogates operate by a far different set of rules than does the United States. We do not favor countering their efforts by mirroring their tactics. However, the United States requires a realistic assessment of the threats it faces, and it must have the best intelligence capability in the world. Republicans pledge this for the United States.

A Republican Administration will seek to improve U.S. intelligence capabilities for technical and clandestine collection, cogent analysis, coordinated counterintelligence, and covert action.

We will reestablish the President's Foreign Intelligence Advisory Board, abolished by the Carter Administration, as a permanent non-partisan body of distinguished Americans to perform a constant audit of national intelligence research and performance. We will propose methods of providing alternative intelligence estimates in order to improve the quality of the estimates by constructive competition.

Republicans will undertake an urgent effort to rebuild the intelligence agencies, and to give full support to their knowledgeable and dedicated staffs. We will propose legislation to enable intelligence officers and their agents to operate safely and efficiently abroad.

We will support legislation to invoke criminal sanctions against anyone who discloses the identities of U.S. intelligence officers abroad or who makes unauthorized disclosures of U.S. intelligence sources and methods.

We will support amendments to the Freedom of Information Act and the Privacy Act to permit meaningful background checks on individuals being considered for sensitive positions and to reduce costly and capricious requests to the intelligence agencies.

We will provide our government with the capability to help influence international events vital to our national security interests, a capability which only the United States among the major powers has denied itself.

A Republican Administration will seek adequate safeguards to ensure that past abuses will not recur, but we will seek the repeal of ill-considered restrictions sponsored by Democrats, which have debilitated U.S. intelligence capabilities while easing the intelligence collection and subversion efforts of our adversaries.

All of this could not be done in a day. At midyear of 1981, no new legislation had been passed and a simpler Executive Order replacing much of Carter's 12036 was still in the drafting process. Almost imperceptibly, however, a new style and new attitude surfaced. Accountability to Congress as well as to the President had been worked out on a reasonable basis and readily accepted by the new government officials.

## The Casey Case

The extraordinary sensitivity of everything about the CIA and the inevitability of rough bumps in the path forward are well illustrated by the major news story concerning the CIA in the first seven months of 1981. Despite his professional and political qualifications, Bill Casey very nearly lost his job in July 1981. Looking back immediately after the treatment of the Casey case in the media, one cannot fail to be astonished at the sudden fire storm feeding on very thin fuel that hit the CIA and its new director quite unexpectedly. It burned out as quickly as it started, but not before three senior Republican Senators had called for Casey's resignation on the basis of casual Congressional criticism and vague speculation in the news media.

The real tinder that fed the fire was an administrative appointment in CIA. Casey wanted a skillful and loyal professional layer of deputies and assistant deputies under him and his principal deputy, Admiral Bobby Inman. He moved John McMahon, an able and experienced professional manager risen from the ranks of CIA operations from the post of DDO to the post of DDI. Most previous DDIs had been more known in the outside world of academic achievement than McMahon, but his appointment met with general approval because of his administrative skills, agency experience, brains, and congenial personality.

The trouble arose over filling the DDO slot, almost always heretofore occupied by clandestine operations professionals from the time of Allen Dulles and Dick Helms. Casey apparently felt that he could break that tradition because he himself intended to monitor clandestine activities closely and because he had confidence in the very professional assistant DDOs already selected. He decided to give the DDO post to an outsider, a businessman named Max Hugel, who had worked closely and loyally with Casey during the Reagan presidential campaign.

His main reasoning evidently was to let the professionals run operations but use a politically oriented businessman to build bridges back to the world of international entrepreneurs who had largely severed all relations with the CIA after the Church Committee inquisition. Useful, legally acquired information, and know-how about foreign economics, as well as operational support possibilties all needed substantial upgrading, which Hugel might have been expected to achieve.

The choice was opposed by many, most importantly by Senator Barry Goldwater, now Chairman of the Senate Select Committee on Intelligence as a result of the Republican capture of a Senate majority in the 1980 election. The Senator had made clear around town that he would have preferred Admiral Inman, whose professional knowledge of intelligence he admired, as DCI instead of Casey. He grumbled to anyone who raised the matter that he thought the Hugel appointment was a mistake—a view widely shared.

Selection of deputies at this level in government seldom makes big news in Washington, however, and the news media paid little attention until reporters learned that Hugel was involved in a messy business finance scandal with disappearing assets and company officials. No specific charges were made and Hugel denied all wrong doing. Nevertheless, in keeping with time-honored Washington principles of political operations, the White House quickly reached the conclusion it would be better to have Hugel go and keep the details of his earlier business life, whatever they might be, from rubbing off on the CIA and the Reagan Administration. Hugel resigned promptly, claiming innocence but wanting to avoid trouble. By most logical standards the incident should have been over with no great harm done.

Ordinary logic is not necessarily Washington political logic, however, and the flames suddenly flared. Newsmen published stories about Bill Casey himself being involved in a totally different business problem of a decade ago where he had been accused of persuading investors to put their money in a business called Multiponics, a firm that went bankrupt. Although he lost $150,000 of his own money in the investment, it was reported that he may have acted unethically in advising other investors. It was even speculated, quite groundlessly, that he had made a profit somehow on the ill-fated venture. Oddly, the Hugel matter blended in a vague, unstructured way into the speculative questioning of Casey's private business life and generated news story after news story repeating the few known facts and the interesting suspicions about the two cases.

Then Senator Goldwater, elder Republican statesman *par excellence*, undertook to explain in a TV interview that he put no stock in the old suspicions about Casey's business behavior, which he really considered irrelevant, but let himself be put on the air strongly criticizing the Hugel appointment and recommending that Casey step down from his job on that ground alone. The fire storm quickly got out of control. Military intelligence officers, active and retired, hoped for a military successor to Casey. Some civilian professionals, active and retired, agreed that the Hugel decision showed very bad judgment. Two unusually sensible Republican Senators, Bill Roth and Ted Stevens, joined Goldwater in asking for Casey's resignation. The press stories got longer and longer, and the TV news networks carried a capsule every night on the Casey case without much information but with a generally negative slant. Even the White House staff began sounding cautious as if they thought President Reagan might decide to let Casey follow Hugel into oblivion. As of the week ending July 25, 1981, things looked bad for Casey and the CIA.

At that point cooler views began to be heard. If an experienced public servant like Casey could lose his job on such frothy charges, unproven, anyone could lose his job. If an exceptionally well qualified DCI with the complete confidence of a new and popular President could be destroyed by Congressional gossip and media speculation, how would it ever be possible to rebuild the CIA? If Casey lost his job for no very compelling reason, it seemed a long way from due process in government and an open invitation to keep the CIA from stabilizing itself, recovering morale, and improving competence.

The turning point came when a volunteer group of old friends of Casey, mostly old-boys from OSS who knew Casey well and wanted him to have a fair deal, organized a grass-roots movement of surprising effectiveness across the country to persuade media editorialists and Congressmen to counsel caution in jumping to conclusions in such an important matter. They rallied some influential citizens like former Secretaries of the Treasury, George Shultz and William Simon, to support Casey. They also scheduled mass meetings of the alumni of OSS and other friends of Casey for luncheons in New York and Washington as testimonials to his competence and respectability. The announcement of these events made new stories.

*The Washington Post* on Sunday, July 26, printed an elegantly judicious editorial recommending against a rush to judgment and summary decision on the Casey affair. The front page news headlines in most papers featured support for Casey rather than an attack on him. Senator Henry ("Scoop") Jackson, a respected Democrat, went on TV to urge careful Senatorial examination of the facts before final conclusions. Letters to the editors of newspapers poured in. The tide turned rapidly toward deliberation and fair play. President Reagan strongly endorsed Casey. Within a few days it was over.

The Senate Select Committee on Intelligence listened to Casey for two days and examined the evidence of his business affairs he presented. By the end of the day, July 29, Senator Goldwater read to the waiting reporters and TV cameras the unanimous view of the committee that no evidence had surfaced to suggest Casey was unfit to hold office as DCI. *Ipso facto,* the earlier Senate confirmation that he was suited to the job held. The Congress soon went on August recess, and Casey, having in the meantime appointed John Stein, a career professional as DDO, went back to the business of running the intelligence community.

The lesson was plain. The DCI ought to cultivate and consult the Congressional oversight committees with great care. Congressmen, especially intelligence committee members, ought to keep their private views on the CIA within the committees. The White House ought to resist media murder of its key officials, most particularly the crucially important Director of Central Intelligence.

## Issues Ahead

The CIA must be administered in a way that reflects a realistic view of the world. This view recognizes the existence of nations firmly persuaded that our free society will perish, and that some of those nations employ large, ambitious secret intelligence organizations to collect information on our political and social weaknesses. They then exploit these vulnerabilities to create or hasten a process of political disintegration in the United States and in other countries where the United States has interests. No President can be permitted to preside over the disruption or dissolution of our society through ignorance of the efforts by foreign governments to subvert or destroy it.

The Reagan Administration is committed to the preservation of our internal security, to maintain our mutual defense alliances, and to insure adoption of wise defense and foreign policies. To this end, it is essential to support the most sophisticated intelligence community possible. As in military strength, second best is not nearly good enough in intelligence capabilities.

Analyzing situations affecting the security of the United States, directly or indirectly, and making estimates of future dangers and opportunities are at the heart of the strategic intelligence system. These intelligence processes are needed for decision-making at the National Security Council level, for giving Congress objective briefings on security issues before it, and to assure the people of this country that national policies are based on sound understanding of the facts of international life. This scholarly, legal, analytical, and estimative enterprise must be separated from the more controversial field of clandestine operations. Bill Casey clearly understands these principles and will try to carry them out in practice.

Many nations whose actions and plans materially affect the United States' economic and diplomatic interests abroad try to conceal them from us. In these countries, especially the Soviet Union, and the People's Republic of China, everything that is not expressly mandatory is prohibited and secret. For this reason our intelligence system must include programs for clandestine collection abroad, designed to discover what other people are trying to hide from us. Every major country tries to collect such data about other nations. An open society like ours especially needs solid evidence about those dictatorships that threaten our interests and that cultivate secrecy in every sphere. We can rely heavily on technical methods of collecting such information, but we must also collect information from human beings, who often supply indispensable evidence of forward plans and intentions, something that cannot be photographed or overheard. We need a competent espionage and counterespionage service, serving the analytical and estimative process but not linked so closely with it as to confuse and tarnish the image of the scholars in central intelligence.

Finally, in those rare circumstances where social order and democratic political processes in areas of strategic importance to the United States are endangered by violence and external pressures toward dictatorship, the United States should supplement open diplomatic, economic, or military help with covert programs of advice and practical political aid. Responsible leaders in Congress ought to be aware of such programs, but to succeed they *must* be covert and not disclosed to the general public. I do not think that we should intervene broadly in foreign situations, but I believe that we should not stand by when the liberties of a friendly country are being destroyed before our eyes. If we are on principle in favor of freedom, we must support it everywhere in accordance with our capabilities. When others intervene to destroy political and personal liberties, I cannot see how U.S. interests or moral responsibilities can allow us to follow the path of indifference, which is ultimately the road to isolation. Hence, I believe our intelligence system must include a potential for covert political action abroad when national interests dictate it. To avoid damaging operational conflicts, this covert operational capability should be maintained in the same organization that is responsible for espionage and counterespionage. It is my impression that President Reagan, Vice President Bush, and DCI Casey all hold this viewpoint.

High-level decision-making in Washington must take place under the President's direct guidance through an orderly process of study and debate in the National Security Council, with both military security considerations and diplomatic programs getting a fair and equal hearing, and with other Cabinet departments being brought into the debate when their interests are involved. Objective information and analytical findings based on all sources of intelligence ought to be fed into this system through the Director of Central Intelligence so that the President, the Secretary of State, and the Secretary of Defense can adopt the most realistic policies that can be devised. The safety and welfare of the nation demand it. Only a highly skilled intelligence system monitored closely by the White House and by a responsible Congressional oversight committee can provide this data base for decision-making.

The National Security Council should meet regularly with the President in the chair to hear unvarnished, straightforward intelligence reports and estimates by senior intelligence officers from State, Defense, and the CIA on matters likely to require national security decisions. It is essential for this process to be established as a basic principle in policy deliberations. The Secretary of State and the Secretary of Defense should be present to bring in foreign policy and military policy recommendations. The Assistant to the President for National Security Affairs, who should be excluded by legislation from holding one of the other portfolios, would act as an honest broker responsible for insuring that essential information and recommendations from intelligence and policy agencies reach the President. In the low-profile role of the National Security Council staff, under Richard V. Allen, with strong guidance from President Reagan's White House policy monitoring triumvirate, Edwin Meese, James Baker, and Michael Deaver, a method of operation along these lines emerged.

I believe the professional corps of senior public servants, including the heads of intelligence agencies, should be brought into the process of policy planning and decision-making as much as feasible. Not only could they contribute light and clarity to the process, but they also could persuasively explain the realistic reasons underlying policy to appropriate members of the news media, to the members of Congress, and to the interested public. We should move away from the imperial system of policymaking whereby the only information available on the rationale for critical national decisions is in the public pronouncements of top officials after the fact. International agreements and commitments must be worked out in privacy, but they ought to be explained candidly afterwards, not lobbied for as part of a mysterious conceptual framework that hardly anyone is allowed to glimpse, let alone criticize.

The White House should discontinue suppressing dissemination of intelligence data related to international negotiations involving the President and his Assistant for National Security Affairs, a practice that was routine under Kissinger's White House aegis.* At least a few senior officials in the intelligence community should see all data concerning foreign actions or reactions in fields like Soviet policy, China policy, or disarmament. It is not safe to let one man and his personal staff decide what can be known by every other official about key developments in their fields. Keeping the negotiating process as secret as Nixon and Kissinger have done means that the nuances of foreign behavior and views that could be detected by intelligence experts may go unnoted and hence not taken into account in final decisions. Although the Reagan style in these matters is not yet fully established, it seems comparatively open and relaxed, free of paranoia that gripped both Nixon and Carter a great deal of the time.

The details of what foreign officials say in all discussions with the President or his White House emissaries should be made available for examination by professional intelligence analysts expert in the behavior patterns of the foreign countries involved. This means that the positions taken by Soviet, Chinese, or North Vietnamese officials in talks held with White House representatives should be made available for analysis by experts not directly involved. In this way hidden snags or unforeseen long-range consequences are much more likely to be noted and brought out. This is the kind of assessment that the senior U.S. intelligence officers ought to be providing regularly in the interests of objectivity and prudence. That the substance of such conversations has seldom been made available to the State Department and the CIA in recent years,

---

*For a discussion of this problem see my testimony and that of Edward W. Proctor, then Deputy Director for Intelligence, CIA, and William G. Hyland, Deputy Assistant to the President for National Security Affairs, before the House Select Committee on Intelligence on December 17, 1975. I have also discussed this matter in "Policy Without Intelligence," *Foreign Policy*, Number 17, Winter 1974-75, pp. 121-135.

when crucial changes of policy direction were made, is in my view a much greater scandal than any of the intelligence agencies' misdeeds.

All of these recommendations simply require a consensus by Congress and the Administration that a central research and analysis facility in the field of international strategy and foreign policy is essential to provide objective assessments to the National Security Council and Congress. Naturally such a facility needs good data collected for it to study. Assessments of strategic situations should be disseminated to appropriate officials of the U.S. government without the suppression of information and views contrary to White House policy.

The position of Director of Central Intelligence should be elevated by legislation to Cabinet level. Casey has been granted Cabinet status on a personal basis, but the job itself should be permanently made equal in rank of the Secretaries of State and Defense. Any DCI ought to be entitled to report directly to the President on policies and broad programs of the whole intelligence community, the budget for which he should coordinate and defend before the Congress. He would be essentially a Cabinet-level coordinator of all intelligence activities, striving for balance and capability in the whole intelligence community.

This top national intelligence official, sitting *ex officio* on the National Security Council and speaking for the President and the NSC as Chairman of the Committee on Foreign Intelligence (CFI), will have broad supervisory control over all intelligence agencies. The National Foreign Assessment Center under the DDI should consolidate the work of the main analytical staffs now in the CIA, State, and Defense. It should also work out, on an interagency basis, directives for overt, technical, and clandestine intelligence collection agencies to be attached to Defense, State, other Cabinet departments, or to the National Security Council itself. The Director of the National Foreign Assessment Center should be by training a scholar in the social sciences, preferably one who also has wide experience in government, best of all in some aspect of clandestine or covert intelligence work.

The DCI should exercise a strong operational and budgetary influence, if not control, over the central analytical elements of all intelligence agencies, no matter where—in State and

Defense, mainly—they may be physically located. The analytical part of the INR should certainly remain in place to provide access to Foreign Service desks and personnel, and analytical research elements of the DIA ought to continue to work in the Pentagon. Nevertheless, these analytical staffs should be part of the National Foreign Assessment effort for management and planning purposes.

The DCI must establish specific requirements for intelligence collection by agencies not under the operational control of the CIA but subject to tasking by him. CIA should prepare current intelligence reports and strategic estimates for the NSC and other Executive Branch officials as it does now, and it should in addition continue to prepare reports for the oversight committees of Congress. It should also be explicity instructed to make as much of its findings as possible available for public use. The analytical staffs of NFAC and CIA should have close contacts with collection agencies but not be responsible for any operational tasks.

Other agencies of government should not duplicate NFAC and CIA analytical facilities as such. In Defense, the DIA should continue to operate the attache system and provide the intelligence link between the Joint Chiefs of Staff and the individual military service staffs at headquarters and overseas command levels. For national research and analysis, the Secretary of Defense and the Secretary of State should rely upon NFAC.

The rest of the intelligence community should consist of collection services tasked for intelligence purposes by the DCI under the authority of the NSC. These collection services should include the present signals and reconnaissance organizations under Defense administration and supervision.

Clandestine agent collection activities would have to be authorized in broad program terms and carried out in response to intelligence community resources studies and collection guidance priorities. Operational responsibility and control should be exercised by a small professional staff in DDO, reporting directly to the DCI. The DDO should work closely with the State Department, the Defense Department, and NFAC. This DDO staff would assign collection tasks to overseas stations and to special groups to be set up in various agencies for designated secret program purposes. Provisions for these latter must be negotiated by the DCI with Cabinet department chiefs and cleared in general terms with the oversight committee members of Congress. These programs would be limited in number, and the special groups would be specifically tasked to procure only information not available from all the other sources. The programs would change in title and area of responsibility from time to time in accordance with directives evolved under DCI procedures. The total personnel at any one time would constitute the clandestine services of the United States. The aim of this method of clandestine collection would be to deflect and diffuse public and journalistic curiosity by scattering these clandestine efforts and units widely. While some of them might remain physically at Langley Headquarters Building, secrecy as to the size, the location, and the budget of the clandestine services would be maintained. This is a costly and administratively wasteful system of doing business, but essential secrecy could be maintained and cover furnished much better than is now possible; in clandestine operations, as in war, waste of resources is inevitable in the process of providing overall security. Bill Casey issued instructions to cut down briefing contacts with the news media to keep secret the mechanics and personal responsibilities involved in clandestine and covert operations at Langley.

No permanent organization for covert political and paramilitary actions beyond the small groups now on the DDO staff should be established. Programs of support to groups abroad whose existence is vital to U.S. security and foreign policy aims should be small, exceptional, and carried out covertly only when and if the President makes a formal finding based on the recommendation of the NSC that secret rather than open support of the foreign action envisaged is essential to success. These covert operations should not be too frequent nor too large. The operations themselves should be carried out by specially trained personnel assigned to the clandestine services or members of the clandestine services staff. Only one secret foreign agent operation should exist—mainly for collection purposes but available when tasked to handle a covert action project.

The heart of these additional steps to put our intelligence on a sound footing is to change the popular image of intelligence by demonstrating that most of the work is neither illegal nor immoral. Thus, NFAC could nominally replace the CIA as the known administrative element at the Langley Headquarters Building, which could then be more open to scholars and journalists interested in consultation and substantive research findings. It would, in these circumstances, be feasible for the Central Intelligence Agency to abandon the famous acronym that has become a worldwide public relations liability. Sentiment at Langley runs against this at the moment, but perhaps some incidents abroad will make the President and the DCI consider dropping "CIA" in the interest of security. Many of CIA's liabilities are no fault of its own, but realism suggests we might do better with a new label.

If Casey were to emphasize that his job is to preside over a central analytical research facility, the fact of his emphasis would focus attention on the open-society aspects of U.S. intelligence. Our first principle ought to be to do nothing secretly that can be done openly, to do nothing in this country not provided for by law, and to do nothing abroad not called for in the legislative charter given our intelligence agencies. This principle should not diminish the CIA's positive determination to conduct intelligence operations vigorously and analyze the strategic situations confronting the United State thoroughly.

Every great nation with responsibilities for prudent behavior in the international arena must have a sophisticated intelligence system to help the key officials of its government in decision-making. The fact that the United States maintains such a system is no secret; it is a necessity that only the irresponsible or our enemies would oppose. My preference would be to structure research and analysis services along the lines of the simplified RAS chart on page 324 and to make public the fact that these functions are being performed as part of the American political process.

On the other hand, we should keep the specifics of our intelligence operations and the staffing of the clandestine services closely guarded. As long as analytical reports do not reveal intelligence sources and methods, their findings should be distributed wherever they are useful to enrich the public dialogue and provide a sound factual footing for political debate on defense and international affairs.

If we rebuild and reinvigorate a research institution of this kind, tasked with setting priorities for the secret collection of intelligence but engaged in no clandestine work of its own, it could not only report its findings to the President and Cabinet on a secret basis, as now, but also could make from 50 to 75 percent of its reports available to Congress to improve legislative understanding of international issues as they affect national policymaking. Moreover, where secret sources and methods were not involved, such reports could be released publicly for the benefit of university scholars, journalists, and citizens who need objective facts to guide them in thinking about pressing policy issues involving international developments.

CIA has a quasi-fiduciary responsibility in the field of national intelligence analysis under the direct supervision of the Director of Central Intelligence. It would serve the people as well as the government by candid presentation of demonstrable facts and reasonable anticipation of future problems. This would be a novel approach to an old problem; it would help in reknitting a consensus among the opinion-making elements in our society. It would free scientific research on vital international problems from the taint of suspected illegality or deception. Within the tradition of our free society, it would provide a center for the advancement of knowledge and the sharing of it on an open and voluntary exchange basis with the interested citizenry. Knowledge is power, and knowledge of this kind ought, insofar as practicable, to belong to the people whose safety and welfare it is designed to serve. An open Presidency should provide for this kind of public service and insure that it is as free from bias or political pressure as our census data or our economic statistics programs.

There are many other things to be settled in correctly structuring our intelligence system. It is not certain yet how far or how fast DCI Casey wants to go. As of now, mid-1981, the CIA is licking its wounds to heal them and gathering strength for the challenges ahead.

My view is that the people of this nation will respond to honest, candid leadership. The President, the Congress, and the people need access to a reliable, objective view of the world around us, a view that should never be distorted or suppressed

# Schematic Design
# Research and Analysis Services

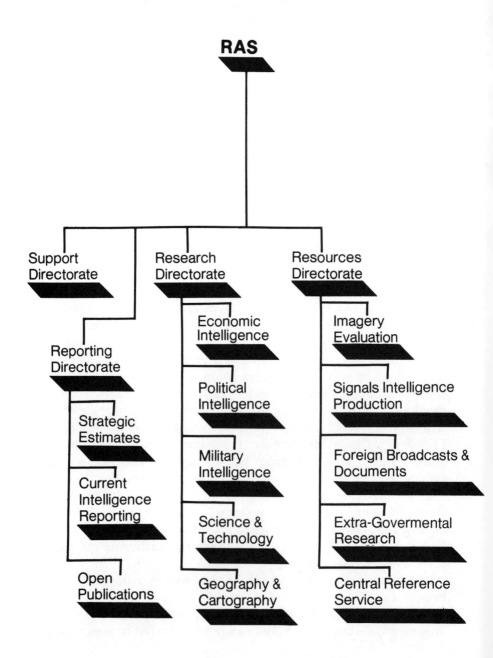

for partisan political reasons. It ought to be possible to persuade Congress and its constituents that this nation needs the best national intelligence system that can be devised to study the international environment in which we live so that we can foresee world problems, exploit opportunities beneficial to our interests, and defuse dangers to our open society and pluralistic way of life. I believe that Reagan, Bush, and Casey can carry out this necessary task.

The nation must be able to protect its own secrets and find out those of others if it is to survive and prosper in the strategic and international arena of the 1980s. If this is made clear to everyone, the peculiarly American combination of spies and scholars, working in tandem, can be mobilized along the lines suggested to do the job of central intelligence better than it has ever been done before anywhere in the world. Doing the job exactly in that way is very high on the Reagan Administration agenda.

# List of Charts

1. U.S. Intelligence, 1940 ...................... 29
2. Office of Coordinator of Information, 1941 ........................................ 68
3. Office of Strategic Services, 1945 ............ 73
4. U.S. Intelligence, early 1947 ................ 116
5. Central Intelligence Agency, 1950 ........... 132
6. Central Intelligence Agency, 1953 ........... 138
7. Central Intelligence Agency, 1961 ........... 210
8. Central Intelligence Agency Leadership, 1962-1965 ................................... 218
9. Central Intelligence Agency, 1975 ........... 246
10. Central Intelligence Agency, 1976 ........... 267
11. Directors and Deputy Directors of Central Intelligence ................................ 280
12. Director of Central Intelligence Command Responsibilities ............................ 305
13. DCI/CIA Organization ...................... 306
14. The Intelligence Community ................ 307
15. Direction, Supervision, and Coordination of National Intelligence ....................... 308
16. Schematic Design, Research and Analysis Services .................................... 324

# List of Acronyms

| | |
|---|---|
| **A-2** | Air Force Intelligence. |
| **BSC** | British Security Coordination Office. |
| **CA** | Covert Action. |
| **C&D** | Censorship and Documents unit in OSS. |
| **CAT** | Civil Air Transport airline. |
| **CE** | Counterespionage—active oeprations aimed at penetrating foreign secret intelligence agencies or operations. |
| **CFI** | Committee on Foreign Intelligence. |
| **CHAOS** | Domestic security files and operations, CIA. |
| **CI** | Counterintelligence—active and passive measures undertaken to protect organizations, individuals, and information against foreign secret intelligence penetration. |
| **CIA** | Central Intelligence Agency. |
| **CIFAR** | Central Institute of Foreign Affairs Research—proposed analytical intelligence agency. |
| **CIG** | Central Intelligence Group—direct predecessor of CIA. |
| **COI** | Office of the Coordinator of Information, predecessor of the Office of Strategic Services. |
| **COPS** | Chief of Operations in the DDP. |
| **CSS** | Clandestine Services Staff—proposed clandestine intelligence collection agency. |
| **DCI** | Director of Central Intelligence. |
| **DDA** | Directorate of Administration. Also the term used for the Deputy Director responsible for DDA. The same unit has been designated DDS. |
| **DDCI** | Deputy Director of Central Intelligence, CIA. |

| | |
|---|---|
| **DDI** | Directorate of Intelligence—the intelligence analysis side of CIA. Also used to refer to the Deputy Director responsible for the DDI. |
| **DDO** | Directorate of Operations—formerly called Directorate of Plans. The change occurred in 1973 during James Schlesinger's term of office as DCI. |
| **DDP** | Directorate of Plans—the clandestine services side of CIA. Also used to refer to the Deputy Director responsible for the DDP. |
| **DDS** | Directorate of Support. Also the term used for the Deputy Director responsible for the DDS. The same unit has been designated DDA. |
| **DDS&T** | Directorate of Science and Technology. Also the term used for the Deputy Director responsible for the DDS&T. |
| **DIA** | Defense Intelligence Agency. |
| **FBI** | Federal Bureau of Investigation. |
| **FBIS** | Foreign Broadcast Information Service. |
| **FI** | Foreign Intelligence—clandestine collection of intelligence in the DDP. |
| **G-2** | Army Intelligence. |
| **G-3** | Army Operations. |
| **IAC** | Intelligence Advisory Committee. |
| **INR** | Bureau of Intelligence and Research, Department of State. |
| **IOB** | Intelligence Oversight Board, subcommittee of PFIAB, later independent. |
| **IPC** | Intelligence Priorities Committee. |
| **JANIS** | Joint Army—Navy Intelligence Surveys. |
| **JCS** | Joint Chiefs of Staff. |
| **JEDBURGH** | World War II Allied paramilitary teams, also known as "Jeds." |

| | |
|---|---|
| **JIC** | Joint Intelligence Committee of the Joint Chiefs of Staff. |
| **KGB** | Soviet secret security and intelligence service—the Committee on State Security (Komitet Gosudarstvennoy Bezopasnosti). |
| **MAGIC** | Translations of decoded Japanese messages during World War II. |
| **MI-5** | The British internal intelligence organization. |
| **MI-6** | The British external intelligence organization. |
| **MO** | Morale Operations unit of OSS. |
| **MONGOOSE** | Covert action plan against Castro's Cuba. |
| **NIA** | National Intelligence Authority, the policy group supervising CIG. |
| **NIE** | National Intelligence Estimate. |
| **NIO** | National Intelligence Officer—analytical officer designated by the DCI to prepare estimates on a regional basis comparable to those prepared collectively by the Office of National Estimates. |
| **NIPE** | National Intelligence Programs Evaluation. |
| **NSA** | National Security Agency. |
| **NSC** | National Security Council. |
| **OAG** | Operations Advisory Group—subcommittee of NSC to review proposals for covert action abroad. |
| **OCD** | Office of Collection and Dissemination in CIA. |
| **OCI** | Office of Current Intelligence in CIA. |
| **OG** | Operational Group Command of OSS. |
| **ONE** | Office of National Estimates of CIA. |
| **ONI** | Office of Naval Intelligence. |

| | |
|---|---|
| OO | Office of Operations—overt collection unit of CIA, which included FBIS and Domestic Contacts. |
| OPC | Office of Policy Coordination—covert action section of CIA. |
| ORE | Office of Reports and Estimates in CIG and CIA. |
| ORR | Office of Research and Reports in CIA. |
| OSI | Office of Scientific Intelligence in CIA. |
| OSO | Office of Special Operations, intelligence collection unit in CIG and CIA. |
| OSS | Office of Strategic Services. |
| OWI | Office of War Information. |
| PFIAB | The President's Intelligence Checklist. |
| POTUS | President of the United States—used by Winston Churchill in his messages to President Franklin D. Roosevelt. |
| PURPLE | Japan's pre-World War II diplomatic code. |
| R&A | Research and Analysis unit in OSS. |
| SACO | Sino-American Cooperative Organization. |
| SI | Secret Intelligence unit in OSS. |
| SIGINT | Signals Intelligence. |
| SNIE | Special National Intelligence Estimate. |
| SO | Special Operations of OSS. |
| SOE | Special Operations Executive—British World War II unconventional warfare unit. |
| SSU | Strategic Services Unit—the espionage and counterespionage sections of OSS which were transferred to the War Department in 1945. |
| TORCH | 1942 Allied landings in North Africa. |
| ULTRA | Translations of German messages intercepted and deciphered during World War II. |
| USIB | United States Intelligence Board. |

| | |
|---|---|
| **X-2** | Counterintelligence unit in OSS. |
| **10/2 Panel** | NSC subcommittee, including State and Defense officials, which was set up to review covert action proposals. |
| **5412/ Special Group** | The NSC subcommittee which succeeded the 10/2 Group. |
| **303 Committee** | The NSC subcommittee which succeeded the 5412/Special Group. |
| **40 Committee** | The NSC subcommittee which succeeded the 303 Committee. |

# Footnotes

### Footnotes to Overview

1. Sherman Kent, *Strategic Intelligence for American World Policy* (Princeton, New Jersey: Princeton University press, 1949), pp. vii-viii.
2. See interview of the Vice President with the American Press Institute at the White House, February 24, 1979.
3. *Republican Platform*, proposed by the Committee on Resolutions to the Republican National Convention, July 14, 1980, Detroit, Michigan, pp. 60-61.

### Footnotes to Chapter One

1. An authoritative, detailed account of the establishment of OSS and its relationship with the birth of CIA is now available in a book published by CIA: Thomas F. Troy, *Donovan and the CIA*, 1981.
2. According to William Stevenson's account of this period, Churchill got permission from King George VI for this procedure, which would have been even more irregular. See William Stevenson, *A Man Called Intrepid* (New York: Harcourt Brace Jovanovich, 1976), p. 69.
3. For the most recent information on the Stephenson-Donovan relationship, see *Ibid.*
4. *Ibid.*, p. 203, and H. Montgomery Hyde, *Room 3603* (New York: Farrar, Straus and Company, 1962). Hyde's book was the first British account of Stephenson's work in the United States during the war. See pp. 43-44.
5. Stevenson, *op. cit.*, p. 249.
6. James G. Kellis, "The Development of U.S. National Intelligence, 1941-1961," (unpublished Ph.D. dissertation, Georgetown University, Washington, D.C.: 1962). Used with the permission of the author, who had access to the papers of William Donovan.
7. Donald McLachlan, *Room 39* (New York: Atheneum, 1968), pp. 234-236.
8. *Ibid.*, pp. 230-234.
9. Hyde, *op cit.*, p. 153, and Stevenson, *op. cit.*, p. 249.
10. Kellis, *op. cit.*, Appendix C.
11. See page 46 of *The Secret War Report of the OSS*, edited by Anthony Cave Brown (New York: Medallion Books, 1976). This report was prepared by the OSS under the direction of Kermit Roosevelt and was declassified in February 1976.
12. Samuel I. Rosenman, compiler, *The Public Papers and Addresses of Franklin D. Roosevelt: The Call to Battle Stations, 1941*, Volume X (New York: Harper & Brothers, 1950), pp. 264-265.

### Footnotes to Chapter Two

1. The first unvouchered money, $100,000, came from Roosevelt's Emergency Fund in September of 1941. In the period 1944-1945, OSS was given $37 million in unvouchered funds. See Brown, *op. cit.*, pp. 10-11.
2. Professor Langer has written of this period and of his later work with the Office of National Estimates in a privately printed autobiography, *In and Out of the Ivory Tower*, in 1977.
3. Kellis, *op. cit.*, p. 17.
4. Stewart Alsop and Thomas Braden, *Sub Rosa: The OSS and American Espionage* (New York: Harcourt, Brace and World, Inc., 1946), pp. 80-81.
5. Kellis, *op. cit.*, Appendix H.
6. *Ibid.*, pp. 20-21.

7. U.S., Congress, *Hearings Before the Joint Committee on the Investigation of the Pearl Harbor Attack* and *Report* 79th Congress, (Washington, D.C.: U.S. Government Printing Office, 1946), 39 Volumes.
8. For the early organization of the war planning process, see Ray S. Cline, *Washington Command Post: The Operations Division*. (Washington, D.C.: U.S. Government Printing Office, 1951), Chapters III-VI.
9. Kellis, *op. cit.*, Appendix E.
10. *Ibid.*, Appendix G.
11. *Ibid.*, p. 45.
12. *Ibid.*, p. 65.
13. Alsop and Braden, *op. cit.*, p. 35.
14. First published in 1949, *Strategic Intelligence for American World Policy* was reissued with a new preface by Kent and published by Princeton University Press in 1966.

**Footnotes to Chapter Three**

1. This memorandum and Tab A appear in Edward Hymoff's *The OSS in World War II* (New York: Ballantine, 1972), pp. 367-369.
2. *Ibid.*, p. 370.
3. Kellis, *op. cit.*, p. 213.
4. Walter Mills, editor, *The Forrestal Diaries* (New York: Viking 1951), p. 37.
5. Harry S. Truman, *Memoirs by Harry S. Truman*, Volume 1: *Year of Decisions* (New York: Doubleday, 1955), pp. 98-99.
6. Lyman B. Kirkpatrick, Jr., *The Real CIA* (New York: MacMillan, 1968), p. 100.
7. Harry S. Truman, *Memoirs by Harry S. Truman*, Volume II: *Years of Trial and Hope* (New York: Doubleday, 1956), p. 58.
8. R. Harris Smith, *OSS: The Secret History of America's First Central Intelligence Agency* (Berkeley: University of California Press, 1972), p. 364.
9. U.S., Congress, Senate, Select Committee to Study Governmental Operations with Respect to Intelligence Activities, *Foreign And Military Intelligence*, 94th Congress, 2nd Session, 1976, *Book I*, p. 102.
10. U.S., Congress, Senate, Committee on Armed Services, *National Defense Establishment: Hearings on S. 758*, 80th Congress, 1st Session, March-May 1947, pp. 525-528.
11. This point is accepted in the Senate Select Committee's *Book I, op. cit.*, p. 105. Also see pp. 26-29 of U.S., Congress, Senate, Select Committee to Study Governmental Operations with Respect to Intelligence Activities, *Supplementary Detailed Staff Reports on Foreign and Military Intelligence*, 94th Congress, 2nd Session, 1976, *Book IV*.
12. For NSC papers and related documents on Italy, see U.S., Department of State, *Foreign Relations of the United States, Volume III: Western Europe* (Washington, D.C.: Government Printing Office, 1974), pp. 724-789.
13. *Ibid.*, pp. 848-849.
14. Senate Select Committee, *Book IV, op. cit.*, p. 27.
15. Senate Select Committee, *Book I, op. cit.*, p. 144.
16. Senate Select Committee, *Book IV, op. cit.*, p. 31.
17. Senate Select Committee, *Book I, op. cit.*, pp. 48-49.
18. Glenn D. Paige, *The Korean Decision* (New York: The Free Press, 1968), pp. 58-61.
19. Senate Select Committee, *Book IV., op. cit.*, p. 13.

**Footnotes to Chapter Four**

1. Senate Select Committee, *Book IV, op. cit.*, pp. 31-32.
2. *Ibid.*

**Footnotes to Chapter Five**

1. Senate Select Committee, *Book IV, op. cit.*, p. 62.
2. *Ibid.*, pp. 45-46, p. 82.
3. For discussion of assassination planning see: U.S., Congress, Senate, Select Committee to Study Governmental Operations with Respect to Intelligence Activities, *Alleged Assassination Plots Involving Foreign Leaders*, 94th Congress, 1st Session, 1975.
4. *Ibid.*, pp. 92-93.
5. *Ibid.*, pp. 181-187.
6. *Ibid.*, p. 274.
7. *Ibid.*, p. 149.
8. Haynes Johnson, *The Bay of Pigs* (New York: W. W. Norton and Company, 1964), pp. 64-69. Theodore C. Sorensen, *Kennedy* (New York: Harper and Row, 1965), pp. 304-307. For a discussion of the entire Bay of Pigs episode, see pp. 291-309. Arthur M. Schlesinger, Jr., *A Thousand Days* (Boston: Houghton Mifflin, 1965), pp. 251-252.
9. Sorensen, *op. cit.*, p. 305.
10. *Ibid.*, p. 308.
11. Johnson, *op. cit.*, p. 175.
12. Senate Select Committee, *Book IV, op. cit.*, p. 73.
13. Senate Select Committee, *Alleged Assassination Plots, op. cit.*, pp. 98, 132-135.
14. *Ibid.*, pp. 140-142.
15. See Robert F. Kennedy, *Thirteen Days* (New York: W. W. Norton and Company, 1969), p. 139.

**Footnotes to Chapter Six**

1. For the main facts see U.S., Congress, Senate, Select Committee to Study Governmental Operations with Respect to Intelligence Activities, *Covert Action in Chile: 1963-1973*, 94th Congress, 1st Session, 1975.
2. *New York Times*, December 22, 1974.
3. The Rockefeller Commission's findings were made public on June 10, 1975 in the *Report to the President* by the U.S. Commission on CIA Activities within the United States.
4. For the official proceedings of the committee see U.S., Congress, House Select Committee on Intelligence, *U.S. Intelligence Agencies and Activities*, Volumes I-VI, 94th Congress, 1st Session, July-December 1975. *The Village Voice* published the Committee's secret report on February 16 and 23, 1976.
5. See Senate Select Committee, *Book I* and *Book IV, op. cit.*
6. See the Rockefeller Commission Report, *op. cit.*, Chapter 2 on "The Need for Intelligence," pp. 6-8.
7. *Commission on the Organization of the Government for the Conduct of Foreign Policy* (Washington, D.C.: U.S. Government Printing Office, June 1975). See also Appendix, Volume 7.
8. A great deal of information on FBI operations of questionable legality or propriety is contained in: U.S., Congress, Senate, Select Committee to Study Governmental Operations with Respect to Intelligence Activities, *Intelligence Activities and the Rights of Americans*, 94th Congress, 2nd Session, 1976, Book II.
9. *New York Times*, November 5, 1977. See a competent biography of Helms by Thomas Powers, *The Man Who Kept the Secrets: Richard Helms and the CIA* (New York, Alfred A. Knopf, Inc., 1979).
10. Moscow Radio, Domestic Service in Russian, September 9, 1977, as translated and reported in the *Foreign Broadcast Information Service* (FBIS), September 12, 1977.

11. The California case involved Andrew D. Lee and Christopher J. Boyce. Their motivation and personalities are examined at length in a book using their operational code names as title: Robert Lindsey, *The Falcon and the Snowman* (New York: Simon and Schuster, 1979).

**Footnotes to Chapter Seven**

1. U.S. Senate, 94th Congress, 2nd Session, *Final Report of the Select Committee to Study Governmental Operations with Respect to Intelligence Activities, United States Senate, Foreign and Military Intelligence*, Book I, April 26, 1976. (U.S. Government Printing Office, Washington, D.C.: 1976), pp. 435-436.
2. *The Writings of George Washington from the Original Manuscript Sources, 1745-1799*, edited by John C. Fitzpatrick, Volume 8, May 1, 1777-July 31, 1777 (U.S. Government Printing Office, Washington, D.C.) See letter to Colonel Elias Dayton, pp. 478-479. The original letter is in the extraordinary private library of veteran intelligence officer and scholar, Walter Pforzheimer. The library is called the Walter L. Pforzheimer Collection on Intelligence Service, Washington, D.C.
3. All of these statements from AFIO officials are taken from formal papers prepared at the time, copies of which were given to me as one of the founding members of AFIO and are still in my private possession. They were collected and preserved as part of my work in support of the National Intelligence Study Center.

# Index

Acheson, Dean 34, 36, 156
Adams, John Quincy 34
Adenauer, Konrad 231
Africa 41, 69, 89, 96
Agee, Philip 268
Ailes, Stephen 265
Air America 202-203
Air Asia 202
Algeria 64, 88, 92
Allen, Edward 169, 228
Allen, Richard V. 317
Allende, Salvador 16-17, 249-251
Alsop, Stewart 82, 100, 239
Amory, Robert, Deputy Director for Intelligence 136, 155, 172, 174, 209, 218
Angleton, James 83, 114, 185-186, 244
Armas, Castillo 155
Army and Navy: Military collection and evaluation 34-35, 37, 48, 59
Army intelligence 37-39, 59, 76, 78, 111; collection and evaluation 34-35; "Black Chamber" 37; clandestine activity 65-66
Arnold, General Henry H. 69, 127
Assassination planning 153, 208-215, 218, 265
Association of Former Intelligence Officers (AFIO) 275, 300-301
Babbitt, Theodore 127, 172
Baker, James 317
"Baker Street Irregulars" see Special Operations Executive
Balaguer, President of Dominican Republic 237-238
Barnes, General Earl (Ret'd) 143, 226
Barnes, Tracy 209
Barrett, David 95
Barron, John 240n
Battle of Britain 27, 51
Battle of Midway Island 74
Baxter, James Phinney 62
Bay of Pigs 153, 208-216, 219
Becker, Loftus, Deputy Director for Intelligence 136

337

Berlin, West Germany 120; blockade, 126, 165; tunnel 184-185
Betts, Brigadier General Thomas 146-147, 150
Billington, James 187-188
Bissell, Richard 179-181, 207, 209, 211-214, 218
Blake, John F. 275, 280, 301
Bohlen, Ambassador Charles E. (Chip) 131, 181
Borel, Paul 144, 235
Bowie, Beverley 99
Braden, Tom 100
British Broadcasting Corporation 32-33
British Chiefs of Staff 43, 70
Bross, John 217, 232-233
Bruce, Colonel David K. E. 93-94
Budget, CIA 138, 233-234, 266, 283, 296, 303, 321
Bull, General Harold R. (Pinky) 143, 163-164
Bunche, Ralph 98
Bundy, McGeorge 61n, 74, 154, 211, 219-222, 223-225, 235, 239
Bundy, William 155-156
Bureau of the Budget 59, 71, 107
Bush, George, Director of Central Intelligence 19, 265-266, 269-270, 280, 301, 309, 325; Vice President 19-20, 277, 302, 309, 314
Buxton, Colonel Edward 97
Cabell, General Charles Pearre 174, 207, 280
Cabinet status for Director of Central Intelligence 319
Carlucci, Frank C. 280
Carroll, General Joseph 233

Carter, Jimmy, President of the United States 18-19, 268-275, 278, 293, 299, 301-303, 310, 318
Carter, General Marshall S. (Pat) 220, 280
Casey, William, Director of Central Intelligence 19, 98, 100, 270, 278, 280, 298, 302, 304, 309, 315-316, 319, 324-325; the Casey case 20, 311-315
Castillo, Armas 155
Castro, Fidel 208-215, 218
Censorship and Documents (C & D, OSS) 84-85
Central Intelligence Agency (CIA): appropriations and budget 129, 233-234, 266, 283, 296, 303, 321; Bedell Smith Reforms 129; charter 117-119, 298-302; director: office and duties 129-130; domestic activities 254-256, 258-260, 297; employees 125, 136, 141; establishment 101, 103-104; Foreign Broadcast Information Service (FBIS) 32, 114; see also National Security Act of 1947
Central Intelligence Group (CIG) 113-115
Central Intelligence system 15-16, 51-57, 59, 103-106, 139, 268, 303-309
Central Reference Service (CIA) 136
Chamberlain, Neville 44-45
CHAOS 258, 297; see also domestic activities
Charter (CIA) 298-302; see also National Security Act of 1947
Chennault, General Claire (14th U.S. Air Force "Flying Tigers") 95

Cherne, Leo  265
Chiang Ching-kuo  205
Chiang Kai-shek  95, 153, 199, 205
Chile, covert action in (CIA)  249-252, 271
China, People's Republic of (PRC)  31, 198, 261, 315; Communist control 126, 128, 139, 148, 153; defector 202; intelligence of 165, 169, 172-173, 175, 180, 196, 200-201, 227; Japanese war 24; Office of Strategic Services 95-96; nuclear explosion 227; support of North Korea 103, 148; Vietnam 226
China, Republic of (ROC)  149, 153, 165, 167, 196-207, 211; Quemoy and Matsu 153, 198-200
Church committee  17-18, 252, 261, 266, 269, 271, 275, 288, 299, 301, 312
Churchill, Winston  27, 42, 45, 63; First Lord of the Admiralty 44, 103; intelligence liaison with United States 47, 50, 52; iron curtain 121
Civil Air Transport (CAT)  202-203
Clandestine intelligence and operations  86-92, 114-115, 119, 133-139, 154, 169, 174, 183-185, 208, 299-300, 310-311, 315
Clandestine Service (CS, CIA)  63-66, 72, 76, 82, 134-135, 166, 184-185, 191, 195, 197, 243-245, 270; issues ahead 314-325; *see also* Office of Policy Coordination and Office of Special Operations
Clark, Bruce  230
Clark, General Mark  90-91

Clark Amendment  293
Clarke, John  233
Clay, General Lucius  120
Clifford, Clark  125
Cline, Ray S.  25-26, 74, 274; Central Intelligence Agency 126-131, 142-146, 156-157; Cuba missile crisis 220-221; Deputy Director of Intelligence 169, 219, 226-235, 237, 284; Geneva summit 181-183; Khrushchev's speech 185-187; London 146-147; net estimate 163-166; Office of Current Intelligence 172-173, 177, 181; station chief: Taipei 195-207, 211; Bonn (special adviser to ambassador) 239-240; Office of Strategic Services (OSS) 74-75, 78-79, 85; State Department: Intelligence and Research (INR) 172, 173, 177, 181, 241, 242; world trip 187-193.
Codes and ciphers: Germany 27, 44-45; Japan 30, 37; United States 28, 36-38, 136
Colby, William E.  301, 303; Congressional investigations 252-253; Director of Central Intelligence 243-245, 266, 280; "Family Jewels" 245, 253, 265; Office of Strategic Services 87, 98
Combined Chiefs of Staff  70
Commandos  71, 87
Committee on Foreign Intelligence (CFI)  263, 319
Conein, Lucien  99
Congressional oversight  244, 253, 279-298, 300-302, 316; *see also* U.S. Congress oversight committees
Cooley, James  143
Cooper, Chester L.  231, 235

*The CIA Under Reagan, Bush and Casey*  339

Coordinator of Information (COI)   24, 41-42, 54, 62-63, 66-67, 70, 82, 89, 94; establishment 50, 55; facilities 61, 92; military order 55; radio propaganda 66; research and analysis 57, 61-63, 80; role and mission (clandestine collection and intelligence analysis) 55, 63, 66-69, 89; special activities 86
Coordinator of Strategic information   55
Corcoran, Thomas G. (Tommy)   60
Correa, Matthias F.   134
Counterespionage   29-30, 40-41, 49-50, 63, 82-83, 109, 114, 119-120, 139, 150-154, 185, 256-257, 260, 282, 294, 299, 315
Counterintelligence   33-36, 82-84, 109, 114, 148-149, 185, 238, 294, 310
*CounterSpy*   268
Covert action   15, 119-126, 133-135, 139, 171, 174-175, 209, 216, 230, 238, 264, 270, 316, 321; Bay of Pigs 208-215; congressional oversight 289, 291-293, 298-302; Chile 249-252, 271: China (PRC) 86-87; China (ROC) 203-205; executive order 300-301; Iran 154-155; Italy 121-124; Vietnam 244; *see also* Hughes-Ryan Amendment
Covert action (OSS)   82-83, 89-97; TORCH Operation 89-92
*Covert Action Information Bulletin*   268
Covert political action   282, 286; in Guatemala 154-156; in Iran 154-156
Cox, Archibald   242
Cryptanalysis   33-34, 36-38, 50, 74, 150; British "bomb" 43-44;

collaboration with Great Britain   46, 50
Cuba 20; Bay of Pigs 208-214, 220; support of Allende (Chile) 250-251
Cuba missile crisis   14, 219-222, 230-232, 281
Cuneo, Ernest   54
Current Intelligence Staff (CIA) 227-228; 230; (OSS) 76-77, 103
Cushman, Lieutenant General Robert E., Jr.   280
Czechoslovakia   14, 25, 31, 44, 120, 126
Dahl, Roald   52
Darlan, Admiral Jean   91
Davis, Elmer   67
Deak, Nicholas   98
Defense Department   125, 132, 134, 154, 157, 161, 166, 211, 230, 232, 263; secretary 125, 132, 232
Defense Intelligence Agency   233, 319
DeGasperi, Alcide   122
De Gaulle, General Charles   91
Despres Emile   98
Diem, Ngo Dinh   99, 223
Director of Central Intelligence, 165, 188, 232, 295; cabinet status 318; issues ahead 314-325
Directorate of Administration (DDA)   136
Directorate of Intelligence (DDI) 134-136, 165-166, 169-170, 178-179, 218-219, 223, 231, 306, 309, 319; *see also* Office of Current Intelligence and Research and Analysis
Directorate of Operations (DDO)   244n, 309; issues ahead 314-325

Directorate of Plans (DDP) 134, 218
Directorate of Science and Technology 223
Directorate of Support 136
Disclosure of identities 301, 311
Doering, Otto C. 99
Domestic activities, legality of: break-and-enter operations 259; dissident groups 254-256, 258, 297; opening mail 259-260, 297; telephone taps 259
Domestic Contact Service 114, 245
Dominican Republic crisis 236-238
Donovan, William J. (Wild Bill) 24-26, 41, 46-54, 59-63, 66, 69-71, 77, 79, 85, 87-88, 90, 94, 96-97, 100, 129, 131, 138; Coordinator of Information 23-24, 55, 66-69; liaison with British 26, 47, 81, 88, 92; Office of Strategic Services 71-72, 77-91, 95, 97-100, 104; plans for a central intelligence agency 103-112, 115-119
Douglas, Frances 144
Douglass, Kingman 280
Downes, Edward 79
Drumright, Ambassador Everett 198-199
DuBois, Cora 98
Dulles, Allen Welsh 16, 56, 79, 81, 114-115, 135, 139, 141, 155-156; Deputy Director of Central Intelligence 134, 280; Director of Central Intelligence 134, 138, 176-177, 179, 181, 184, 197n, 216, 240, 271, 278, 280; Deputy Director for Plans 134-135, 140-142, 156; Bay of Pigs 208-215, 311; covert political action 139, 155-156, 174-175, 207; current intelligence 174-175; Khrushchev's speech 14, 185-187; net estimate 163-166; Office of Strategic Services 78; 80-82, 114; Penkovskiy papers 222-223; research and analysis 61-63, 166-168, 171-172, 174; world trip 187-193
Dulles, Foster, Secretary of State 134, 139, 175-176, 181, 183, 187, 193, 199
Eberstadt, Ferdinand 112
Eddy, Colonel William A. 65, 89-90
Edward, Sheffield 209
Einstein, Albert 45
Eisenhower, Dwight D., President of the United States 15, 36-37, 91, 110-111, 131, 133, 135, 139, 164, 181-183, 189, 206-207, 226, 240, 309; Bay of Pigs 208, 211-212; covert action: in Guatemala 206; in Indonesia 207; National Security Council meetings 172-178; relations with Central Intelligence Agency 131; Summit conference in Geneva, 1955 181-182; Supreme Allied Commander (Europe) 90-92, 133, 143, 150; War Department 37-38
Ellsberg, Daniel 248-249
"Enigma" 44
Espionage 13, 34, 39-40, 50, 63-66, 82-83, 113-114, 118-119, 134, 139, 147, 151, 260, 270, 282, 299, 315
Espionage Act 257
Ewen, Barbara 147
Executive Order (Truman) 107
Executive Order 11905: Reform of Central Intelligence Agency 263-265, 272, 279

Executive Order 12036 272, 311
Fahs, Burton 98
Fairbank, John K. 98
"Family Jewels" 244-245, 253, 265; *see also* domestic activities; CHAOS
Farm 197
Federal Bureau of Investigation (FBI) 39-41, 46-47; counterintelligence 39-41; responsibilities 290, 294, 297; South American and Caribbean 41, 112, 132; Watergate era 245, 248, 254, 257-259, 264, 272
Federal Communications Commission 32
Field Experimental Unit (OSS) 86
Fitzgerald, Desmond 217, 223, 237-238
5412 Committee 264
"Flap" (CIA) 252-260
Fleming, Ian 54-65
Ford, Corey 100
Ford, Franklin 98
Ford, Gerald R., President of the United States: Reform of Central Intelligence Agency 260-266, 269, 279, 293
Ford, Harold 232
Foreign Broadcast Information Service (FBIS) 32, 114
Foreign Intelligence Surveillance Act of 1978 273
Foreign Nationalities Branch (OSS) 83, 114
Foreign Service 32-33, 241
Forgan, Russell 93
"Former Naval Person" 44; *see also* Winston Churchill
Forrestal, James 112, 120
40 Committee 154, 249, 264
Franklin, Benjamin 34

Freedom of Information Act 301, 311
Frei, Eduardo 16
Friedman, William F. 37
Fulbright, Senator William J. 214
Gardner, John W. 99
Geneva, "Spirit of" 181-182, 193
Geographic and Cartographic Division (CIO) 67
Germany: Nazi 23-25, 28, 31, 38, 43-44, 47, 53, 57, 79, 82, 87, 92, 107, 227; air attacks against Great Britain 27; ciphers 28; submarines 26, 51
Germany: West 121, 149, 183, 191, 240; Berlin blockade 126; tunnel 184-185
Gilpatric, Roswell 219
Giraud, General Henri 90-91
Gisevius, Hans 82
Gleason, S. Everett 75, 79, 103, 109, 133
Global Survey Division 172
Godfrey, Rear Admiral John 54
Goldberg, Arthur 98
Goldwater, Senator Barry 275; Casey case 311-315
Goodfellow, Colonel Preston 98
Goodpaster, Andrew 182
Great Britain 23-30, 41, 51, 55, 83, 183; cryptanalysis 37; intelligence 27, 35-50; press 30-32
Greenslade, Rush 228
Grew, Ambassador Joseph 32
Guatemala 154, 206
Guevara, Che 209
Guthe, Otto 169, 228
Hall, Thayal 147
Halperin, Maurice 98
Harriman, Averell, special adviser to the President 223

Harrington, Congressman Michael  251
Harvey, William  211
Helms, Richard  135, 301; Central Intelligence Agency: Chief of Operations  174, 183-185; Deputy Director for Plans  207, 216, 235, 311; Deputy Director Central Intelligence  235-236, 280; Director of Central Intelligence  226, 239-240, 241, 243, 248, 257, 271, 280; Bay of Pigs  212-213; domestic activities  254-256, 258, 259, 297; Watergate  249; Central Intelligence Group  114, Office of Strategic Services  98
Hersh, Seymour  252
Hillenkoetter, Rear Admiral Roscoe, Director of Central Intelligence  129-130, 280; Central Intelligence Group  113, 119, 128, 172
Hilsman, Roger  220, 223
Hitch, Charles  98
Hitler, Adolf  25-26, 31, 43-44, 51-52, 74, 79, 82, 213
Holborn, Hajo  98
Hoover, Calvin  143
Hoover Commission  134
Hoover, J. Edgar, Director of the Federal Bureau of Investigation  39-41, 46-50, 63, 107, 119, 257-258
Hopkins, Harry  70
Horton, Philip  114
Houston, Larry  117n, 203, 217
House Permanent Select Committee on Intelligence  279, 298-302; see also United States Congress, oversight committees and Senate and House committees and subcommittees

Howley, John  99
Huebner, General Clarence  143
Hugel, Max: Casey Case  20, 311-315
Hughes, H. Stuart  98
Hughes, Thomas L.  233
Hughes-Ryan Amendment of 1974  293, 301-302
Huizenga, John  157, 226
Hull, Cordell, Secretary of State  32-34, 62
Human agents  233
Hungary  14, 173
Hunt, Howard  248-249
Hyland, William G.  317n
India-Burma area  93-94
Indonesia: covert political action  155, 205-207
Inman, Admiral Bobby R., Deputy Director of Central Intelligence  280, 309, 311-312
Intelligence Advisory Committee (ICA)  132, 137, 171-172
Intelligence and Research, Bureau of (INR) see State Department
Intelligence Authorization Act for Fiscal Year 1981  302
Intelligence collection and analysis  290, 299, 303, 311
Intelligence Collection Guidance Staff  303
Intelligence Community Staff  266
Intelligence Coordinating Committee  39-40
Intelligence Oversight Board (IOB)  265, 272
Intelligence Priorities Committee (IPC)  184

*The CIA Under Reagan, Bush and Casey*  343

Intelligence Reform Act of 1980 301
Intelligence Sources and Methods 258, 298, 301
Intercepts: MAGIC 38
Internal security *see* domestic activities and CHAOS
INTREPID *see* William Stephenson
Iran 154, 273, 310
Irvin, John 242
Italy, Fascist 25, 28, 47, 250; postwar 121
Jackson, Senator Henry ("Scoop") 269, 314
Jackson, Robert 53
Jackson, William H. 134, 280
Japan 25, 28, 32, 34-35, 39-40, 94-106; atom bomb 107; code 36-37; purple diplomatic 37; Pearl Harbor 23-24, 27, 38, 69, 158; surrender 107
JEDBURGH (JEDS, OSS) 87-88, 94, 100
Johnson, Alexis 219
Johnson, Kelly 179
Johnson, Lyndon, President of the United States 125, 145, 223-225, 228, 235, 257, 294; domestic activities 258; Dominican Republic crisis 236-238; Vietnam 238, 240
Joint Army-Navy Board 38
Joint Army-Navy Intelligence Committee 39
Joint Army-Navy Intelligence Surveys (JANIS) 80-81
Joint Chiefs of Staff (JCS) 60, 67, 70-72, 76, 78-79, 81, 90, 103-106, 110, 117, 132, 134, 154, 163, 165, 215; William Donovan's memorandum for Central Intelligence Agency 104, 117; Joint Intelligence Staff 113
Joint Intelligence Committee (JIC) 132, 146; Weekly Summary 78
Jones, Geoffrey 99
Kachin Tribesmen, China-Burma-India Theater 94
Kaltenborn, H. V. 31
Kampiles, William 273
Karamessines, Thomas 99
Kaysen, Carl 98
Kellis, James 114
Kellogg-Briand Pact 37
Kennan, George F. 31, 120-121, 124, 125
Kennedy, John F., President of the United States 61n, 74, 154, 216, 224-225, 227, 240, 269, 309; Bay of Pigs 207-215; Cuba missile crisis 15, 219-222, 230-231; death 222
Kennedy, Joseph P. 48
Kennedy Robert F. 219-221, 230-231
Kent, Sherman: Central Intelligence Agency, Director, Office of National Estimates 62, 144-145, 155, 172, 174, 200, 217, 226, 231; Office of Strategic Services 12, 34, 62, 82, 101; Strategic Intelligence for war policy 34, 100
KGB (Soviet Secret Policy Organization) 41, 83, 171, 182, 240n, 260, 272, 300
Khrushchev, Nikita 15, 177-178, 181, 212, 220-221, 228; secret speech 14-15, 185-187
King, Admiral Ernest J. 69, 112
Kirkpatrick Lyman B., Jr. 217, 235
Kissinger, Henry 17, 154, 226, 240, 242; Assistant to President for National Security

Affairs and Secretary of State 242, 249-251, 318
Knight, Ridgeway 90
Knoche, E. Henry, Deputy Director of Central Intelligence 266, 270, 280
Knox, Frank, Secretary of the Navy 30, 48, 53, 63
Komer, Robert 145
Korea, North 20, 103, 128, 172
Korea, South 153, 165
Korean War 16, 130, 137, 138, 143, 153, 165, 281
Kunming (OSS) 94-95
Kuznetsov, Vasiliy 15
Langer, Walter 99
Langer, William: Central Intelligence Agency, Office of National Estimates 62, 133, 136, 142-146, 155; Office of Strategic Services: Chief of Research and Analysis Branch 62, 67, 75, 80, 86, 109
Laos 153; covert action 239, 250, 285-287
Lay, James 128
Leahy, Admiral William D. 64, 113
Legacy of Office of Strategic Services 95
Lehman, Richard 225
Lemnitzer, General Lyman 214
Lend-Lease Act 51
Li, General Tai 94
Liddy, Gordon 248
Lodge, Ambassador Henry Cabot 223
Lothian, Lord 50
Lundahl, Arthur 178-179, 181, 230-231
MacArthur, General Douglas 86, 88

MacBain, Alistair 100
MacLeish, Archibald 61
McCarthy, Senator Joseph 156
McClelland, General Harold 137
McCone, John A.: Director of Central Intelligence 177, 190, 215-235, 239, 271, 278, 280; Cuba missile crisis 220-221, 230-231
McCormack, Alfred 109
McGhee, Ambassador George 240
McKay, Donald 75
McMahan, Knight 130, 168, 172
McMahon, John 311
McNamara, Robert, Secretary of Defense 214, 223, 225, 238
Magruder, Brigadier General John: Office of Strategic Services, Deputy Director for Intelligence 76-77, 79-82, 85-86, 98, 109; plans for a central intelligence agency 103-112
Mao Tse-tung 187, 199, 202, 204-205
Marchetti, Victor 212n
Marcuse, Herbert 98
Maritime Units (OSS) 86
Marks, John 212n
Marshall, General George C. 15, 24, 35-37, 39, 65, 69, 91, 110, 120, 131
Masaryk, Jan 120
Mason, Edward 98
Mathias, Senator Charles 212
Matthias, Willard 145, 226
Meeker, Leonard 79
Meese, Edwin 317
Menzies, General Sir Stewart 43-44
Meo army 239, 285-287

MI-5: counterintelligence and counterespionage (British) 42, 83
MI-6: secret intelligence service (British) 42, 81, 83, 86, 147
Miles, Admiral M. E. 94
Miles, Brigadier General Sherman 35, 39, 65
Millican, Bowie 78
Millikan, Max 168-169
Minh, Ho Chi 95, 99
Mondale, Walter, Vice President of the United States 18, 268-275, 293, 299, 301
Montague, Colonel Ludwell Lee: Central Intelligence Agency 126, 128-129, 143, 157, 226; Joint Intelligence Committee 78
Morale, Operation (MO) 86
Morell, William 169, 228
Morgan, Henry 97
Morgan, Junius 97
Mossadegh, Mohammed 154
Moynihan, Senator Daniel P. 274, 301
Murphy, Admiral Daniel J. 266
Murphy, James 83
Murphy, Ambassador Robert 64, 89-90; Intelligence Oversight Board 265; Murphy Commission Report 262, 264-265
Murray, Henry A. 99
Murrow, Edward R. 31
National Estimates *see* Office of National Estimates
National Estimates Board 142-143, 163
National Foreign Assessments Center (NFAC) 303, 306; issues ahead 314-325
National Foreign Intelligence Board (NFIB) 306

National Foreign Intelligence Program 264
National Intelligence Authority (NIA) 113, 115
National Intelligence Estimate (NIE) 133, 143-144, 146, 156-162, 164-165, 169, 171, 226, 306
National Intelligence Officers 303
National Intelligence Program Evaluation (NIPE) 232
National Intelligence Reorganization and Reform Act of 1978 (S. 2525) 299, 302; son of S. 2525 (S. 2284) 301
National Intelligence Study Center 278
National Photographic Interpretation Center 227, 245
National Security Act of 1947 (CIA Charter) 104, 115, 117-125, 157, 253, 255, 258-259, 263, 281, 289, 298-302
National Security Affairs, Assistant to the President for 249, 263-264, 317-318
National Security Agency (NSA) 234, 309
National Security Council (NSC) 166, 299, 316; Bay of Pigs 208-215; establishment and function 104, 112, 115-119, 128; Central Intelligence Agency briefings 172, 174-176, 177; decline 225; directives 153, 253, 255; NSC 1, 2, 3 122, NSC 4 124, NSC 4/A 124, NSC 10/2 125-126, NSC 68 129, NSC 50 134, NSC 5412 153; Cuba missile crisis 220-221, 232; issues ahead 314-325; Net Estimate 163; officers and participants 133; policy studies 226

NATO  228, 240n
"Naval Person" *see* Winston Churchill
Navy intelligence *see* Office of Naval Intelligence
Net Estimate of 1954  163-166, 171-172, 174
Neutrality Act  24
*New York Times*  187, 229, 244, 252-253, 274
Nicaragua  155
Nimitz, Admiral Chester  86, 88
Nitze, Paul  129, 214
Nixon, Richard M., Vice President of the United States 209; President of the United States 226, 240, 242, 247, 257, 262-263, 282, 318; covert action in Chile 250-251; domestic activities by CIA 252, 258, 294; Watergate 18, 243-244, 248-249, 287
North Africa: TORCH Operation  64
Office of Collection and Dissemination *see* Central Reference Service
Office of Current Intelligence (OCI, CIA)  135, 167-168, 172-174, 176, 181, 227; *see also* Sino-Soviet Staff
Office of National Estimates (ONE, CIA) 133, 135, 142-146, 166, 172; abolished by Schlesinger 243, 245, 303; corporate structure 142, 267; drafting 144-145, 230; Dulles interest in 174; officers and staff 156, 165, 217, 235
Office of Naval Intelligence (ONI) 35-36, 39; "Black Chamber" 37; collection and evaluation 36; foreign branch 35
Office of Policy Coordination (OPC, CIA) 125, 134-137, 146, 157
Office of Reports and Estimates (ORE, CIA) 113, 125, 135, 166-167, 172; Global Survey Division 127-128, 143; Korean War 129-130
Office of Research and Reports (ORR, CIA) 135, 169, 228, 230
Office of Scientific Intelligence (OSI, CIA) 135, 169
Office of Special Operations (OSO, CIA): relations to Office of Policy Coordination (OPC) 125, 134-137, 146; Special Procedures Group working on Italy 124; Staff 114, 136
Office of Strategic Services (OSS) 62, 75, 85; covert action 82, 89-92, 153, 191; Current Intelligence Staff 12, 19-20, 126, 144, 147; establishment ᶠ 23-24, 71; field units 92; legacy 94, 96-101; research and analysis 78-81, 93, 100, 143, 241; termination of 107; theater operations, World War II 92-96; visual presentation 67, 109, 227, 278
Office of War Information (OWI) 67, 71, 86
O'Gara, John  97
Open skies  181-182
Operation CHAOS *see* CHAOS
Operation Mongoose  219
Operation Advisory Group (OAG, NSC)  264
Operation Group Command (OG, OSS)  82, 88
Operations Center (CIA)  236
OSS Detachment  94, 101,
Oversight committees *see* U.S. Congress: oversight committees

Overt collection of intelligence 84, 135, 166, 235, 243
Paramilitary operations 286; Chile 249-252, 271; Cuba 208-215, 220; Indonesia 155, 205-207; Laos 239, 250, 285; North Africa 89-92; Vietnam 250, 286-287
Parker, Barrington D. District Court Justice 271-272
Patterson, Robert 120
Pearl Harbor 23-24, 27, 35, 38, 69, 74, 103, 158
Peers, General W. Ray 94
Penkovskiy, Colonel Oleg 222
Persico, Joseph 278
Personnel strength 136
Peurifoy, John E. 155
Pforzheimer, Walter 117n, 335
Photo interpretation 228, 230-231
Photo reconnaissance 170, 178-181, 191, 211, 216, 233, 304; China 200-203, 227; Cuba missile crisis 15, 220-222, 230-231; U-2s 178-181, 201
Pike committee 252, 261, 288
Poland 48, 173
Poole, Dewitt 83
"POTUS" 44; see also Franklin D. Roosevelt
Presidential directives 23, 115
Presidential orders 71
President's Foreign Intelligence Advisory Board (PFIAB) 265, 272, 278, 303, 311
Press: American 187, 228-230, 245, 256, 268, 274, 288; Casey case 20, 311-315; radio 230
Privacy Act 311
Proctor, Edward W. 317n
Psychological and political warfare 150, 229

Putzell, Edward 99
Raborn, Vice Admiral William (Red), Director of Central Intelligence 235-239, 280
Raczkowski, Marcelle 147
Radford, Admiral Arthur 163, 164
Radio Free Europe 151, 203
Radio Liberty 151
Radio propaganda see Office of War Information
Ragsdale, Maurice 79
*Ramparts* 255
Read, Conyers 98
Reagan, Ronald, President of the United States 277-278, 293, 298, 302, 309, 314; Casey case 311-315; issues ahead 315-325
Reagan Administration 275, 315, 324
Ream, Louis 97
Reconnaissance satellites see Photo reconnaissance
Reitzel, William 127
Republican Party Platform 310-311
Research and Analysis: Central Intelligence Agency 166-171, 303, 309, 310
Resource management 303
Resources Technical Staff 95
Richard, Atherton 97
Richardson, Elliot, 242
Robbins, Rear Admiral Thomas H. 163-164
Robinson, Geroid 98
Rockefeller, Nelson 63; commission 252, 256, 261-262; recommendation for CIA reform 261-262, 265
Rogers, William, Secretary of State 242
"Rogue elephant" 18, 261

Roosevelt, Franklin D., President of the United States: central intelligence system 25, 50, 52, 55; Churchill and British intelligence 42, 44, 46, 103; establishment of Coordinator of Information 23-24, 42, 55, 59; establishment of Office of Strategic Services 23, 72; "POTUS" 44; World War II 27, 31, 38, 90
Roosevelt, James 98
Rostow, Walt W. 98, 154, 225, 239
Rowlett, Frank B. 37
Ruddock, Merritt 79
Runge, Eugene 240n
Rush, Ambassador Kenneth 240, 242
Rusk, Dean, Secretary of State 214, 220, 225, 227, 238
*Samizdat* protest literature 152
Sarson, Rosie 147
Satellite reconnaissance 285; *see also* photo reconnaissance
Sato, Premier of Japan 228
Sawyer, John E. 98
Schlesigner, Arthur, Jr. 74, 76; OSS 79; special assistant to President Kennedy 211-212, 214
Schlesinger, James, Director of Central Intelligence 243-245, 280
Schorske, Carl 76, 79
Schow, Colonel Robert 64
Schuirmann, Captain R. E. 36
Secret Intelligence (SI) 77-78, 98, 109
Secret Intelligence Service (British) *see* MI-6
*Secrets, Spies, and Scholars* 22n
Senate Select Committee on Intelligence 279, 299, 301, 302, 311; Casey case 20, 311-315; *see also* United States Congress, oversight committees and Senate and House committees and sub-committees
Service, John 95
Shah of Iran 16, 154
Shastri, Premier of India 228
Sheldon, Huntington (Ting) 168, 172, 174, 234
Shepherdson, Whitney 98
Sherwood, Robert E. 66
Shirer, William 31
Sidey, Hugh 274
Signals Intelligence (SIGINT) 168, 211, 233-234
Sino-American Cooperative Organization (SACO) 95
Sino-Soviet relations 173, 199, 201
Sino-Soviet Staff (OCI, CIA) 172-173
Smith, Abbott 145, 226
Smith, Harold D. 107
Smith, R. Jack 79, 127-128, 225, 227, 231
Smith, General Walter Bedell (Beetle), Director of Central Intelligence 130, 142, 166, 168, 171, 208, 280; National Intelligence Estimates 171; reforms 129-139, 141, 146, 157; Under Secretary of State 138
Sontag, Ray 143, 145
Sorensen, Theodore C. (Ted) 269-270
Sourers, Rear Admiral Sidney 112-114, 122n, 280
South America 41, 44, 46
Special Group 154; augmented 219

"Special Intelligence Service" 40
Special National Intelligence Estimate (SNIE) 226
Special Operations (SO, OSS) 86-87
Special Operations Executive (SOE, British "Baker Street Irregulars") 49, 54, 69, 86
Special Procedures Group 124-125
Special Projects Unit (OSS) 86
Sputnik 1 178
Stalin, Josef 14, 120, 185, 192
Stalin-Hitler Pact 23
Stark, Admiral Harold R. (Betty) 39
State Department 20, 70, 166, 211, 227, 230, 241, 263; diplomatic reporting 33; Division of Foreign Activity Correlation 34; Intelligence and Research, Bureau of (INR) 220, 228, 232, 233, 241; "Black Chamber" 37; Policy Planning Staff 120
Stein, John 314
Stephenson, William (Little Bill) 45-46, 48, 52; INTREPID 50
Stevenson, Adlai 231
Stilwell, General Joseph W. (Vinegar Joe) 94
Stilwell, General Richard 300
Stimson, Henry L. 30, 53, 63
Strategic military research analysts 230
Strategic Service Unit (SSU, OSS) 109, 114
Strong, Sir Kenneth W. D. 150, 150n
Sukarno, President of Indonesia 155, 205-206
Tangiers 65, 88
Taylor, Vice Admiral Rufus L. 280

Technical Services 85
Thailand 94
Thompson, Llewellyn E. 31, 221
303 Committee 154, 219, 265
Tibet 205
Tidwell, William 231
Tokyo-Rome-Berlin Axis 24
TORCH Operation 82, 89-92
Trohan, Walter 107
Truman, Harry S., President of the United States 15, 122n, 130-131, 138; Central Intelligence Agency 107, 112, 120, 133; establishment of National Security Council 129; termination of Office of Strategic Services 108-109
Truscott, General Lucian 146
Tunisia 64
Tunney, Gene 46
Turner, Rear Admiral R. K. 35-36
Turner, Admiral Stansfield, Director of Central Intelligence 269-272, 280, 303-304; replacement of 309
20th Party Congress in Moscow 14
U-2 14, 178-181, 201, 220, 285
Ulmer, Alfred 114
ULTRA 44-45, 50-51
Undercover Intelligence Service *see* Clandestine Intelligence and operations
Unick, Dolores 147
Union of Soviet Socialist Republics (USSR) 199, 201, 251, 315; agriculture shortage 228; atom bomb 128; BACKFIRE Bomber 273; intelligence of 167, 169, 175-176, 178, 180, 200, 310; KGB 41, 83, 171, 182, 241n, 260, 271, 300;

Khrushchev's secret speech 14-15, 185-187; missiles 165, 177-178, 180, 201, 273; Net Estimate 156-157, 163-164, Sputnik 1 178; support of foreign powers: Chile 17, 250; Cuba 230-231; Guatemala 155, 206; Iran 154, 273, 310; North Korea 20, 103, 128, 172; Yugloslavia 128; 160

United Fruit Company 155

United Nations 231

United States Army in World War II 110

United States Congress: Appropriations Committee 283-285, 300; Armed Services Committee 283, 289, 300; Casey case 20, 311-315; Charter legislation for CIA 298-302; Church and Pike committees 17-18, 252, 261, 266, 269, 271, 275, 288, 299, 301, 311; oversight committees, CIA 244, 253, 279-298, 300-302, 316; Senate and House committees and subcommittees 249-250, 274-275, 279-299

United States Constitution 296, 299-300

United States Intelligence Board (USIB) 137, 232-233, 241, 306

United States Intelligence system 303-309

United States Joint Intelligence Committee (JIC) 70

Vandenberg, Lieutenant General Hoyt S. 113-115, 280

Vanderbilt, William 98

Van Slyck, DeForest 127-129, 143, 167

Veterans of Office of Strategic Services (VOSS) 99

Vichy France 63-64, 90

Vietnam 153, 172, 203, 222-223, 225-226, 230, 235-236, 238-240, 243; covert action 250, 286-287

*Village Voice* 261

Visual Presentation Branch (COI) 67; (OSS) 77

Walters, Lieutenant General Vernon A. 249, 280

War Department 34, 70; General Staff 110; Military Intelligence Division 35

Warner, Senator John 117n, 300

Washington, George, President of the United States 300

*Washington Post* 107, 244

Watergate, break in 18, 247, 249; post-Watergate era 230, 242-243, 287

Wedemeyer, General Albert C. 95

Welch, Richard 268

Welles, Sumner 62

Wheelon, Albert (Bud) 224

White, Frank 98

Wilbur, Martin 98

Wilkinson, Captain T. S. 35

Wisner, Frank: CIA 125-126, 134-135, 151, 185-187, 197, 207

Wohlstetter, Roberta 38

Wright, Brigadier General Edwin K. 280

Wright, Penny 147

X-2 (OSS) 82-83, 85, 109

Yenan, China 95

Yu Ta-wei 200

Yugoslav resistance 51